Dad —

Merry Christmas 1990

From your 1st, 2nd & 3rd

Cougar...

i love you

& Jen

Gary

Kellie

CREATING THE PEOPLE'S UNIVERSITY

Washington State University Centennial Histories

Creating the People's University

Washington State University, 1890-1990

GEORGE A. FRYKMAN

Washington State University Press
Pullman, Washington
1990

Washington State University Press, Pullman, Washington 99164-5910
Copyright 1990 by the Board of Regents of Washington State University

All Rights Reserved
First Published 1990
Printed and bound in the United States of America

00 99 98 97 96 95 94 93 92 91 1 2 3 4 5 6 7 8 9 10

Library of Congress Cataloging in Publication Data

Frykman, George A. 1917-
    Creating the people's university: Washington State University,
1890-1990/ George A. Frykman
    p. cm.
    Bibliography: p.
    ISBN 0-87422-058-0 : $24.95

ISBN 0-87422-058-0 (hardbound)

This book is printed on pH-neutral, acid-free paper.

DUST JACKET PHOTO: *President E. O. Holland and the graduating class of
1922. Bryan Hall is in the background.* (Historical Photograph Collections,
Washington State University Libraries)

Table of Contents

Foreword by President Samuel H. Smith

It is fitting that George A. Frykman's *Creating the People's University: Washington State University, 1890-1990* is being published in conjunction with the school's hundredth anniversary on March 28, 1990.

This is an important book, one that recounts a century of dramatic institutional growth, effective teaching, influential research, and dedicated public service. In telling this marvelous story, Centennial Historian George Frykman ranges from accounts of personal experiences on the Pullman campus to descriptions of research and teaching in Western Europe, the Soviet Union, China, Pakistan, Antarctica, Jordan, the Sudan, Indonesia, and elsewhere. The book is truly a monumental undertaking.

With its companion volumes—William L. Stimson's *Going to Washington State: 100 Years of Student Life* and Richard B. Fry's *The Crimson and the Gray: 100 Years with the WSU Cougars*—*Creating the People's University* completes WSU Press's trilogy, the *Washington State University Centennial Histories*. Together these three books constitute the most comprehensive, in-depth examination of WSU ever undertaken.

We are proud of our authors and of the important past they have made accessible to us. I hope you will join with Washington State University's faculty, staff, students, alumni, and friends in celebrating WSU's first century and the beginning of its second.

Samuel H. Smith
President
March 1990

Foreword
by Weldon B. Gibson

One hundred years ago this year Washington's first Governor Elisha P. Ferry signed legislation creating the state's land-grant school, the institution that would one day become Washington State University. Two years later the school opened its doors for the first time to a small band of young students. Those who made the trek to register for classes at the tiny Pullman campus that first day did not come from wealthy families, nor were their parents members of an elite intelligentsia. Instead, they were the sons and daughters of farmers, laborers, and shopkeepers, representatives of America's working and middle classes.

It is therefore appropriate that George Frykman has chosen *Creating the People's University* for the title of this comprehensive and in-depth study of Washington State University's first century. From its inception, when the school was popularly known as Washington Agricultural College, WSU has remained true to the egalitarian, tripartite mission of teaching, research, and public service that is implicit in its land-grant heritage.

This book stands as a testimonial to the achievements of the faculty, researchers, staff, and administrators who have worked to make this dream of a hundred years ago an ongoing reality. *Creating the People's University* also is a tribute to the tens of thousands who have come to Pullman to get an education. Being one of that number myself, I can say with emphasis that the education I received at WSC, as the school was called in when I attended in the 1930s, sharply changed the course of my life. College at Pullman opened up a whole new future for me, just as it has done for countless others.

Those of us connected with WSU take great pride in what it has done and what it continues to do: to educate and train young men and women from the state, region, and world. We look to WSU's future with pride, optimism, and enthusiasm. This is what we celebrate when we say: "Happy one-hundredth anniversary Washington State University!"

Weldon B. "Hoot" Gibson, '38
Stanford, California
March 1990

Dedication

When Edward Danforth Eddy, Jr., completed his *Colleges for Our Land and Time, The Land-Grant Idea in American Education*, in 1956, he paused to acknowledge a debt that he as an institutional historian had not repaid in his volume. "The quality of institutions," he wrote, "is measured best by the quality of the men and women who serve them. This volume . . . tells the story of the thousands of men and women who, through the years, devoted their lives to the development of the institution of which they were a part." Eddy then expressed a sentiment I share upon finishing this present work. He wrote: "I wish it were possible to mention all of the past and present pioneers. . . . To each of them ultimately must go the credit for whatever quality this story of their efforts contains." My dedication, too, of this work, *Creating the People's University*, is to the people—students, faculty, staff, and administrators—who witnessed and contributed to one hundred years of history.

The story contained in the following pages is meant to be comprehensive but not encyclopedic. For each epoch, attention has been centered upon significant innovations, major developments, disasters, noteworthy happy events and perennial conditions—good or bad—that shaped the character of the institution or affected the lives of its people. Attempts have been made to disclose the roles of faculty, students, and of the administration as the institution has evolved. Chapters have not been drawn strictly along the lines of presidential administrations. Thus, I have tried to permit events themselves to illumine boundaries, pinpoint chronology, and determine the narrative flow.

Acknowledgments

I wish to express my gratitude first to Stanton E. Schmid, Vice-President for University Relations, who has supported this project from its inception through publication. On his staff, Sonja Hussa was especially helpful to me in the early stages of development. In the WSU News Bureau, Allan J. Ruddy provided much assistance in my many forays into the files and in many public relations aspects of the project. Pat Caraher, editor of *Hilltopics,* generously gave me access to his photographic files and provied working space in his own busy office.

Professors David H. Stratton and Richard L. Hume, former and present chairs of the Department of History, good friends and colleagues, have my deepest gratitude for obtaining my appointment as University Centennial Historian and author. Acting in their capacity as successive departmental chairs, they provided me with office space, equipment, research assistance, and secretarial assistance. The department, of course, also provided funding for my project and kept me in an active teaching capacity until retirement.

Director Thomas H. Sanders, Editor in Chief Fred Bohm, and the fine staff of Washington State University Press have published this work as a part of the trilogy, *Washington State University Centennial Histories.* I owe many thanks to them for their work.

The entire staff at the Manuscripts, Archives, and Special Collections of the WSU Libraries (termed WSU Archives in the end notes) has been extremely helpful and has shown me every courtesy in carrying out my requests for research assistance. Special thanks are reserved for Assistant Archivist Lawrence R. Stark whose knowledge of the WSU Archives is phenomenal and whose ability to find certain abstrusely cataloged items and unprocessed materials is gratifying.

Registrar James Quann and his staff have my thanks for tolerating my incursions into records housed in their suite of offices. The President's Office staff also has my gratitude for providing me with working space, a precious commodity there, and easy access into the *Regents Record.* Executive Assistant Gen DeVleming deserves special mention for the staff's hospitality. Finally, I wish to thank the Graduate School for providing research assistantship funding early in the project.

My research assistants on this project have been four graduate students from the Department of History. Patricia and David Hall and Christine Hadlow assisted in the early stages of research and for that I am grateful. Robert W. Hadlow remained with the project from the start virtually to the finish and has proved to be not merely skilled at collecting data but a useful sleuth at finding new material and a valued adviser on statistical and research problems.

I want to thank my wife, Betty, for patience and good humor when my work has come before recreation, social activities, or has even threatened trips to Europe, at a time when *emeritii* are supposed to put such frivolous matters first.

Preparation for writing the *People's University* might be said to have begun in 1950 when I completed my doctoral studies at Stanford University and moved the family from California to Pullman. In the course of the next thirty-seven years I taught most of the American history courses (at one time or another) but became especially involved in teaching Pacific Northwest and American intellectual histories. Both specialties prepared me—by inclination at least—for the present project. Practical experience in serving as assistant librarian and chief of the Social Science Division of the University Library (1951-1953), assistant to the dean, the Graduate School (1961-1964), in charge of academic programming and admissions, and finally as chairman of the University Senate (1977-1978) materially assisted my understanding of certain of the inner workings of the University. I received appointment as the University Centennial Historian in 1985 when the work on the project began. The volume is herewith presented. The text, written in Wilson Hall 338, at the top of College Hill, is mine, with whatever errors it may contain. Hopefully, it tells a useful and felicitous story.

George A. Frykman
Washington State University Centennial Historian
Professor of History, Emeritus
Pullman, Washington
March 1990

Chapter One

Founding the College, 1890-1899

WASHINGTON STATE UNIVERSITY IN PULLMAN OPENED ITS DOORS FOR the first time on January 13, 1892, under the name Agricultural College, Experiment Station and School of Science of the State of Washington.[1] This event at the newest of the nation's land-grant colleges failed to arouse much interest among prospective students or the general public. A mere forty-seven students enrolled that first day and ultimately only eighty-four signed up for the first two terms. After a hasty evaluation of students' credentials by the faculty of five men and one woman, only sixteen applicants were placed in the freshman class, the remainder being relegated to the preparatory department, a necessary unit since the State of Washington had only three recognized high schools and few acceptable academies to prepare young men and women for college.[2] When the first class of seven students graduated in June 1897, the collegiate departments could boast of only eighty-nine enrollees, thirty of whom were listed in an anomalous "special collegiate" category, while the preparatory and other non-collegiate programs dominated the campus with their total of 219 students.[3]

The founding of the college could hardly have been expected to arouse great enthusiasm in 1892 since the State of Washington, having been admitted to the Union little more than two years before, on November 11, 1889, had scarcely been organized politically or thoroughly exploited economically. Attention turned to the seemingly unlimited opportunities for profit and power; a new college in its far southeast corner did not persuade the public that the road to progress and profit lay in higher education.[4]

Nevertheless, Pullman joined in a spirited contest with other towns to obtain the new college. It is entirely possible that Pullman's leaders initially may have sought publicity and were not entirely serious in their effort to obtain the site of the new college. Subsequently, they became deeply interested and, along with numerous rivals, offered a quarter-section or more of land for a campus (a matter discussed below in this chapter). The townspeople made a favorable impression when the commissioners visited Pullman in May of 1890, but the

OPPOSITE: *A turn-of-the-century college gathering to hear a performance by the Glee Club and Orchestra in what was then the new gymnasium.* (Historical Photograph Collections, Washington State University Libraries)

selection body became deadlocked after traveling to competing towns and soon resigned without rendering a decision.

In the spring of 1891, a second commission failed to make a choice on its first ballot. In accordance with an 1891 law, all counties west of the Cascades were eliminated from eligibility as were those in eastern Washington already possessing state institutions. Thus, influential counties like Spokane, Kittitas, and Walla Walla were not considered. After a lengthy and controversial site selection process, lasting more than a year, the competition essentially narrowed down to Yakima and Pullman.

The three-member site selection committee, which had been appointed by the governor, finally chose Pullman at a meeting in Olympia on Saturday, April 25, 1891 and reported their decision in a dispatch dated Monday, April 27. Immediately, E. H. Letterman, one of the four citizens sent to the capital to watch over Pullman's cause, telegraphed home to the anxiously waiting townspeople: "The fight is over. Whitman wins. Pullman gets the agricultural college and school of science. Three cheers for the little star of the Palouse." The message touched off a celebration lasting for two days. All stores closed, according to the town's historian, "with the exception of the three saloons which were indispensable to the occasion. In the victory celebration some enthusiasts hung the vanquished towns in effigy."[5]

Once the celebration ended, it would have been difficult to find anyone outside of Pullman who might have predicted a great future for the college that existed only on paper. The town, located in the Palouse hill country in the eastern borderlands near the Washington-Idaho boundary, was a thriving wheat-ranching community but was not more than fifteen years old. Indeed, as one of the youngest farming communities in the Palouse, Pullman had few advantages to lift it above its rivals except, perhaps, enterprising leaders. It shared with other Palouse towns a highly useful pattern of rail connections to Spokane and Portland, which undergirded claims to commercial advantages and cultural attachment with the outside world. On the other hand, competing Palouse towns constricted its immediate commercial hinterland so that at no point might its domination of trade have been described as extending more than ten miles from the town center.[6] Nevertheless, Colonel F. J. Parker, editor of the Walla Walla *Statesman* in December 1891, recognized Pullman as "better situated for business" than any rivals. He prophesied for Pullman a glorious future that no other city in the state could match. Perhaps the only uncertainty remaining in his mind concerned whether its promise would be delivered by the agricultural college or the recently discovered artesian wells, which the Colonel compared with the healthful waters of Bath, England.[7]

E. V. Smalley, a publicist, writing in September 1892, described Pullman's main street as "well-built for two squares, with brick." The largest enterprise "is a general merchandise store in the fullest sense of the word," providing for all the community's needs. Though obviously a farmer's town, a matter dealt with in detail by Smalley,

Pullman had special educational attractions. In addition to the agricultural college it possessed attractive public schools and a military college. He concluded that it "has now a good right to call itself the educational center of the Palouse Country." Since the agricultural college was in its infancy and the small military school would burn to the ground in March 1893 and not reopen, Smalley's accolade was premature.[8]

The legal and intellectual roots of the small college that would become Washington State University reach back to 1862 when, in the midst of the American Civil War, President Abraham Lincoln signed into law the Morrill Act. This legislation provided a grant of federal lands to each state as an endowment for establishing a college "where the leading object shall be, without excluding other scientific and classical studies, and including military tactics, to teach such branches of learning as are related to agriculture and the mechanic arts . . . in order to promote the liberal and practical education of the industrial classes in the several pursuits and professions in life." Established states had readily grasped these federal grants and, with varying degrees of success, had used the landed endowment either to create colleges of agriculture in connection with already existing state universities, or had established separate institutions. In each case, attempts to realize the ideals outlined in the Morrill Act were products of gradual evolution.[9]

Indeed, the realization of the primary objective of improving agriculture required additional federal direction and support beyond that provided by the Morrill Act. The opening of vast Western lands to agriculture laid bare the need for scientifically improved farming techniques and innovative new production technology. Consequently, in 1877 Congress passed the Hatch Act, which provided regular funding for scientific experimentation and application of findings to plant and animal life through agricultural experiment stations attached to the land-grant colleges. The Hatch Act required these stations to disseminate the results of research widely, free to the public, especially to farmers. Such stations quickly sprang up and their activities were coordinated by the U. S. Commissioner of Agriculture in Washington, D. C. In the early years, however, the work accomplished was essentially practical, rather than scientifically innovative. Before World War I agricultural improvements often waited upon raising the general level of botanical, chemical, and other fundamental scientific advances.[10]

On August 30, 1890, a second Morrill Act became law. Edward D. Eddy, Jr., in his *Colleges for our Land and Time: The Land–Grant Idea in American Education*, described the new measure as "an important milestone in the history of the Land-Grant Colleges. The Institutions that had struggled to survive were now ready, with this additional federal aid, to become permanent and progressive segments of American higher education."[11] Washington, along with other states and territories, also benefited from an additional largess that began with a $15,000 annual grant, which would increase to $25,000 in ten years. This money, according to the law, could be applied only to teaching agriculture, mechanic arts, English, "and the various branches of mathematical, physical, natural, and economic science *with special reference to their applications in the industries of life. . . .*" Support for classical and humane studies clearly was not granted under this measure.[12]

Washington first became eligible for Morrill land-grants when it gained statehood on November 11, 1889, at last shrugging off its stifling territorial existence. The state was, in fact, a party to the notable "Omnibus Bill," which admitted Washington, North Dakota, South Dakota, and Montana to the Union in 1889. The enabling act granted Washington not only 90,000 acres for an agricultural college, to which it was entitled under the Morrill Act of 1862 (30,000 for each senator and representative in the United States Congress), but provided an additional 100,000 acres for establishing a school of science.

The State of Washington's first legislature convened shortly after gaining statehood and continued for some weeks into the spring of 1890. In spite of its myriad tasks, many seemingly more pressing, the legislature approved an enabling act, put into law on March 28, 1890, by which the State of Washington accepted the land offered for the endowment of an agricultural college and the school of science, naming the authorized institution as the Washington State Agricultural College and School of Science. The legislation also authorized the governor to appoint a three man Commission on Technical Education to function much as a combined Board of Regents and college administration. It should locate the college and collect information on technical instruction in the United States and Europe in order to carry out the law's objective, which was "to train teachers of physical science, and thereby to further the application of the principles of physical science to industrial pursuits."[13]

The legislators, thus, ignored the broad mandate of the first Morrill Act to provide a liberal and practical education for the "industrial classes" in placing their emphasis upon training teachers of physical science. Agriculture, however, was to be coequal with industry, for the chemical, physical, and biological laboratories, the chief facilities for instruction proposed, were to provide studies of the morphology and physiology of animal and plant life, principally for the "breeding and feeding of livestock, and the best mode of cultivation of farm produce." Reaching into another, potential source of industry, the commissioners were to promote instruction in mining and metallurgy. They were to establish an agricultural experiment station and provide also for military training.[14]

When the Technical Commission failed in its task of locating a site for the college, its other functions also ceased. As a consequence, on March 9, 1891, the legislature passed a second law concerning the organization of the college. It returned to a broader view of education for the "industrial classes," approaching that found in the first Morrill Act. Gone was the Commission of Technical Instruction, replaced by a five member Board of Regents. The legislature commissioned the Regents not only to organize the agricultural and technical curriculum but also to add a large number of arts and science courses in

Washington Agricultural College's first classroom building, the Crib, was a one story, thirty-six by sixty foot structure that stood at the top of college hill. (University Relations, Washington State University)

history, philosophy, and political and household economy, not previously enumerated. The Regents might authorize other courses as they saw fit, in addition, and were required to inaugurate an agricultural experiment station as a part of the agricultural college and school of science. They also were to appoint a president to manage the day-to-day affairs of the institution.[15]

Lieutenant Governor Charles E. Laughton, presiding during the long illness of Governor Elisha P. Ferry, selected five Regents: Dr. S. B. Conover of Port Townsend, A. H. Smith of Tacoma, George W. Hopp of Sedro Wooley, Captain Eugene J. Fellows of Spokane, and J. H. Bellinger of Colfax. On May 1, 1891, several days after Pullman had been chosen as the site for the school, the Board met in Tacoma and elected Professor George W. Lilley as President of the Agricultural College and School of Science and Director of the Experiment Station. Lilley's nomination was presented by Regent George W. Hopp, a long-time friend of the candidate, and Treasurer Andrew H. Smith seconded the motion. Regents Smith, Hopp, Fellows, and Conover voted unanimously for Lilley. The victor then was brought before the group to accept his appointment as college president and experiment station director.

Lilley's selection foreshadowed an early "time of troubles" for the institution. In the first place, the Regents declared that his term "shall be for one year and until his successor shall be elected and qualified." Then, they introduced political considerations when appointing professors. Inevitably, in an institution not yet established, they participated so much in its internal affairs as to increase its instability. Judge Thomas Neill, a friend and promoter of the college, years later looked back in dismay at its early operation. In 1892 and 1893, he recalled with some exasperation, "the institution was a miserable excuse for a college. As a rule, politicians and those having a political pull were made professors."[16]

Judge Neill's criticism might have begun with President Lilley, whose background was obscure and whose dossier contained ambiguities concerning advanced and honorary degrees. Lilley was a native of Illinois, probably born in 1850. The best-established portions his formal training were four years of study at Knox College in Illinois from 1869 to 1873, and the following year as a special student of mathematics at the University of Michigan. He also earned the degree of Master of Arts from Washington and Jefferson College in 1878. Lilley's previous professional experience included the presidency of Dakota Agricultural College from 1884-1886 and four years there as a professor of mathematics after heading the school. His May 1, 1891 appointment to the presidency of the Washington Agricultural College came about, in all likelihood, because of his long-standing friendship with Regent George W. Hopp.[17]

Three weeks later, at a meeting in Pullman on May 22, the Regents were served a restraining order initiated by North Yakima interests making a desperate stand to prevent the issuance of funds for the construction of college buildings. This last legal measure did not, however, prevent Pullman from holding fast to its newly acquired institution. The board proceeded to approve plans, drawn up by Spokane architect Herman Preusse, for a modest brick building—soon called the "Crib." A contractor, W. White, built the structure for $1,500.[18]

At a meeting in Tacoma on November 16, 1891, the Regents expressed a note of urgency in their resolution that the college should be opened "at the earliest possible moment." Since Lilley was absent, their instructions took on a note of asperity. They ordered the president to appear in Spokane on November 28, "to assist Regent A. H. Smith and Architect Preusse in the perfection of plans for the necessary buildings." Furthermore, they directed Lilley to meet with the Regents in Pullman, on December 1, to make recommendations regarding curriculum and appointments to the new faculty. Since his hiring on May 1, 1891, in fact, Lilley had spent most of his time in the Midwest, settling personal affairs and interviewing potential instructors for the new institution. This probably contributed to his eventually weakened position as head of the college, since during his absence the Regent's increasingly took control of many of the specific duties normally handled by a chief executive.

At the Pullman meeting on December 1, which convened downtown in the Bank of Pullman office, the Regents approved plans for the classroom building and also for a dormitory. They also directed Lilley to open the school's doors on January 13, 1892.[19] The Board also selected a faculty of five instructors. Outright nepotism and favoritism, which were not uncommon in higher education, were evident in the recommendations for these faculty positions. At least three of the new staff members were from Brookings, South Dakota, where each had known Lilley either as friend or colleague: John O'Brien Scobey, a businessman and politician, became professor of agriculture; Dr. Charles E. Munn, Lilley's brother-in-law, was appointed professor of veterinary science; and Nancy L. Van Doren became professor of English and preceptress of the women's living quarters. The remaining two educators also came from the Midwest: Edward R. Lake, with a Master of Science degree from Michigan Agricultural College, would teach botany, forestry, and horticulture; and George G. Hitchcock, trained at the University of Nebraska, was appointed as an instructor in chemistry. In addition, President Lilley would teach mathematics and elementary physics.[20]

Having taken their various paths to the wintry Palouse country, the faculty assembled as ordered in Pullman on January 12, 1892, with all members present.

On the same busy day, and apparently with little debate, the Board decreed that there would be three collegiate fields of study: agriculture, mechanic arts, and domestic science. In addition, the Regents established a two-year non-degree pharmacy course and a one-year preparatory department. Lilley's involvement in these latter decisions seems to have been minimal, but the Board proposed a large role in the future for the president, as well as the faculty. The Regents resolved that the president and the faculty were required to make recommendations regarding the curriculum, and prescribe rules concerning conduct, examinations, and scheduling. In a final momentous decision that day, the Board ruled that tuition and housing would be free to citizens of Washington.[21]

Having taken their various paths to the wintry Palouse country, the faculty assembled as ordered in Pullman on January 12, 1892, with all members present. They agreed to open classes the next day without formal exercises, and, in regard to the prospective students, they decided to make "a rough examination of qualifications, and classify them chiefly according to the work desired by them."[22] The faculty's desire for simplicity and informality did not quench enthusiasm for the start of classes. The Pullman *Herald* found the opening day events "most gratifying." The editor, in a report understandably touched with pride, stated that a "large number of citizens were present at the opening exercises, and all expressed great satisfaction at the brilliant beginning." At the same time, he seized upon the college's first opportunity for providing public service by proclaiming that its work "is not confined to any one locality, but its field extends over the entire state." This notable pronouncement followed a reported epidemic among horses in Kittitas County, which caused President Lilley to offer the services of Dr. Munn, the veterinarian. Whether he went or not apparently is lost to history, but the editor's words were not: "This is but one of the many benefits that farmers and stockraisers of the state will receive from the college."[23]

The events of the first few weeks of classes in that winter's first term belied any optimistic prophecies for immediate success. On February 10, 1892, President Lilley reported that a mere fifty-nine students were enrolled on campus and that most were doing preparatory work. Though the college's catalog listed an elaborate curriculum, in actuality students' choices were limited. In fact, no clear distinction was made between freshmen and preparatory students or the classes they took. The subjects actually made available ranged from Arithmetic, Grammar, and Literature to Algebra, Geometry, Botany, Rhetoric, Shop, Physics, German, and Mechanical Drawing. As yet, there was little class work available to support either an agricultural or mechanic arts degree, while Domestic Economy and Pharmacy did not materialize as studies at this time.[24]

Much of the work of organizing the college and constructing its facilities remained to be accomplished after classes started. On February 10, 1892, for instance, the Regents awarded a contract to build a five-story brick dormitory, designed by Herman Preusse, to contractors Taylor and Lauder. The Board accepted bids for other

On February 10, 1892, President Lilley reported that a mere fifty-nine students were enrolled on campus and that most were doing preparatory work.

work on the fledgling campus as well. Meanwhile, Professor Hitch-cock, who had yet to teach a class, had been granted a leave of absence without pay until the new term opened on April 1, 1892. The Regents accepted his claim that he could not leave his previous position before that date.

Doubt was cast on the stability of the new institution when the state auditor withheld $1,333.33 of Lilley's $4,000 salary, nurturing suspicion that the president had not fulfilled his obligations. In actuality, there were legal and administrative reasons for the reduction in payments in the summer and autumn of 1891, when Lilley remained in the Midwest clearing up personal obligations. Also, though Lilley had been appointed president on May 1, 1891, his one year appointment, in effect, did not start until several months later, apparently due to legal challenges and administrative requirements. The Regents, however, passed a resolution supporting Lilley's claims for funds from the state's treasury. The faculty had greater reason than the Regents to worry about the new college's integrity, since the Regents did not set their salaries until February 18, about five weeks after classes began. At that time, male professors were granted stipends of $2,000 per year, whereas Nancy Van Doren had to be content with $1,500.[25]

The first recorded extracurricular activity for students, a "Spell-down," took place on a Friday afternoon, January 31, when Professor Lake quizzed students encircling him. The contest came to an end when Orin Stratton "went down on the word 'lily,'" perhaps having confused it with the spelling of President Lilley's name. Allie Fariss was declared winner, after which President Lilley, ever popular with the students, closed the meeting with a speech, while Mrs. Lilley looked on.[26]

Such activities could hardly satisfy the expectation of college students. So, on February 22, a group of them organized a literary society to engage in literary and oratorical exercises. On March 4, the faculty sought to widen the narrow intellectual content of the curriculum by encouraging more intensive "society work" in literature and oratory. Next, the faculty sponsored an Arbor Day celebration on April 15, an appropriate conservation and aesthetic gesture on the treeless hills of the Palouse. A full program of music and speeches accompanied the tree planting.[27]

A student newspaper also appeared in February 1892. Known as the *College Record*, and originally edited by William D. Barkhuff, the monthly publication reported on student and faculty activities, often with humor, and contained feature articles about agricultural and scholarly subjects. Unfortunately, it ceased publication in April 1893, after only ten issues, due to financial problems. It provided an interesting, delightful, and sometimes controversial record of the college's first year.[28]

The students organized an athletic club within a few days of beginning literary work. Baseball began in March, with the first game being a 26-0 victory over the Pullman Military College. Challenged by the "Moscow U.S." team (which was not connected with the University of Idaho), players and most of the supporters boarded a Union Pacific train for Moscow at eight in the morning of April 16. A few hardy souls rode to the game on horseback. After "a fine repast" at the Commercial Hotel in Moscow, the WAC team defeated its hosts 10-4. The Pullman athletes and their fans, having been royally entertained, returned in triumph. During the remainder of the spring, the men from the college played nine more games—four of them with Moscow U.S. The only loss came in one of the contests with the latter team. Athletics that year ended in a "Field Day" celebration including track and field events, tennis, tug-of-war, and baseball.[29]

The college's abbreviated first academic year of two quarter terms ended in June 1892 with final examinations that revealed a heavy emphasis on sub-collegiate courses. Tests were conducted in subjects ranging from spelling and reading to history, botany, and chemistry. The faculty and Regents, of course, were well aware of the need to introduce new courses in the curriculum, in order to fulfill the program proposal in the First Annual Catalogue for full instruction in the fields of agriculture, mechanic arts, domestic science, and pharmacy.[30]

The Regents responded to that need on June 16, 1892, by first adding the teaching of physics to the duties of Chemistry professor George Hitchcock, a dubious decision in view of Hitchcock's absence from the campus for a good part of the first year. In an even more questionable motion, the Regents appointed Dr. Charles Munn, the veterinarian, to teach Physiology and Zoology. In July, they adopted courses in Chemistry, Assaying, and Mining, Civil, Mechanical, and Electrical Engineering.[31]

No additional instructors for these new programs were authorized at the time, nor was the board able to address this need until months later. At a meeting on November 17, 1892, Regent Bellinger recommended that a civil engineer be hired to teach in the college and survey the campus. The board adopted the resolution 3-1 and immediately hired Ernest L. Newell of Tacoma, thereby perpetrating a comedy of errors.[32] They had relied heavily on the recommendation of Edmond S. Meany, a Seattle legislator and journalist (and later a noted Pacific Northwest historian at the University of Washington), who had persuaded influential politicians and business leaders to support Newell. Meany claimed that Newell could organize an orchestra, teach history, coach athletics, and instruct in engineering. The young man quickly proved to be an embarrassment, since he could not fulfill any of the tasks assigned to him. He soon resigned.[33]

Thus, the Board of Regents continued to treat faculty appointments as minor political patronage, perhaps actually taking turns in selecting new instructors. The new appointees often were unqualified or inept, but there were notable exceptions. One of those was Charles V. Piper, also hired in November 1892. Meany, a close friend, rallied support among politicians, and personally recommended Piper as "a loyal young man." Fortunately, Piper, who was largely self-taught as a naturalist, was destined to become a distinguished professor of biology, and some years later transferred to the headquarters of the U.S. Department of Agriculture.[34]

Within six months of WAC's opening, formal social events had become an important part of campus life. Shown here is a printed invitation addressed to W. M. Brainard to attend a "Social Ball" given by the Young Men's Social Club on June 3, 1892. (Private Collection)

Elisha P. Ferry, first governor of the State of Washington, signed the legislation creating the institution that would one day become Washington State University. (Historical Photograph Collections, Washington State University Libraries)

On December 28, 1892, the board chose George H. Watt, Superintendent of Schools in Yakima, as professor of chemistry. Watt would serve honorably on the faculty, later becoming the first head of the Pharmacy Department. Professor John D. Hendricks became professor of agriculture at that meeting, but resigned within a few months due to the fact that he had been a candidate for the college presidency.[35]

When the Board of Regents hired James Ferguson on December 12, 1892 as professor of typing and shorthand it ventured into studies questionable for college credit from the standpoint of the Morrill acts. Ferguson proved to be exemplary in character and skills, but when Enoch A. Bryan became the third president in 1893 he quickly persuaded the Board to abolish the position. Perhaps the most bizarre case of irresponsibility in faculty hiring arose when Lee Fairchild appeared on the campus. In late 1892 he apparently began teaching, perhaps English Literature or Political Economy or both, without having been formally appointed by the Regents. Characterized by the Pullman *Herald* as "Well known as a poet, humorist, and newspaper man," and by Bryan as "an odd genius, half newspaper man, half public entertainer, and wholly free lance," he remains a mystery. Whether or not he received compensation is unclear, but his pretensions ended on May 8, 1893, when the Regents refused his application for a professorship.[36]

By the start of the fall 1892 term, it had become increasingly apparent that certain members of the Board of Regents lacked confidence in President Lilley. From the beginning, in fact, the Board had usurped the president's authority by engaging in administrative tasks on campus. In particular, Regent Andrew H. Smith, a Tacoma architect, was intimately involved in overseeing construction activities at the college, including even such minor projects as the building of a root cellar and other facilities for a branch experiment station at Sumner. He and the other Regents took it unto themselves to purchase supplies, machinery, and other equipment for the campus, and has been shown above, they retained direct responsibility for hiring staff.[37]

In an annual report published on November 1, 1892, the Regents proudly noted their accomplishments and made a rather naive prophecy "that the most critical period in the life of the institution is safely passed. . . ." Proudly describing the campus which sustained their high hopes, they stated that it consisted of twenty–five acres with two main buildings, the first being a two-and-a-half story College Hall which housed the president's office, all classrooms, laboratories, the library, and an assembly hall. A dormitory of five stories, serving both sexes, was the second structure. These buildings, along with the smallish Crib, farm buildings, and shop, were located on "a commanding eminence which overlooks the town."[38]

Writing with more imagination and verve, a contributor to the *College Record* stated that the buildings were situated on "the Hill of Science, surrounded on all sides by finely cultivated farms . . . looking north we see the mountains of Steptoe and Kammiack, [*sic*] famed in the pioneer history of our state as the scenes of two battles between the early settlers and the Indians. On the west and south, in the distance, we see the Blue Mountains. . . . On the east a spur of the Coeur d'Alene mountains. Thus, you see, we have a scene of which the most exacting could not complain."[39]

According to another student journalist, the college farm of 225 acres was a "beautiful tract of fertile land comprising bottom land and north and south hillsides. Some . . . is yet in its natural state . . . covered with sunflowers and bunchgrass." The effort was already under way to cultivate the virgin soil. Professor E. R. Lake reporting to the Regents, described the planting of numerous species of forest trees, an orchard, and a garden. Though the results of this work were unclear, the purpose was not: this investigation was to adapt plants and trees to the region, not to engage in original research.[40]

Professor John O'Brien Scobey, agriculturalist, reported that his crew had "sown nearly all kinds of small grain," on the farm. While he expressed confidence of good results, he admitted that he did not possess adequate equipment to measure the harvest. The extent and variety of plantings suggest that he, like Lake, had started no truly scientific experiments but he had, in effect, put the students, in training as apprentices. The *College Record* summed up the primitive nature of the work by remarking that the abundant wildflowers "are now being analyzed by the class in botany."[41]

President Lilley never became a leader in developing policy nor did he satisfy the Regents in his daily administration of the school. On December 13, 1892, eleven months after the Washington Agricultural College held its first classes, the Regents dismissed him from the college presidency and the directorship of the experiment station. Regent A. H. Smith led the movement to drive Lilley out of office, declaring that the president lacked "the moral courage and independent force" to govern the college successfully. More specifically, Smith criticized Lilley's poor accounting practices and blamed him for overcrowded dormitories. Smith discounted Lilley's claim that he did not have sufficient office help and described him as a teacher who was slovenly, neglectful and careless in his ways." There is reason to suppose that Smith victimized Lilley, possibly with the hope that he might thereby dominate the Board of Regents.[42]

George W. Lilley, President of Washington Agricultural College and School of Science from May 1891 to December 1892 (Historical Photograph Collections, Washington State University Libraries)

The most damning imputation regarding Lilley, however, had to do with rumors concerning experiences he had before joining the Washington Agricultural College. For some time, stories had come from Iowa and South Dakota alleging that Lilley had misappropriated property of his employers when he had worked as a broker selling wheat on commission some years earlier. With the permission of the Board, Lilley had gone to the Midwest to gather documentation to demonstrate his innocence. Subsequently, however, the Board did not permit him to state his case. Years later, in 1943, Professor Rolland B. Botting, having studied the dismissal, stated that the Board had been as culpable of poor management of the college as had Lilley. The evidence concerning the wheat sales remained unclear, although Lilley claimed he had been absolved of wrong-doing.[43]

At the December 13, 1892 meeting at which Lilley and Scobey were fired, the Regents turned to the task of selecting Lilley's successor. Upon Smith's nomination, after three ballots it elected John W. Heston, principal of Seattle High School. The decision revealed that sentiment still existed to retain Lilley, as on the third and final ballot Heston received three votes while Lilley held one. On the previous two ballots, John D. Hendricks, the only other candidate, tied Heston with two votes. The board, two weeks later, chose Hendricks as the new professor of agriculture.[44]

The Heston administration suffered an inauspicious beginning when on December 21, Regent A. H. Smith appeared on campus to introduce President Heston to the students. The latter demonstrated a continuing loyalty to Lilley by singing a parody of "John Brown's Body," substituting the words "We'll hang Regent Smith to [Regent] Bellenger's gate post" and "We'll have George Lilley for our next president." Then, when someone read a letter from Smith accusing Lilley of misappropriating funds, the students angrily chased Smith and Heston off campus, throwing snowballs, rotting cabbages and eggs at them. The students later assured Heston that they were angry only at Smith. The latter, a few days later, in Spokane professed to believe the incident was only an undergraduate prank, declaring that he had not been hit by any eggs but admitting that he indeed had run all the way to the town center.[45]

A storm of controversy and outrage arose in the press over the egging affair. The Colfax *Commoner*, for example, depicted the "disgraceful episode" as having been perpetrated by "heathen ruffians" among the students, who should be expelled. William R. Hull, the student editor of the *College Record* and a leader in the assault, countered by declaring that the event had been exaggerated and the students had not meant to include Heston in the pelting.[46] The Spokane *Review* saw the firing of Lilley as an effort to turn the spotlight away from the Regents, who were the real culprits. The editor asserted that they should be investigated for misusing their authority. The egging indeed became a rallying point for dissident elements critical of the efforts to establish the agricultural college.[47]

John Heston, the new president, stood at the center of the storm in which opponents accused each other of lacking moral courage and competence in administering the school. He had no means of controlling his own administration. Indeed, he never gained the attention and respect of his own faculty or of the Regents required to develop leadership. The latter, for example, undercut his position by appointing his rival, Hendricks, to the chair of Agriculture.

Heston's election had been legitimate, if ill-advised. Thirty-nine years old, he appeared about ten years younger, a matter that probably did not help gain respect. His description, found in the Spokane *Review*, that he was of "medium height with fairly good looks and light complexion," suggested that Heston did not stand out in a crowd. He came to his task with a respectable academic career, having graduated from Pennsylvania State College in 1879 and later served as principal of its preparatory department and as professor of pedagogy before organizing the Seattle High School in 1890.[48]

John W. Heston, President of Washington Agricultural College and School of Science from December 1892 to August 1893. (Historical Photograph Collections, Washington State University Libraries)

The winter term opened on January 9, 1893, with high hopes, according to the *College Record*, with "nearly all" old students returning "and all determined to make good use of their time." President Heston apparently delayed his arrival in Pullman until early February, but soon had to depart for the legislative session in Olympia, to represent the college. One of his first letters from Pullman to a regent revealed the primitive state of his administration when he wrote of his office that "we ought to have a book case with a cupboard underneath. . . . There are a few crude shelves along one end of the office where everything lying there is exposed to the dust and presents a very untidy appearance."[49]

Political difficulties soon eclipsed minor worries about a barren office. The 1893 legislature responded to rumors and reports of difficulties and corruption at Pullman by appointing an Agricultural College Joint Investigating Committee. Its report, first noted in the Pullman *Herald* on March 3, 1893, reviewed charges and the condition of the campus with a fine tooth comb. Accusations of corruption in locating the college and in the contracts let for construction and improvements were quashed. The committee failed to uncover political influence in the making of appointments, but criticized the Board of Regents for poor judgment in assessing the needs of the institution and incompetence in running it. The main buildings, the dormitory, and college hall were termed unsuitable, the livestock on the College farm of poor quality, printing charges extravagant, and the record-keeping abominable.

The legislators concluded that the Board of Regents, whose appointment the governor had never confirmed, should be removed and that Professor Hendricks, who "not working for the best interests of the school. . . ." ought to be fired. The committee further advocated that the Regents should be sharply limited in compensated expenses, but that a generous budget was essential for the welfare of the college, including a large sum for a new college hall and administration building.[50]

There was small comfort for Heston in the succeeding political steps. Governor John H. McGraw removed the Board of Regents but failed to consult Heston when appointing its successor. In fact, Heston, quite confused, mistakenly wrote to J. W. Arrasmith of Colfax, on April 4, 1893, that "I see by the papers that you have been appointed a regent of the Agricultural College and School of Science." Actually, Arrasmith did not join the Board until 1895. Subsequently, an informed Heston sent congratulatory messages to the new Board: John W. Stearns, Tekoa; E. S. Ingraham, Seattle; H. S. Blandford, Walla Walla; Charles R. Conner, Spokane; and General Thomas R. Tannatt, Farmington.[51]

The new Regents would not accept a president appointed by the discharged Board, forcing Heston to send in his resignation on May 10, 1893 (though the letter itself was dated May 6, 1893). For its own convenience, the Board resolved not to accept the resignation until June 30. Later, Heston demonstrated his own dissatisfaction by complaining that the abrupt dismissal of Dr. Munn, the veterinarian,

●

John Heston, the new president, stood at the center of the storm in which opponents accused each other of lacking moral courage and competence in administering the school. He had no means of controlling his own administration. Indeed, he never gained the attention and respect of his own faculty or of the Regents required to develop leadership.

●

had destroyed the latter's research into glanders, wasting money spent to prepare an extension bulletin on that disease of horses. Heston's lack of acceptance was so great that, when the Board dismissed Professor Hendricks, Heston's rival, the students clearly sided with the professor. The *College Record*, apparently expressed a popular attitude when it editorialized that "The Professor may be assured of our continued confidence and esteem."[52]

Heston's forced service after May 10 produced additional complaints but enabled him to prepare for end-of-year exercises. At that time, the college offered its first graduate, Thomas O. Steine, who received the Bachelor of Science degree. A resident of Brookings, South Dakota, Steine had completed most of his work at the agricultural college there, taking only his final year in Pullman. Those studies consisted to a considerable extent of individual, informal work, signifying the unreadiness of the school to present upper division courses. In the spring of 1898, at the approach of the first commencement ceremonies, the Regents validated the award by issuing Steine another diploma.[53]

During the early summer of 1893, Heston requested permission to withdraw his letter of resignation and asked for an increase in salary. It was his last attempt to take the initiative. The Regents, instead, simply ignored both requests, instead moving the date for termination from June 30 to August 31. George Lilley, who evidently had remained in Pullman, received more consideration than did Heston. He applied for the professorship of agriculture and the directorship of the experiment station. The Board rejected the first application, although somewhat hesitantly. Then, on reconsideration, the Regents debated the whole issue thoroughly but again turned Lilley down, 3-2.[54]

Clearing the slate of old candidates was followed by the election on July 22, 1893 of Enoch A. Bryan as the third president of the Washington Agricultural College. In a ceremony scarcely more formal than on the two previous elections, the Regents chose Bryan over a dozen other applicants, none of whom seems to have been formidable. Indeed, the whole process suggests nothing more than another casual liaison between candidate and institution. Bryan later admitted that he had not even heard of the college when he learned that a friend in Oregon had nominated him for the post. After a brief investigation of the circumstances at the school, Bryan accepted the position.[55]

The third president of Washington Agricultural College, Enoch Albert Bryan, came to Pullman from the presidency of Vincennes University in Indiana, a small two-year college with a grandiose title. He had been born on May 10, 1855, on an eighty-acre farm in Monroe County, Indiana, three miles east of Bloomington, home of Indiana University. His father, a minister, baptized the infant Enoch Albert into the Presbyterian Church. It is evident that the father farmed at least part of the time.

Enoch Bryan expected, at first, to become a farmer but entered Indiana University, probably after some experience at teaching school at age eighteen. His college studies were intermittent but encompassed classical languages, mathematics, philosophy, history and economics. He graduated at twenty-three years of age, in 1878, having established a good record. All thoughts of farming disappeared when the farm, heavily mortgaged, fell to creditors. Bryan first went to work in harvest, but soon obtained a teaching position in the Grayville, Illinois, schools. Later he became superintendent of schools in Grayville and in 1882 became president of Vincennes University in Indiana. While at Vincennes, he took leave to engage in graduate study at Harvard University, obtaining a Master of Arts Degree there in 1893. He then returned briefly to his duties at Vincennes,which included teaching Latin, Greek, and literature.[56]

He expressed a strong preference for character training, indelibly written in what originally may have been a student oration which became expanded into a full-blown didactic piece as president at Vincennes. Progress, he defined, as the product of character rather than materialism. On that occasion and numerous others, down at least to 1905, he embellished and repeated the speech. In it he defined character as "an inward spiritual grace". . . involving [a] "strength of mind and body as well as depth of soul." Character, he thought, produced stability in the individual, the nation, and society. Character, rather than sheer intellect marked his philosophy and to both he added the ideals of religion while seeking to direct his students at Vincennes. He came to Pullman well-equipped with administrative experience, but with a philosophy more attuned to nineteenth century liberal arts than to sheer intellectualism or the practical mission of the land-grant institution of a raw, new state.[57]

The president's first impressions of Pullman were favorable. He later recalled that, though it was a small town of approximately 900 people, Pullman had "long rows of wheat wagons lined up near the warehouses." The presence of three banks, a new high school, a flour mill, and stock yards indicated that it had developed a vigorous commercial life and a heavily populated hinterland. These facts did not obscure for Bryan the reality that Pullman was suffering from an economic depression. At the moment, though, the town was especially lively as both a temperance meeting and a county teachers' institute were in session. The latter, if not the former, perhaps accounted for a heavy patronage at the numerous saloons. Pullman citizens filled the high school auditorium to greet Bryan. He described his reception as kindly but deprecated his own extemporaneous speech and appearance. Of the latter, this thirty-eight year old educator stated: "I was a small man weighing 130 pounds, wearing a full beard to add age and dignity and must have been somewhat disappointing in appearance on this my inauguration."[58]

Preparations for a new beginning became evident in the spring of 1893—while Heston occupied the presidency—when the legislature had appropriated $97,000 to the college for the 1893-1895 biennium. Two-thirds was reserved for construction, with $50,000 for an administration building and $10,000 for mechanical engineering facilities. The proposed construction immediately revealed a serious land

Enoch A. Bryan, President of Washington State College from 1893 to 1916. (Historical Photograph Collections, Washington State University Libraries)

shortage on the campus, compounded by the odd configuration of the property. The main campus stood aloof from the college farm, the two portions being joined only by a narrow "neck" of land. These pieces of property had been donated by a number of civic-minded Pullman residents in the wake of the college location being awarded to their town. The land, consisting of more than 200 acres, was made up of individual gift parcels that now constituted the entire site of the institution. In fact, townspeople had oversubscribed the original pledge by as much as twenty acres. Difficulties soon arose when certain donors procrastinated in giving up title to a strategic four-acre plot on which the college had carelessly constructed a power plant and several other buildings. Probably as much as $23,000 had been invested in public structures built on lands not owned by the state.[59]

The narrow "neck" of land connecting the two parts of the college offered little in the way of development possibility for needed recreation facilities, a matter which caused the Regents to encourage town leaders to make additional property available to the school. The necessity of an amicable settlement became obvious to both sides as confusion fueled rumors that the college itself might be moved from Pullman to Spokane.

To settle issues, the Regents first held a public meeting in downtown Pullman on June 16, 1893, to explain the need for additional land, as well as to speed the transfer of already pledged acres. Subsequently, the board met with the six town leaders who had been responsible for gathering the more than 200 acres already donated. At that meeting, each side assumed certain responsibilities for enlarging the college site. Townspeople guaranteed the transfer of the four acres on which the power plant stood and promised to find additional lands that the college might purchase. The Regents accepted these proposals and agreed to seek funds from the 1895 legislature for the purchase of additional property.

From this point, the course of action becomes unclear. Regents records for September 1893 indicate that the Board ordered an enclosure for the bonded lands, a reference in all likelihood to the pledged four acres. Without waiting for the legislature to act, the Regents obtained several other plots of land. In due course the legislature appropriated $4,000 to pay for additional property "in front of and south of the campus." Probably the Regents' purchase on June 27, 1895, of two lots for relocating the heating plant represented the first of many transactions covered under that appropriation. Numerous additional purchases over the years would be required before the campus could fully support the full development of a modern university.[60]

In the summer of 1893, also before Bryan's arrival, the Regents appointed two men who joined Charles V. Piper in forming the core of a strong faculty. Elton Fulmer became professor of chemistry, geology, and metallurgy. He had been an instructor in chemistry at the University of Nebraska and had had practical experience in metallurgy and in propagating sugar beets. Bryan later recalled that Fulmer "was one of that band of men, who, in the summer of 1893 had come to Pullman, to reorganize the young college and put it in line for a useful career." Osmar L. Waller was another of that group. A native of Ohio who was serving as superintendent of schools in Colfax, Washington, he became professor of mathematics and engineering.

Although he was not hired until the Spring of 1894, Professor William J. Spillman formed a part of the nucleus of Bryan's loyal and efficient faculty. Spillman, who had taught under Bryan at Vincennes University, had earlier graduated from the University of Missouri. Trained in several sciences, he became a strong head of the Agriculture Department. Bryan remembered, years later, that Spillman "was bubbling over with enthusiasm, was a good teacher, and could gather knowledge as rapidly as any man I ever knew."[61]

President Bryan, of course, could not effect major changes in calendar or curriculum during his first year, 1893-1894, since he took office only thirteen days before classes began. Alterations were ordered for the academic year 1894-1895, beginning with the replacement of the quarter (term) system with a semester schedule. In addition, the college offered a revamped and enlarged list of courses. Nine departments appeared, covering (I) mathematics and civil engineering (including mining engineering), (II) chemistry, (III) botany and zoology, (IV) agriculture, (V) horticulture, (VI) English language and literature, (VII) economic science and history, (VIII) mechanical engineering (Including electrical, steam, and hydraulic), and (IX) military science and tactics. Since the small faculty faced approximately 100 students the first semester, all but eleven of whom were sub-collegiate, there was no need to staff fully Bryan's ambitious new curriculum in the first or second year. There were no upperclassmen present.[62]

In general, the enlarged and more diversified program reflected a support for a practical education. Waller's courses in mathematics were "to render the student capable of using them as tools in the various engineering courses." Only in the future would the faculty introduce the study of pure mathematics. In chemistry, Fulmer assured students that he would present enough theory so that "the different operations conducted by the student will be performed with a clear understanding of the principles involved." Piper's botanical and zoological courses emphasized "the economic phases of the subjects." Spillman's agricultural students, on the other hand, although avowedly pursuing a practical subject, were to be thoroughly grounded in zoology, botany, and chemistry.[63]

Bryan, who headed the Department of Economic Science and History, emphasized the goal of providing "adequate means of studying the social and economic development of the race." His courses supported the Anglo-Saxon interpretation of the history of England and the United States, especially courses in Medieval and Modern History, English and American Constitutional History, and Political Economy. But, Bryan denied that he offered any "theoretic system of politics or economics," insisting instead on the superiority of "the wisdom which comes through a knowledge of the facts of human history, and a close observation of social and economic conditions."[64]

English and foreign languages, it was thought, should play a prominent role in collegiate studies since skilled use of them was essential to clear thought and expression by all graduates. Annie Howard, Instructor in foreign languages, asserted that understanding "advanced technical courses are [sic] next to impossible without a command of one or more languages other than English." Hence, she proposed to teach scientific and engineering students to read French and German scientific treatises. Drilling in foreign languages, in addition, would discipline the minds of students, a traditional role for studies deemed esoteric in the popular mind. Elevation of student thought through bringing it into contact with great British and American authors also formed a strong motive for offering literature courses.[65]

Though the practical aspects of all fields of study were emphasized, the collegiate curriculum was not intended to be simply technical in orientation. Students had to pass, in addition to a major line, two years of a foreign language. They also had to complete a one semester course in the history of medieval and modern Europe, two semester courses in English language and literature, and two semester courses in mathematics. All male students were required to take military drill. Music, athletics, and informal activities in domestic science (for the women) were listed as voluntary activities.[66]

President Bryan probably worked harder and for longer hours than anyone else. Certainly, he had more duties than anyone else. As president, he had no staff, so he served as recruiting officer, concerning himself intimately with admissions procedures and policies. He supervised or worked personally in developing public relations, keeping records, selling textbooks, supervising discipline, and maintaining correspondence with parents.[67] As professor, he taught his several courses in history and political economy, at first with little assistance. He also was director of the agricultural experiment station, a task foreign to his previous experiences. Bryan also spent a good deal of energy watching for machinations, real or rumored, by Lilley's local supporters.[68]

Treasurer A. H. Smith of the deposed first Board of Regents constituted a great annoyance to President Bryan by refusing to transfer $17,000 in Morrill Act funds to his successor. Smith's intransigence forced Bryan to delay payments to beseeching creditors for long periods. Finally, on August 21, 1894, Smith surrendered the money to new treasurer John W. Stearns at a meeting at the Fidelity Trust Company Bank in Tacoma, putting an end to a miserable episode.[69]

Smith's surrender of the college's funds did not end financial problems. State appropriations proved wholly inadequate for funding instruction. Perhaps as serious for good relations with federal authorities as well as for proper administration, were the difficulties in classifying and justifying expenditure of Morrill funds. The infancy of the institution, with attendant unsettled conditions and turn-over

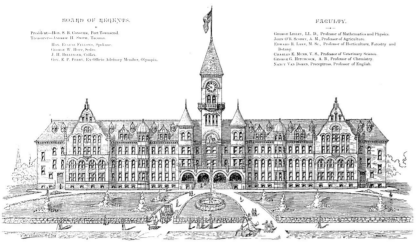

THE PROPOSED BUILDING FOR THE STATE AGRICULTURAL COLLEGE AND SCHOOL OF SCIENCE.

WAC's promoters had a set of grandiose architectural plans drawn up for the new institution. Pictured here is a frontal view of what they hoped would be the school's main structure. College President E. A. Bryan subsequently declared the design to be ". . . wholly visionary and impractical." (Private collection)

of administrators and faculty, rendered it difficult to determine just what had been taught by each faculty member. "For example," Bryan reported, there were unusual circumstances, such as "the teaching of physics by the professor of Economic Science, and the teaching of a class in Algebra by the professor of Horticulture."[70]

Bryan, as director of the experiment station, incurred the criticism of Alfred C. True, director of all experiment stations of the United States Department of Agriculture, by permitting Lyman C. Read, an assistant in horticulture at the station, to give music lessons in addition to his regular duties. Expecting opposition, Bryan instructed Regent Charles R. Conner, visiting True in Washington D. C., to seek permission to use Read to teach music, arguing that the new state of Washington did not have sufficient resources to meet all needs in an orthodox manner and had to resort to makeshift arrangements. Conner was to assure True that "we are really doing a great deal of station work, only a small portion of the time of the staff [is] being devoted to teaching." Furthermore, he wrote, the teaching was not paid for out of station monies. True denied the petition, a decision no doubt appropriate from the standpoint of the national program, but one that indeed overlooked the infancy and small scope of the entire program in Pullman.[71]

As he approached the end of his first year at Washington Agricultural College, in the winter and spring of 1894, Bryan still feared the machinations of the "Lilley Crowd." His worst fears soon seemed to be realized. Disturbing accusations against the integrity of the Board of Regents, evidently arising from the dissident Pullman group, led Governor John H. McGraw first to visit the campus and town and later to dispatch an investigator to search out charges of corruption in connection with building construction and malfeasance in office by the Regents. When confronted, the accusers, would neither swear to their charges nor supply evidence. The governor absolved the college administration of any wrongdoing in the matter and, in Bryan's view, became a strong supporter of the institution. Subsequently, the Board of Regents determined that Professor E. R. Lake, head of the work in horticulture, forestry, and botany, had joined a group of men making charges, seemingly with the intent "to wreck the college." Lake refused to resign his position, but at the end of the term was "retired," to use Bryan's expression.[72]

Regent H. S. Blandford responded optimistically to the Lake's ouster, writing to "Friend Bryan" that "I may say that I do not propose to pay any more attention to the Lilley crowd. So far as I am concerned, I shall pay no regard to charges of any kind, signed or unsigned." Bryan soon displayed his own optimism about the future, commending his colleagues for faithfully carrying out their work in the face of many hardships and predicting new levels of student achievement that would accompany the improvement of facilities, as well as a quieting of off-campus criticism.[73]

Sometime later, when reviewing the first two years of his administration, Bryan called to the Regents' attention what he believed was the greatest fallacy they could fall heir to—pinning hopes for success upon purely materialistic or practical goals. He offered what by then must have begun sounding like a familiar homily regarding the purpose and role of the land-grant college. Higher learning, he stated, must be "collegiate work; that is *advanced* scientific and technical work and a liberal education." But, this broad education also must be designed for the welfare of the "industrial classes." Hence, it must always be oriented to economic values and to the growth of citizenship, rather than to intellectualism for its own sake. Optimistic that science would, in the long run, open the door to individual achievement and progress in society, Bryan recognized that the bulk of his 1895 collegiate students chose practical majors in engineering or economics, rather than courses of study that entailed long-range searches for scientific truth. He noted that majors in agriculture or horticulture were few, while many farmers' sons seemed more interested in careers as engineers, merchants, and accountants, rather than succeeding their fathers on the family farm.[74]

Bryan had no doubt that this "difficulty," whereby students overwhelmingly chose practical studies, "will right itself largely as the institution grows older." Such optimism might have seemed justifiable because of the nucleus of gifted faculty already assembled. But, Charles V. Piper, one of the most talented of the group, had such a heavy teaching load, as Bryan reported, that he had to curtail his research at the experiment station. In the laboratory and lecture hall, Piper emphasized the practical aspects of botanical and zoological studies, rather than fundamental knowledge. Professor Elton Fulmer, the chemist, may have had the most unenviable set of tasks, as the Bryan took full advantage of his skills and rationalized that "the nature of the work in the Chemical Department enables Professor Fulmer to instruct more classes at one time than is possible in most departments." He also taught geology and mineralogy. Indeed, Bryan had personal knowledge of the severity of teaching problems. As professor of economic science and history, he taught all the courses in that department, which certainly left little time to explore new discoveries and theories in the fields covered by his chair or even to contemplate theories of administration.[75]

Sometime later, when reviewing the first two years of his administration, Bryan called to the Regents' attention what he believed was the greatest fallacy they could fall heir to—pinning hopes for success upon purely materialistic or practical goals.

Lack of proper facilities and equipment, of course, handicapped educational advance, a matter which the Regents had attacked with modest success amid glaring errors and misguided steps. The "Crib" and the first college hall had provided little more than stop-gap shelter for classes. First plans for a permanent academic structure yielded, on paper, a gargantuan "castle," as Bryan contemptuously termed it. Lack of funds, rather than a return to common sense, prevented the first Board of Regents from trying to build it. That Board did, however, build an "ungainly and inefficient dormitory," later named Ferry Hall.[76]

The second Board adopted a more circumspect attitude toward means and designs. Between 1894-1896 it succeeded admirably in constructing a mechanic arts hall, an administration building, and a women's dormitory, later named Stevens Hall. Though not greatly celebrated as architecture, the mechanic arts hall soon became very popular, as it was completely equipped for engineering laboratories, machine work, woodworking, and mechanical drawing. Stevens Hall provided the women students with a splendid residence, heralded locally as representing "the old colonial style." It also offered the most modern conveniences, including an "upper porch . . . [which] will in winter be enclosed with glazed sash, thus affording an opportunity for exercise in the sunlight without the inclemency of the weather."[77]

The Administration Building, located on the western edge of the campus, closest to Pullman, became the center of campus life and the epitome of the first years of the college. With dimensions of 156 by 89 feet, large by standards of that day, its exterior of brick and granite, it stood impressively on the brow of College Hill. The granite exterior trim represented a departure from the sandstone used on other buildings. As on all the early buildings, however, the authorities manufactured the brick from a clay deposit up the hill from Stevens Hall. The necessity of using local materials provided a homogeneous appearance. The four story structure housed laboratories, library, class rooms, an assembly hall, and offices.[78]

The dedication of the Administration Building on June 26, 1895, served as a substitute for Commencement, there being no senior class. It was a grand two-day celebration, with many notables present according to the *Evergreen*, the student newspaper. Inspired by the new building, Bryan seized the moment to advocate a broad and liberal education. The enlightenment of the people, he stated, requires that they recognize that "the mind grows by what it feeds upon. We have come to know that it may feed upon the common things of nature about it and receive as true a growth as from words." The sciences, he stated, would free humanity as completely as would philosophy and literature. He believed that the Washington Agricultural College was ready to provide true enlightenment of the people with the opening of the new building, concluding that "If we are true to our trust, we will here offer the best that science has to offer."[79]

Bryan's more immediate concerns were with the introduction of several new non-degree or sub-collegiate programs in the next two

●

The dedication of the Administration Building on June 26, 1895, served as a substitute for Commencement, there being no senior class. It was a grand two-day celebration, with many notables present according to the Evergreen, *the student newspaper.*

●

years. The catalog for 1895-1896 announced a two year school of pharmacy, designed to prepare druggists for state certification. Classes began in 1896 under the direction of chemist George H. Watt, who had joined the faculty in another capacity in December 1892. Dr. Sophus B. Nelson, a young veterinarian trained at Copenhagen and the State College of Iowa, headed a program in Veterinary Science. Nelson was to provide service courses to agriculture students and two years of preparation for majors who might then finish in an Eastern veterinary college. A school of business also opened to offer commercial subjects. Practical training in farming and dairying now replaced the previously offered short courses in those subjects.[80]

The Sixth Annual Catalogue of 1896-1897, announced that the college "takes pleasure" in providing training in vocal music and piano, thus finally attaining a desire for artistic expression harbored from the opening of the institution. The Regents hired Lillian A. Bolster to teach piano, reporting that she had studied under the "best teachers in the east." Mrs. W. J. Windus, "well known as a vocalist and teacher of voice culture," would handle vocal music. Students could not major in music and special fees for this work emphasized its seminary or non-collegiate standing.[81]

Since, by law, the college had the duty to train teachers of science, a program in education was introduced in 1897. This included courses in psychology, the history of education, and theory and practice of teaching. There is no indication as to who might have taught these new courses but Bryan seems the most likely candidate. He had already shown considerable interest in Washington's high school curricula and had begun evaluating high schools for accreditation of programs. He had, of course, also taught and supervised public schools in the Midwest.[82]

In this period, extracurricular activities took on greater variety and formality, due in part to the faculty's continued involvement and direction. No doubt, it was hoped that well organized literary and musical societies would fill a gap in student education, since the curriculum offered few classes in the humanities. The 1896 catalogue, for instance, listed three literary groups: the Che-Wa-Wa Society serving preparatory students, and the Washington and the Columbian societies, which included both collegiate and preparatory students as members. These organizations met on Friday evenings. An English Club, on the other hand, met once a month under faculty supervision to discuss papers prepared by its members, and the *Faust-Verein, Schiller-Verein,* and French Club specialized in German and French discussions and readings respectively. In addition, a Mechanical Engineers' Club and a Civil Engineer's Club studied technical literature and topics in their fields. To balance the offering, the YMCA and YWCA met each Sunday for Bible study.[83]

Oratorical exercises drew large audiences, as well as the critical attention of the faculty. Prizes could be at stake and winners were lionized as much as, or perhaps even more than, star athletes. Indeed, when the Che-Wa-Wa and the Columbian literary societies had held their first contest on the evening of November 25, 1893, they introduced an outside set of judges, headed by President F. B. Gault of the University of Idaho, to select winners and award literary volumes as prizes (in this case, *Longfellow's Poems, Ben Hur, Tom Brown's School Days,* and *Tom Brown at Oxford*). Interest in the societies remained high. For example, the *Evergreen* in April 1896, while reporting that a new oratorical society had been formed, proclaimed that rhetoric had "been predominant in the minds of our college students" in the past few months—a gratifying matter since it was "one of the principal constituents of a symmetrical and well-rounded intellect."[84]

Special occasions, such as George Washington's birthday and other holidays, brought forth patriotic gatherings with speeches and singing. Within the first few weeks of the college's opening, in fact, President Lilley and the original faculty held an Arbor Day celebration and had planted trees on the campus. This exercise remained a popular annual event for many years.

The Arbor Day festivities of April 24, 1896, for example, were a great success according to the Pullman *Herald.* In the morning, school children planted fourteen saplings at the town's public school grounds, and then proceeded on to College Hill to join local residents and the students and faculty from the college in exercises at the auditorium. Speeches were presented, in which Bryan, for one, foresaw Pullman as being transformed into a city of trees and parks, and a committee was formed to beautify the town with landscaped greenery. John A. Balmer, the professor of horticulture, then led the crowd in the planting of seedlings on campus. Trees gathered from Moscow Mountain the day before were distributed free. The saplings were attended with much care, as each class ceremoniously planted and dedicated individual trees.[85]

Intercollegiate athletics, which began with baseball contests a few weeks after the opening of the institution in 1892, continued with the first football game in November 1894. The Washington Agricultural College team, called the "Farmers," played the University of Idaho, defeating the latter 10-0. A sizeable delegation travelled to Moscow to witness the contest and cheer for "the Pink and Blue [to] wave Victoriously Over the Orange and White." They filled the air with the college cheer: "W.A.C. hu-rah! hu-rah! hu-rah!—W.A.C. hu-rah! hu-rah! hu-rah."[86]

Next spring, thirty students began training for track and field events, and competitive baseball also was played, though the field was unplayable until early April. The climax of spring athletics came on Field Day, when WAC and the University of Idaho competed in seventeen track and field events in Pullman. An excursion train brought 300 to 400 Moscow, Idaho, residents to downtown Pullman, where the visitors were hosted at hotel luncheons before proceeding up on campus. Meanwhile, Pullman's merchants closed their shops, and "the town people turned out en masse to witness and enjoy the contests, in which they entered with as much zest as the participants themselves," the University of Idaho athletes were defeated, winning only four events, while the home team won thirteen.[87]

Professor William J. Spillman, hired by Bryan in the spring of 1894 formed a part of the nucleus for a loyal and efficient faculty. Spillman had taught under Bryan at Vincennes University and was trained in several sciences. He soon became a strong head of the agriculture department. (Historical Photograph Collections, Washington State University Libraries)

When the college reopened in the fall, the 1895 football squad had enough players for two teams, and played two games that season. Captain Francis M. Lowden coached the squad, assisted by Professor William J. Spillman. A mid season scouting report in the *Evergreen* stated that the team was weak in "interference," but they had set about correcting it. The result for that year? They defeated the University of Idaho 10-4 and the Spokane Amateur Athletic Club 26-4.[88]

The Pullman campus was a tightly knit community, permitting the president and faculty to be intimately concerned with student life. Of course, collegiate tradition dictated that the administration and faculty should act out the role of parents to their youthful charges.

Problems regarding amateurism and sportsmanship existed from the beginning, and remained matters of concern both to Bryan and student leaders. On August 20, 1895, for instance, President F. B. Gault of the University of Idaho complained that the Pullman college had enticed an Idaho athlete to change schools, and other problems in athletics arose in the following year.[89] The Field Day between the two colleges, held in Moscow on May 29, 1896, was a victory for Idaho 26-18, but the results were difficult for some to accept with equanimity. The *Evergreen* reported that several of the victors "forgot their positions as gentlemen, one man being carried so far as to use strong language in loud and boisterous terms [*sic*]." The partisan reporter then noted: "In regard to our boys, we are pleased to say that their conduct in victory or defeat has been above reproach."[90]

Athletic relations with the University of Idaho worsened when Bryan cancelled the 1896 football game at the request of Pullman citizens and the town council. He stated that a diphtheria outbreak in Moscow might spread to Pullman residents if the populations of the two towns were allowed to mix. Since Bryan did not believe the outbreak was serious, he may have had other reasons for the cancellation, for indeed the neighboring colleges had haggled over disputes arising at the Field Day and football contests.[91]

No football game or track meet was scheduled with the University of Idaho in 1897 as ill feelings persisted between the schools. Finally, in the spring of 1898, the two institutions resumed athletic competition. Meanwhile, Bryan appointed a faculty committee, consisting of instructors John A. Balmer, Osmar L. Waller, and S. H. Webster, to recommend a system for regulating athletic competition.

On June 25, 1898, the committee presented a plan that was quickly adopted. Taking matters out of the hands of the old student-guided Athletic Association, the committee recommended that three members of the faculty, plus three student athletes, should control and supervise intercollegiate athletic events. There were to be no more than six football contests, with none after Thanksgiving, and a maximum of ten baseball games, and "due care" was to "be taken to eliminate undesirable contests with clubs of little or no standing." The reorganized Athletic Association, however, boldly attempted to exert control over the sportsmanship and behavior of all students, not just the athletes, when recommending "that some system of demerits ought to be devised for use on the athletic grounds, and campus, to cover the vices of swearing, smoking, trespassing on the grass, picking flowers, using the space outside laboratory windows for a dustbin, and other offences against decency."[92]

Trouble arose again during the 1898 football game with Idaho, when the WAC team walked off the field before the opening kickoff, protesting that Idaho halfback McFarland, who had been a star with the Carlisle (Pennsylvania) Indians, and two other players, had enrolled only a few days before the game. It appeared to the Pullman players that the men had signed up at the Moscow college just to play in the contest, though an administrator from the University of Idaho later denied the charge. The WAC team was willing to play if McFarland was benched, but the offer was refused. The referee picked up the ball and declared the game forfeited to the University of Idaho. Matters were patched up in time for the 1899 season, when WAC won 11-0.[93]

The Pullman campus was a tightly knit community, permitting the president and faculty to be intimately concerned with student life. Of course, collegiate tradition dictated that the administration and faculty should act out the role of parents to their youthful charges. Indeed, Bryan originally had hoped to be spared some of the tasks of surrogate parents by not establishing a dormitory system. He reluctantly acknowledged, however, that the remote location and the small size of Pullman made dormitories necessary. He must also have recognized that the presence of very young prep school pupils imposed a special parental responsibility.[94]

To fulfill the parental obligation, Bryan appointed certain professors as proctors for the boys' dormitory and designated student assistants, called "inspectors," to assist in maintaining good order, decorum, and the rules of curfew. These were unpaid positions. Nancy Van Doren, an English professor, presided over the girls' dormitory as preceptress.[95]

To the faculty fell the larger task of governing the student body in matters which reached far beyond the tasks of proctors and the preceptress. On October 1, 1894, for example, Professor Piper presented a set of regulations for the boys' dormitory which the faculty approved. The Spartan schedule adopted awakened students at 6:30 a.m. and turned off the lights at 10:30 p.m. They were to attend class or study individually from eight in the morning to noon, and from one to three in the afternoon, and to study again from seven to 10:15 in the evening. Proctors and inspectors not only monitored study hours but the cleanliness of the rooms, which, among other things, meant patrolling to make certain tobacco was not used in the building. The faculty passed similar regulations for the women soon thereafter.[96]

The Faculty entered conscientiously into the parental role. On October 19, 1894, Secretary Piper, representing a new faculty Committee on Student Affairs, announced that it would "keep an eye on the moral, social and intellectual life of the student body and make suggestions both to the individual students and to the faculty that may promote a higher and better life." Bryan recognized that he had imposed "arduous duties" which would require "rare wisdom."[97]

The faculty, indeed, did spend much time in counselling students on academic problems, on occasion dropping them from school for

To the faculty fell the larger task of governing the student body in matters which reached far beyond the tasks of proctors and the preceptress.

grade deficiencies. Since Lilley's administration, many students had remained in school due to the many part-time jobs that were made available. Then, in 1896, the Regents joined the faculty in developing a constructive program of scholarships in 1896, whereby the commissioners of each county granted an award relieving one student of special fees and dormitory charges (there was, as yet, no tuition charge for Washingtonians). This was a welcome boon to poor students, but its possible effect on scholarship or behavior is not known.[98]

Unfortunately, professors had to devote an inordinate amount of time and energy to curbing disruptive student behavior. Infractions of dormitory and campus rules carried demerits. When these reached fifty, offenders were suspended from school for a stated period, being required, at least in some cases, to demonstrate constructive and corrective activity before being re-admitted.[99]

On one day in October, 1895, President Bryan wrote letters to three parents reporting with "deep regret" that he had suspended their sons for becoming drunk in Moscow and then visiting houses of ill-fame there and in Pullman. "It is absolutely necessary," he wrote, "where a large number of young men are committed to our care to use every precaution to prevent debauchery and to insure good conduct." Punishments did not prevent other visits to disorderly houses, or drunkenness, and at least one case of adultery carried into a court of law.[100] In addition, the faculty's Committee on Discipline discovered students visiting gambling establishments in Pullman. In one instance, four students who confessed and promised to reform were shown leniency, according to the faculty minutes. They lost the usual dormitory privileges for three months, which included forfeiture of the right to play cards in the dormitory or to leave the campus except Saturday afternoons, without written permission from Bryan.[101]

Close supervision of life in Ferry Hall, the boys' dormitory, led intermittently to attacks on the proctors and, inevitably, to other pranks. On one day in April 1897, a student attempted to flood the proctor's room with water, which led to his "banishment from the dormitory for the rest of the year."[102] On June 3, 1897, a bomb exploded in Ferry Hall, breaking windows and damaging walls and hallways in the first two floors. It appeared at first that the proctor might have been the target. But, as his room was some twenty-five feet away from the blast, the perpetrators, two students, were absolved of that charge. Later, it became clear that the object had been merely to shock the residents. Though the students were suspended indefinitely, there is no evidence as to who paid for the damages.[103]

Bryan seized numerous opportunities to lecture guilty students and their parents. Often, he attempted to involve the latter in a rehabilitation of their wayward offspring. When a Spokane attorney protested as too drastic Professor Piper's refusal to permit his son "to attend a place of amusement in the village" along with other students, Bryan tried to enlist the father to impress upon his son the need to live up to the rules. Other letters testified to Bryan's close observation of student study habits, academic performance, dress and deportment. Virtually all of the correspondence concerned male students.[104]

The epitome of expectations of genteel student behavior and beliefs may have been expressed in an incident which began when students were congratulated for their patriotic observance in raising the American flag over the campus every day. Judge Norman Buck, Commandant of the Grand Army of the Republic for Washington and Alaska, conveyed these seemingly uncontroversial greetings to President Bryan in early April 1896. A few days later, a reply by Joe Smith, student, appeared in the Spokane *Spokesman-Review* denying the judge's prerogative to pass judgment on the acts of patriotism by the students and querying whether he would accept student criticism of his behavior in court. In the eyes of the Spokane editor and those of the editors of the Pullman *Herald*, and the Portland *Oregonian*, Smith's comments were insulting and unpatriotic.

In the outcry that occurred, Joe Smith seemed alone in his position. The faculty resolved that the article was "disrespectful and uncalled for" and condemned "its sentiments in the severest terms." So that it would not happen again, the faculty recommended that such letters must be first submitted for the president's approval before mailing. This minor tempest apparently produced a rally of students who drew up resolutions condemning Smith's actions. General T. R. Tannatt, a Regent, gathered up the evidence to use in placating the Grand Army of the Republic. Joe Smith, in any event, soon left the college and his studies, having taken the measure of the political climate and finding it unfavorable for criticism of patriotic symbols and the status quo.[105]

In 1896-1897, state-wide political turmoil brought a new challenge to the college, one that Bryan considered to be the most serious of his career. Washington's Populist Party, after fusing with Democrats and free-silver Republicans, swept the state's elective offices and the legislature in the general election of November 1896. The new fusionist party was dedicated to making drastic, if not draconian, cuts in state expenditures, which many voters, justly or not, had considered as extravagant. These events followed in the wake of the Panic of 1893, when economic depression affected large segments of rural and urban America. All state supported institutions, including Pullman's struggling new college, could expect serious difficulties with funding.

In the spring of 1897, the newly elected Populist governor, John R. Rogers, paid a political debt to C. W. Young, who had been instrumental in his election, by appointing two Pullmanites, Walter V. Windus and Dr. John L. Powell to the Board of Regents. This development shocked Bryan since it suggested once again the presence of a local cabal hostile to him, the Board of Regents, and most of the faculty.

Bryan acceded to Rogers's second challenge: in which the governor demanded a reduction in professors' salaries in order to meet budget stringencies. The faculty supported Bryan by voluntarily accepting salary cuts in September 1897, for a two-year period. In the

Nancy L. Van Doren, WAC's first woman faculty member, was one of the five original instructors hired by Lilley in 1891. She taught English, served as school librarian, and was Preceptress of Stevens Hall until she left the institution in 1905. (Historical Photograph Collections, Washington State University Libraries)

Bryan expected to succeed, too, by placing on the faculty robust individuals who possessed the same confidence in the institution and in their own abilities and strength as he possessed.

midst of these negotiations, Bryan threatened to resign but colleagues dissuaded him from doing so.[106] Though many difficulties remained, unusually mild weather in the winter and spring of 1898 reduced heating costs, which in part alleviated the crisis and mitigated Governor Rogers' stern warnings that school must close when the money ran out. During the emergency, Bryan demonstrated his own ability to manipulate funds, transferring all expenditures possible to the Morrill and Hatch acts, since state funds were scarce.[107]

Subsequently, Rogers removed the offensive pair of Pullman Regents, rendering Bryan's life easier. The governor then appointed three new Regents, including George H. Witt of Harrington. Bryan wooed Regent Witt, a prominent Populist politician, by declaring his adherence to efficient business practices in running the school. But he warned that "the life and reputation of an educational institution are very delicate, quick to receive injury and slow to recover. Slowly and painfully, we have won a strong place in the confidence of the people and the outlook in that regard is splendid and assures us a rapid and enduring growth."[108]

Bryan expected to succeed, too, by placing on the faculty robust individuals who possessed the same confidence in the institution and in their own abilities and strength as he possessed. Thus, when, in June 1896, Dr. Albert E. Egge, of Iowa City, Iowa, sought to relinquish his recent appointment as professor of English literature, Bryan refused to release him, instead "heartily" welcoming him to the Palouse. The president felt dismay at signs of weakness and handicap when he learned that Egge's wife would not accompany him that first year. He felt impelled to lecture the new professor, writing: "It is our desire to gather in as a faculty young, strong, competent men who will enter heartily into the work of building this institution and. . . . [to that end] we would prefer men with families and men who would wish to make their home here rather than elsewhere. . . ."[109]

If Bryan investigated a new male faculty member's family and religious backgrounds, he seldom, if ever, entertained the idea of appointing women candidates to positions of prestige and power. He defended his largely male faculty as best he could before the Regents. In his report to the Board on June 30, 1898, Bryan stated that most faculty were overworked and faced with impossible expectations that they should teach full time and also carry a significant research program. His own position, he reported, was difficult. He received no salary as president. One-fourth of his remuneration was as Director of the Experiment Station and the remainder he received for teaching four classes in Economic Science and History. Salary restorations attributable more to the return of prosperity than to executive skill, were made in September, 1899. At that time, Bryan's salary returned to $4,000 per year while most professors were restored to a scale ranging from $1,500 to $1,600.[110]

In the midst of financial difficulties and unsettling regent appointments, the faculty prepared for the first commencement, to be held in June 1897. On April 30, the faculty approved the degrees of Bachelor of Science in Civil and Mechanical Engineering, Geology,

Chemistry, Agriculture, Horticulture, Botany, and Economic Science and History. It also approved of the degrees of Bachelor of Letters in English and Modern Languages. Notably, recipients of college degrees must not only have completed thirty full courses, but also must have submitted and defended a senior thesis, "the results of an exhaustive study, and in so far as the equipment of the college affords facilities, it must show original research in some topic connected with the candidate's major subject."[111]

Commencement, in time-honored fashion, began on June 18, 1897, and for the next week displayed artistic, literary and musical talents as well as a baccalaureate sermon and the graduation of senior preparatory students. At the college graduation on June 24, Governor John R. Rogers handed out five bachelors of arts degrees and two bachelor of letters degrees.[112]

According to the Spokane *Chronicle*, the seven graduates faced "a vast throng . . . far beyond the capacity of the hall." The paper editorialized approvingly that "the Agricultural College is no kid glove shop. There are no students here who have been brought up to think lightly of the dignity of labor. . . ." An irony may have been hidden to the reporter—of the seven graduates none was in agriculture or horticulture. In addition to the two bachelor of letters degrees, there were degree recipients in civil engineering, botany, economic science and history, and electrical engineering.[113]

The editor of the Spokane *Spokesman-Review* acknowledged that the college was a helpful and elevating influence, in spite of some of the rowdyism which had been reported, as he contemplated Bryan's "scholarly" and "masterful" address on "characteristics." Directing his remarks to the graduates, Bryan spoke not at all of the land-grant mission or the scientific method, but of the "insatiable" urge to knowledge and to power, reminding his hearers of a deep moral obligation to use both wisely.[114] Bryan, no doubt, hoped that Governor Rogers had listened intently and had agreed with him. To a regent who evidently had not attended Commencement, the president wrote that the affair had been "pleasant" with the governor having expressed himself as highly satisfied with the college. Bryan's chief political anxiety remained—that the governor might want to run the institution himself. That development, Bryan remarked, would result in his resignation.[115]

Five months later, on the night of November 23, Ferry Hall burned to the ground, making about one hundred male students homeless and destroying most of their personal property. The fire started in the kitchen and spread rapidly, soon engulfing the entire structure despite the bucket brigade formed to carry water to the blaze. Fortunately, there was no loss of life, and the entire Pullman community rallied to aid the young men with food, shelter, clothing, and money. The college rented an unused building downtown for a nominal sum and furnished it as a temporary dormitory. Churches provided turkey dinners on Thanksgiving, which came only a few days after the fire.

•

In the midst of financial difficulties and unsettling regent appointments, the faculty prepared for the first commencement, to be held in June 1897. On April 30, the faculty approved the degrees of Bachelor of Science in Civil and Mechanical Engineering, Geology, Chemistry, Agriculture, Horticulture, Botany, and Economic Science and History. It also approved of the degrees of Bachelor of Letters in English and Modern Languages.

•

Bryan reported to the Board of Regents that these developments demonstrated "a cordial relation between the College and the people of Pullman, which cannot but add to the usefulness of the college and its good name throughout the state." The boys added their own solemn thanks for the help and resolved to practice rigid economies in order to finish the school year. But, humor abounded, as well. The *Evergreen* carried jokes about the fire, such as that of a young man who might write home to his father: "Dear Father—Dormitory burned last night; dressed in fig leaf; send money. B. D. B." The camaraderie of the moment was revealed in J. B. Winston's remark to a dormitory mate at the height of excitement, trying to save valuables, "Crossen, throw the wash bowl and looking glass out the window, and I will carry the bedding out." A hope which all dwellers might assent to was wrapped up in the remark by Clemons, "Dave, did the demerits burn up?"[116]

In the Autumn of 1898, Bryan found a platform from which to introduce his ideas and institution to a wider audience than previously when he addressed the National Association of Agricultural Colleges in Washington, D. C. Speaking under the title, "Some Recent Changes in the Theory of Higher Education," he reminded his peers that the land-grant mission required that they provide the industrial classes with the best practical as well as liberal education. Science, he stated, provided the method of inquiry, adaptable to all fields of study, including education. That method applied "common sense to the acquirement of accurate knowledge." He reduced theory to a mere "rational explanation . . . to modify, strengthen, or defend the existing process." The method of science, when employed in a highly individualized elective system, whereby students chose their studies without interference, such as at Harvard, would be democratizing and liberating. It would destroy outmoded tradition and permit individuals to develop the practical, pragmatic culture needed to satisfy the common needs of humanity.[117]

Many years later, in 1929, Bryan recalled happily, but somewhat extravagantly, the wisdom of President Charles W. Eliot of Harvard in developing free election, which had led "the way out of the slough of despondency into which the American college had sunk," bringing it into "the promised land of freedom and light." In 1898, on the contrary, he had recognized that for Washington Agricultural College escaping the "slough of despondency" and attaining the goals of the land-grant college required, not free election, but the addition of a full college curriculum. He admitted that in order to concentrate on the main purpose of both federal and state legislation they had "omitted many of the subjects of a literary nature which might be included." He vowed, once again, "to make the central thought of Senator Morrill the central thought of this institution, viz., to bring to human industry of whatever kind, the best results of modern science." To attain that objective, no doubt, some modified free-elective system might be needed.[118]

Actually, at the opening of the legislative session in January 1899, Bryan had more pressing concerns than educational philosophy. He

This photograph, taken relatively early in the development of the WAC campus, looks east over the site where Johnson Hall stands. (Historical Photograph Collections, Washington State University Libraries)

dreaded the possibility that the University of Washington, out of jealousy, might force a reduction in capital funds he intended to request for a new Ferry Hall and for a science building. His fears were unfounded, for in late February he witnessed passage of the building measure. Bryan then possessed $40,000 for rebuilding Ferry Hall and $60,000 to construct a central core structure to house all the sciences.[119]

The rivalry with the University of Washington warmed up again when legislators were confronted with the charge of duplication of programs. It began when Senator Herman D. Crow of Spokane (later a regent from 1901-1905), introduced a bill to change the name of the institution to Washington State College. Friends of the college joined President Bryan and the Board of Regents to support Crow's proposed name, which they believed would properly represent the broad offering of the school. Opponents raised the specter of duplication, accusing Bryan of seeking to create a second state university.[120]

Senator Harold Preston, of Seattle, in particular, claimed that Bryan and the Regents wanted to duplicate the University. Bryan confined his rebuttal largely to a defense of the legal obligation of his school to offer engineering and engineering education. The editor of the Seattle *Post-Intelligencer*, on May 5, 1899, arrogantly lectured Bryan for neglecting his one true function–that of providing a good agricultural education. He wrote that not only had it been a mistake to separate agriculture from the state university in Seattle but he assured Bryan that the "people" would "rebuke" him for trying to create a second university. The president responded with a ponderous defense of his position, which the *Post-Intelligencer* published on May 15. The editor stood his ground, however, reporting that before publication he had handed Bryan's article around to friends of both schools "and [it] has been commented upon with much disfavor."[121]

On the other side of the coin, Editor William Goodyear of the Colfax *Commoner*, a populist journal published in Colfax, found a special animus in Seattle's attitude toward the Washington Agricultural College, which he believed to result from its success in outstripping the University in attendance and reputation. The fact that the agricultural majors were in the minority at Pullman he attributed to "the gold standard, trust—breeding tariff and imperialist policies" advocated by the *Post-Intelligencer*, which made unattractive to many young people. Goodyear insisted that Bryan had carried on splendidly, but opponents insisted the farmers would be cheated out of their identity and farming devalued if a new name were adopted.[122]

In the midst of controversy, Bryan never lost faith in his institution. He wrote to a friend in the East "that there is no institution in the northwest with so settled a policy, where tenure is so stable, and where the future of the institution is so bright." He also believed strongly in himself, stating "when I tell you that I am a staunch republican, and notwithstanding that fact, I have gone through a wildly populistic administration [that of Governor J. R. Rogers], and that this was about the only institution in the state which did so successfully, you will understand what I mean." The acid test for his leadership might be summed up in his statement that "it would be utterly impossible for anyone to have political pull enough, or any other kind of pull [for] that matter, to secure even the humblest position in the college." Bryan needed patience in 1899, for the legislature defeated the motion to change the name. He would need much more resolve and determination in the next decade and a half to meet more serious challenges to the integrity of the Washington Agricultural College and School of Science than that involved in the name dispute.[123]

Chapter Two

The Embattled College, 1900-1915

PRESIDENT BRYAN, THOUGH NOT UNMINDFUL OF DIFFICULT PROBLEMS ahead, wrote with satisfaction in June 1900 that "there have been many things upon which the institution may well be congratulated." He pointed out that 386 students had been enrolled in the 1899-1900 academic year, as opposed to 300 the preceding year. A recently started summer science school, he believed, would raise the total to more than 500. The student body had grown to a point where it included residents from thirty-one of the state's thirty-six counties, an indication that the Washington Agricultural College might soon realize its land-grant mission of providing services and meeting the educational demands of the entire state.[1]

The College celebrated its fourth Commencement in June 1900, granting fourteen bachelor's degrees and two pharmacy diplomas. Shortly after, a more portentous event occurred when the Regents dedicated Science Hall (the older half of the present Morrow Communications Center). Governor John R. Rogers served as President of the Day, and other celebrities also took part in the proceedings. Once again, President Bryan delivered the pertinent message. He envisioned the new structure as a "temple to science," tangible evidence that new facilities would mean an improved curriculum. In his address, he repeated a familiar refrain that science would solve mankind's problems and that "every building erected in the name of an advancing humanity is a sacred building."[2]

Certainly, the completion of Science Hall answered the faculty's pleas for more classroom and assembly space, as well as laboratories. Bryan himself had been forced to teach in his own office, due to scarcity of classrooms. The chemistry professor had to sacrifice even more; he loaned his personal laboratory and equipment to advanced students. Perhaps most unhappy of all was the veterinary faculty, which held "its recitations in the small, crowded, ill-smelling laboratory where pathological and other specimens are kept."[3] Now, there would be suitable lecture rooms for the science students and literary societies, plus space for laboratories, specimen collections, and museums. As an added structural feature, the eastern

OPPOSITE: *WAC women students gathered around Preceptress Nancy Van Doren on the porch in front of Stevens Hall.* (Historical Photograph Collections, Washington State University Libraries)

ends of the building's wings were given a "unique semicircular shape. . . [as] an adaptation of the structure to the uses of the flatiron microscope tables, affording better lighting and economy of space." Also much appreciated was the large amphitheater where veterinary clinics and demonstrations would soon be held.[4]

On the same occasion, the college dedicated a new, redesigned Ferry Hall (standing on the site of the old hall) as the men's dormitory. According to architectural historian J. Meredith Neil, the "very simple Georgian façade . . . dismayed contemporary observers," but they "hastened to admire the efficient and attractive interior" of the four-story structure. The building housed 180 students and contained a dining room that seated 200. Bryan found "the student rooms well-adapted to the purpose." Certainly, the president must have been pleased that this well-planned, fire-proof dormitory also promised to permit the faculty to maintain close student discipline.[5]

A year later, in June 1901, the president expressed confidence to the Board of Regents that "the general theory of the scope and character and aims of the college . . . may be accepted as determined." In an additional burst of optimism he noted that the "curriculum . . . is approaching a definitiveness which is gratifying." Bryan's constant wariness and occasional critical outbursts against threats posed by the University of Washington did not die. But he regarded his faculty and the student body as providing strength against such outside threats. He looked with favor, for example, on the expansion of Dr. Sophus Nelson's veterinary program from two years to three in 1900, after only three years of operation. When that program required a small hospital, several faculty drew the plans and supervised construction. Similarly, engineering professors made plans for a water works and an electrical system, to serve the needs voiced by Bryan.[6]

Students sometimes assisted in formulating the curriculum. On May 29, 1900, for instance, a hundred or more of them petitioned the faculty to establish a debate class. Professors Spillman, Beach, and Howard prepared a proposal for such a course, which the faculty adopted three weeks later. During the following year, the faculty also required participation in literary society exercises by all junior and middle preparatory pupils, as well as by students in the School of Agriculture.[7] Likewise in 1901, the faculty approved a regular collegiate course titled "Declamation and Dramatic Reading," in which one of Shakespeare's plays, *MacBeth* or *Julius Caesar*, would be studied "with especial view to vocal expression."[8]

President Bryan, who had served as Professor of Economic Science and History since his arrival, now retired from teaching, although he remained as chairman. The burden had been heavy since his teaching encompassed Medieval History, modern History of Europe and the United States, English and American Constitutional History, Political economy, and the Social History of the Laboring Classes. Now, however, Bryan instituted new courses in transportation studies and economic geography, as well as a course in sociology that he had

•

Students sometimes assisted in formulating the curriculum. On May 29, 1900, for instance, a hundred or more of them petitioned the faculty to establish a debate class.

•

always been too busy to offer. The president dared to extend the course burden because he had great confidence in his successor, Walter G. Beach, possessor of an M. A. from Harvard, who had joined the staff in 1898 and who had taught courses in education as well as the social sciences.[9]

The two men, however, held contrasting social philosophies. Beach was a liberal—indeed, Bryan characterized him as not a socialist, but as having some tendencies in that direction. Beach raised questions as to whether the conservative Bryan would place trust in him. Years later, the president stated that their personal differences did not matter, for the work was scientific. Confident that Beach was not a propagandist, Bryan stated that he had no fear of his results in the classroom. He had instructed Beach: "You will teach your students how to think and find the truth and will be concerned with that chiefly and with the methods of research." Beach succeeded in his task and became Chairman of the Department of Economic Science and History in September 1904.[10]

In 1903, at the close of his tenth year as president of the college, Bryan expressed pride in his achievements. The curriculum was, in his view, unfolding logically from the simple to the complex. He noted, in particular, that the technical short courses had justified their development by successfully training young people for occupations. In particular, they had produced professionals for business careers, dairying, shop work, agriculture, and the pharmaceutical trade. The preparatory department and the School of Agriculture had attained a similar objective: that of "preparing young people coming from country districts and the smaller towns for collegiate work."[11]

By 1905, steady increases in enrollment placed so much pressure on facilities the college's administration had to spend precious funds to construct a temporary four-classroom "shack." Hardly an architectural gem, it at least provided a warm and dry haven for professors and students for several years before being converted to lesser uses.[12]

New departments and formal collegiate programs were also created to meet increases in student interest, as well as well as to raise the prestige of particular disciplines. For instance, Geology profited from expansion and became a department in April 1904. Professor Solon Shedd, the sole member, gained the title of chairman. At that time, fifty-five students were enrolled in geology courses, and Shedd noted with pleasure that all were collegiate students (preparatory and other non-collegiate students not being permitted to enroll). Nevertheless, the actual number of students majoring in Geology remained small. In 1915, for example, Shedd reported only five candidates for the bachelor of science degree and but two graduate students. The total of 175 enrollees, however, pleased him since it revealed that many students elected Geology for general educational purposes and because Bryan appointed a second faculty member to teach Economic Geology.[13]

The Pacific Northwest fruit industry offered the most important stimulus to agricultural research in the first years of the new century.

Unfortunately, constant staff turnover left WAC's horticultural teaching and research sections in disarray. When Professor N. O. Booth resigned in 1904, Bryan seized the opportunity to reorganize, with the goal of placing the college and experiment station at the center of horticultural activities in Washington. Bryan's first move was to merge the departments of Agriculture and Horticulture, a step designed to provide greater efficiency and cooperation in research. Professor W. G. Thornber, appointed as the horticulturist, proved to be a capable director

Research findings by Charles V. Piper, Carl Melander, and Eldred Jenne were especially successful in controlling fruit pests, particularly the San Jose scale and the codling moth. These discoveries greatly stimulated the tree fruit and berry industries in the Pacific Northwest. The "very fever of enthusiasm" also extended to increasing student enrollments in Horticulture classes. Years later, Bryan recalled that "the number of students enrolled in this subject was equal to any other subdivision of the college." One result, in 1908, was that horticulturalists once again gained separate departmental status, a tribute to their success.[14]

In 1903, Professor Edith F. McDermott, noted for her work at Eastern institutions, inaugurated a program in Domestic Economy (Home Economics). Fitted out with laboratories in Morrill Hall, the program quickly became popular, so that two years later the Regents elevated it to a department that offered the baccalaureate degree. Indeed, development was so rapid that the Domestic Economy Department produced its first graduate the next year. By 1908, it moved into its own building, Van Doren Hall.[15]

In the spring 1906, the college inaugurated a fully collegiate curriculum in Latin, Pharmacy, and Veterinary Medicine. In each case, the Regents created departments, elevating the existing short, practical curricula in order to offer bachelor's degrees. In spite of these revisions, they retained existing short courses for practical training. In June 1906 the Regents authorized a sub-collegiate School of Forestry, which later would be a source of annoyance to the University of Washington and would trigger arguments about the duplication of the Seattle school's authorized curriculum.[16]

The two-member Latin Department offered a full range of classical courses, including "Livy, Cicero, and Horace," "The Letters of Pliny the Younger," "Tacitus," and "Roman Satire," as well as a course in Latin nomenclature for pharmacists. By the middle of the first decade of the twentieth century seven faculty offered an impressive array of foreign language studies. In addition to Latin, students could take courses in German, French, Spanish, and Scandinavian languages, all of which were designed to present cultural and literary studies, as well as training for the reading of scientific treatises in German and French.[17]

A deep commitment to teacher training and educational administration became evident in 1905 when the Regents approved more than a dozen courses, covering the methods of instruction in school subjects and administration of public schools. In doing so, the board went far beyond the college's meager offerings and the narrow intent of the original mandate to train teachers of science. As a further sign of commitment to pedagogy, Bryan appointed H. C. Sampson as the first professor of education, transferring him from an assistant professorship of English. Earlier, Sampson had served on the faculty of the Cheney Normal School, and after moving to Pullman, had distinguished himself in reorganizing the WAC preparatory department. Sampson, no doubt aided by Bryan, had to obtain the cooperation of interested departments in order to insure that many of the new courses were taught.[18]

Also in 1905, Bryan's dream of elevating the arts to a prominent position within the curriculum came closer to realization when the Regents approved a three-year School of Music that offered the degree of bachelor of music. Though music had not been among the studies enumerated in the Morrill Act, nor had it been provided for in the college's budget, Bryan did not doubt the legality or desirability of musical instruction. Recalling his early education, Bryan asserted: "In the olden day music was deemed a vital part of education and it was looked upon not as 'an accomplishment' but as an essential element in the education of the human soul." He also believed that the "somewhat isolated conditions such as we have in a new region," made music a necessary and desirable part of the curriculum.[19]

Some musical instruction and activity had been available in WAC's earliest days, when an extension staff member briefly offered choral singing (a matter discussed in chapter one). After that, the college employed piano and voice teachers whose income came largely from special fees paid by pupils. For example, in 1900, Anne Evanden taught piano on a guaranteed income of eighty dollars per month plus one-half of all proceeds over that amount. As Evanden pointed out when asking for her salary increase the next year, however, she did much more than teach piano. She prepared all musical programs and directed quartettes and musical club work, tasks covering six days per week. An art teacher, hired in the same year, taught drawing and painting also on an individual fee basis, but with less prospect than Evanden had for speedy attainment of collegiate status. Bryan acknowledged that art had a refining influence, but evidently agreed with a faculty committee in deciding that only advanced free-hand drawing might carry collegiate credit.[20]

A marked advance in music instruction occurred when Herbert Kimbrough arrived to teach piano in the fall of 1902, with a guarantee of $1,000 in fees per year (the college to retain any additional income). He had just completed two years of study in Germany. His popularity gradually built the respectability for the School of Music. In 1906, a group of Pullman private citizens constructed a conservatory and leased it to the college until such time as a purchase could be arranged. The Regents imposed a small surcharge on lesson fees in order to provide funds to furnish the sixteen practice rooms, six teaching studios, and the conservatory's assembly hall.[21]

Whitman County rancher and State Representative Peter McGregor played an important role in getting legislation passed to change WAC's name to Washington State College in 1905. (Historical Photograph Collections, Washington State University Libraries)

In 1907, the regents appointed Kimbrough Principal of the School of Music, a position that forced him to cut back his piano instruction, but which also provided him with a salary of $500 to compensate for the loss of instructional fees. Although the Regents offered no explanation for the promotion, Bryan sought to mitigate any charges of favoritism toward Kimbrough. Professor W. B. Strong, who directed the band and orchestra, also played a significant role in maintaining a successful music program. Bryan placated Strong by explaining that the Regents had granted the partial fixed salary and new title to recognize Kimbrough's superb administration, not in recognition of his musicianship. The upshot was that, late in the next month, for reasons unknown, the Board rescinded the title, though not the responsibilities or the compensation.

In any case, Kimbrough led the department, sans title, until he was again made its "Principal" in 1911. Although he continued to sustain mightily the program's popularity and provided a model administration of it, music occupied only a secondary status on the campus.[22]

The sciences remained the most prestigious disciplines. Prompted by institutional responsibility to offer scientific studies for economic and other practical ends, Bryan and the faculty sought new and better ways to train science instructors, researchers, and students. In 1900, the college offered an on-campus "Summer Science School for Teachers," a six-week program catering to high school teachers and education majors. One hundred and eighty-eight students enrolled, including twenty-four principals and teachers. Other programs at the time included small groups of investigators engaged in research at Tokeland, on Willapa Bay, and Dog Fish Bay, on Puget Sound.[23]

Displaying energy, wisdom, and promotional skill, Bryan literally led the way in the college's development and expansion of summer programs. He wrote countless letters to attract teachers and principals, and even advertised campus amenities and pleasant Palouse summers. To one person, Bryan urged that if he would only "work up a little party of the teachers of whom you speak . . . I shall be glad to make as good arrangements as possible for them." There would be no tuition or laboratory fees, he assured his correspondent, while room and board in the dormitory would be nominal. Meanwhile, the college faculty contributed its time, energy, and knowledge without additional salary.[24] The program continued in 1901, but then was suspended for financial reasons. When resumed in 1905, the summer school covered the full curriculum and the faculty enjoyed the novelty of extra compensation.[25]

The financial crisis which closed the summer school threatened next to deprive the college of a desperately needed modern chemistry building. In 1902, the legislature proceeded on the assumption that it might allocate the income from the sale of School of Science lands, which had been granted to the college by the federal government. Construction proceeded under the belief that funds from this source were available. But Washington's attorney general subsequently ruled that the principal of the endowment could not be used

A group of turn-of-the-century students pose with a placard announcing their allegiance to President Bryan. The hand-lettered sign reads: "Thou shalt speak good of Prexy for he who does not, 'flunketh.'" (Historical Photograph Collections, Washington State University Libraries)

for construction. Only the interest earned from subsequent investment of receipts from land sales might be utilized by the college.
Thus, the expected money was unavailable. When the legislature met
in 1903, however, the college finally succeeded in obtaining a
$33,000 appropriation to complete the structure.[26]

Assurance of completing the chemistry building did not end the
financial crisis, for Bryan announced that the school might close at
the beginning of February 1903, if it did not receive before that date
a deficiency appropriation of $125,000. Addressing several legisla-
tors, he pleaded that the emergency grant be made before they
considered the regular budget. To the chairman of the House
Committee on the Agricultural College, he affirmed that "you are
representing the farmers of the entire state and the children of the
state and its future material development. . . . I ask you, therefore,
to lay aside all local and temporary points of view and bend your
energies to the accomplishment of this great task." Fortunately, the
request brought almost immediate passage of a measure which
covered the deficiencies. The doors of the college remained open
while the legislators took up the regular budget.[27]

Relief proved to be temporary, however, as the promise of a rich
return from the federal endowment of 90,000 acres for the Agricultural
College and 100,000 acres for the Scientific School proved illusory.
The state's land commissioner in 1905 reported that only 2,367.5
acres had been sold, with an income on land and improvements
totalling $62,587.10. Selection of the lands and their validation as a
part of the college endowment proceeded slowly and unsatisfactorily
for quick and profitable earnings. But an even greater difficulty lay in
the scarcity of investment possibilities. By state law, the income from
granted lands could only be invested in state and local bonds bearing
interest of five percent or more. Bryan reported to the Board of
Regents on June 30, 1905, that such investment opportunities seldom
were available. Thus, he observed, the greater part of the endowment
was not being re-invested, depriving the college of any substantial
benefits. The principal, of course, could not be reduced.[28]

The president had for some time striven earnestly to find means to
improve financial returns from the granted lands. For instance, he
watched intently for opportunities to convert acreages to crop lands
from lower-valued grazing uses, and also sought ways to obtain
more financial returns for timber sales. In the summer of 1903, he
toured Douglas and Okanogan Counties where a sizeable portion of
the school's endowed lands were located, and reported choice
holdings in the vicinity of Brewster which might be converted to
irrigated farms using water from the Methow River. He also specu-
lated that valuable coal deposits might be found if surveys were
conducted. He reasoned, too, that once the authorities sold or leased
choice irrigated or mineral lands, buyers would be more easily
attracted to the remaining lands. Unfortunately, his hope that the
federal or state government might provide irrigation systems proved
to be no more than wishful thinking.

From 1907 through the early years of World War I, according to a historian, "the Washington Agricultural Experiment Station grew at a fast pace, with more and more of its scientists having completed advanced studies in special fields of agriculture."

To Bryan's great frustration, the State Commissioner of Public Lands administered the granted lands. The President and the Board of Regents had no formal role in determining the financial transactions. Bryan was particularly incensed that the state rented the college's grazing lands for five cents per acre and farmland for ten cents, his wish being that the first price be doubled and the second rise six fold. Finally in the legislative session of 1905, Bryan and the Board of Regents induced Senator D. L. Pogue, a physician and stock rancher at Alma, to introduce a bill designed to give the college control over 8,000 acres of its best land in Okanogan County. The measure called for construction of private irrigation systems under the watchful eye and authority of the Regents. Opponents, including the Land Commissioner, saw to it that the bill died in committee. Thereafter, Bryan resumed his role of angry critic, seeking in vain to modify the rules that aided buyers and tenants at the expense of the college.[29]

The president also persisted in seeking the legislature's approval in changing the image of the college by adopting a more appropriate name. Senator Herman D. Crow's futile endeavor to introduce the name Washington State College in 1899 was discussed in chapter one. Other bills, with varying titles, failed in the legislative sessions of 1901 and 1903. Many friends of the college, especially farm groups and agriculture professors, opposed any title devoid of the word "agriculture," fearing loss of attention to that subject. Many suspected that Bryan sought to create a second state university, which they opposed. Indeed, Bryan found that he had many supporters who wanted the school to have a name that more accurately represented its comprehensive program and future possibilities.

Finally, in the 1905 session, Representative E. E. Smith, of Whitman County, introduced a bill to change the name to the State College of Washington. Taken up and strongly supported by the Chairman of the House Committee on the Agricultural College, Peter McGregor of Whitman County, the measure became law on March 2, 1905.[30] The law contained an explicit guarantee of the status quo in every particular except the title, a matter which satisfied both opponents and supporters of the name change. (Variant titles for the college in this work will be "State College" and "Washington State College").[31]

The president, of course, faced other critical matters of more substance. For some time, A. C. True, Director of Experiment Stations for the United States Department of Agriculture, had urged Bryan to step down from the direction of the agricultural experiment station. From experience, True knew that difficulties often arose at institutions in which the post of president of the college was joined with that of the experiment station director. Conflicts of interest often were prejudicial to the experiment station. Bryan, perhaps, recognized the validity of True's criticism of the dual administrative posts. He may well have recognized his own limitations in dealing with agricultural and scientific policy decisions. In the early years, the college had not

Captain John Kinzie poses for a formal portrait with a group of his senior WAC cadets. (Historical Photograph Collections, Washington State University Libraries)

been in a position to divide the tasks due to the small size of the institution and the scarcity of funds to hire another administrator. Circumstances had changed by 1907: Bryan needed relief from the burden of his many duties, and relatively generous federal and state funding made it possible for him to resign from the directorship. When he did so in January 1907, the Regents elected Roscoe W. Thatcher, a chemist at the station, as the new director.[32]

Thatcher's election signaled a new era in experimental work. Earlier, except for the trio of Spillman, Piper, and Fulmer, the staff generally had less than desirable training and the work in many lines of research developed slowly. When Congress passed the Adams Act in 1906, federal funds available for research were doubled. Thus, with the Hatch Act of 1887 and the new Adams Act, the experiment station experienced an infusion of cash that greatly increased research possibilities. State money also supplemented federal support, mainly in the establishment of more laboratories, offices, and facilities that were scattered about the campus.

From 1907 through the early years of World War I, according to a historian, "the Washington Agricultural Experiment Station grew at a fast pace, with more and more of its scientists having completed advanced studies in special fields of agriculture." Scientists focused attention largely on Washington's agricultural problems, without making distinctions between basic and applied science. Notable successes were attained in developing pesticides, in the discovery of the nature of "Stinking Smut" while studying the growth characteristics of wheat, in the development of berry hybrids, and in testing varieties of corn and peas as high-yield alternatives to the wheat monoculture that dominated the Columbia Plateau at that time.[33] While studying the San Jose scale, an insect harmful to fruit trees and ornamental shrubs, Alex L. Melander made a pioneering

Bryan's first assistant, Professor of Mathematics and Civil Engineering O. L. Waller, was one of the college's most capable early administrators. He assumed the post of vice president in 1909 at a time when the president's health began to deteriorate. (Historical Photograph Collections, Washington State University Libraries)

discovery that "repeated applications of insecticides produced strains capable of surviving the toxic effect of chemical sprays or dusts." According to a recent historian of the experiment station, Melander's "pioneering in the field of entomology came years before other scientists pondered the question of insect resistance to powerful and complex chemical insecticides such as DDT."[34]

While reporting to the Regents in 1911, Bryan noted with candor that research based on the Adams Act funds had not been entirely successful. Most satisfactory had been the studies of cereals, soil moisture, and veterinary and zoological subjects. On the other hand, he found the work in horticulture, entomology, botany and swine breeding as being generally unsatisfactory. Bryan attributed these failures to the youth and inexperience of many researchers and to a diversion of their time, presumably to teaching.[35]

Although authorities and the public focused most of their attention on the Main Experiment Station in Pullman, the state's charter of 1891 also required the establishment of at least one research station in western Washington. Thus, when the town of Sumner offered a tract of land for such a facility, the Board of Regents quickly accepted it and began to make plans for the installation. Unfortunately, the site proved of little value and in 1893 the new board conveyed it back to Sumner.[36]

In 1894, Denman and Charles Ross offered a tract in Puyallup that became the permanent location. Serious work did not begin until the arrival, in early April 1899, of David A. Brodie as superintendent. He set out hop vines, had the ground ploughed while considering other crops, and erected modest but suitable buildings. Though a man of energy and fidelity, he resigned because the station was not yet ready to function properly. The problem was a shortage of funds, which caused the station to be closed for a period of more than two years.[37]

The greatest difficulty at first appears to have been the U. S. Department of Agriculture's position that the Puyallup Station was not a part of the Main Experiment Station, hence it could not receive federal money. The state legislature, for its part, reluctantly accepted the financial burden of the Western Washington Experiment Station, as the Puyallup unit came to be called. Reopened in 1905, it faced the severe criticism of W. H. Paulhamus, president of a local fruit growers association in Sumner and Puyallup, who wrote in 1907 that "the great trouble with the Puyallup Station in the past has been, that it is more of a lawn tennis proposition than farming." In 1911, he wrote again, criticizing the station for continuing to drift, doing little work of value. To the Regents, Bryan acknowledged the validity of the criticism, pointing out that the state again had cut the experimental station funds, this time by twenty-five percent. Recognizing that Paulhamus's criticism represented a general demand of western Washington agriculturists that their needs be served better, he resolved that the Puyallup Station should concentrate on the agricultural needs of western Washington, pointing out that they had that year begun to study plant and animal pathological problems of the western part of the state.[38]

Limitations on research at the experiment stations arose not only from shortages of state funding but because of the myriad duties and responsibilities of each member of the staff. In fact, when wealth came, it bred difficulties. For instance, the availability of Adams Act funds greatly increased research possibilities, a matter that severely taxed the energies of existing personnel. Furthermore, many station staff members in many cases had heavy teaching loads, as well as responsibilities for the agricultural extension work.

The influx of large numbers of immigrants into the new state with its inviting farm lands increased the volume of extension activity. In particular, a great many farming families descended upon the vast arid portions of central Washington, the Big Bend country, just east of the Columbia River. There, in the mid-1890s, they enjoyed several years of bumper wheat harvests. Thereafter, the sparse rainfall, together with the fact that these crops had used up the moisture and diminished fertility, brought about crop failure. The poor crops and financial losses brought an exodus of farmers that alarmed promoters, bankers, and scientists, as well as the farming community itself. Among the promoters, the Spokane Chamber of Commerce urged the State College to open a demonstration farm to bring the latest techniques to the dry land farmers.[39]

In 1910 R. D. Thatcher of the Main Experiment Station viewed dry farming negatively as a "fad". He asserted that there was a "very real danger that the present tide of popular enthusiasm in and for dry land farming will result in attempts to extend these areas far beyond the limits to which former studies will apply." Nevertheless, publicists and special interests prevailed. Bryan recognized that a great many failures had resulted from dry farming experiments but he bowed to the public's demands. The Regents, in 1915, established a dry land experiment station at Lind, known as the Adams Branch Experiment Station. From it they hoped to learn much concerning soils, climate, and tillage. In addition, they opened a practical demonstration farm at Waterville, in Douglas County, to reveal new cultivation techniques, especially with forage crops.[40]

The Lind experiment station and the Waterville demonstration farm illustrate the close relationship that had existed from the earliest days between collegiate teaching and research, on the one hand, and extension, or popular education, on the other. In 1892, even before they had much, if any, new data, WAC scientists had gone to Colton, a small town just fourteen miles south of Pullman, and into Pomeroy and Garfield, to show farmers how to cultivate wheat and care for their animals. Although they probably met with a good deal of skepticism—which would have been the norm at that time—the college staff members persisted. Aided by free passes from the railroads, they traveled over the entire state year after year, operating with a growing sophistication and deepening experience.[41]

In 1901, with railroad sponsorship, the college developed demonstration trains which steamed to all parts of the state, bringing faculty and exhibits on wheels to townsfolk and farmers. A long train might exhibit an orchard being sprayed for the codling moth or it provide

•

The influx of large numbers of immigrants into the new state with its inviting farm lands increased the volume of extension activity. In particular, a great many farming families descended upon the vast arid portions of central Washington, the Big Bend country, just east of the Columbia River. There, in the mid-1890s, they enjoyed several years of bumper wheat harvests.

•

evidence of how to increase egg production or how to detect diseases in horses and cattle. Professors would lecture from thirty to forty minutes and, not incidentally, pass out literature on the virtues and uses of the State College of Washington. The instructional staff actually lived on the trains, finding some of the amenities of home in the dining and sleeping cars attached to the train. Many people were reached in this fashion but, in the absence of follow-up studies, the measurement of impact could not easily be made.

Farmers' institutes and short courses provided opportunities for more in-depth instruction. Winter short courses were held in Pullman, whereas the farmers' institutes were brief lecture demonstration courses held in communities around the state. These were scheduled in towns where local interests were willing partly to underwrite them. Once again, professors were called on for duty as lecturers and demonstrators at any time of the year. Such programs had become very popular—so much so that in the year following July 1907, 14,000 people attended a total of seventy-one institutes. In that same year, three dairy institutes had approximately 400 enrolled in each.[42]

In 1911, Acting President O. L. Waller expressed great satisfaction at the growing interest around the state in agricultural education. He noted, in particular, an "extra-ordinary demand" for home economics extension work, which he believed ought to be undertaken immediately. Bryan not only agreed with Waller's assessment of the demand for extension work, calling it "a tidal wave," but expressed fear that the new high schools were not teaching the essentials of home, industrial, and agricultural life. Especially trained high school teachers were needed, a matter which caused Bryan in 1912 to conduct a six-week summer school for teachers at the Puyallup station. In 1915, in a further attempt to meet demands for extension work, the college offered a Winter School for Farmers at Puyallup.[43]

In 1913, Bryan appointed J. A. Tormey, formerly superintendent of the Spokane schools, as director of the burgeoning extension services. Tormey was given responsibility to "conduct a great propaganda for industrial education in the rural schools and in city and county high schools . . . not only [concerning] the agricultural industry but all other types of industrial education." Faculty of all departments were put on notice that they might be enlisted in this service, receiving expense money but no additional salary. Tormey began to work vigorously with farming schools and exhibits but also set up displays at numerous county fairs and other meetings.

A comprehensive federal extension program replaced the local program when, in 1914, Congress passed the Smith-Lever Act. Under the supervision of the U. S. Department of Agriculture, this new law provided funds to each land-grant college for an agricultural extension service. A few months later, in 1915, the State College came under the new federal program, with the Regents naming W. S. Thornber. Under federal as well as state sponsorship, the future promised large-scale developments in bringing home economics and agriculture to the "industrial classes."[44]

Legislative appropriations for the State College in the spring of 1907 were unusually generous; $555,754 was granted for three major buildings and three other capital projects. Years later, Bryan still enthused: "Six important buildings! A goodly sum for maintenance! Was it any wonder that the hearts of the college people should rejoice?" Included among buildings that would serve programs and functions down to the centennial of the institution were the library and assembly hall (later named Bryan Hall), a recitation building (College Hall), and a domestic economy building (Van Doren Hall). Under the appropriation for 1907 farm buildings, a hydraulic laboratory, and a veterinary hospital wing also were completed.[45]

In 1907, as commencement approached, Bryan soberly reflected that while "a gratifying success," it still would be necessary for WSC to maintain the usual "careful economy" in regard to daily operations. New buildings, although welcome, increased the burdens of maintenance. Yet, Bryan could not help but express pleasure, that enrollments had risen to 1,100, with 773 men and 327 women. The sixty-one graduates of that year were dispersed as follows—twenty-two in Engineering, ten in Pharmacy (most receiving the short course diploma), seven in Botany and Zoology, and five each in Agriculture and Economic Science and History. The remaining graduates represented the following studies: Domestic Science, English, Geology, Latin, Music, and Veterinary Science.[46]

Personal problems pushed college concerns into the background that summer as Bryan contracted typhoid fever, which left him debilitated. The Regents responded sympathetically by granting him three months of sick leave, from November 1907, until the first of February 1908. He traveled on the continent of Europe and in England most of that time, returning refreshed from his first extended vacation since arriving in Pullman. The incident forced Bryan to realize that for the sake of his health, at least, he would have to share major administrative burdens with others. O. L. Waller because his first assistant, being named vice president. Waller, a professor of mathematics and civil engineering, had served as acting president when Bryan was out of town. He assumed his new post in June 1909.[47]

In October 1909, Bryan appointed Elton Fulmer, a chemist, to be the first dean of the faculty. The president instructed his new aide that he was to conduct all academic committees, oversee the development of the curriculum and the teaching, advising, and disciplining of students. "These functions," he stated, "will give you a large oversight over the student from his entrance into the freshman class until his final graduation with the Bachelor's degree." Though a sweeping injunction, this statement did not remove Bryan entirely from the daily scene. He assured Dean Fulmer that he would follow matters closely, adjudicating difficult cases.[48]

Despite unavoidable preoccupation with his administrative duties, Bryan remained concerned that students receive a broad education, emphasizing the need to prevent overspecialization. He argued that the faculty, administration, and the Regents needed to make a concerted effort to guarantee "that subjects appertaining to general culture and general training and the bearing of the curriculum upon the individual student be protected against the onslaughts of the specialist." The faculty supported Bryan's objective in the spring of 1910 by recommending a bachelor's-degree program in general studies. It also approved a four-year curriculum in Mathematics and new courses in Economics, Biology, and new four year courses in Music and Forestry. The Board of Regents adopted these recommendations on April 13, 1910. Advances in liberal arts continued to be balanced, or counter-balanced, by new practical studies, as witnessed by the introduction of business courses in the Department of Economic Science and History.[49]

The Department of English, which had fallen heir to belles lettres and oratorical exercises, once monopolized by extra-curricular societies, had also moved in the direction of practical training. Bryan's Commencement Report to the Regents on June 10, 1914, summarized the expanding scope of instruction beyond preparing future teachers. "More and more," he asserted, "we are endeavoring to put the major work of this department on an 'instrumental' basis. That is to say, the preparation which it offers is an preparation to do something with—mayhap to teach but just as likely to engage in 'journalism,' public speaking, argumentation and the like." Courses in newspaper and magazine writing, public speaking, and debating found in the department's offering, strongly suggest an engagement with professional or pre-professional training for reporters, lawyers, and even for those entering certain branches of business.[50]

Unfortunately, Bryan still suffered the effects of the typhoid attack, and felt that he needed relief from the burdens of office. His wife, too, had been exhausted by seventeen years of presiding as the first lady on campus. It was for purely personal reasons, then, that Bryan submitted his resignation to the Regents in 1910. The unexpected move shocked the campus, alumni, and the general public, all of whom voiced their disapproval. Deferring to the constituents he had

This 1908 photograph of the main part of campus shows College Hall (to the left) and Bryan Hall (to the right of center) under construction. Both buildings were designed by Architect J. K. Dow and were completed in 1909. In the foreground to the right stands the "Old Gymnasium" (completed in 1899); Science Hall (completed in 1901) is in the background to the left; just over the crest of the hill, the upper stories of the Administration Building, now called Thompson Hall (completed in 1894) can be seen. (Historical Photograph Collections, Washington State University Libraries)

served with such devotion, Bryan reluctantly withdrew his resignation. Instead, the Regents granted him a leave of absence from April 15, 1911, until February 17, 1912. As in 1907, he planned a trip to Europe. This time, however, he delayed departure until mid-September, "directing the policy of the institution" largely from the President's mansion, despite the presence of Vice-President O. W. Waller.

Family illness disrupted and shortened the trip, but Bryan managed to visit educational institutions in England and The Netherlands, and he assured friends in Pullman that he would return with many new ideas for higher education. England he found impressive in substituting modern vocational education for the outmoded industrial apprenticeship system. Indeed, he thought England was ahead of America in that regard. His visit to The Netherlands yielded little of use in the United States, for in his view the agricultural educational system there seemed geared only to training peasants to produce more food for domestic and international trade, with no thought for the higher learning of the "industrial classes."[51]

Soon after Bryan's return from Europe, he and the Regents publicly acknowledged the fact that they no longer needed the preparatory school. The number of Washington high schools able to prepare college students had increased dramatically. Bryan, however, argued that the rural areas and small towns of the state still harbored young people needing advanced technical training. He proposed making the Department of Elementary Science, as the preparatory school had become known, into a "finishing school" for young men and women desiring to prepare themselves for a lifetime of farming, factory, and foundry work, clerical work, or home-making. Even so, he retained a lingering hope that some might yet advance to college studies; thus, he suggested that such students should also study pure science, or at least be introduced to the scientific method. Subsequently, the Department of Elementary Science functioned as a trade school. By the 1920s it had become an anachronism, and finally closed its doors in 1926.[52]

Homemaking, indeed, had not been confined to a trade-school status but had become a major line of study, with departmental status granted in 1905. In less than a decade, domestic science studies had evolved from mere extra-curricular demonstrations and exercises into formal studies, which an anonymous spokesman, probably Bryan, called "the most efficient department of the kind west of the Mississippi Valley." Professor Edith F. McDermott, the professor, set goals to promote middle-class virtues centering on an efficiently-run, economical households. The young women of the State College hosted eminent visitors at luncheon, including William Jennings Bryan, Robert La Follette, and Governor Folk of Missouri "and many others of fame equally inspiring." Perhaps those occasions and the opportunity to study and imitate the latest fashions in dress and millinery, allowed the young women to peer above the immediate horizons suggested by "domestic science." Actually, by 1914 a new level of professionalism had been introduced into the curriculum, with majors being trained in institutional nutrition management and dietetics, Research in those fields and in textiles was also offered.[53]

The faculty, operating within the limitations imposed by professional demands and trade-school curricula continued, as it had from the early years, to provide a somewhat narrowly conceived general education. The latter had been developed as requirements for all collegiate students. From time to time, the faculty rephrased statements outlining minimum standards, but did not substantially alter requirements. In 1915, as earlier, heavy emphasis was placed on the physical and biological sciences and foreign languages. Students had to take at least fifteen semester hours in the sciences and two years of languages. Mathematics began prominently, with one year required in 1897-1897, but later that figure dropped to one semester, and then was eliminated entirely as a graduation requirement in 1913. Due to financial stress, all instruction in that discipline had to be concentrated on providing service courses for engineers. In addition to course work, each graduating senior had to investigate a topic in his or her major field and write a senior thesis. A mark of growing educational accountability arose in 1911 when the oral examination of theses became a vehicle for testing a student's "general grasp of the field of his thesis subject."[54]

Bryan had long advertised the State College campus and the Pullman community to prospective students and faculty as an attractive environment. The *Eighth Annual Catalogue* described Pullman as "a prosperous town of 2000 inhabitants" and listed six Protestant churches and two railroad lines as evidence of stability and connection with the outside world. In 1899 Bryan related to a scientist in the East something of the living conditions in Pullman. To rent a house, a professor would pay about fifteen dollars per month, "a little more or less as your fancy would dictate." Meats cost from ten to twelve cents a pound. Fruits are abundant and cheap. . . . The cost of living is cheaper than it was in Vincennes [Indiana] in many respects . . . and the style of living not expensive." Living standards inevitably remained modest, for salaries improved slowly for male professors, in spite of Bryan's optimism. Sexual prejudice guaranteed that women continued to be paid less than men, a discrepancy so firmly intrenched that Bryan did not even discuss the matter.[55]

Bryan maintained firm control over the campus, frowning on deviations from the norm on economic and social questions, a matter made clear in his reaction to the notorious Ross case, a headline item in late autumn of 1901. Edward A. Ross, a professor of economics and sociology at Stanford University had been dismissed by President David Starr Jordan, who had been Bryan's mentor at the University of Indiana. Mrs. Jane Lathrop Stanford, the sole trustee of Stanford, had forced the dismissal, charging that Ross had been disloyal by supporting views she firmly believed to be heretical. He had sought the prohibition of oriental immigration, had supported the Populist attempt to introduce free silver into the coinage, and had advocated public ownership of the means of transportation. Such proposals were perceived as direct attacks on the Stanford family and, not incidentally, on the endowment of Stanford University.

Bryan argued that Jordan should have seized the initiative from Mrs. Stanford, and protested Ross's right to academic freedom, thus protecting the stability and respectability of the university. Nevertheless, Bryan had no praise for Ross, characterizing him as an "illy balanced" scholar who had falsely taken refuge in the contention that his writings were scientific when, in fact, they were partisan tracts. To Bryan, misuse of the scientific method, as he conceived of it, was anathema. The stern Bryan concluded that his sympathies lay with the university and that he never would have anyone on his faculty who had been associated with "the Stanford fracas."[56]

Faculty members at the young college in Pullman, however, had more to fear from the demoralizing effects of a seemingly endemic budgetary crisis than they did from an attack on theoretical freedom and political ideology. When Professor Charles A. Barry, head of foreign languages, contracted an illness in December 1900, which required a three months leave of absence, the Regents required that "the cost of his substitute . . . be deducted from his salary." No ulterior motive—certainly not punishment—seems to have entered this action. It was simply standard operating procedure. Less than two years later, in June 1902, the Regents conferred the degree of Master of Arts on Barry, a strong mark of approbation.

Budgetary deficiencies in 1902 struck hard at the lower ranks of teachers, too, forcing the administration to dismiss summarily seven recently appointed instructors, a loss of fourteen percent of the teaching force, collegiate and preparatory. Senior professors were largely unaffected, except that they were obliged to assume additional teaching responsibilities.[57]

Hearings for those dismissed for cause might be granted but could also be quickly disposed of, as Professor J. A. Mitchell discovered in 1902. Suspended for repeating "street rumors" about immorality among certain members of the faculty, he also was one of the seven teachers dropped for financial reasons. Though he confessed to his guilt in spreading false tales about fellow faculty, and expressed contrition, Mitchell obtained no relief from the Regents, who refused to reinstate him.[58]

When, in 1903, Captain John Kinzie, the professor of military science, asserted to higher authorities that the State College of Washington did not properly support military training, Bryan counterattacked. The President described Kinzie as the worst instructor he had ever encountered and avowed his own deep commitment to the military training program. Bryan was not finished: he obtained the appointment of Captain Edward Kimmel, Artillery Corps, to the professorship. Kimmel had graduated with the college's first class in 1897 and had served in the Philippines during the Spanish-American War.[59]

Bryan did not expend all his zeal in dismissing undesirables from the faculty but he had little to offer professors beyond what he often acknowledged as "very low" salaries. Women suffered more than men not only because they automatically received less pay but because they seldom, if ever, were considered as candidates for

Campus social occasions were elaborate affairs in the middle of the first decade of the twentieth century. This eight-page printed booklet, complete with a photograph of Stevens Hall on the cover, announced one such event sponsored by the "Faculty Bachelors" in honor of Dennis C. Mooring. It contained a formal plan that included a schedule of "toasts," a "dance programme," space for autographs, and a dinner menu complete with: oyster cocktail, potatoes, turkey, cranberry sherbet, hot rolls, cheese wafers, stuffed olives, plum pudding, coffee, candy, and salted almonds. (Historical Photograph Collections, Washington State University Libraries)

promotion. Furthermore, they were discouraged from seeking training for the prestigious science or social science disciplines. Unfortunately, the inadequate pay was not relieved by many professional or personal perquisites, such as sick leave or sabbatical leave. The time had not arrived when colleges and universities granted such absences as a matter of policy. Indeed, the State College of Washington required work during the full calendar year, if demanded. Ordinarily, only full-time faculty with no experiment station responsibilities might expect to be awarded as much as two or three months of summer vacation. Finally, in 1912, Bryan established one month vacations for experiment station workers, administrators, librarians, and the architectural staff.[60]

The faculty's small size and the absence of budgetary support meant that Bryan could not grant funded sabbatical leaves. Lacking a far-sighted policy, the administration resorted to expediency when allowing a few leaves with pay. Bryan vigorously defended his own leave with pay, which everyone recognized as justified. Other such actions might have aroused some criticism, including those made in 1913. At that time, O. L. Waller and Elton Fulmer, who divided time between administration and teaching, were granted one semester leaves with pay.[61]

When Dr. Frank Golder, historian, proposed in 1913 that he be given leave and additional salary to travel to St. Petersburg, Russia, to engage in historical research, Bryan demurred. The progress made by Golder's department pleased Bryan greatly but the president apparently did not put great value upon Golder's reputation as one of few American scholars possessing language skills necessary for historical research in Tsarist Russia's archives. In this case, according to the president, the college rules had to be followed: "He is an excellent man," Bryan stated, "but the general system of the college would not justify us in modifying greatly the hours of teaching or the salary paid." Golder actually obtained leave in 1914, supported by the Carnegie Institution of Washington, D.C., and the outbreak of World War I found him deep in St. Petersburg's archives. He escaped war conditions in Russia by fleeing to Vladivostock on the Pacific Coast, via the Siberian Railway. Golder remained with the State College until 1920, when he became a curator of the Hoover Institution on War, Peace and Revolution.at Stanford University.[62]

Professors who sought outside consulting work to supplement their salaries found that the Regents circumscribed their actions closely. In 1910 Professor W. S. Thornber, horticulturist, asked the Regents about the extent to which he might be allowed to work on projects outside his school duties. Board members replied that he and his colleagues were totally obligated to their employer and that the products of their labor became college property. On one occasion, Bryan softened that harsh restriction when he argued that engineers and other technicians might accept pay for consulting jobs in order to keep in touch with the latest developments in their fields. Teachers, in the same fashion, might with reason accept work at county teachers' institutes. Nevertheless, it became clear in 1912 that Bryan had to proceed warily, for the Regents decreed that no employee could undertake outside work for compensation unless the college had previously entered into a contract for such work.[63]

President Bryan accepted and supported such restrictions with equanimity, but when Governor Marion E. Hay, in 1908, ventured the opinion that extra pay and expense money given to professors lecturing at county teachers' institutes might be illegal, Bryan leaped to the defense of his colleagues. Evidently, Attorney General Bell agreed with Bryan rather than with the governor, knowledge that strengthened Bryan's resolve to preserve the county institute perquisites, small as they were. He was especially incensed that the public seemed to think a professor was "a public servant," who was at the beck and call of any tax-paying citizen, to provide services ranging from agricultural to medical and for satisfying curiosity on countless matters. The issue raised by Hay died without confrontation.[64]

Faculty had few opportunities to take the initiative to improve their status or salaries, except in rare instances when another institution might try to hire one of them away. Even then, outside inquiries seldom resulted in the president's resorting to bargaining. In 1902, the Regents instructed Bryan to counter a University of Illinois offer to H. V. Carpenter, a highly valued instructor in mechanical engineering. The latter rejected the outside offer when Bryan proposed a salary of $1,800, an increase of but a few hundred dollars. F. D. Heald, a noted plant pathologist, whose reputation if not his personality, endeared him to Bryan, brought in an offer from the North Carolina Agricultural College. Bryan raised his salary to $2,700, equal to that of departmental chair. Heald stayed, later to have a building named for him.[65]

Strict control of student behavior and faculty prerogatives might yield a quiet campus in which the status quo prevailed, but the administration reacted strongly to preserve individual liberties against outside pressure groups. Demands for change at the college came from the Washington State Grange at its annual convention in June 1907. The Grange had fought unsuccessfully to establish a five mile zone around the college that would be free of saloons, obviously a plan to remove liquor from students. Though most of the faculty had been sympathetic, a minority had supported saloons. Reacting strongly against this minority, the Grange had passed a resolution demanding the replacement of those faculty with individuals who had "the moral well being of our boys and girls at heart." In the meantime, saloons had been closed by local governments. Still the board uncompromisingly indorsed academic freedom in the following words: "Relative to the views of the members of the faculty on temperance legislation, or on other political questions, the Board does not deem it expedient to interfere with the religious or political opinions of members of the faculty, believing them to be personal rights with which the Board has no desire to interfere."[66]

Actually, Professors H. V. Carpenter and Elton Fulmer had led the Pullman anti-saloon forces from their positions on the city council and had been successful in the first weeks of 1908 in rendering the

The Grange had fought unsuccessfully to establish a five mile zone around the college that would be free of saloons, obviously a plan to remove liquor from students. Though most of the faculty had been sympathetic, a minority had supported saloons.

Herbert Kimbrough joined the college faculty as a piano teacher in the fall of 1902, having just completed two years of study in Germany. By the end of the decade he had greatly enhanced the respectability of WSC's School of Music. (Historical Photograph Collections, Washington State University Libraries)

town dry. Bryan fully supported their efforts.[67] The victory over the saloon forces did not end the series of events. It drew the attention of the local chapter of the Women's Christian Temperance Union, which then sought to raise further the public morality of town and campus. The local chapter passed along a "common report" that students drank beer in their rooms and smoked on the campus. The women directed special animus, however, at Charles Timblin, Head of the Department of Elementary Science. Timblin reportedly not only drank beer openly, but stocked it in his home and scoffed at religion and the Bible. In the estimation of his detractors, he ought to have been removed from contact with students. The Regents answered, however, by promoting Timblin to assistant professor of mathematics.[68]

But, despite occasional attention focused on faculty foibles and folkways, life at the college remained centered on undergraduate students. On March 8, 1901, the Spokane *Spokesman-Review* reported that eight students marched into Ferry Hall for supper dragging a ball and chain. Some moved in "lock step," to suggest that they lived under prison rules in the dormitory. Spectators were amused. The editor, however, was not, as he had to amend his story the next day to admit that the mocking of the prison regimen applied only to a few students who were being punished for deficiencies in their studies and excessive demerits for poor behavior.[69]

The faculty's disciplinary committee, a redoubtable trio of Fulmer, Waller and Nelson, also was not amused. At about the same time as the prison burlesque, another student had fired the college's cannon as a prank. While the committee members rejected exaggerated reports that the episodes represented "rebellion against dormitory discipline," they nevertheless invoked the principle *in loco parentis*. As a result, the President reprimanded the chief perpetrator in the cannon episode in the presence of the faculty.[70]

Such measures might impress a single student generation, but every four years a new group of restless youth repeated the follies of its predecessors. Hence, faculty discipline and the patriarchal authority of Bryan remained an overarching presence on campus for many years. The faculty's and Regents' records and Bryan's correspondence files are a constantly repeating litany of the same student transgressions. Young men (apparently not young women) continued to sneak liquor into their rooms and smoke openly on the campus. Locks were jammed or picked and other property damaged.[71]

A rare occurrence arose, in December 1909, when Bryan had to chastise three young women who had crawled through a window into the kitchen of Stevens Hall to raid the larder. A more daring action occurred on May 28, 1911, when a number of male students, under cover of darkness, entered Stevens Hall and upset beds with sleeping women in them. Fortunately no one was injured but the three men were expelled. The affair drew so much public attention that Bryan felt compelled to defend the decorum and morality of the institution, stating: "Just as any family suffers from the dereliction of any of its members, so the college suffers from such an episode[,] but to the sane and wise citizen there was nothing in the action or attitude of the faculty or student body before or since which was worthy of other than approval."[72]

Students living in dormitories took their meals at Ferry Hall as members of a dining club, joined by some who dwelt in town. Undoubtedly they often complained about mess hall fare, as students have always done. In early April 1910, however, even President Bryan felt the necessity to complain to the club steward, J. A. Crosby, about lack of cleanliness in the kitchen and the dining room, noting the presence of cockroaches. Students, he reported, characterized the food as unappetizing, the bread, in particular, often being poorly baked. The president also sent the steward suggested menus, designed to silence criticism. The upshot was inevitable: the steward resigned and Bryan appointed a faculty committee to oversee the cooking.[73]

Students' recreational and service activities became more diversified as the student body grew in size. In the autumn of 1913, students and alumni celebrated the first Homecoming, along with a football game, an event that strengthened the loyalty to the school of both groups. By that time, students already observed the traditional Campus Day, an exercise in service and fun derived through the ritual and actual cleaning of the campus. In 1914, the Associated Students took another important step in community service by opening a student book store, operated by a student corporation in which certain of the faculty also participated. Probably for the first time the possibility existed of providing current trade books and popular magazines for the campus community in an informal atmosphere.[74]

Perhaps no student event, apart from sporting contests, drew as much publicity as did seventeen domestic science students at the National Apple Show, held in Spokane from December 7 through 12, 1908. The headline in the Spokane *Spokesman-Review* called attention to the fact that "College Girls Demonstrate Apple Cooking." These young women tested forty-one varieties of Washington apples, served 1,500 people on the peak day, and spread good will as they sought to raise $7,000 for equipping the kitchen in their new building (later christened Van Doren Hall). Evidence of their success arises from an announcement in the 1908-1909 catalog that this fully equipped building was "the only college building west of Chicago devoted wholly to the work of domestic economy."[75]

Campus Days and apple shows probably warmed the hearts of the president and faculty, but as time passed student attention turned more and more to athletics, fraternities and sororities, and entertainments. On June 15, 1911, the faculty created a committee to regulate student activities in the interest of better scholarship. Two weeks later, Bryan reported to the Board of Regents that student interest in literary, oratorical, and debate contests was declining while interest had risen in general social life and athletics. He accepted fraternities and sororities as facts of life, noting at the end of his administration

Students' recreational and service activities became more diversified as the student body grew in size. In the autumn of 1913, students and alumni celebrated the first Homecoming, along with a football game, an event that strengthened the loyalty to the school of both groups.

that five national fraternities and four national sororities were located
in houses on the WSC campus. What was his remedy to bring
proportion to bear on this burgeoning social life? First, to recommend
appointment of a Dean of Women to have "oversight" of all women
students. Second, he admonished Dean Fulmer to practice closer
surveillance of all student activities and organizations.[76]

President Bryan remained ever vigilant to serve the students and
the state in the most expeditious and frugal manner possible. When
he and his family moved into a new $25,000 presidential mansion
in June 1913, Bryan worried that some might question whether the
apparent munificence of the home could be justified. More than a
comfortable house, the building, especially the first floor public
rooms, was designed to be a community center permitting the
entertainment of distinguished guests, faculty, and students. He
reported to the Regents on June 30, 1913, after the briefest
experience in the house, that It was already serving as a social
center, assisting in the development of the college. As such, it ". . . will
tend to give unity to the life and culture of the college and perform
its services as a means of culture and education of the students of the
state as well as any other part of the plant."

Any anxiety Bryan felt over the expenditure involved in constructing the house should have been allayed when Governor
Marion Hay earlier recommended raising the proposed expenditure
from $15,000 to $25,000 and by the admission by Regent R. C.
McCroskey, after doubting the project's validity, that it gave him
"deep satisfaction," and that "no building on the campus has been
more useful or necessary."[77]

Bryan found allies in the Spring of 1914 for a re-emphasis on
scholarship at the expense of activities. The faculty had created a
committee to seek means of reducing activities and the students had
formed a comparable group for the same purpose.

Indeed, a sympathetic student attitude was expressed in the
Evergreen. The newspaper's editor acknowledged the need to
reduce student activities detrimental to ". . . the more serious pursuits
of college life." He did not wish the State College to be classified with
". . . some of the larger institutions of the country where society seems
to be the main concern and studies merely secondary." When Bryan
reported to the Board of Regents at Commencement, however, his
feelings were mixed. The academic year 1913-1914 had been "one of
the best years in the history of the college," he wrote. There had been
no internal "complications." Extracurricular activities, he still asserted,
weighed heavily on students, causing "overstrain" and "ragged class
work." On the other hand, when writing to the Regents, he recognized
that they should not "lose sight of the somewhat broader and more
wholesome participation in life movements" that the extra-curricular
activities provided.[78]

The faculty and student committees spent a year studying rules to
govern student activities and in the end the latter agreed to continued
faculty governance. Cigarette advertisements were to be banned
from the *Evergreen;* smoking on campus was prohibited, as was

Among the many competitions to take place on the campus early in the twentieth century were events triggered by the rivalries between various classes. Here, members of the freshmen and sophomore classes are shown engaged in a tug-of-war across Silver Lake on October 8, 1909. (Historical Photograph Collections, Washington State University Libraries)

cutting across lawns. On the other hand, the student body narrowly upheld the use of the "Give 'em Hell" yell, which aroused team spirit and supporters at football games.[79]

Thereafter a standing faculty committee administered rules limiting the number of general student functions, restricting gatherings in size and frequency, and reserving certain nights for studying. First evidence of the more stringent application of these traditional rules came on November 3, 1915, when the faculty as a whole supported its committee, voting to close all parties and entertainments at no later than 11:30 in the evening. The committee also undertook the task of promoting worthwhile activities in Ferry Hall, the men's dormitory.[80]

The latter point arose from a faculty committee survey of social life, which found that much of the student body did not take part in social affairs. Men in Ferry Hall were conspicuous in this matter, one reason being that they had no suitable social room. Off-campus young men were in a similar plight. These disadvantaged groups thought that their social opportunities were consciously restricted by fraternity and other social leaders. By and large, fraternity men and Stevens Hall women were at the center of social life, the former seeming to be but "dimly conscious" that others might be outside their social circle, the latter feeling "constrained" against consorting with "undesirables."[81]

On the college's playing fields intramural athletics continued, as evidenced in May 1900, when a faculty baseball team defeated the senior class, 21-20. More attention and energy, however, were directed at fostering inter-collegiate competition. The first football

A long tradition of baseball excellence got a firm foundation in 1906 when the team began four consecutive years in which it won the Pacific Northwest collegiate championship. Again, in 1914 and 1915, it claimed the championship.

game with the University of Washington, played in Seattle in 1900, produced a 5-5 tie. The next year, the WAC decisively defeated the University at Pullman, 10-0.[82]

Athletic competition had, however, grown without careful planning. The faculty soon learned that there had been misunderstandings among the regions schools concerning student eligibility and, particularly, of a tendency to introduce "professionals." In light of these developments, Professor Spillman offered a resolution, which the faculty approved, to create a committee of professors to oversee athletic events and to determine player eligibility—a vexing task.[83] Pullman authorities continued to be sensitive to the contaminating effects of professionalism and shady ethics, including gambling on football games. For example, Bryan dismissed football coach W. E. Allen in August 1903 upon learning of allegations that he had misappropriated the property of an insurance firm that had employed him.[84] Evidence was clear that intercollegiate sports were popular. When the Athletic Association incurred an eleven-hundred-dollar deficit in 1902, the faculty called on "all members of the college to devise some plan to raise the deficit." It was, in fact, the students who provided the significant response, raising funds and reorganizing the Athletic Association to float loans and devise stratagems for minimizing expenses until the debt was paid off.[85]

But, the main concern was that one college might trick another by using players who covertly accepted money to enroll to play football. Though the number of "ringers" could not have been large, for the total group of players was small, Bryan passionately denounced such deceptions. He proved especially sensitive to the criticism that college football, which he regarded as the most intellectual of sports, might be compromised by professional participation. For the most part, the so-called professionals were young men—often good students—who played "semi-pro" baseball on town teams in the summer. Others were men who simply moved from campus to campus with the change of seasons. Town baseball might be associated with beer, gambling, and games on Sundays: all anathema mocking amateurism, in Bryan's view.[86]

The Northwest Association of Colleges, which became moribund in 1905, failed to govern intercollegiate athletics, a dilemma that forced Bryan and President Thomas F. Kane, of the University of Washington, to attempt to assume control of athletics by reason of their positions and prestige. The attempt failed for want of cooperation and compromise. Bryan sought to revive the Association but Kane accepted its demise. The latter argued that each institution must make and enforce its own rules. Bryan's obdurate opposition to leniency in the eligibility rules on summer baseball doomed intercollegiate agreement as much as did Kane's desire to omit hard and fast rules on the subject.[87]

The two presidents, as a result, agreed that their football teams could not play each other in the fall of 1905, Bryan reluctantly but Kane with firm resolve. Fortunately, for State College players and supporters, the two schools mended fences in time for their football teams to meet in 1907. It was a memorable season in which the State College defeated the University of Washington, 11-5, and won 6 out of the 7 remaining games, losing only to the University of Idaho, 5-4. If Bryan had sufficient foresight, he might have wondered at the meaning of one game, played in Spokane, in which the State College defeated the University of Saint Louis, 11-0. This first intersectional game might have suggested to Bryan and his associates that the future held not merely problems of scheduling distant foes, but a much higher level of financing than they had yet envisioned.[88]

Other men's sports included basketball, baseball, and track and field athletics. High schools and athletic clubs offered much of the early competition but the main attention fastened upon contests with the University of Idaho, Whitman College, and the Oregon Agricultural College. In 1910, under the leadership of Coach J. Fred ("Doc") Bohler, the basketball team claimed the Pacific Northwest championship. Bohler, who had arrived in Pullman in 1908, and was beginning a long career in physical education at the State College, developed a team in 1912 which exhibited "some of the best team work in years," according to a local chronicler. The Oregon Agricultural College defeated the local team, preventing another claim of the Northwest Championship.[89]

A long tradition of baseball excellence got a firm foundation in 1906 when the team began four consecutive years in which it won the Pacific Northwest collegiate championship. Again, in 1914 and 1915, it claimed the championship. Track and field obviously were developing satisfactorily in 1909 when Jack Nelson broke the broke the world's record in the 100-yard dash in 1909. Unfortunately, the course failed to meet specifications, being about one foot lower at the finish than at the start. Hence, he was denied the record. He broke the region's 440 yard run record and won numerous honors in national competition. The college contested dual track and field meets with most Pacific Northwest colleges, including the University of Washington.[90]

Enthusiasm for jumping, running, and throwing weights ran deep at the Pullman school. In fact, beginning in 1905, the college sponsored a "Field Meet" for eastern Washington high schools. It sought not merely to provide competition but to foster school spirit as well. High schools were new in the fledgling state and the administration sought to incite a sense of belonging and pride in achievement. Many groups in the college worked hard to promote the first and succeeding meets. The first also included oratorical and declamatory contests. These events ran annually for a number of years.[91]

Women were not entirely cut off from intercollegiate athletics. They played basketball perhaps as soon as did the boys. It is clear that the sport existed in 1904, when negotiations were concluded to play the Colfax High School girls. More important than victory was a genteel atmosphere. A Colfax official wrote that "I will personally guarantee to control the people who attend and allow

•

Women were not entirely cut off from intercollegiate athletics. They played basketball perhaps as soon as did the boys. It is clear that the sport existed in 1904, when negotiations were concluded to play the Colfax High School girls.

•

nothing to be done that could possibly make it unpleasant for any of your young ladies." They would be chaperoned and put up in the hotel or in the homes "of our best citizens." After such hospitality, the score of the contest seemed inconsequential.[92]

Obviously, far more time, money, and effort went into the men's program than into women's competition and, very often, Bryan was at the center of the stage. In April 1906, the Regents directed him to build a grandstand at the athletic field, a modest edifice to be paid for from income derived from selling tickets to games. In the Spring of 1909, the college athletic association petitioned the Board of Regents for a graduate manager to direct all student activities including athletics. The Regents "heartily approved" of the idea of a graduate manager and Bryan appointed John Jones, of Lewiston, Idaho, to the position.

Bryan did not, however, relinquish all direction of athletics to Jones. Indeed, he responded eagerly to a suggestion from President W. J. Kerr of Oregon Agricultural College that the two land-grant schools might play an annual football game. Bryan asserted to Kerr that the University of Washington had tried to isolate their two schools, claiming further that the Seattle institution "has constantly endeavored to cut the State College from athletic and literary contests with itself [sic] and the other universities of the Northwest."[93]

Bryan again had to defend American intercollegiate football when its brutality, and often unsportsmanlike play, came under attack by public figures. President Theodore Roosevelt, for example, had excoriated the prevalence of uncivilized action on the playing fields, threatening at one point to outlaw the game. Bryan became particularly disturbed when others advocated substituting English rugby for the American game. He refused to consider a substitute for the American game which remained for him the most "intellectual" American game, not merely "a clash of brute force" as its critics claimed. To Bryan, it fostered, instead, "manliness, courage, loyalty and many similar virtues which ought to be cultivated in the midst of any people rather than purely effeminate sports."[94]

Regardless of his vigilance to prevent evil, Bryan soon faced a threat to his ideals, for after the 1910 football season two players accused Coach W. S. Kienholz of having offered bribes. Allegedly using money supplied by Pullman businessmen, Kienholz promised to pay certain athletes to return to school to play for him. The Coach apparently had failed to live up to the bargain. Nevertheless, Bryan immediately appointed a faculty committee of three to investigate the allegations; they decided that Kienholz was "guilty as charged." The Regents, more lenient than the professors, absolved Kienholz of bribery charges but, nevertheless, fired him as football and baseball coach and instructor in biology for use of coarse language and attempts to corrupt the morals of youth.[95]

The president reported to the Board of Regents in February 1914, that students and alumni had criticized the coaches for lack of success in football, but that now the alumni had rallied with "a splendid spirit . . . and it would appear that we will be able to stand

Blessed with a talented squad led by Captain Asa Clark, Dietz enjoyed an undefeated season (seven victories against no defeats) in 1915, which brought an invitation to play in a game at Pasadena's Tournament of Roses (later called the Rose Bowl game) on January 1, 1916.

as a unit in all our sports in the future." Although student and alumni support have been important to athletic success, Bryan's hopes depended more upon the hiring of a new football coach. In this matter he was fortunate when he hired William H. "Lone Star" Dietz two months later. Dietz, of Carlisle, Pennsylvania, had taught art and served as assistant coach at the Carlisle Indian School for several years before arriving in Pullman. He brought to the State College, in the two years before World War I forced suspension of football, a flamboyant spirit as well as a thorough knowledge of the game and equal skill in teaching it.

Blessed with a talented squad led by Captain Asa Clark, Dietz enjoyed an undefeated season (seven victories against no defeats) in 1915, which brought an invitation to play in a game at Pasadena's Tournament of Roses (later called the Rose Bowl game) on January 1, 1916. There, before 25,000 spectators, the largest crowd yet achieved in Southern California, Washington State College defeated Brown University, 14-0. Referee Walter Eckersall, famous quarterback from the University of Chicago, bestowed bountiful praise on the men from Pullman, saying "It [W.S.C.] is the equal of Cornell. There is not a better football team in the country. I do not believe I ever saw one at any time." With that game, Washington State College experienced a high point in its early-day sports program—attaining national acclaim.[96]

Bryan never lost the feeling of being embattled in his relations with politicians, legislators, and the University of Washington. He remained continually troubled by what he perceived to be the state's careless and even callous handling of the State College's endowed lands. Thus, he expressed great anxiety in May of 1908 on discovering, quite by accident, that the Land Commission had advertised 8,000 acres of college land at Brewster, in north central Washington, for a minimum price of ten dollars per acre. He called a special meeting of the Regents, who, on May 13, resolved to seek a reappraisal at a much higher value per acre. To their dismay, the land commissioner, in a decision Bryan called "monstrous," refused to order a reappraisal or to grant to the Regents any of their power over the granted lands. Bryan, who advocated improving certain lands for irrigation in order to realize greater revenue found himself without authority—reduced to urging many people to bid on land purchases in order to drive up the sale price.[97]

In 1910, Bryan labelled as "intolerable" the continued intransigence of the legislature and the land commission, neither of whom would give the State College relief from low valuation of the lands. In the summers from 1912 to 1914, Bryan and the Regents took matters into their own hands: they sent Professor George Clothier out with several forestry students to re-cruise some 55,000 acres of endowed lands. Bryan expressed amazement at Clothier's reports, for it appeared that his earlier fears might have been exaggerated. Clothier reported that, of the acreage re-cruised, only eight percent had been sold and that trespassing had produced only small losses. The total value of the timber examined was estimated to be $4,000,000.

•

Bryan never lost the feeling of being embattled in his relations with politicians, legislators, and the University of Washington.

•

Through heroic efforts, Clothier and his students had covered some-what more than approximately forty percent of the timbered lands possessed by the college, suggesting that it might have been a more accurate guide to the total holdings than frightening headlines engendered by earlier and smaller surveys.[98]

A legislative investigation of the college in 1909 once again stirred the embers of the old rivalry with the University of Washington. A Joint Legislative Committee on Higher Education inspected the campus during commencement week. Three members, all from King County, returned during the spring semester of 1910. They had nothing but praise for work in agriculture, horticulture, experimental work, and scientific studies. But, they found "jealousy and rivalry" between the Pullman and Seattle schools deplorable. They raised a familiar cry that each school should strive for perfection in its own realm—the college devoting "its efforts primarily to experimental, agricultural and scientific work and the university at Seattle [continuing] to develop into a university of the highest type. . . ." Accompanying the declaration that the institutions must be different in aim carried with it the accusation that Washington State College duplicated university courses. With a practiced hand and pen, Bryan brushed aside the imputation of guilt, pointing out that the University of Washington had duplicated courses in home economics and engineering, fields mandated to Washington State College.[99]

Bryan again submitted his resignation on December 14, 1914, asking that it take effect in slightly more than one year, on January 1, 1916. This time the Regents accepted it without question. But, he put on his armor once more in January 1915, when another legislative committee raised the question of duplication of courses and programs. Bryan boldly argued that the state needed two major institutions of higher learning, turning the arguments of his opponents back upon them. He could find no legal provision, federal or state, which limited the State College to one field, agriculture, or granted to the University of Washington the right to encroach upon fields mandated to the former, namely engineering and home economics. His testimony reached beyond the immediate arguments, however, to demonstrate the absurdity of the contention voiced by some opponents that the State College should seek to become the best agricultural college in the nation by abandoning all other studies. The absurdity arose from more than twenty years of history in which the State College had been developing a compre-hensive collegiate program, and by the fact that no college could provide higher education without a full complement of liberal arts, as well as technical courses.[100]

But, while he argued his case from the high ground of legal rights and moral responsibility, Bryan also feared that there were many people who threatened the integrity of his institution. He could, of course take some satisfaction that when President Kane retired during the 1912-1913 academic year, the State College had a record high enrollment of 1,537. Unfortunately, his anxieties were fed by University of Washington enrollment figures of 2,824 students that same year. Concern also arose that the University of Washington might grow at the same pace as the City of Seattle itself, which was outstripping growth in the rest of the state. The effect of this rapid expansion was evident in 1909 when the State College's engineering enrollments seemed to Bryan to be declining, while reports showed that the University of Washington's electrical engineering class lists rose forty-one percent in one year and the school's mechanical engineering registrations climbed 100 percent.[101]

In his final report to the Regents, in June 1915, Bryan abandoned circumspection to state that the two institutions should be free to meet the needs of "a rapidly growing population which has great expectations for the future." He further asserted that "The logic of the situation demands that both institutions should have a fairly free and unhampered opportunity for development in response to the needs of the entire state, and particularly the needs of the respective centers of population to which they minister." The cost of higher education to the state was not an insurmountable obstacle for he found it, "all things considered . . . not unreasonable, nor is it greater than in any other states, population and wealth considered." The issue of geography entered into "the logic of the situation," for Bryan recognized two sections within the state, east and west, each relatively heavily populated, but with a thinly settled central sector, as yet in its pioneering phase. The western section, the Puget Sound Country, had its university. Now, the eastern portion, the Spokane and Palouse country, 300 miles from the University of Washington, required its own university.[102]

When Bryan presided over his final Commencement in June 1915, the impressive numbers of teachers and graduates strongly suggest that the State College of Washington had a bright future. With the president sat a faculty of approximately 140 members and 142

Members of the graduating class of 1904. (Historical Photograph Collections, Washington State University Libraries)

Bryan's influence on the president's office had not ended when, in October of 1915, the Board of Regents sent its president, Edward T. Coman, east to seek a new chief executive for the college. Quietly, Bryan orchestrated the search by enlisting the aid of his brother, William L. Bryan, President of Indiana University, and that of President Nicholas M. Butler, of Columbia University.

recipients of degrees. These included eight winners of master's degrees, plus single recipients of professional degrees of electrical engineer and mining engineer. Six Doctors of Veterinary Medicine also trod the platform as did 116 new bachelor's degree candidates. The largest delegation of the latter, which numbered forty-five, was in liberal arts and sciences. Agriculture (including horticulture and veterinary science) numbered forty, engineering included nineteen, and home economics added twelve more. Although pharmacy had no graduates with a bachelor's degree, seven received diplomas which entitled them to work as pharmacists or to go elsewhere to finish work for the bachelor's degree. There were, also, three graduates in music.[103]

Bryan's influence on the president's office had not ended when, in October of 1915, the Board of Regents sent its president, Edward T. Coman, east to seek a new chief executive for the college. Quietly, Bryan orchestrated the search by enlisting the aid of his brother, William L. Bryan, President of Indiana University, and that of President Nicholas M. Butler, of Columbia University. If Coman conferred with others, it was of little consequence. He came back to Pullman with but one candidate he wished to propose to the Regents. Undoubtedly, the fine hand and firm grip of the retiring president dictated that the candidate should be Ernest O. Holland, the Superintendent of Schools of Louisville, Kentucky. Holland had close associations with the Bryan family and Indiana University, having earned his bachelor's degree at that institution in 1894. As for Butler, he had already placed Holland, a Ph.D. from Teacher's College, Columbia, high on his list of candidates for a college presidency.

The upshot was that on October 20, 1915, the Regents chose Holland as the new president, without seriously considering another candidate. Bryan and the Regents had worked in virtual secrecy, without seeking the advice of the faculty and apparently only consulting with the eastern presidents mentioned above. It was, perhaps, enough to know that Holland, forty-one years old and a bachelor, was a Hoosier like his predecessor, came from a professional family, and had taught in the Department of English at Indiana University before moving into public school administration. Delighted at the smooth changing of the guard, Bryan allowed himself moments of exultation years later when recalling the event. "So smoothly did the change of administration take place," he wrote, "that an outside observer would not have perceived anything unusual on the campus in January 1916, just twenty-four years after the college opened the doors of the little crib for the reception of students. . . . Faculty and students alike were unconscious of any change other than a new face in the president's office and on the platform at assembly." Would a new day dawn without any major change?[104]

Chapter Three

War, Reorganization, and the State College in the 1920s

WHEN PRESIDENT ERNEST O. HOLLAND TOOK CHARGE OF THE STATE College during the first week of 1916, he immediately faced serious challenges to the existence of the institution. He came with the philosophical weapons and rhetorical armor needed to comfort friends and discomfit critics, a matter disclosed in his inaugural address, delivered a few weeks later. The State of Washington, he proclaimed on that occasion, possessed the "best stock of American-born, who have come from the East and Middle-West, and their immediate descendants." They were engaged in increasing the population rapidly and want the best education for their children, adapted to their needs. Thus, he saw that "every industrial activity in the state and the Inland Empire and in the Northwest, in fact, must have its counterpart in this great institution of higher learning." Only in that way might the great wealth be tapped for social uses. "In a word," Holland concluded, "colleges and universities, to be efficient, must function in the lives of the people."

But Holland, like Bryan, made it clear that he was not referring to a technical school. Washington State College would continue, as it had in the past, to "promote the liberal and practical education of the industrial classes in the several pursuits and professions of life." Basic sciences would be essential to learning but would be coupled with the liberal arts and humanities, which were necessary to produce fully developed individuals. Music and physical education must be studied for their contribution to "human happiness and appreciation." Associated with physical and culture would be "clean, manly intercollegiate athletics."[1]

When Holland became president the old animosity between WSC and the University of Washington took on the dimensions of a personal feud with President Henry Suzzallo of the Seattle school. Before they took up their respective presidencies, Holland and Suzzallo had been close personal friends. As a result, many people hoped that they might work in harmony in their common educational

OPPOSITE: *A 1910 winter view. Looking down the hill from the old Administration Building toward the steam plant and downtown Pullman.* (Historical Photograph Collections, Washington State University Libraries)

field. Each, however, stood ready to advance his institution toward its goals, at the expense of the other if need be. There were early gestures of friendship, including appearances by each man on the campus of the other, but to no avail. The political urgency and the clashing missions of each institution militated against friendship.

When the battle was joined, Holland enjoyed strong support. Enoch A. Bryan, ready in the wings, personified the struggle. The Board of Regents, through its president, E. T. Coman, bluntly reminded Suzzallo that the State College had a strong legal basis for offering a full collegiate curriculum. On the other hand, numerous critics of higher education supported the legislative inquiry because they believed that too much state funding had been directed to the institutions. Ironically, others believed that "Bryan had been too successful in building his people's university and it was draining the resources of the state." Whatever the roots of the controversy, the issue once again boiled down to questions about the State College's mission.[2]

In March 1915, precisely a year before the harmonious inauguration of the two presidents, the Legislature had created a Commission of Educational Survey of Washington, charged with reviewing the status of higher learning in the state. The body was "to determine more definitely the purpose, sphere and functions of the University, the State College and the State Normal Schools, and the lines along which each should be encouraged to develop for the better service of the State." In reality, the only serious debate concerned the University and the State College, the real issue being the mission of the latter.

To conduct the inquiry, the Legislative Commission chose a trio of experts: Dr. S. P. Capen, a specialist in higher education, and Mr. H. W. Foght, a specialist in rural education, both being officials of the United States Bureau of Education. The third member, Dr. Alexander Inglis, taught pedagogy at Harvard University.

To conduct the inquiry, the Legislative Commission chose a trio of experts: Dr. S. P. Capen, a specialist in higher education, and Mr. H. W. Foght, a specialist in rural education, both being officials of the United States Bureau of Education. The third member, Dr. Alexander Inglis, taught pedagogy at Harvard University. None was conversant with conditions in Washington as they had developed over the preceding quarter century. Nevertheless, within a year of their appointment, the experts issued a report that both sides in the controversy soon attacked.

The report did, however, set the record straight on a number of points and recognized several important realities. To begin with, it dismissed the popular complaint of excessive expenditures, finding in fact that the State of Washington ranked twenty-fourth in the nation in spending on higher education, per $1,000 of wealth. The experts refused to accept the criticism that the State College provided needless duplication of undergraduate curricula on the grounds that any higher educational institution must offer the basic sciences, social sciences, and humanities. The report recognized that the State College's entrance standards and the caliber and diversity of the instructional staff made it, in effect, a university "doing work of equal rank with that offered by the university proper."[3]

To reduce expensive duplication to a minimum, the commission divided the fields of study. The State College should develop "major lines" in agriculture, veterinary medicine, and "economic science in its applications to agriculture and rural life." It should also train those interested in home economics, and mechanic arts, and agriculture. In emphasizing that these fields must be developed to the highest degree, including graduate study and research (except in teacher training), the experts stated that "The institution would be, with respect to these departments, of full university rank . . . ."

More controversial, however, were the recommendations of the commission regarding graduate and professional training in other areas. The high cost of such programs dictated specialization on one campus, contended the experts. In furtherance of that goal, the University of Washington was identified as being the suitable home for major lines in law, medicine, all graduate studies in the liberal arts and sciences, commerce, journalism, and "the professional training of high school teachers, superintendents, and educational administrators . . . ." Also the University should offer exclusively majors in architecture, forestry, and pharmacy, although rural architecture and "wood-lot cultivation" "might well be retained as service lines at the State College," said the report.

Since both schools were relatively strong in engineering, the experts recommended that each continue undergraduate offerings in civil, mechanical, and electrical engineering. Graduate study in those fields, however, and work in all chemical engineering should be lodged exclusively at the University. The commissioners evaded the hotly-debated question of where to locate mining engineering by suggesting that an out-of-state panel make the decision. The experts revealed uncertainty, and perhaps a bowing to the cross-currents of political debate, by deciding that each institution might offer home economics—after first awarding that field of study exclusively to the State College.[4]

Overall, the report struck harshly at the mission and accomplishments of the State College. The University, likewise, remained unhappy with its assigned role. The legislative commission, perhaps cognizant of the unpopularity of the report, altered some of the portions outlining exclusive assignments when submitting the final version of the report to the legislature. It recommended that both institutions might offer pharmacy as a main line, that both might carry on studies in mining and engineering, and that in other respects that the State College should broaden its scope. Nevertheless, supporters of the State College repudiated the document when it reached the floor of the legislature in January 1917 as the Zednick Bill.[5]

E. A. Bryan led the fight, speaking to the Spokane Chamber of Commerce only a few days after Representative Zednick introduced the bill in the House: "The present phase of the struggle is more critical and serious than anything which has occurred in the past," said the former president. Regarding the controversial bill, he warned: "It will be a question of might at the outset. If the university has the power she will crush her rival. If not there will be little change." Following Bryan's speech, the Chamber expressed its hearty support for WSC by passing a resolution, stating:

> That there is no demand from the people or from any
> business or farmers' organization for this arbitrary transfer of
> vital departments from the state college of Washington to
> the city of Seattle;
>
> That we protest against taking away from the state college
> any department that is a proper part of its work of educating
> the boys and girls of this state in agriculture, the mechanical
> arts, and the sciences; [and that]
>
> The industrial professions of the state college must con-
> tinue to have as respectable and eminent a place in our
> democracy as are given to the so-called learned professions
> of the university.[6]

Community organizations across the Inland Empire rallied to the call. The Almira Farmers' Union and Commercial Club called for an end to attempts to limit the work of the State College. In Chewelah the Chamber of Commerce protested transferring any departments to the University.

Three days later in Spokane, Board of Regents President E. T. Coman marshalled the combined forces of the Chamber of Commerce, the Spokane Ad Club, the Rotary Club, and the Spokane Board of Realty in support of the state college. Not surprisingly, the Pullman Chamber of Commerce threw its unanimous endorsement behind the college, even going so far as to raise approximately $2,500 to fund lobbying efforts in Olympia. The Chamber's strongly-worded resolution was sent out to other groups in eastern Washington towns, asking them to pass similar pleas:

> Resolved, That the Pullman Chamber of Commerce will
> resist to the utmost any and all efforts, direct or indirect, to
> emasculate the state college of Washington for the benefit of
> the state university, or for any other purpose, and that we ask
> all friends of scientific and industrial education throughout
> the state to join us in such resistance . . . .[7]

Community organizations across the Inland Empire rallied to the call. The Almira Farmers' Union and Commercial Club called for an end to attempts to limit the work of the State College. In Chewelah the Chamber of Commerce protested transferring any departments to the University. In Pasco the Chamber of Commerce endorsed the State College's record and protested "any change."[8]

With battle lines clearly drawn, leaders and lobbyists of the opposing camps descended upon the Legislature in Olympia for what promised to be a prolonged fight. Presidents Suzzallo and Holland and WSC Regents President Coman testified in a joint hearing of the Senate and House committees on educational institutions, which were considering a draft compromise bill dealing with the two schools. The press characterized a four-hour evening session as "a lively cross-examination" by legislators, with responses from the educators eliciting "applause from rival partisans." Questions regarding the State College's possible loss of federal aid if courses were transferred to the University produced "hot discussion" and a surprising denial from Suzzallo: ". . . we were not seeking to take anything away from the state college. We have no intention or idea of ever doing so." To that disclaimer Regent Coman responded, "That's the most reassuring statement I've had since my arrival here."

When Senator W. J. Sutton of Cheney, Chairman of the Educational Survey Commission, publicly denounced the findings of the experts, legislation introduced to enact the recommendations was all but dead. Sutton and Suzzallo urged Governor Earnest Lister to intervene. The governor called the warring factions together at an all-night meeting, during which compromise legislation was drafted and agreed to by both Holland and Suzzallo. Signed into law on 10 February, 1917 and titled "Regulation of Instruction in State University, College, and Normal Schools" it recognized the legitimacy of the State College, and established the fundamental curricular tasks and academic relations between it and the University, which still remain in force, though with modifications induced by time and circumstance. Section four stipulated that the State College shared equally with the University in undergraduate offerings in the liberal arts, "pure science," home economics, pharmacy, mining, and in all engineering fields except marine and aeronautical. WSC also had equal right to train high school teachers and school administrators.[9]

Without serious challenges, the State College retained exclusive right to develop agriculture, veterinary science, agricultural economics, and rural sociology. The University, on the other hand, took full degree-granting privileges over architecture, law, human medicine (when it should be developed), forestry, fisheries, commerce, journalism, library training, and marine and aeronautical engineering. Supporters of WSC had challenged for but lost the privilege of granting degrees in architecture and forestry.

Graduate work, as yet in infantile state at both institutions, received little attention. The one sentence on the subject, section seven of the act, stipulated that once a major line, or degree-granting privilege, was established, "it shall carry with it the right to offer and teach graduate work . . . ." That provision signified victory for the State College's expectations for growth into a university.[10]

Though generally satisfied with the law's provisions, President Holland regretted the harm done by the complete revelation in the legislature and the newspapers of the affairs of the two institutions. Had he and President Suzzallo "exercised a little more common sense" and "a rather broader spirit toward each other," Holland admitted, the issues might have been settled without fanfare and political maneuvering. Instead, the feud encouraged outside meddling and broke up a long-standing warm friendship between the two men.[11]

In spite of legislative successes Holland remained acutely aware of the public's limited acceptance of the land-grant mission. As the legislature prepared to debate the educational commission's findings, on January 2, 1917, the editor of the Seattle *Post-Intelligencer* offered an editorial advising the governor to settle the matter adversely to the interests of the State College, for the latter should strive only to offer the best agricultural training available. At the end of the legislative session, Holland confided to the editor of the Spokane *Spokesman-Review*, a strong supporter, that the college had just weathered the most serious crisis in its short history. But the President learned that condemnation by faint praise might come even from friends when W.H. Cowles, publisher of the *Spokesman-Review*, enthusiastically approved of Holland's plan to seek increased funds

The governor called the warring factions together at an all-night meeting, during which compromise legislation was drafted and agreed to by both Holland and Suzzallo.

for all of the agricultural work, but then offered his opinion that most people in eastern Washington thought primarily of that work rather than of a full-fledged college. When invited, Cowles declined to visit the campus to learn more about the institution.[12]

Difficulties with the University of Washington continued after the legislative settlement when Regent E. T. Coman, a Spokane banker, expressed concern over what he regarded as an attempt by the Seattle school to enter the field of agricultural education, recently reaffirmed as a State College prerogative. He warned President Holland and his fellow Regents that Professor Henry Landes, Professor of Geology at the University and State Geologist, announced that he would make a survey of the soil of Spokane County in the Summer of 1917. In his agitation, Coman asked Governor Ernest Lister to intervene and prevent the University from conducting a project seemingly related to agricultural development and education. Lister refused to be drawn into the controversy. Holland, on the other hand, fully accepted Coman's fears, stating to him that "If we are not careful, the University is going to project itself into many agricultural lines." Far from attempting to usurp State College rights, however, Landes sought merely to carry out a legislative mandate to survey the soils of the state. Any vestige of paranoia probably evaporated when Holland learned that Landes had hired two State College faculty to assist him in the survey, thus fulfilling the president's stated hope that he would be "magnanimous in spirit, [by] turning over this part of the work to the college."[13]

A second confrontation with the University of Washington proved more painful to Holland and reinforced his feud with Suzzallo. A quarrel arose over implementation of the Federal Vocation Act of 1917, more popularly known as the Smith-Hughes Act. Under its terms, colleges and universities might receive federal funds for training teachers of vocational and trades subjects. The State Board of Education, of which Holland was a member, commissioned the WSC president to prepare a plan of operation in which the State College would train all such teachers. Suzzallo opposed the proposal and, in Holland's absence, redrew the plan placing the training at the University. When Mrs. Josephine Preston, State Superintendent of Public Instruction, sided with Suzzallo, his plan won approval.

Once again Holland agonized over possible consequences for the State College, fearing that if the trend continued, his institution would lose touch with the common people. He concluded that "the State College cannot survive unless it can serve in a broad and vital way the economic and social interests of the state." The passage of time would dispel such fears, for Holland did not lose control of the training of agricultural and home economics teachers. Furthermore, no great advantage occurred to the University from Suzzallo's victory, since vocational training remained a small part of its curriculum. Two decades later, New Deal programs altered the administration of such grass-roots education.[14]

A financial crisis in the first few months of Holland's administration proved to be a far more serious threat to the existence of the State

College than any machinations emanating from Seattle. The president's "honeymoon period" ended less than three months after its beginning when Auditor William C. Kruegel informed the president that financial resources were dwindling rapidly. About $80,000 of departmental funds had been spent for salary increases, new positions, improvements and repairs, extension work, and other matters, leaving only $12,000 for the second year of the biennium. Of the total budget, about two-thirds had been spent the first year, leaving only one-third available for the second year, ending March 31, 1917.

Holland responded vigorously to the crisis by slashing $100,000 across the board. He cut departmental budgets and other expenditures to the minimum, positions were left unfilled, and staff employees in some cases were laid-off for the summer. Extraordinary handicaps were imposed as Professor George Severance of the Department of Agriculture discovered to his dismay. He and his students were not permitted to exhibit livestock at fairs "unless there is excellent probability that the prizes will defray the expenses of the exhibiting." Professor Herbert Kimbrough must have noted the irony that popularity might not pay—$300 in extra tuitions earned in piano and music instruction had to be handed over to the general treasury. Thus, early in his administration, Holland began practicing an economy which often appeared to be an all-consuming enterprise.[15]

Indeed, Holland's first months in office epitomized the small college presidency and recapitulated much that had been familiar in Bryan's era. Holland found in necessary to keep in close touch with the discipline committee, which monitored absences from class and other infractions of rules. He undertook public relations work, personally answering inquiries about admission, describing the living conditions at the college, extending assurances that discipline would be enforced, and reporting that the college has an infirmary with a nurse in attendance. With the assistance of his aide Joseph Ashlock, Holland promoted automotive excursions to the campus by businessmen and farmers who, he believed, if better informed, might support the college's claim to larger appropriations. In the natural course of his duties, he also assisted numerous needy students in finding jobs or suitable accommodations.[16]

Holland's handling of criticism by a Tonasket farmer, who attacked provisions of the 1916 budget, reveal the president's considerable fund of tact and an even temper. Writing angrily, the man decried a $400,000 college budget as excessive and indicative of the college's indifference to farmers. He warned Holland that a lot of "smoldering" radicalism lay in the farming communities and predicted that socialists would take over and remake the institution for the benefit of farmers. The president replied soothingly that the taxes in questions amounted to no more than $0.90 per $100 valuation of private property.[17]

Looking inward to the campus, Holland felt compelled to develop a new organization and a more satisfactory chain of command. Under Bryan, chairmen or heads of twenty-one departments reported directly to the president. Faculty and student body growth had

In 1909 President Bryan appointed Chemist Elton Fulmer to be the first Dean of the Faculty. The president instructed his new aide to conduct all academic committees, oversee the development of the curriculum and the teaching, advising, and disciplining of students. (Historical Photograph Collections, Washington State University Libraries)

Professor Edith F. McDermott inaugurated the study of Domestic Economy (Home Economics) in 1903. The program quickly became so popular that the Regents elevated it to the status of a department that offered baccalaureate degrees two years later. (Historical Photograph Collections, Washington State University Libraries)

brought to light the cumbersome and fearfully time consuming nature of this organization. The matter became urgent as the president surveyed the faculty for strong leaders who might ease some of his many burdens.

Though Holland discussed reorganization with trusted advisors in 1916, the controversy involving the UW forced postponement of action until the legislature had given its mandate for the curriculum in March of 1917. In June of that year, apparently without consulting the faculty as a body, the president announced creation of five colleges and four schools. The colleges were to be: Agriculture, Mechanic Arts and Engineering, Sciences and Arts, Veterinary Science, and Home Economics. The schools included: Mines, Education, Pharmacy, and Music and Applied Design. A dean or head would be in charge of each of these nine divisions, providing the intermediaries Holland wanted between himself and the department chairmen.[18]

America's entrance into the World War in April 1917 soon overshadowed college organization. By January 1918, two-thirds of the student body had disappeared from the campus. More than 700 students and alumni were in military or naval service or working in factories and on farms to produce food and war materiel for American military forces, the allies, and the home front. Ten faculty had been called to the colors, including Dr. Frank Golder, a specialist in Russian history, who left "to assist the United States Government in important war work," probably an assignment in military intelligence. LeRoy F. Jackson, professor of American history, accepted an Army commission, expressing regrets at leaving his department in a shambles. Four young instructors of short tenure at the State College also departed for service elsewhere, but they and Jackson need not have worried excessively about their colleagues left behind, as the student load, for the moment, had dropped sharply. The Regents voted to pay departing faculty salaries for the whole year, minus the stipends paid to their substitutes. They were assured that their jobs would be waiting for them at the end of the war. Students inducted into the armed services were given generous terms upon which they might gain credits in the courses not completed.[19]

Perhaps surprisingly, the first outside criticism of changes produced by the war came from Acting Governor Louis F. Hart. As a politician, he might have been expected to advocate enlistment, but instead urged State College students to work producing foodstuffs. On April 27, 1917, he informed Holland that he had read a news report stating that 600 WSC student cadets were learning map reading and range finding, digging trenches, and soon would be fighting a mock battle at a military encampment with University of Idaho cadets. He remonstrated mildly, expressing fear that food production would suffer if too many students chose military service over farming. Holland assured Governor Hart that, while about fifty had enlisted, from fifty to sixty others had already gone home to farm. To encourage the latter enterprise, the faculty had voted to grant such students credit for the courses they left.[20]

Holland, however, soon took a strong stand justifying the war against "the autocratic government . . . of Germany" and subsequently thought deeply about the contribution that the State College might make to the conflict. Not only should the college comply with the government's requests for special training programs but it might, he told the Regents, establish a College of Military Science, elevating the existing department to a much larger, permanent place in the collegiate program. Though the Regents agreed with him, the subsequent wide-spread disillusionment with the effects the war had on campus probably contributed to the demise of that idea.[21]

Faculty eagerly demonstrated their own patriotism, rendered perhaps even more intense by the feeling that they remained on the sidelines, while others fought in the glorious battle for humanity. Atonement came in the form of generous academic credits granted to those students who dropped studies for military or farm service. A few weeks later, the faculty, perhaps recalling its parental role, agreed to counsel students to stay in school until receiving the call to service. For those who departed for active duty, the professors memorialized (probably unsuccessfully) the military authorities at the San Francisco Presidio, the induction station, to protect the young men from "the terrible effects of commercialized prostitution upon military efficiency and upon the morale and heredity of the coming generation." Enthusiasm for the war produced vicarious participation such as the faculty's reorganization of morning schedules to inaugurate voluntary military drill for teachers and students. Holland, too, was given the opportunity to display patriotic enthusiasm when, in June 1917, Food Commission Herbert Hoover contacted WSC requesting that an intensive summer course in food conservation be instituted at the school. The president immediately agreed to undertake the task at the College's expense.[22]

A rapid increase in military training accompanied the decline in collegiate teaching and research. The federal government and the State College signed a contract in May 1918 which converted considerable portions of the campus and educational facilities to military instruction. Recruits were organized as the Students Army Training Corps (SATC). Numerous regular faculty and temporary instructors were to offer practical instruction in engineering, carpentry, auto mechanics, machine shop, and communications. On June 15, 1918, the Army began sending units of 300 recruits to the campus every two months. Holland watched developments, over which he had no control, with mounting dismay. The Army's contracted schedule broke down when it began to flood the campus with more than twice as many soldiers as had been promised. Living facilities proved inadequate in spite of temporary housing construction. Change was piled on change and Holland feared for the harmful effect on facilities and on education in general. Finally, welcome relief came when the war ended with the Armistice signed on November 11, 1918. The Army then cancelled its contract with the State College on December 14.[23]

If short-term military training courses proved disillusioning to Holland and the Regents, the need for much increased food produc-

The federal government and the State College signed a contract in May 1918 which converted considerable portions of the campus and educational facilities to military instruction. Recruits were organized as the Students Army Training Corps (SATC). Numerous regular faculty and temporary instructors were to offer practical instruction in engineering, carpentry, auto mechanics, machine shop, and communications.

tion and its better preservation and use did not. Feeding America and her allies remained the top priority of the nation. The State College responded by greatly increasing efforts of the new cooperative extension service to teach citizens to produce and utilize food more efficiently. A federal emergency act to increase food production, adopted early in 1917, spurred the State College to develop programs enabling county extension agents and home demonstration agents to instruct large numbers of people in production and preservation of food through canning. Satisfied with the result, Holland told Food Commissioner Hoover that additional agents could be utilized as soon as they were available. These successes on the home front did not, however, cause Holland to lose his critical sense to a thoughtless patriotism. When an official of the Food Administration asked him to try harder to persuade the people of the state to use corn meal in place of wheat flour, Holland replied pointedly: "It is impossible to persuade people to use corn instead of wheat when the cost of corn has been so thoroughly padded by the millers and the dealers. We feel that the U.S. Food Administrator should at once take action to force the price of corn meal down to where it ought to be . . . . This is really a serious matter and our extension workers find it next to impossible to persuade the women . . . to pay almost $.03 more per pound for corn meal and use it in lieu of wheat flour when as a matter of choice they prefer to use wheat."[24]

The faculty and administration did not neglect the war-time training and indoctrination of the civilian students. In early August 1918, the faculty approved courses in "Sanitation and Hygiene" and "Literature of the Great War," and six weeks later certified the teaching of a "War Aims Course." Similar classes were being widely taught across the country. The title of the latter course suggests that its intent was to be a vehicle for strengthening war morale and the students' resolve to fight. Under emergency plans, students were to enroll in the War Aims instruction, as well as to elect preparedness-oriented technical studies. Surprisingly, students might choose to study German, the language of the enemy, a sign that the faculty had not resorted to the prevailing hate-mongering toward the enemy. Students might also choose French, of course, in order to appreciate more fully the virtues of an ally.[25]

The State College terminated patriotic instruction after the war ended. The war program, much of which had been in operation only two months, had little course work to offer which could not be accomplished more satisfactorily by regular curricula or other means. The quarter system for dividing the academic calendar, which had been introduced as a means of providing an accelerated, full year schedule, also perished. Debate on the matter was circumscribed by the need for quick decision to accommodate the next annual curricular catalog. Further debate on the quarter system was promised, but discussions occurred only intermittently over the years.[26]

In the last days of the war, a new enemy struck army cantonments across the nation, bringing a lethal pandemic which had already killed thousands in many other parts of the globe, including the battlefields of Europe. It was the Spanish Influenza, which raged relatively unnoticed amid the destruction of warfare. Soldiers transported to the State College in early October 1918 came bearing the dreaded disease. By October 7 authorities recognized the presence of the influenza and virtually all public places on the campus had been closed. The twenty-five cases were not yet enough to cause serious alarm. Classes were canceled, although light drill continued on campus. The Pullman *Herald*, on October 18, expressed little concern despite the fact that the college gymnasium was being used as a hospital. By Sunday October 20, however, the situation was alarming. Eleven persons had died, most of them soldiers, and doctors from numerous surrounding communities were called in. The enlarged infirmary of the community now included beds in a fraternity and in the town's churches. The college was quarantined.

By November 15, the city health officer lifted the quarantine, but the gruesome statistics led him to caution the public that the disease might strike again. Fortunately, it did not. Six hundred people had contracted the influenza in town and on campus. There were forty-eight deaths, of which forty-two were soldier-students and six were civilians. According to terms of the contract between the college and the War Department, the Army was responsible for the care (including medical) of men undergoing military training. Nevertheless, college students, faculty, and administrators worked closely with townspeople and military authorities in caring for the sick. The College of Home Economics aided by several extension specialists played an especially vital role in the crisis, serving as many as 900 meals in a single day to influenza victims. Fifty-two women students joined in the work serving as waitresses and in other capacities. Whether such hastily organized vital services would have sufficed in a long siege fortunately never had to be tested. Without warning, the Spanish Flu left as abruptly as it had come.[27]

Financial problems arising from the Army contract and the presence of student-soldiers remained to be dealt with after the war ended. Indeed, to accommodate the influx of men in uniform, the Regents had upset their carefully-balanced budget by building a mess hall and barracks, improving sanitary conditions and plumbing, and repairing and altering some of the academic buildings. They did not begrudge such expenditures but worried lest the War Department should fail to provide timely reimbursement. Pointing out that their actions had been motivated by seeking the comfort and safety of the men and were appropriate to the college's wartime service, the Regents asked the legislature to appropriate $30,000 to cover deficits.[28]

Inflation, too, had taken its toll on lowered faculty living standards and morale. Indeed, at the entry of America into the war, J.N. Emerson, a Pullman merchant, advised President Holland that many faculty, regular and valued customers of the Emerson Mercantile Company, were falling as many as six months in arrears in paying clothing bills. Furthermore, he warned Holland that among the new merchandise there would be few cheap clothes available.[29]

Though Holland apparently did not reply in writing to Emerson, he took seriously the matter of faculty salaries. He met with Suzzallo and other Pacific Northwest college presidents in December 1919. At that time, he emphasized the need, first to reward merit and, second, teaching efficiency. He also advocated advances based on the amount of administrative responsibility a person exercised. In some ways, he thought, the "spirit of cooperation or lack of it" might be the most important point worth noting. On the other hand, a committee of seven faculty, representing an "Association of Professors," expressed a wish to have faculty salaries governed by a new, fixed scale on a plane with other, comparable institutions.

Holland acknowledged that State College salaries on the average were more than $500 lower than at the University of Washington. In the end, he fell back upon his priorities stated above, but added—perhaps for the first time—that the criteria for increases should include "substantial research contributions." When Holland awarded salary increases in 1919 and 1920, the greater rewards generally went to those already enjoying higher incomes, with money being reserved, also for promising faculty recruits.[30]

If the administration fretted over ways and means to recruit bright young teachers, the existing faculty explored other possibilities for providing better education at the school. It was not a matter of attracting students of higher abilities, for the institution's mission called for educating the offspring of the "industrial classes" who would, of course, display the entire range of intellectual powers. As early as February 1918, the faculty had expressed its confidence in the state's high school education by approving the admission to full-standing of all graduates of the state's accredited four year high schools.[31]

Granting blanket admissions did not relieve the faculty of further obligations, for sharply increased post-war enrollments greatly strained

Ernest O. Holland, President of Washington State College from 1916 to 1945. President Holland is shown here going through a Campus Day "bread line." (Historical Photograph Collections, Washington State University Libraries)

their ability to respond to varied student needs and demands. Administrators and professors recognized that while the average student might be easily satisfied with the programs, the students at the lower level of ability or performance, and those at superior levels, might require special consideration. To meet the needs of the latter group, the faculty, in January 1921, recommended that various departments establish honors courses for juniors and seniors who might profit by independent research experiences. When it was learned that one-fourth of the freshman class regularly suffered poor academic performance and needed special assistance, rules were established requiring freshmen in the lower quartile of the class be counselled by special advisors and take a limited number of courses until they demonstrated adequate college work.[32]

Unfortunately, the faculty's recommendation for honors courses did not meet with favor, and apparently none were established. It may be assumed that resourceful individuals, faculty and students, would find means to informally overcome the curricular barriers to independent study. But the faculty continued to study the problem, as reported in the *Ten Year Report* of the Regents, issued in 1936. "It is hoped," said the Regents in a pious mood, "That a plan best fitted to local conditions can be devised."[33]

In 1921 the faculty attempted to address student artistic abilities and aesthetic appreciations by offering a bachelor of arts degree in art and design. To make such an offering possible, the program was lengthened to four years and a Department of Art (of the School of Music and Fine Arts) created. The new department placed emphasis upon developing professional artists and teachers, and the aesthetic values of art as well. The department forced attention of the faculty and students on the fact that research did not stand alone as the means to achieving intellectual advancement. The *Ten Year Report* noted that "Contributions made by art teachers take the form of creative work rather than research. Each member of the staff produces on the average about twenty-five pictures each year. These are exhibited on the campus and elsewhere throughout the state and the nation. The cumulative effect of this work is of considerable cultural value to the people of the State and to the student body." Each gifted student could partake in this work, gathering inspiration from his mentors and developing his own expression and creativity.[34]

An important benchmark in the progression toward the highest academic attainment was struck on April 8, 1922, with the organization of the Graduate School and appointment of C.C. Todd, professor of chemistry, as the dean. Holland told the Regents at that time that in the previous 19 years some 78 graduate degrees, master's and professional, had been granted. Formal organization of graduate studies now signalled that the State College would seek the best candidates for advanced degrees and invited expansion and increase of numerous programs. In the following month, the faculty formally defined a uniform set of requirements for master's degrees which actually restated existing regulations. In general, the rules provided parameters still followed today. Terms were also set whereby active engineers might write a thesis to receive the professional degree of engineer.[35]

To encourage scientific and scholarly production, a blue ribbon committee of twelve professors formed a Research Council, following the 1923 Commencement exercises, to encourage faculty and graduate student research. The Council, which did not include experiment station personnel, soon numbered fifty-three professors and graduate students. Holland enthusiastically endorsed the organization, suggesting that he might provide salary increases to those members making significant contributions to science.[36]

While the war still raged, and in the midst of hectic scheduling, President Holland anticipated significantly reduced enrollments on the campus. Viewing declines as indefensible, he called for appointment of a director to develop a general college extension program to bolster student rolls. The Regents readily agreed to the idea that alternative off-campus programs might safeguard the budget of the State College. The Board added a more substantial justification, stating that there were "increased numbers of people, who, although they have reached adult years, wish opportunities to study under competent instructors." The Regents had in mind countless individuals in cities, towns and in the countryside of the state who had not yet been given the opportunity to take extension classes.[37]

Holland had additional incentive for acting quickly in this matter when he learned from a candidate for the directorship, Dr. Frank F. Nalder, that the University of Washington contemplated opening an extension service in Spokane. The president employed Nalder, a loyal WSU alumnus and assistant director of general extension services at the University of California, as director in mid-July 1919; he quickly vowed to bring Spokane into the State College's orbit.[38]

Nalder wasted little time establishing a four part program including (1) renting movies and stereoptican slides, (2) holding extension classes, (3) offering correspondence courses, and (4) providing extension lectures and musical recitals. Nalder brought to his job an expansive optimism, as found in one report in which he stated that his division "has more than fifty miles of educational moving picture film in circulation among the high schools" and other organizations. He also reported, perhaps with exaggeration, that "more than 180,000 persons have been reached . . . in the last year" by his program.

Nalder proposed to leave no area untouched and energetically sought to involve as many communities as possible in his programs. Above all, he directed his energies to create a Spokane center. Encouragement came in November 1919 when the *Spokesman-Review* reported approvingly of a music appreciation course Nalder had scheduled in downtown Spokane. Lectures accompanied by selections played on a phonograph delighted an appreciative audience, noted a reporter. About the same time, Nalder organized classes in chemistry for industrial workers, economics, French, social psychology, and English.[39]

•

To encourage scientific and scholarly production, a blue ribbon committee of twelve professors formed a Research Council, following the 1923 Commencement exercises, to encourage faculty and graduate student research.

•

Extension enrollments remained small in the early 1920s, with little evidence that courses were taught outside Pullman, Spokane, and occasionally Walla Walla. In 1924, the Spokane enrollments in music appreciation, health, classroom measurement of arithematical reasoning, and newswriting totaled 206. Class lists for leisure courses in formal gymnastics and folk dancing, also offered through extension, are not available. A course in salesmanship, which met for several nights in a circus-like atmosphere in Walla Walla, drew 424 persons.[40]

Nalder rose in stature and usefulness to the president. He traveled extensively to every corner of the state, even seeking to bring the State College's message to the shadow of the University of Washington's campus. As he moved about, he became a well-informed confidant of Holland, ever deploring the apparent advantage another school might have in the competition not only for extension students but also for resident students in Pullman. Though cordially received in the high schools everywhere, he was handicapped by the general public's ignorance about Washington State College. Common reference to it as "Pullman College" assailed Nalder's sensibilities, reinforcing his aversion to the view that it was merely a "cow college." On one occasion, Nalder could not contain his anger. Dipping his pen sharply, he wrote that the location of the college was "a grim and silly mistake." A few lines later he testified that "the College is simply off the earth, as far as the great majority of people in Southwestern Washington are concerned." Holland appreciated Nalder's candor and loyalty but did not yield to pessimism as he sent numerous faculty envoys to all parts of the state offering the services of the State College.[41]

While striving to recruit all possible students, Holland and his cohorts could not forget that enrollments already far outstripped official housing. At the end of the war, the State College possessed only Stevens Hall, with a capacity of seventy women, and Ferry Hall, housing 175 men. Fortunately two new women's dormitories, McCroskey, built with state funds, and Community, a private venture, were ready for occupancy in September 1920. Together, they raised the capacity for women to 250. The Community Building Corporation, a group of Pullman businessmen, built Community Hall, which it leased to the college for a number of years until the latter could purchase it. The venture was so successful that the corporation also built Stimson Hall which, when finished in 1923 added 219 beds for men.

The college possessed space for 644 students when school opened in September 1924. It was hardly a matter for congratulation, however, as enrollment continued to outrun the increase in rooms, as there were now 2,528 students on campus. Some 1,884 students remained unhoused, a small number of whom became members of sororities and fraternities. The great bulk of the unhoused had to go into town, where space already was at a premium. Unfortunately, the college would not construct another dormitory for more than two years.[42]

The college possessed space for 644 students when school opened in September 1924. It was hardly a matter for congratulation, however, as enrollment continued to outrun the increase in rooms, as there were now 2,528 students on campus.

Holland wanted to build new academic facilities, but financial stringency throttled initiative. This came about when, in August 1921 Governor Louis F. Hart demanded severe reductions in expenditures. He declared that budgets must be balanced by April 1, 1923, the end of the biennium. Compliance was to be immediate. There was nothing for Holland to do but request all department heads to save not less than fifteen percent, and if possible, twenty percent, from the current budget. Yielding as gracefully as possible to an unhappy situation, Holland termed the initial faculty response gratifying.[43]

By the end of the biennium, the State College had reduced expenses by $30,000, a feat accomplished only by neglecting repairs, failing to purchase needed supplies, and by raising student fees. In addition, the Regents closed Veterinary Hospital Number Two, located in Spokane. They put off completion of Wilson Hall and the Mechanic Arts Building, both of which subsequently stood unfinished for about a decade. The Regents' Biennial Report of 1916 described a condition which still existed a decade later: "Only parts of the buildings are now occupied, and this is under conditions not conducive to general satisfaction. Such items as plastering, painting, varnishing, the installation of heating and ventilating systems, and the construction of entrances are yet to be completed in these buildings."[44]

Fiscal difficulties could not be separated from the continuing animosity between the State College and the University. In fact, financial problems were more deep-seated than sporadic attention by the legislature to proposed budgets. In 1911, the legislature divided a portion of the millage tax on property and granted it to the normal schools, the State College, and the University. Bryan had expected that the higher education tax millage would provide a stable, permanent fund for creating a great institution. Experience taught otherwise as costs mounted more rapidly than income, in the war years and after. Furthermore, millage apportionment fell victim to political maneuvering, at least in the eyes and experience of Holland and his regents.[45]

In 1921, the legislature decreed that the Joint Board of Higher Curricula, an advisory group which came to be dominated by Suzzallo, should recommend a restructured tax millage. Subsequent Board meetings provided yet another cockpit for Holland-Suzzallo quarrels, as seen in the millage recommendations that were finally proposed in 1924. The Board advised that the University of Washington should receive a thirty-eight percent increase, from 1.10 to 1.25 mills, while the State College gained only a fifteen percent raise from .67 to .77 mills. In the end, the 1925 legislature responded strongly in favor of the Joint Board's report. Indeed, the legislature granted somewhat larger millages to both institutions, but without altering the proportions. To the State College, it appeared as a form of discrimination. Earlier, the school had sought to obtain support for a permanent construction fund of .08 mills to compensate for the inadequate regular millage, but had its proposal turned down by the Suzzallo-dominated board. Fortunately, a supplemental appropria-

The Veterinary Science Building (now simply called the "Ad Annex") in 1915. The bell, to the left, now sits atop College Hall and the Eternal Life Fountain, in the center, is gone. The inscription on the face of the photograph refers to Sophus B. Nelson, a Veterinary Science professor at WSC for many years. (Historical Photograph Collections, Washington State University Libraries)

tion provided sufficient funds for immediate construction needs. As a result, Wilson Hall and the Mechanic Arts Building could be completed and a gymnasium constructed. But Holland did not easily forget the defeat of his hoped-for greater millage, the frustration of his plans for a permanent building fund, or the discrimination, as he perceived it, in favor of the University of Washington.[46]

Through the agency of the Joint Board, Suzzallo remained a thorn in Holland's side for curricular as well as fiscal reasons. The Board had been commissioned to oversee development of the curricula decreed for the University and the State College at the 1917 legislative session. Squabbles resumed in December 1922 when the University challenged the offering of a major in architecture by the State College, claiming that the program had been reserved to it. Subsequently, University authorities insisted that the College illegally offered full programs in commerce, journalism, and forestry. Bitter exchanges resulted, as on one occasion a University professor criticized the architectural offering at WSC in the familiar patronizing terms which suggested the school should stick to agricultural studies: "A curriculum [architecture] more carefully designed to lead the student away from the rural districts into the larger cities could not be conceived."[47]

Though a dean from the University called the journalism program at WSC "an outlaw curriculum," going far beyond what the law permitted, the State College simply pointed out that it did not offer a degree in that subject or in any of the other questioned programs and, hence, had not broken the law. The Joint Board of Higher Curriculum, on January 9, 1923, upheld the position of the State College, finding the charges against it without foundation.[48]

Holland's difficulties with Henry Suzzallo came to an end when Governor Hart's successor, Roland H. Hartley, forced the University of Washington's president out of office in October of 1926. The feud between Governor Hartley and Suzzallo antedated the political strife then engulfing higher education, but the State College may have contributed materially to its termination through the influence of Regent Duncan Dunn. The latter claimed that he had exacted Suz-

Significant building activity on the campus occurred during the peak years of the nation's prosperity, 1928 and 1929. The home economists opened a new building (later named White Hall) of three and one-half stories which provided first-class dining facilities and the most modern laboratories and classrooms.

zallo's dismissal as payment for Hartley's political debts. In any case, the dismissal "simplified the problem of the Holland administration, at least for the time being," according to a close student of the subject.[49]

In fact, Holland did not enjoy a peaceful interlude, as Governor Hartley offered new challenges and confrontations to educators. Difficulties arose when Hartley vetoed special legislative appropriations to the five institutions of higher learning in the 1926 session. The legislature at first failed in an attempt to override the veto but, upon reconsideration, overrode it. Hartley, however, ordered all state agencies and institutions to withhold expenditures until the constitutionality of the legislative maneuver could e determined. For the State College, the considerable sum of $446,500 hung in the balance.[50]

When Holland learned that the appropriation would not be available in April 1926, he declared it would be a "great calamity," if the funds were lost and expressed severe disappointment to the Regents. The ultimate release of the money in no way diminished the validity of his criticisms. He noted with concern the poor record of the state of Washington in supporting the State College as opposed to the more generous example set by the federal government. Rising enrollment proved a mixed blessing, for in the preceding decade WSC had had the largest increase of students among separate land-grant institutions (those not attached to state universities), except for Oregon. On the other hand, according to Holland's calculations, his institution had fallen to near the bottom of capital expenditures among such schools, surpassing only the State College of New Mexico which had increased by only forty-five students in the decade. Until completion of Troy Hall, the dairy industries building, in February 1926, the 2,800 member student body had been jammed into the same academic buildings as had existed in 1914 when only 1,300 students were enrolled. Furthermore, Holland noted that administrators' and faculty members' salaries lagged as much as ten to twenty-five percent below those of twelve other separate land-grant colleges, a matter of special concern because of possible professorial exodus to other colleges.[51]

Significant building activity on the campus occurred during the peak years of the nation's prosperity, 1928 and 1929. The home economists opened a new building (later named White Hall) of three and one-half stories which provided first-class dining facilities and the most modern laboratories and classrooms. The edifice attested to the popularity of the discipline and to the transformation of the curriculum from imparting domestic arts to training skilled professionals in institutional economics, nutrition, and the scientific study of child and family life. Other building projects belied the contribution of the State of Washington, for it shared the costs with the students and with outside benevolent agencies. Everyone felt the need for extensive health, physical education, and sports facilities; but to obtain them, the Associated Students contributed special fee revenues toward construction of the men's gymnasium (later called Bohler) and to a field house (named after Coach Hollingbery).

When the State College sought a legislative appropriation for a hospital, Governor Hartley vetoed the measure, but offered to start a private giving campaign with an out-of-pocket pledge. Joining the students in financial support was the Finch Memorial Trust, of Spokane, whose $40,000 grant was most instrumental in the construction of the Finch Memorial Hospital.[52]

Students profited from the better facilities, but the president hoped to accelerate the improvement of the student body through better preparation of high school graduates. Strong evidence of that improvement came in 1926 when the Board of Regents abolished the sub-collegiate Department of Elementary Science-Vocational School, which had long served to prepare students whose secondary training had been inadequate or non-existent. The growing list of the state's accredited four-year high schools also indicated that preparatory work was not as necessary as it once had been. This development plus a fiscal shortage that made it exceedingly burdensome to accept all high school graduates applying, caused Holland to introduce more stringent entrance requirements. Beginning in 1926, the top three-quarters of a high school graduating class might enter the State College without condition. The bottom fourth could enter only with the special recommendation of a principal or superintendent and would remain closely supervised and counselled throughout the freshmen year. Such students might return after the first year only if their work proved satisfactory.[53]

On campus, the rise in popularity of business courses and secretarial studies produced serious problems in organization and administration for the Department of Economic Science and History, in which they were housed with the social sciences. To remedy the cumbersome operation, the Regents agreed with the administration and faculty that the old department should be transposed into three: Business Administration, Sociology, and History and Political Science. The first two retained incumbent faculty H.W. Cordell and Fred

A student dormitory room in 1915.
(Historical Photograph Collections, Washington State University Libraries)

Yoder, respectively, as chairmen, but the third received as chairman Claudius O. Johnson, a political scientist from the University of Chattanooga.[54]

Bringing in Johnson as a promising scholar might have been intended to raise the level of scholarship and research in the social sciences, but there were few resources which he and his colleagues could utilize to that end. Johnson's original assignment made no mention of research and, indeed, strongly suggested he should teach summer school instead of engaging in writing. It remained that no division other than the College of Agriculture had funding above minuscule levels for basic research studies.[55]

Under the circumstances, a surprising number of graduate students pursued advanced degrees. Prior to 1926, 159 Master's degrees had been granted. In 1927, the college began offering the Doctor of Philosophy degree in several fields of study. An orthodox set of degree requirements were instituted, including three years of study (beyond the bachelor's degree), passing of tests in two foreign languages, and passing an oral examination over the candidate's field of special study. In addition, an acceptable dissertation was required. By 1935, seventeen Doctor's degrees had been granted, along with 380 Master's degrees.[56]

The College of Veterinary Science entered the post-war years troubled by small enrollments and low esteem for the profession, which many believed would soon be rendered obsolete through the eclipse of the work horse by the internal combustion engine. The small faculty, which one expert observer termed inbred academically, mirrored the small graduating classes, there were twenty graduates in 1920, but only four students graduated each year from 1922 through 1925. The nadir was reached with three in 1927. Interestingly, in that year, the college enjoyed a notable rise in enrollment of sixty-eight students, suggesting that earlier qualms about the profession were giving way to a realization that many opportunities lay ahead in the field of animal medicine. A name change in 1925 to College of Veterinary Medicine (forsaking College of Veterinary Science) may also have foretold that the veterinary studies were moving closer to an alliance with human medicine. Revitalization of the program took on a very tangible form in 1935 when a fifth year was added, a pre-professional year which would not only bolster the scientific training but would permit broader cultural education for the veterinary students.[57]

A steady, albeit unspectacular, growth of the student body, crowded facilities, and financial shortages characterized the 1920s and 1930s. Teaching demands on all faculty intensified proportionally. By 1936, the size of the faculty had remained unchanged for a decade despite a thirty-five percent increase in student enrollment. The result was that there were 15.9 students for every teacher. A comparison of the WSC with sixteen other institutions yielded the disheartening information that the State College had the highest student/teacher ratio. The other institutions averaged only 12.3 students per teacher. For

A name change in 1925 to College of Veterinary Medicine (forsaking College of Veterinary Science) may also have foretold that the veterinary studies were moving closer to an alliance with human medicine. Revitalization of the program took on a very tangible form in 1935 when a fifth year was added . . .

WSC to reach that admired average would require the hiring of sixty-four additional faculty.

Inevitably, teaching loads became heavier. The largest classes might be divided but the same instructor might teach both. Laboratory sessions might become overcrowded or occupy odd hours. Makeshift and overcrowded facilities threatened to undermine the creative energy of faculty and students, a matter which Holland could only lament. He noted that many faculty labored eleven months of the year, receiving no additional pay for the summer, often working at maintenance tasks instead of research projects. His assertion in 1936 that "all too often the State College has had to lose excellent faculty members to other schools or private employment because this institution could not pay the small additional amount for which the persons would have stayed." The president's papers attest to such losses but also to successes which support Holland's claims that a few hundred dollars extra might hold people in Pullman.[58]

Emphasis remained primarily on teaching, with little provision for research, performing arts facilities, laboratory equipment, or an adequate library—the life blood of scholarly and creative activity. Indeed, Presidents Bryan and Holland had both asserted that the library might be the center of intellectual activity on the campus but neither had allocated sufficient funds to make it so in practice. When W.W. Foote became the head librarian in 1915, he inherited a substandard collection not only for research but also for undergraduate use. Working energetically to enlarge the library, which had been moved into the north half of Bryan Hall in 1909, Foote's successes permitted the president in 1936 to proudly claim that the State College had "the distinction of possessing the fourth largest educational library on the Pacific Coast." But Foote had attained that position by indiscriminately gathering material not wanted by other libraries. Much of it had been available simply for the taking. The result was that he increased the size of the library from the 33,000 volumes present when he arrived to 275,000 volumes in 1935. Some 52 percent of the increase in the preceding decade had come as gifts, subject to selection by the donors and not by Foote, Holland, or any professors at the State College. The result was not a collection dedicated to the activities of faculty or students, though some of the material might incidentally be useful.[59]

Graduate study and faculty research operated largely without special financial assistance, except in agriculture, although there were some exceptions. A notable instance occurred when the State College financed publication of a second edition of Piper and Beattie's *The Flora of Southeastern Washington*, first published thirteen years earlier. Holland relieved Dr. Harold St. John of one-third of his teaching load for 1927-1928 so that he might revise this widely used work, first assembled by two prominent scientists of the Bryan years. The president justified the modest relief given to St. John on the grounds that the State College had in the past two decades published several works "of a scientific character which have been

With the assistance of his aide Joseph Ashlock, Holland promoted automotive excursions to the campus by businessmen and farmers who might support the college's claim to larger appropriations from the state legislature. Ashlock served the university in a variety of other ways. In addition to teaching Journalism, he was also a news correspondent for the Spokesman-Review, *the Seattle* Post-Intelligencer, *the Seattle* Times, *and the Portland* Oregonian. *(Hilltopics)*

helpful in the education work of the State and also in the development of the natural resources of Washington."[60]

Sabbatical leaves with pay were so rare as to evoke special attention, which indicated that the average faculty member could not aspire to them. Director E. F. Gaines, Cerealist at the Main Experiment Station, applied in 1930 for leave to make a six month tour of Europe to collect specimens of cereal grains strongly resistant to rust. He also planned to visit agricultural experiment stations in England, on the continent, and in the Scandinavian countries. Gaines, who had begun a brilliant career in wheat hybridization, received detailed instructions for his movements, which included a visit to Russia to study wheat production. He rendered a full report to the college upon his return. In 1932, Professor Hans A. Bendixon, Dairy Scientist, sailed for Germany under a special grant to engage in advanced studies and to investigate dairy production on the continent, with the objective of reporting his findings but also to write two popular magazine articles for publication.[61]

The first major effort to involve the social scientists in research arose in 1934 when Claudius O. Johnson proposed to travel to Washington, D. C., for a semester's research in the papers and activities of Senator William E. Borah of Idaho. Holland responded enthusiastically to the project. Looking to the future, the president envisioned Johnson's study as grounds for building a research library devoted to the political, economic, and social development of the Pacific Northwest. Johnson, who had just published the first edition of his popular *Government in the United States*, brought his *Borah of Idaho* into print in 1936. His contribution to the library's general research materials on the region, however, was limited to the materials collected on the Borah project.

Holland did not let the moment pass without a deeper verbal commitment to excellence. To him, Johnson represented the kind of scholar needed to elevate the academic calibre of the State College. Johnson was, Holland stated to the Regents and, undoubtedly, to the faculty as a whole, "included in the small group of faculty folk, who, we believe, should be given preferential consideration when our financial condition has improved. It is my hope that this group of persons can be rewarded in such a way that they will feel justified in remaining with this institution indefinitely."[62]

The golden age of adequate financial support had not arrived. Nevertheless, the State College acquired a coterie of young men in the last years of the 1920s who fit Holland's mold of efficient and loyal professors, teachers who would remain to build the school's reputation for teaching and research. Among the innovative faculty Holland hired were professors who contributed to the development of research facilities as well as those who published. Professor J. Horace Nunemaker became Head of the Department of Foreign Languages in 1928. He served for many years and did little research, but strengthened the social sciences as well as foreign languages by collecting a priceless archive on Mexican colonial history. Murray W. Bundy joined the faculty in 1928 as well. He elevated the teaching of English literature in his long tenure.[63]

Harry Weller, appointed Assistant Professor of Architecture that same year, brought a great deal of practical experience to his field. J. C. Knott, Assistant Professor of Dairy Husbandry, represented a strong test of Holland's resolve to retain staff. In 1930, when Oregon State College offered Knott a position at $4,000, Holland succeeded in keeping him by raising his salary from $2,500 to $3,400. Knott later served the State College in important administrative positions. Paul A. Anderson came to the State College in 1931 as Head of the Department of Physics. Holland recognized his potential value in graduate work. Anderson, a much traveled professor, had taught at Peking and Berlin but had also served as National Research Fellow in Physics for three years. Holland placed Anderson's salary at only $2,400 for the first year but soon increased it to $4,500 because he saw Anderson as "among the best prepared and most promising physicists in the country."[64]

For the faculty as a whole, fewer perquisites and safeguards to unfettered teaching and research were available. Leaves without pay to complete professional training might be gained by a few, but little else.[65] Displays of "disloyalty" or less than polite behavior occasionally surfaced and were sometimes dealt with by summary dismissal. Dignified retirement after years of devoted service as an administrator or professor proved impossible for many since they had no retirement annuities. On the other hand, when Dr. Sophus Nelson experienced difficulties with the administration and with farmers over his conservative handling of the Extension Service, the Regents sought to ease him gently out of office. They offered him a $4,000 a year position teaching and researching in Veterinary Medicine, his original field of expertise. The salary would have provided comfort to this veteran of 34 years of service to the State College, but he refused all overtures. The Regents finally removed Nelson from the job without salary or benefits.[66]

The problem presented by President Emeritus E.A. Bryan was how to provide a comfortable and dignified retirement for the elder statesman. After leaving office in 1915, he served to several years as Idaho's Commissioner of Education. That task finished, he faced an unhappy, poverty-stricken future, as he had not been able to save any money. President Holland and the Regents lamented Bryan's plight and his lack of a pension. They also feared the anger of the older alumni if the revered administrator was not adequately provided for by the school he had built. Bryan, thereafter, received appointment as research professor at a salary of $4,000 per year. Later, when he lost his eyesight and could work no longer, the Regents reduced the amount of $1,800.[67]

The size of the student body quickly surpassed pre-war levels during the 1920s. Enrollments for the full year of 1919-1920, including summer school, reached 2,532, an increase of 402 over the previous record enrollment in 1916-1917. By 1925-1926, that number had risen to 3,388. President Holland reported that "more than one-third of the students . . . have come from west of the Cascade Mountains and more than one-half have come from west of the

The inscription on this photograph from the second decade of the twentieth century simply reads: "Young lady and gentleman in front of Sigma Nu House." (Historical Photograph Collections, Washington State University Libraries)

Columbia River." Obviously, the State College could now justifiably claim that it truly represented the whole state. Eleven hundred and twelve (approximately one-third) of in-state students came from the three metropolitan counties, King, Pierce, and Spokane, suggesting the significant presence of urban influences. Out-of-state students numbered only 255, while foreign students remained a hidden number, not mentioned in the records.[68]

One professor characterized the student body as relatively naive and unsophisticated when compared with students at the University of Montana in Missoula, attributing the difference in part to the location of the Montana institution on the main railroad trunk lines. The continuing practice of surrogate parentage by administrators and professors probably inhibited deviant behavior and independence. Could it be said to have reinforced naivete? The YMCA and the YWCA endeavored to provide a strictly Christian atmosphere on the campus, bolstering the *status quo.* According to the report of the YMCA in 1924, eight mainstream Protestant churches and one Roman Catholic church in Pullman attracted perhaps as many as 1,800 students to worship, at least once in a while. "The clergy," according to one professor, "even objected to Saturday evening dances because the students would not be in a good frame of mind for Sunday morning services."[69]

In spite of strict regulations, a wholesome environment, and surrogate parental guidance, the sophomores began to haze the freshmen boys soon after school opened in September 1916. Freshmen Ernest Marchand wrote secretly to a younger brother at home, describing three nights of hazing. The first night began mildly enough as Ernest and companions in Ferry Hall swept floors, shined shoes, and washed windows under the watchful gaze of sophomores. Having attained some semblance of organization the next day, the freshmen ran rampant: "armed with buckets of paste . . . [they] 'plastered the town good.'" In subsequent battles the sophomores retaliated by paddling and ducking the younger students in the lake. By the end of the third day the freshmen were "completely exhausted." Parents protested and Holland quickly assured them that he would stop such barbaric practices. This meeting of minds exhibited by president and parents later extended to the leaders of the sophomore class who agreed to cease hazing for the good of the institution. That the president remained in command of the campus was acknowledged by at least one parent who wrote that his son would enter the State College the next fall, confident that there would be no hazing.[70]

Certainly, not all regulations denied individual choice or permissive behavior. When the Anti-Narcotics Department of the Women's Christian Temperance Union in Spokane protested the propriety of tobacco advertisements appearing in the *Evergreen,* Holland declined to interfere, stating that the students could make their own decisions. He and the faculty gave grudging recognition to changing values and behavior in the wake of the catastrophe of the world war. An example of such change on the campus came when the faculty abandoned the tradition of reserving Friday evenings solely for literary and oratorical exercises or musical recitals. Instead, they agreed that social events might be scheduled that night from 8:30 to 11:30 p.m.[71]

The faculty continued, as it had for many years, to permit annual tours by the Glee Club. In 1918 the singers traveled to several eastern Washington towns for a week, missing (incredibly) only two days of classes. Tours in the spring and fall of 1919 encompassed two weeks each, such losses of class time no doubt being rationalized by the successful role the tours played in recruiting new students. Several western Washington towns received Glee Club visits, as did communities closer to Pullman.[72]

Grievous minor problems upsetting to the moral climate of the campus continued to justify the parental code. In fact, *in loco parentis* took on additional meaning in the spring of 1924 when Holland became perhaps excessively sensitive to the content of student publications. He appointed a faculty committee to censor the *Cougar's Paw*, a student publication. The reason? Some issues of the preceding year had been subjected to "severe criticism" from high schools to which they had been sent. Portions of the 1925 edition of the *Chinook*, the student annual, were censored, with a number of pages being removed before copies were distributed to high schools around the state. The incident resulted in creation of another faculty committee to advise the student editor.[73]

If student editors sometimes troubled the administration in the mid-twenties, the political leaders of the Associated Students were less likely to do so. On July 7, 1927, under the strong leadership of Graduate Manager Earl V. Foster, they petitioned the Regents for the privilege of levying a five dollar fee each semester to establish a students' building fund. That fee was to be charged in addition to a $6.50 activity ticket already exacted to support extra curricular activities. The students now proposed an ambitious construction program, to include building a college hospital and for improving physical education grounds and facilities. Holland and the Board of Regents wasted no time approving the building fund and in making the needed hospital the first project. The Associated Students floated bonds worth $75,000 to obtain the funds promised as their share of the construction costs. Plans were completed quickly and the hospital opened in 1928.[74]

The Associated Students also underwrote a field house (later christened Hollingbery Field House) in 1929, selling bonds worth $125,000 to finance it. When completed, it provided all-weather facilities for a variety of athletic activities. The next year, at the insistence of the student body, the Regents increased the Associated Student ticket in price from $6.50 to $7.50. A required purchase, it gave students access to all football, basketball, baseball, and track contests. It also funded the YMCA and YWCA, debate, Glee Club, band, and, in part, the *Evergreen*.[75]

Increased funding for athletics and construction of the new field house were evidence of the tremendous enthusiasm for sports on campus in the 1920s. Intercollegiate athletics, nevertheless, were in their formative stages. The Rose Bowl victory of 1916 did not

On Armistice Day, November 11, 1918, WSC students, faculty, and administrators gathered with people from the community in downtown Pullman to celebrate the victory. Shown here, a military band, "Uncle Sam" flanked by an honor guard, and a large crowd look on as German Emperor Kaiser Wilhelm II is burned in effigy. (Historical Photograph Collections, Washington State University Libraries)

drastically change the sports program at WSC. Coaching assignments were short-term or casual, an indication of the innocence of the era. Even college presidents might give locker room pep talks. Dr. Holland reportedly delivered inspiring speeches to the football team, and on at least one occasion praised the competitive spirit of WSC student rooters at Missoula. He also criticized an alumnus in that 1925 season for suggesting that the football coach had failed to arouse a fighting spirit in his team.[76]

By 1916, Washington State College had joined the new Pacific Coast Conference and its education in big-time athletics began. Ironically, (it may seem to the reader in this day) the conference leaders insisted that coaches should be hired for the entire year in order to advance the *amateur spirit* in college games. The State College, however, continued to employ football coaches exclusively for a four months' season plus spring practice until 1926. In spite of an abbreviated work schedule, the football coach, A. A. Exendine, received the highest salary on campus in 1925 ($5,250), except for the salary paid to President Holland.[77]

To meet the requirements of the Pacific Coast Conference that coaches serve all year, the Regents hired Orin E. "Babe" Hollingbery to direct the football program in September 1926 at $6,000 for the full year. Although he was not a college graduate, Hollingbery had coached successfully in a San Francisco high school and for the San Francisco Olympic Club, which played a schedule largely against college teams. Indeed, Hollingbery's arrival inaugurated a modern coaching program with personnel remarkably stable and of relatively long tenure.[78]

Other coaches hired were Arthur B. "Buck" Bailey, assistant football and head baseball coach, Karl Schlademan, track and field, and, in 1928, Jack Friel as basketball coach. Friel was also to serve as an assistant to any other branch of sport "that may be deemed necessary." Hollingbery coached seventeen seasons, achieving the best record among the institution's football coaches, including a Rose Bowl appearance in 1931. Friel coached for three decades and produced the highest achievement in the college's basketball history with his 1941 team which reached the final round of the National Collegiate Championship. Defeated at that point, it nevertheless had won the championship of the western portion of the nation and proudly rode home by train to a tumultuous reception on campus.[79]

Hiring the new coaching staff immediately raised the salary budget from $17,850 in 1925-1926 to $21,000 the following year and foreshadowed other increases. Most notably, expenses for travel to the far-flung reaches of the conference and entertainment of visitors from the same places promised to tax the athletic budget heavily in the future. The January 1, 1931, Rose Bowl game netted $60,000 in athletic revenue. Without those receipts, football would have produced only a $12,000 net profit while other sports suffered deficits.[80]

Though College authorities had good reason to rejoice over a good revenue-producing football season in 1931, some critics questioned the entire extra-curricular program. Indeed, some went so far as to link consideration of football as an appropriate college function with questions about the nature of the institution. On September 10 of that year, A. S. Goss, Master of the Washington State Grange, reported to President Holland that there was a "growing feeling in the state that inter-collegiate athletics are of questionable merit," and quoted an anonymous letter that accused the State College of reserving a "large part" of campus jobs for athletes. Holland quickly turned a considerable part of his energies to gathering data personally from all department chairmen to disprove the accusation. Indeed, the charge was buried under an avalanche of data. Most impressive was the fact that only three percent of the regular-year jobs were held by athletes. In addition, during a special summer renovation of the quarter-mile running track in the stadium, athletes received only one-fourth of the total salaries.[81]

Holland had to remain vigilant, for Goss's inquiries concerned not simply a preference for athletics, but called into question the very character of the College. In June 1932, while addressing the state Grange's annual convention, Goss called for the State College to remove "useless courses which the public ought not to be called upon to pay for, such as golf and esthetic dancing." In addition, he recommended that the school "eliminate extravagant expenditures for athletic coaches." Holland went to some lengths to show that golf was not in the curriculum. Ace Smith, an undergraduate student, simply gave lessons as a means of paying for his school expenses. Esthetic dancing he defended as appropriate training in physical education for women students. Nothing seems to have been said about coaches' salaries.[82]

The wearying public relations tasks Holland found himself forced into were lightened somewhat when Goss joined the president in opposing a proposal by Governor Hartley to place all five state institutions of higher education under a single board of regents. Such a body, with its members chosen by the governor, both Holland and Goss feared would seek to reduce the State College to a purely agricultural school. Hartley's proposal never found acceptance in the

Stevens Hall Residents in the late 1920s. (Historical Photograph Collections, Washington State University Libraries)

legislature or with the public, but it did complicate Holland's public relations work.

The State Grange's attitude revealed an equivocal position for WSC in the affairs of the state. The school's functions and mission remained ambiguous, a fact illuminated by an editorial that appeared in the *Seattle Times* on June 24, 1932, supporting the Grange's view of the State College and, by implication, the views of President Holland. Arguing supportively, but in terms that were outmoded by developments, the editorial stated that "The State College was founded as an agricultural school many years ago; its basic purpose remains; but the world has moved on since then. Agriculture is now something more than a matter of soils, seeds and crops, it is business." There followed a narrow concession to the liberal arts and sciences as the heritage of all students. The editor went on to say "Moreover, the amenities of farm life have become such that a larger measure of general education is needed for their enjoyment." Master Goss expressed appreciation for the support of his position and that of the Grange by a member of the urban press. For President Holland, the editorial could only yield misgivings in the long run. It fell far short of being a statement that envisioned the creation of a genuine "people's university," meeting the intellectual and cultural needs of a diverse society and its youth in a democratic way.[83]

*C*hapter Four

Depression and World War II

BUDGETARY DEFICITS DOMINATED HIGHER EDUCATION IN WASHINGTON as the world-wide depression deepened in 1932 and 1933, reducing state funds available to administrators. Representatives from Washington State College, the University of Washington, and the three normal schools gathered in Tacoma on February 5, 1932, to plan ways and means to meet yet another demand from Governor Roland H. Hartley to reduce salaries drastically in order to balance the state's budget. The representatives drew up a schedule, ranging from a ten percent reduction for professors earning $3,600 per year or more, 7.5 percent for those earning between $2,600 and $3,599, five percent for those between $2,100 and $2,599, and no reduction for those earning $2,100 and less. Washington State College immediately adopted the proposal and put it into effect.[1]

Governor Clarence D. Martin, who succeeded Hartley in January 1933, proved to be as stern as his predecessor in handling the financial crisis. He demanded yet another round of salary reductions, which brought counter-proposals from Holland and from Lyle Spencer, President of the University of Washington. Negotiations settled the total reduction at twenty-five percent for all administrators, faculty, experiment station staffs, and extension workers. Holland reduced his own salary by 26.6 percent. Left out of this scheme were teaching fellows and part-time staff, who were already living close to the poverty level. Their salaries were soon reduced but only by fifteen percent.

Holland saw the crisis as an opportune time to force resignations from faculty members he regarded as inefficient, and to place others on half-time if they attracted only small classes or otherwise did not meet his standards. Professor Frank F. Potter, who taught Latin, Greek, and later, philosophy suffered one severe reduction and almost a second because so few students studied the classics. Potter escaped a further reduction only because he consented to the indignity of writing scripts on Greek and Roman culture for presentation on KWSC, the college radio station. Dr. Hannah Aase, Assistant Professor of Botany, a ten-year veteran who was neither

OPPOSITE: *Up the Administration Walk.* (Historical Photograph Collections, Washington State University Libraries)

inefficient nor disloyal, was told that her salary would be cut to $2,100. She chose, instead, to accept a three-quarter time appointment and a further reduction of salary to $1,575 in order to pursue research more vigorously.[2]

Severe salary reductions injured morale and threatened to destroy the middle class standards of living to which most faculty and staff had grown accustomed. President Holland, recognizing that his teachers, researchers, and scholars had been "greatly disturbed" by stories of the impending reductions, sought to involve a faculty committee in allocating pay cuts. Although the committee cooperated, little could be gained from this gesture at improving the climate of opinion. The salary cuts were simply part of a staggering state and college-wide decrease in operating expenses and capital outlay. The budget granted to Washington State College by the legislature for 1933-1935 represented a loss of 36.5 percent over previous budgets, a total of $764,000.[3]

The 1933 cut had been preceded by six years of attrition in which state appropriations had been reduced $314,650. Extension and experimental work had also suffered from the loss of state funds, particularly after the 1927-1929 biennium. For that two year period, a special grant of $178,572 had been made for extension and experimental work.[4] Thereafter, in 1929, a governor's veto removed state funds needed to complement federal monies allotted for experiment stations. Outlying facilities suffered greatly, with research severely limited and some stations closed.[5]

Director E. C. Johnson, of the Main Experiment Station, reported that the elimination of state financial support had forced the firing of staff and the abandonment of some experiments in Pullman and at other locations. Some relief came in May 1934, when Governor Martin granted $38,840 from an emergency fund to keep in operation the Main Station, the Western Washington Experiment Station at Puyallup, four lesser stations, and a set of state soil surveys and land classification projects. Martin also granted $11,160 to maintain agricultural extension work.[6]

Regular academic programs and administration at Washington State College suffered as much as agricultural experimentation and extension services. The total 1933-1934 college budget had been reduced one-quarter over the previous year and stood at $84,995,000. One response to fiscal difficulties had already been made: the administration had closed Ferry and Stevens halls in the spring of 1933. Since enrollment was down and the potential saving might be as much as $6,000, President Holland kept the dormitories closed until September 1934. Few, if any, areas escaped cuts of twenty percent or more, including the central administration. Interestingly, the radio station retained its budget of the preceding year, suggesting that it played an increasingly important role in communication. The library, on the other hand, suffered a cut of thirty-three percent.[7]

In 1934, a year after the drastic salary reductions had been made, President Holland noted anxiously that the federal government, which a year earlier had reduced employees' salaries by about

A junior prom in the Old Gymnasium in the early 1930s. (Historical Photograph Collections, Washington State University Libraries)

fifteen percent, recently had made a partial restoration. The fact, too, that the University of Washington had reinstated some budget reductions increased his anxiety, raising fears that underpaid faculty might leave for other schools. He expressed gratitude for the "devotion and loyalty of all members of the staffs in accepting reductions," noting that "their personal comfort, in some cases, has been placed second to the interest of the college." He realized, too, the urgency of restoring cuts "to keep our faculty folk in a proper frame of mind.[8]

Yet, when Holland and the Regents granted increases in July 1934, only twenty-four administrators and favored professors shared in a pot containing a modest sum of $4,384.00. These were his leaders, for whom he once again applied the characterization that they "are carrying the heaviest administrative and teaching loads." When Holland met with President Lee Paul Sieg, of the University of Washington, in June 1936, he found that Sieg agreed that professors salaries should be restored in full at the earliest moment. But, Holland hesitated to act, favoring instead the plan to reward only the "superior members," to retain them and drive others away.[9]

Holland also resented what he thought to be a trick by which Sieg promoted a considerable number of faculty without giving them pay increases. The WSC president suspected that his counterpart at the University of Washington planned to ask for extra appropriations later, on the grounds that the newly promoted professors had not been compensated adequately. His suspicions were confirmed and his frustrations were evident when, in a meeting with the Regents, he brandished figures showing that the University of Washington had 26.3 percent of its faculty at the full professor rank while at the State College the percentage was only 16.3. Furthermore, he pointed out that the University gained another advantage over the State College by the fact that the latter had an embarrassingly high forty percent of its faculty at the instructor level while the former had but thirty-one percent. Holland's solution was to borrow Sieg's practice. He recommended twenty-seven promotions without pay increases, a move approved by the Board of Regents.[10]

With no solutions having been found to the problem of low salaries, Holland demurred when asked by Director F. E. Balmer, of the Extension Service, to restore full salaries to his staff. Individual members, he affirmed, had to demonstrate worth to gain restoration, thus, when the salaries were restored in 1937, Holland also fired staff members he considered to be unworthy. Unfortunately, the elevated salaries did not include funds for increased costs of living or reward for superior services rendered since 1932. Those fundamental improvements had to wait for a later day and a new administration.[11]

Departmental appropriations reached a low point in 1933-1934 at $85,195 and rose only to $91,000 in the next year. Holland nervously compared those figures with the increased enrollment of more than 600 students in that second year, and worried about adequately housing, feeding, and teaching them. Though operating funds rose to $102,415 for 1935-1936, the faculty and administration had no cause to cheer when they noted the student-faculty ratio that made good teaching difficult. It had risen to 15.9 to 1, the highest among colleges in the region. The Regent's minutes also reveal Holland's concern that "supplies in many scientific departments had been exhausted and that not even needed small equipment had been purchased during the past two or three years." Departmental appropriations rose substantially for 1937-1938 to $159,455, giving promise that immediate needs, if not long-term commitments, would be satisfied.[12]

Most teachers and researchers might suffer in silence, but a crisis in central Washington's fruit industry produced a strong demand for an immediate infusion of funds for extension work. In April 1935, when a lack of financial resources threatened to end fruit pest extermination campaigns conducted by the Chelan County Fruit Laboratory, Washington State College responded with assistance. Indeed, the college had for eight years supplied two scientists for the laboratory, although the work was locally financed in other respects. Holland and the Regents joined Yakima and Wenatchee Valley fruit growers in petitioning Governor Martin to provide emergency support to keep the projects going. On May 29, 1935, the governor not only granted $10,000, but instructed his subordinates to put as many unemployed men to work on the projects as possible, thus reducing the number of unemployed on the relief roles.[13]

When, in 1936, the Western Washington Experiment Station in Puyallup desperately needed facilities for testing cattle for Bang's Disease, and also for testing poultry, there were no funds for those purposes in the budget. Dr. J. W. Kalkus, the Superintendent, appealed to Holland who, once again, petitioned the governor. Martin granted $5,000 from his emergency fund and Holland found $3,000 more so that Kalkus could build his facility.[14]

By contrast with outlying stations, the Main Experiment Station continued to be supported at a reasonable level, thanks to federal funds (not available to outlying stations) and to $12,000 which the Regents squeezed from various sources. A small amount of the funds kept open the Dry-Land Station at Lind. In addition, a sum of $3,100 bolstered the fruit laboratory in Chelan County, now, in effect, part of the college's experiment station system.[15]

Scientists at the Main Experiment Station made important strides in agricultural experimentation in the decades after 1935, which prepared the way for transforming eastern Washington agricultural practices after the war when water and hydro-electric power from the Grand Coulee project would become available to the farmers. The partnership with the federal government became especially important to farming in the Columbia Basin, since it co-sponsored research in erosion control and moisture conservation in an experimental plot in the Palouse Hills, near Washington State College.

Workerts at the Main Experiment Station complemented the research on cultivation with their own studies of new fertilizers that would increase the food production. In projects begun as early as 1927, Orville A. Vogel and O. E. Barbee studied ways to improve crop yields and disease resistance of wheat and other cereal grains grown in six counties of eastern Washington. In 1940 they issued a report recommending varieties specifically suited to those areas. Other research of major significance included studies of wheat smut and fungi that attacked forage grasses and fruits. Resources were also directed toward improving farm management and economics, as well as the study of rural society.[16]

Unfortunately animal scientists continued to make redundant trial-and-error studies of basic animal feed, finding little support from the Federal government for experimentation. As Margaret Rossiter wrote in her study on "The Organization of Agricultural Sciences," they were "seemingly unaware of the great triumphs taking place in vitamin research between 1910 and 1920." By the 1930s, however, "basic nutritive experiments on feeds for cattle, hogs and lambs" were taking place. Notably, too, home economists, at the direction of Dean Velma Phillips, turned much of their attention away from the practice of domestic arts and toward scientific nutritional study. Then, in the late 1930s, at the suggestion of officials from the United States Department of Agriculture, Dr. N. S. Golding, a dairy bacteriologist, began concentrated investigation of molds that might be used to manufacture cheese. A decade later, he perfected the inimitable Cougar Gold cheese, which has become a famous trademark of the university. This "invention" stood as a symbol of the many significant findings in dairy science that were the product of work done by a number of scientists.[17]

When Holland sought to encourage research among the college's social scientists, he once again cited the example of political scientist Claudius O. Johnson. In a 1935 Regents' meeting, the president described Johnson's researches into the career of Senator William E. Borah, of Idaho. He called attention to Johnson's pledge to contribute ten percent of the royalties on the proposed biography, along with the first installment of $160, to purchase books that would strengthen the library's holdings in political science and history. Johnson also deposited in the library a great deal of documentation on Borah for use by the other researchers. The Regents responded favorably, permitting Johnson to devote three

•

When Holland sought to encourage research among the college's social scientists, he once again cited the example of political scientist Claudius O. Johnson. In a 1935 Regents' meeting, the president described Johnson's research into the career of Senator William E. Borah, of Idaho.

•

Holland seized on the talents and initiative of Professor Worth D. Griffin, Chairman of the Fine Arts Department, to do portraits of Pacific Northwest Indians "and other historic characters." The president declared it to be "a rare opportunity . . . to acquire a collection of portraits valuable . . . both from an artistic and historic viewpoint." (Historical Photograph Collections, Washington State University Libraries)

months to full-time work on the manuscript, deducting only a small sum to pay his teaching substitute.[18]

Holland also welcomed the 1935 appointment of Historian Herman J. Deutsch by the State Works Progress Administration, a New Deal-style agency, to make a survey of county and state records pertaining to local and regional history. The project yielded much information, but also produced numerous gifts of documents and books for the WSC library and archives. This work, a byproduct of the New Deal, prepared the way for important historical research and writing for the future, objectives greatly encouraged by both Deutsch and Holland.[19]

In the realm of the fine arts and humanities, Holland seized upon the talents and initiative of Professor Worth D. Griffin, Chairman of the Fine Arts Department, to develop a unique art collection. He proposed an ingenious plan to the Regents for obtaining a large number of paintings of Pacific Northwest Indians "and other historic characters." Holland confided to the board that this was "a rare opportunity . . . to acquire a collection of portraits valuable . . . both from an artistic and historic viewpoint." Expenses would prove negligible, since Griffin consented to work through the summer of 1936 for only his regular salary plus modest expense money.[20]

His success that summer, working at a colony of painters in Nespelem, led to a full-time field assignment during the first semester of 1936-1937. He produced forty-five paintings of Indians and numerous portraits of white businessmen, editors, farm leaders, and others who had served the college well and were, thus, repaid.

Griffin's services in the cause of the arts, along with presidential support, stimulated new interest in the Fine Arts Department. President Holland actually prepared the way for developing art education and a museum collection at WSC shortly after World War I, when he began to visit New York and Chicago on business and vacation trips. He frequented galleries and cultivated the acquaintance of art critics, seeking advice in purchasing American art of the nineteenth and early twentieth centuries. Over the years, he purchased and contributed twenty-seven paintings to the college's collection, which, at the time of Holland's death, was appraised by Griffin at a value of $50,000. Holland also persuaded Regent Charles Orton to donate a valuable art collection to the college in the names of the Virginia and Charles Orton.

The process of strengthening professional techniques and qualities of art education began when Holland appointed Griffin to the Fine Arts Department in 1924. Griffin came to the task with considerable experience in commercial and graphic design, as well as excellent training in portraiture. He did not disappoint the president in either painting or publicizing the fine arts. He served as acting chairman on several occasions and became head of the department in 1935. The field trips of 1935 and early 1936 evoked sufficient interest to permit Griffin to report that the rate of inquiries about art studies had increased "several hundred percent" since news about the Indian portraits reached the public. "It seems," he wrote at one point, "that people have discovered for the first time that we are doing excellent work here at the State College in the fine arts." Indeed, by a more objective measure of progress, Griffin and colleagues had fulfilled the administration's hope for a higher caliber of professional work. In 1928, the Regents approved a Master of Arts program and in 1940 a Master of Fine Arts program. Nevertheless, advanced work developed slowly, with but three Master of Arts degrees bestowed in the years before 1940 and only three more by 1945. The great bulk of the students enrolled were not art majors but undergraduates seeking personal fulfillment and an increased awareness of general cultural values.[21]

It must have been difficult for Holland, who had taught high school English early in his career, to acquiesce to the treatment of the humanities as of secondary rank. On every hand, though, evidence pointed to that truth: Few grants of leave with pay were made to any persons other than scientists. Consequently, when the American Council of Learned Societies awarded Don Cameron Allen, an English professor, $2,400 plus travel expenses to conduct research, Holland joined English Department Chairman Murray Bundy in applauding. Allen was "to investigate the relationship between science and literature from A.D. 1200 to A.D. 1673." The college, however, joined in support only to the extent of granting leave without pay.[22]

The humanities also continued to suffer from the prejudicial treatment of women faculty. For instance, when Ella Clark and Dorothy Dakin joined the English Department with the sub-professional titles of Associate in 1927, they were informed that they might become Assistant Professors but could not hope to rise to higher ranks. Holland confided to the Regents that strengthening the image of English as a virile study required that only men should hold prestigious professorships. Clark and Dakin suffered the consequences of being of the wrong gender but proved to be loyal and competent teachers, rising to associate professorships under a later administration.[23]

Students, however, seemed sometimes to ignore the signals of their elders and frequently made their own choices as to what and who might be significant and attractive. The career of Ida Lou Anderson, instructor of speech, was a case in point. A 1924 WSC graduate, Anderson had been badly crippled in childhood by an attack of polio. She became renowned as an inspiring teacher, and students flocked to her classes in interpretative reading of literature and radio scripts in large numbers.[24]

Edward R. Murrow, the celebrated war correspondent of World War II, a 1930 graduate, acknowledged Ida Lou Anderson's great influence but it was another alumnus who later recalled that she had neither lectured nor had she given final examinations, grades being awarded for personal improvement. "Her goal was to find something in literature that would stir an inner emotion or create a shimmer of intellectual light, however dim, through reading aloud." From her position in a corner at the back of her classroom, she

●

Edward R. Murrow, the celebrated war correspondent of World War II, a 1930 graduate, acknowledged Ida Lou Anderson's great influence but it was another alumnus who later recalled that she had neither lectured nor had she given final examinations, grades being awarded for personal improvement. "Her goal was to find something in literature that would stir an inner emotion or create a shimmer of intellectual light, however dim, through reading aloud."

●

Plowing the sidewalks in the winter of 1935-1936. (Historical Photograph Collections, Washington State University Libraries)

offered criticism and advice that inspired students for more than a decade. At her death in 1941 it was these students who flooded the campus with a tremendous emotional outpouring. President Holland joined the chorus of student responses, acknowledging that she had inspired "hundreds" of students and had helped them "to see themselves objectively and to realize their full capacities." Ironically, such high praise suggests that Anderson might have received one or more promotions and substantial raises in salary during the fourteen years she taught. She did not.[25]

Anderson did not suffer alone in receiving a low salary during the Great Depression. Speech and music teachers in general found their incomes declining since they depended heavily on fees for private lessons. Many students simply could not afford these extra fees. As a result, enrollments dropped off, severely curtailing the income of affected faculty. Thus, in 1942, when the depression had ended, Holland persuaded the Regents to place music and speech teachers completely on a salaried basis, the revenues from special tuition fees being channeled to the general treasury. The cost of these programs remained nominal during World War II, since fewer students were on campus and many of the instructional force, being temporary, drew smaller salaries than members of the regular faculty who had gone off to war.[26]

The long-term financial prospects for faculty improvement troubled the administration. With hope of raising the caliber of professors denied insofar as low salaries impeded it, the president and Regents turned to a second major faculty concern—the adoption of a retirement system. For faculty, retirement annuities obviously would decrease the uncertainties regarding the future. To Holland, such a program offered an opportunity to retire elderly professors and administrators honorably, replacing them with a new generation of vigorous, young faculty.

For a generation, the Carnegie Foundation for the Advancement of Teaching had been offering a blueprint for retirement, which had been adopted by institutions with which the State College liked to compare itself. The plan based on sound actuarial statistics required individuals and the institution to share equally in the payment of annual premiums. But, when the University of Washington and the three normal schools inaugurated retirement systems in 1939, the State College was still considering various options.[27]

Meanwhile, in 1940, Holland and the Regents urgently sought alternative means to remove superannuated administrators and faculty from full-time duty. The only means open to them immediately was to place over-age persons on half-time appointment, utilizing the savings generated to hire younger instructors. Obviously such a plan was a mere stop-gap, granting relief until a system of annuities might be inaugurated. To better plan for the future, Holland traveled east in the summer of 1940, seeking advice on retirement systems in operation. Meanwhile, numerous faculty were placed on partial employment.[28]

A faculty committee, headed by Economics Professor R. B. Heflebower, joined in the quest for a retirement program. In 1942, Aetna Insurance Company installed a system of annuities that soon became inadequate for the needs and desires of the faculty. Finally, in July 1947, after Holland's retirement, the Regents adopted a plan offered by the Teachers Insurance and Annuity Association. With this program, in which faculty and the State College contributed equally to the annuities, a satisfactory solution had been found. Employment of those eligible for pensions now became the exception rather than the rule. Faculty, thereafter, might labor with less concern about the future while a new generation of professors also found greater opportunities for employment.[29]

During the early days of the depression, students, like faculty, often had to reduce their concerns to questions of sheer economic survival on campus. Many did not have the means to remain in school for the full four years, or perhaps even for one year. Whereas 3,270 students registered for classes in the fall of 1930, enrollment steadily declined thereafter until it reached a the low point in September 1933 of only 2,595. After that date, students again returned to Pullman in increasing numbers, which reached 3,587 in 1936 and 4,035 in September 1940.[30]

In the most depressed years of the early thirties, campus life had a somber tone, offering a variety of experiences akin to those found in a frontier community. Many students sought out the most sparsely furnished rooms in town and otherwise lived Spartan existences. Men and women walked or hitch-hiked everywhere. In considerable numbers they prepared their own meals, a practice which campus authorities recognized as a potential health hazard and a reason for distributing menus and advice on nutrition and hygiene.

Adventurous young women were somewhat more favorably situated in this regard than were young men. The administration permitted women students to cook and eat their meals in Stevens

Hall. Men in considerable numbers "bached," as they called it, existing in more primitive ways, sometimes building shacks or huts on college or unoccupied private land in the town. Although "the College had neither encouraged or discouraged this practice," the Regents reported in 1936, "it has, however, endeavored to keep in close touch with the living conditions, the sanitary conditions and problems, and the health of its 'baching students.'"[31]

One student, Peter E. Kraght (pronounced Kraft), who may have been an exceptional but hardly isolated case, proved that the stout heart might be found in even the most depressing conditions. A freshman in September of 1931, he hitch-hiked to the campus from Lynden, nearly 400 miles away on the northwest coast. With great insouciance, he wrote later, he found a vacant lot within an hour, obtained permission to build a shack, "had one thousand feet of lumber delivered," and went to work. "I donned a pair of coveralls, borrowed a saw, square, level, and a shovel and started to erect my house." A week later, after immersion in class work, he finished his "cozy cabin." He claimed to have lived and studied the rest of the term for only $70. This sum included money for the purchase of textbooks, payment of fees, and investment in recreation. Food, he claimed, had cost but $4 to $5 per month. He may have achieved that low figure because he brought food from home as a part of his matriculating "dowry." Certainly, it is clear that many other "baching" students managed to stay in school in part because they brought surplus foodstuffs from the family farm.[32]

Simple living did not necessarily lead to high mindedness or better scholarship, although there is evidence that more students than ever made the honor roll. Holland, on the other hand, decried an apparent drop in scholarship brought on by students who worked at long, fatiguing labor in order to stay in school. The president and the Regents, ever vigilant to moral crises, also watched the end of prohibition with growing apprehension, fearing the return of the saloon. When plans appeared to open a state liquor dispensary in Pullman were divulged, the college authorities donned the armor of opposition. They petitioned the Washington State Liquor Control Board to not establish an outlet in the town. The Dad's Day Committee, in November 1935, commended the WSC authorities "for being constantly on the alert to guard the students of the college from harmful influences and to assure an environment consistent with the highest ideals of college life." This sentiment could only have stirred the college to redouble its efforts to keep the town dry.[33]

Holland's hopes were dashed when, in November 1936, the Pullman citizens voted to permit liquor sales. Although he had argued strongly that the local problem was especially distressing since the students outnumbered the resident townspeople, Holland had to settle for a compromise that removed the state's liquor store from the premises of a drug store heavily frequented by students.[34]

Despite the new temptation of legalized liquor sales within Pullman's city limits, as well as the fact that some students continued to "bach," college officials took increasing satisfaction in the college's accomplishments by the late thirties. In fact, by 1939, the Board of Regents could report to the governor and the public with pride that they had "successfully met the seemingly almost insurmountable series of problems involved in fitting a college community of four thousand students into a town of approximately equal size."[35]

Eight dormitories, each erected by private enterprises, now held 1,273 students. Some thirty-four fraternities and sororities, funded by students and alumni, housed 748 men and 364 women. There were three cooperative houses where 145 men lived. To round out housing used by students, town residents provided rooms for about 1,500, approximately forth percent of the student body.[36]

Living in a fraternity, sorority, or in town did not free students from administrative dictates. The Dean of Men inspected quarters in the town for male students, placing acceptable houses on a preferred list and prodding recalcitrant landlords to come up to the mark. In many cases, Dean Otis C. McCreery reported, householders "have acted *in loco parentis* for the boys who are away from home."

Women off-campus, who represented only one-sixth of the female student body, were as closely supervised as those living on the campus. Fraternities reportedly worked closely with the dean of men's staff to improve living conditions and retain the high level of camaraderie. But the dean acknowledged that ". . . many fraternities still participate in the traditional 'Hell Week' which has been outmoded on most campuses in the country." To the dissatisfaction of the dean, they also overemphasized participation in extracurricular activities. Nevertheless, Greek houses also employed residents and assistants who devoted much time to inculcating the social graces and encouraging intellectual development among their charges.[37]

Close administrative supervision had never deterred students from expressing themselves in campus political matters through their own organizations. Apparent student body cohesiveness often dissolved, as opposing factions took sides on specific issues. Frequently, bickering groups could readily be identified as those students living on campus versus off-campus groups, or dormitory residents opposed to those who lived in Greek houses. The 1930s were a testing time for the viability and strength of each level of student government, permitting a measure of its contribution to campus life.

Senior class and other class governments had their origins in the earliest days of the college, but by the 1930s they had declined in power, energy, and interest to the point where elections of officers represented popularity contests and traditional social events, like the Junior Prom, the Sophomore Tolo, and freshman-sophomore battles proved to be virtually their only activities. Easy and clear class identification had been lost in the turmoil of World War I and in the Great Depression, both of which upset "normal" progress toward degrees for many students. Nevertheless, as a tribute to the power of tradition, class government lingered on for several decades.

Volume 1   Number 1

RESEARCH STUDIES
OF THE
STATE COLLEGE OF WASHINGTON

Pullman, Washington
June 28, 1929

*The origins of Washington State
University Press can be traced to
Holland's founding of the scholarly
journal* Research Studies of the State
College of Washington. *First published
in 1929 it soon fell victim to the Great
Depression. However, Holland revived
the journal in 1935, appointing Paul
P. Kies, Associate Professor of English
as its editor.* (Washington State
University Press)

Realistically in the mid-thirties, it became apparent that the Board of Control of the Associated Students better served the student community than did class government. The campus had become a segmented society of dormitories, Greek houses, and off-campus dwellers that required new modes of cohesion. The fraternities, however, easily developed the superior organization . As a result, they seized control of student politics and maintained their position in election after election. A sub rosa fraternity society, it was alleged, "fixed" elections, sometimes offering only one slate of candidates— that of the Greeks—to a dispirited electorate.[38]

Yet, neither Greek political power nor the viability of the Board of Control permitted students to attain their most immediate political goal, modification of puritanical and repressive social regulations, without an unprecedented confrontation with President Holland and Dean of Women Annie Fertig. A student code of conduct had existed for a long time at Washington State College, and had been supplemented by a set of severe academic regulations. Since the rules had never been codified and published, students were easily persuaded that regulations were merely personal and changeable whims of the president or the dean. In reality, the regulations were the work of college administrators from earlier decades and past student-faculty committees, and were based on orthodox nineteenth century thought and practice. They had, surprisingly, lingered on at Washington State College into the middle of the Great Depression. That they had not been strongly challenged before may be attributed to the power and long tenure of the President Holland and, consequently, to the conservatism of his entire administration.

In early 1936, an organization called the Student Liberty Association sprang up on campus. Its popularity reached across social and political lines to include both Greeks and Independents. Leaders quickly sought the support of faculty by demanding that students and faculty alike be given more control of campus life. To eliminate capricious and arbitrary control of student affairs and to prepare the way for reform, they asked that the college rules be published. Reform proposals were specific on several points. They demanded that dormitory closing hours be extended until eleven in the evening on week nights and until one o'clock in the morning on Friday and Saturday nights. To improve social life, they asked for permission to hold social "mixers" and desserts on Wednesday evenings. In a mood of radical permissiveness, they called for the abolition of compulsory class attendance. They also demanded "abolition of Dean Annie's suggestive picnic and social rulings," including her advice that women should not wear provocative clothing or sit or recline in suggestive postures. Finally, to make their position absolutely clear, student leaders demanded "abolition of Ultra-conservative, dictatorial Administrative policies."[39]

A protest march began on the morning of May 7, when bells rang in every classroom at 11:15 for two minutes, signaling the start of the parade. In spite of a cold rain and strong winds, more than 2,500 students marched in protest of the administration. Assembling in front of College Hall, the students marched around the campus to the beat of a volunteer band of seventy-five performers, many of them ROTC bandsmen. In their anxiety to prove that they were not radical but only wanted justice, the marchers sang the Cougar Fight Song and carried signs that read in one case "We're Not Reds But We Want a White Administration" and in another case, "This May be a Cow College But We're Not Contented."[40]

The impending strike might have turned the good humor of the march and placards sour except for the fact that a faculty committee readily agreed with the student leaders that their specific demands on closing hours, social affairs, and compulsory class attendance ought to be accepted. Holland agreed with the findings, but his statement that the final decision should be made by the Faculty Senate caused the students to vote to strike the next day, May 8, in spite of the disapproval of their leaders. The Faculty Senate condemned the idea of a strike but approved the new regulations and, equally important, provided for the regular review and revised publication of the behavior code.[41]

In the end, students did not strike, instead they applauded Holland, permitting the president to escape criticism. However, Dean Fertig did not escape censure. Ultimately she became the scapegoat for the entire episode. Although she denied having instituted puritanical restrictions, it was to no avail. The following semester Holland put her on leave without pay and later dismissed her. The president, who had received uncompromising support from the Regents, rode out the storm relatively easily. He may have felt keenly the loss of confidence displayed by some students and faculty, but he certainly praised the student body as earnest and hard-working.[42]

One of the most significant changes that took place as a result of the student unrest had nothing to do with the dean of women nor, seemingly, had it been counted among the original student de- mands. It had to do with abolishing the notorious "48 Hour" rule, under which students might not absent themselves from classes two days before a scheduled vacation or during the two days after its official termination. The penalties had always been severe. For each class missed, a grade point would be subtracted from the credits earned in courses missed. In honoring the spirit of the student- faculty agreement that aborted the strike, the faculty amended the rule so that absences in the forty-eight hour period resulted in nominal fines instead of credit loss.[43]

During the next several years the softening of restrictive social regulations gradually took place. More than two years after the strike, on December 1, 1938, the Faculty Senate approved a recommenda- tion from the Board of Deans permitting Saturday "Matinee Parties." These events would be strictly chaperoned, however, as would mixed groups that congregated to listen to radio broadcasts of football games held on other campuses. Liquor, of course, was banned from these events, as was unrestricted smoking of tobacco.

Students smoked only in a few designated rooms in living groups but faculty seemed to be without similar privileges, as classrooms, laboratories, and offices were off-limits. Professors, however, might retire to "Nicotine Lane," below the music building, a wooded area technically off-campus. Additional amenities became available in 1940 when, on petition, living groups were permitted to install "commissaries" where food and soft drinks were sold under the strict control of the deans of men and women.[44]

There was another side to student life and work, that reflected by the graduate student body. This group numbered 379 in 1929, a figure that rose to 686 in 1941, only to fall again to 213 in the war year of 1943. The percentage of graduate students in the total student body ranged from twelve percent in 1929 to eighteen percent in 1941 and did not fall appreciably in the middle of the war when it rested at fourteen percent. While the percentages might suggest a significant graduate student influence on the total curriculum, other factors give reason to doubt a great advancement of the graduate program. There were in the years between 1929 and 1938 only twenty doctor of philosophy degrees granted, an obvious sign that most graduate work was restricted to the level of the master's degree. When Dean F. L. Pickett, of the Graduate School, reported in 1938 that the twenty doctors all were employed at their professions, the satisfaction was evident. He believed that they were the equal of doctoral students elsewhere.

The bulk of master's students afforded Dean Pickett little satisfaction. They were generally of lesser ability, he believed, than doctoral students because many were local and self-selected. Then, too, the State College had few funds available to support their studies. Indeed, instead of offering inducement to superior candidates, the college placed a surcharge of $150 on the tuition fee of non-Washingtonians. Out-of-state candidates could not easily be recruited and foreign graduate students on campus were almost unheard of.[45]

Failing health drove Dean Pickett from office in 1939, giving President Holland the opportunity to place rural sociologist Professor Paul H. Landis in the graduate school directorship. Holland had often praised and supported Landis as a leading scholar, and thus it was not a difficult decision to make. If Holland intended to utilize Landis's reputation to attract graduate students and funds for the graduate program, he negated that objective by making the appointment only one-half time. If, on the other hand, he sought to reward Landis for his research and publication, he must have soon learned that his new dean found administrative work "irksome and exhausting."[46]

But, once in office, Dean Landis strove to increase the number of graduate students by improving working and study conditions. In large measure such improvement centered on urging the president to increase the number of assistantships and fellowships available to graduate students. Holland agreed with him in part because of the economy of using assistants in classrooms and laboratories, especially when the budget did not permit an equal number of professors. The result was that some time before 1943 the number of assistantships rose modestly from seventy to one hundred. Then, reacting to increases in graduate student stripends at the University of Washington, Holland decreed that maximum support for graduate students at WSC would be increased by ten percent—six dollars above the University of Washington figure. To make assistantships even more attractive, those who held them were relieved of the necessity to pay non-resident tuition.

The large number of faculty on eleven month appointments—theoretically, at least, devoting their summers to research—in the estimation of both Holland and Landis, provided a coterie of scientists in agriculture and engineering perfectly capable of handling graduate students and directing their research. Unfortunately, federal or private funds supporting graduate study reached few, if any, students in the College of Sciences and Arts. Landis expressed optimism that the resources of the State College were generally adequate for college-wide graduate study. His faith was based on an unexamined belief that the institution was "building one of the best libraries in the Pacific Northwest in all fields and in several fields the best."[47] Doctoral degrees granted from 1940 to 1945 numbered fourteen, a substantial increase in the rate of degree granting over the previous decade. No evidence exists, however, that any department yet stood out as a leader in graduate study, as none graduated more than three doctors in that period.[48]

Landis, perhaps, first drew the attention of President Holland and the Board of Regents in 1938 as the model research professor outside the field of agriculture. The Social Science Research Council had granted him $1,380 for field expenses incurred while making a study of "defense migration" (migratory farm workers) to the Yakima Valley. The vigorous sociologist had wasted little time in joining two colleagues in producing a carefully researched, dispassionate study of migratory farm labor in the hop fields of the Yakima Valley. The tale of unsanitary conditions, disease, and poor social environment opened the community, area farmers, and even the transient workers themselves to criticism.[49]

Protests poured into the Board of Regents and President Holland from farm organizations. The Associated Farmers of Washington, in particular, challenged the report, which had been published in an experiment station bulletin. Indeed, a member of the Board of Regents, B. A. Perham, protested the report as inaccurate. After investigation, the board agreed with Holland that the report had been prepared with great care and accuracy, justifying its publication. Then, in more general terms, the board recognized that under the Pernell Act the State College had an obligation to present such sociological research.[50]

In supporting publication of the study of Yakima labor conditions, Holland and the Regents supported one of the most important ingredients in scholarly and scientific work—protection of freedom of inquiry and expression. By so doing, they also helped make it possible for Landis to gain additional research funds (apart from his regular salary as a member of the Main Experiment Station). In June 1940, the Brookings Institution in Washington, D.C., awarded him $2,000 to study relief programs in rural Washington.[51]

Professors and graduate students in liberal arts and sciences continued to find that financial stumbling blocks and a concomitant lack of time were serious deterrents to scholarly and research endeavors. Botanist Orlin Biddulph was a notable exception. Characterized as "one of the most promising young men in the field of phosphorus metabolism in plants [studied] by means of radio-active phosphorus," he had received several grants from the National Research Council, culminating in an award of $1,300 for half-time research in 1941-1942. In appreciation, Holland raised Biddulph's salary from $2,600 per year (ten months) to $2,750.[52]

Research without publication, creativity without dissemination, Holland knew, would be self-defeating. The reputation of the school as well as the development of knowledge might be enhanced by publications of the college's faculty. Recognizing the relative scarcity of journals available in which to published, Holland in 1929 had established a scientific quarterly entitled *Research Studies of the State College of Washington.* It had not prospered and disappeared after a few numbers had been issued. Those few issues demonstrated its value, however, and when finances were more readily available in 1935 Holland revived the journal, only this time encouraging publication in its pages from across the entire academic spectrum, from science to literature and history. The editor, Paul P. Kies, Associate Professor of English, stated its purpose very self-consciously: It would be a "medium of publication for articles of research in the pure sciences and arts; it is limited to material making a contribution to knowledge." Perhaps as further encouragement to local research, its pages were open only to professors and graduate students of the State College of Washington.[53]

In 1935, Ernest O. Holland had completed two decades of a personal administration in which the faculty often felt the stinging touch of a benign autocrat who had only the best interests of the institution at heart. Had the professors any reason to suppose that there might be a change in the near future? Certainly, Holland had exhibited no desire to shed the robes or perquisites of office.

When the president addressed new faculty in the fall of 1936 he clearly indicated a desire to continue his close supervision of faculty and interpretation of policy. His warm welcome accompanied a sentiment worthy of the most parochial Westerner when he stated that "Western hospitality is friendly and sincere." It came at a price, however, for he expected new faculty to reserve judgment of policy and traditions until they had gained some experience with the operation of the institution. Traditions and customs in Pullman were different, he declared, from those "in a great city. I shall not discuss these traditions but you can imagine that the members of our faculty are not as free as they would be if they were connected with an institution like the University of California, Columbia University, [or the] University of Chicago, or some other institution."[54]

In 1935, Ernest O. Holland had completed two decades of a personal administration in which the faculty often felt the stinging touch of a benign autocrat who had only the best interests of the institution at heart. Had the professors any reason to suppose that there might be a change in the near future? Certainly, Holland had exhibited no desire to shed the robes or perquisites of office.

Holland once again proclaimed the necessity to preserve academic freedom while, paradoxically, relying on influence and personal relationships to prevent the faculty from organizing independently to affect personnel matters or university policy. If a faculty member, Holland continued, objected to departmental policy or practice laid down by a chairman, he had one "honorable" course to follow. He might take the matter up with his dean. His course thereafter would be as follows: If denied his protest, he might resign promptly, or he might appeal to the president and the Regents. If his petition were denied, his only recourse then would be to resign and go elsewhere.[55]

There were signs that the faculty might seek to loosen these tight administrative bonds when, in January 1934, an independent Faculty Executive Committee was organized, using funds levied on the faculty. Almost immediately, it concerned itself with salaries, even sending a representative to Seattle to make comparisons with the University of Washington. It quickly exhausted its sense of daring, however, for it made no recommendations for salary improvements. Indeed, the committee's members admitted to its constituency in September 1935, that "your Executive Committee finds that the process of defining its function is a slow one. Thus far it believes that its activities have remained distinctly within its proper scope." Perhaps most difficult of all, the members acknowledged their lack of experience in leadership when they wrote: "But each proposed activity must be considered in the light of not-too-well established ideas as to the proper function of a faculty organization."[56]

Despite its caution, however, the Faculty Executive Committee pursued some cherished objectives. Dr. R. B. Heflebower, for example, sought to make its activities more credible by pursuing an exhaustive study of instructional costs, using his own unit, the School of Business Administration, as the model. The committee also strongly urged Holland to introduce a retirement annuity plan. On the other hand, the members, upon looking into problems of student behavior in the classroom, proposed a laissez faire policy whereby each faculty member would establish his or her own punishment for cheating on examinations.[57]

President Holland willingly accepted faculty and Executive Committee financial and moral support in a campaign to defeat Initiative 94 at the Washington's general election in November 1935. Proponents of the measure hoped to limit property taxes for all state purposes to forty mills, reducing the allotment to the University of Washington and the State College of Washington to two mills. Unfortunately for higher education, this restrictive bill became law.[58]

When President Holland contracted a severe cold in early January of 1937 the entire work of the Faculty Executive Committee, as well as the continuity of his administration, came into question. Refusing to slacken his hectic work pace, the president suffered an attack of influenza that forced him to bed in Spokane's St. Luke's Hospital for ten weeks. His difficulties continued after his return to Pullman when he once again fell ill, this time suffering from a "severe attack of indigestion." Slow to recover, Holland traveled to the East where he apparently found a cure in New York City. After that, he continued on to other seaboard centers and then across Canada for further convalescence in Victoria, British Columbia. After three-and-a-half months out of town, he returned to the campus on September 1, 1937.[59]

Even then, Holland described his progress toward recovery as slow and referred to his administration as having suffered through a "critical year." The Faculty Executive Committee agreed "heartily" with his view that it might best serve the cause of the institution by disbanding in order to demonstrate solidarity with the Board of Regents and Holland. The president reciprocated by creating a Faculty Advisory Committee that did nothing but transmit individual professor's suggestions to the administration.[60]

On October 2, 1937, Holland asked the Board of Regents to appoint Dean Herbert Kimbrough as vice president, a position which he held along with his duties concerned with managing the School of Music and Fine Arts. The president had complete confidence in Kimbrough who had served as chief executive officer during Holland's illness and travels. Kimbrough took control of the voluminous correspondence and prepared to substitute at Regent's meetings. Since Holland never regained his stamina, Kimbrough undoubtedly undertook additional tasks. The Regents attested to the continued uncertainty over Holland's health by deciding in April 1939, that the president might remain in office as long as the task was not hazardous to his well being. At such a point, he would be given a lesser office.[61]

The ongoing budgetary crisis of the 1930s provided no medicine to cure Holland's problems, personal or otherwise. Landeen, in *E. O. Holland and the State College of Washington, 1916-1944*, claims that the institution had sunk so low in 1935 that the administration could

President Holland and his staff in the midst of fall 1937 registration in the old Administration Building.
(Historical Photograph Collections, Washington State University Libraries)

not find $3,500 to purchase thirty microscopes for the College of Veterinary Medicine. It had to ask veterinary students to pay for them by means of a special fee of two dollars a semester for ten semesters to amortize the cost. Matters did not improve under the 1937-1939 budget, the college suffering an overdraft of $98,317. The result pushed the institution deep into the red.[62] The new biennium began in 1939 "with something of a financial showdown," within the state's administration. The legislature had increased the percentage of sales tax and other excise revenues sufficiently, it was thought, to yield an income of $3,401,380 for the State College. Governor Martin had other ideas, however, believing that appropriations would exceed revenues by fifteen percent. To escape an impending deficit he ordered the State College and other state agencies to withhold a substantial portion of the allocated funds until further notice.[63]

Holland had not been sanguine about budgetary prophecies, but he could hardly have been more despondent about the governor's decision. The total appropriation for the new biennium barely exceeded that granted for 1937-1939. Plans for improving faculty morale, stability, and achievement by increasing salaries and introducing a pension system were now frustrated. His hope to add thirty-nine faculty and staff positions in order to introduce new programs and specialties and to reduce class sizes appeared chimerical. Noting that numerous large classes of more than 100 students were common, Holland particularly called the attention of the Board of Regents to the four laboratories in chemistry, each of which had the astounding number of more than 100 students. In the end, he reluctantly reduced his request for new faculty and staff to twelve, which did not include even one chemist. His hope to provide salary raises to retain promising young faculty faded in the face or reality.[64]

Agitation and improved revenue forecasts finally produced results. Bursar W. C. Kruegel, on February 26, 1940, revealed that Governor Martin had released funds to the extent that only $92,733 remained impounded. Holland, Kruegel, and Regents B. A. Perham and George H. Gannon then persuaded the governor to release virtually all of the remainder: $54,700 for salary improvements and $38,283 for property and building refurbishings. For the time being, at least, fiscal conditions improved dramatically.[65]

While budgets and appropriations dominated university politics in the middle and late thirties, the world slipped toward war and a future filled with foreboding. Holland felt impelled at successive Commencements to outline a vision which he hoped the degree candidates would respond to in positive ways. In June 1935, for example, he assured graduates that America was strong and good, its democratic system needing only "enlightened, clear-thinking Americans" to fend off fascistic and communistic revolution. The bright young candidates for degrees sitting before him, in his view, represented a coterie of educated men and women who would, at first, sustain democracy at home and, later, transmit its reforming power to the rest of the world. In the more evil days that followed, in 1938

•

Holland felt impelled at successive Commencements to outline a vision which he hoped the degree candidates would respond to in positive ways. In June 1935, for example, he assured graduates that America was strong and good, its democratic system needing only "enlightened, clear-thinking Americans" to fend off fascistic and communistic revolution.

•

for instance, he assured graduates that "straight-thinking may yet bring order to a disordered world." Two years later, graduates were told that they belonged "to this small army of interpreters and defenders of our way of life." America and civilization would be safe if they responded intelligently to the international crisis.[66]

At no time in the ensuing war did Holland lose his faith in America's system of education or in the course of study provided by Washington State College. Although the future remained uncertain, he turned his college's energies to building strength and resolution to win the struggle. The president, for example, in March 1943, broadcast on KWSC, the college radio station, that a good citizen's role on the home front was to cultivate and harvest as much food as possible in his own back yard in order to help win the war. At that moment, the most important service rendered by the college to the public was the publication of an agricultural extension bulletin on "Victory Gardens." It became so popular that within a year 175,000 copies were distributed to Washington families.[67]

He and members of the faculty also sought to promote better understanding of American history and constitutional government in order to increase the public's appreciation of its way of life. To encourage study and discussion of American values and institutions, Professor Herman J. Deutsch, of the Department of History and Political Science, inaugurated an Institute of Americanism in January 1944, which provided speakers, bibliographies, and guidelines for reading circles, as well as articles and editorials for newspapers on the virtues of the American way. Several newspapers, and such diverse civic organizations as the American Legion and the Kiwanis Club, responded favorably to this program.[68]

Many faculty members opened new dimensions in extension teaching when they lectured to workers and their families at the secret Manhattan project at Hanford. The purpose was to acclimate a host of out-of-state workers to their new community, and thus strengthen a disrupted society in wartime. Faculty speakers discussed local and regional history, state government, geography, and general living conditions.[69] At the other extreme in orientation programming, Holland argued at a conference of publicists in Spokane during midsummer 1944 that in default of the family, schools and colleges must provide leadership in strengthening American life.[70]

As early as the Spring of 1939, the State College of Washington responded to a request made by the Civil Aeronautics Authority by offering its facilities and faculty to train aviators and aircraft technicians on campus and at the Pullman-Moscow Airport. Between November 1939, and March 1943, WSC offered ground and flight training—the latter in cooperation with the University of Idaho—to almost 300 regularly enrolled students. The stated purpose, to protect the nation, later seemed justified when the State College reported that it had received superior ratings for its program and because "as a group, these trainees are making commendable records for themselves in the service of their country."[71]

A few weeks after the Japanese attack on Pearl Harbor on December 7, 1941, the demands of war engulfed the campus. The status of normal academic programs was soon cast into doubt as the overwhelming tasks of the war intervened. College enrollment, which had attained the highest figure in the history of the institution at 4,035 in September of 1940, fell steadily thereafter until it reached 1,530 for the first semester, 1943-1944. Thereafter, it rose gradually to 2,708, in September of 1945, reflecting the improved fortunes of America and her allies. Though enrollments of men obviously declined greatly because of the military draft, both men and women students left school in large numbers to join the service or to work in war-related industries or on the farm.[72]

Arrival of soldiers and airmen for technical training arrested the decline in numbers of campus inhabitants, but it also changed the character of the school and affected the tone of life and outlook of faculty, administration, and remaining students. The influx of the military in 1942 added only some 423 students to the campus but the presence of slightly more than 5,000 air crewmen in 1943-1944 (with no more than 1,250 on campus at any one time) created a mood of haste in training and the sense that the "war effort" might be aided from Pullman as well as anywhere else. Several Army Student Training Programs (notably in engineering, veterinary medicine, and a reserve group) and a Cadet Nurses Corps, added 1,600 military students pursuing trade-school and other practical training. These students gave the campus an olive drab coloration and made plausible the speeded-up curricula and the emphasis on "training" as an objective rather than "education."[73]

The faculty responded to the pace of this wartime activity when, only a few months after Pearl Harbor, its Advisory Committee

The protest began on the morning of May 6, 1936 when classroom bells rang at 11:15. Despite cold rain and a strong wind, more than 2,500 students assembled in front of College Hall. Accompanied by a volunteer seventy-five-member band, many of them ROTC cadets, they sang the "Cougar Fight Song" and carried signs that read such things as: "We're Not Reds But We Want a White Administration" and "This May be a Cow College But We're Not Contented." (Historical Photograph Collections, Washington State University Libraries)

proposed a "War Year" curriculum for college students on the grounds that "today trained men and women are sorely needed, soon they will be desperately needed." As they saw, not clearly but with a strong sense of urgency, the need was for a good deal of practical work for college students who might soon be drafted or lured into farming or war industries. The Regents thoroughly agreed and approved this program in September of 1942.

"War Year" curricula were to be run parallel to the traditional academic calendar but were to be planned as two year programs. Many departments were slow to respond and some objected to their participation. In fact, the courses given the greatest attention focused on the nature of war and peace, which was in keeping with the idea that America was fighting to save democracy. Only a few departments actually introduced this option. Among courses introduced were offerings such as, "Civilian War Skills," and "Citizenship in War," both recommended for students whose major interest was remote from engineering, mathematics, and other studies easily related to war activities. The College of Sciences and Arts also offered two courses unusual in character, but obviously possessing a scholarly or scientific basis. These were "Man and the Western World" and "The Meaning of the War," history courses, and "The Human Organism and the War," a biological science course. The Chemistry Department taught two courses in "War Gasses and Explosives."[74]

One professor, who had been deeply immersed in the war curricula, later thought that the program had been a "signal failure," not having met the needs of either the students or the faculty. A colleague, however, characterized "The Meaning of the War" as a very useful and popular course. In 1945, summing up the work, Dean C. C. Todd of the College of Sciences and Arts, praised several courses as having been important to the students and the pursuit of the war.[75]

At the request of the Regents in the Fall of 1942, the Department of Military Science and Tactics increased the technical training of the Reserve Officer Training Corps (ROTC). Fourteen hundred male college students were involved—certainly the bulk of the civilian men—and they must have felt that they were almost a part of the military sector of the campus. They now had to grapple with new skills ranging from "motor maintenance" and "heavy motorized equipment" to "camouflage," "psychology of war," and "Judo wrestling." Close order drill and military history and tactics might have seemed academic by comparison.[76]

For the college, per se, few changes in organization took place and few new programs were started during the late 1930s or during the war period. In 1938, after some investigation, Holland introduced a Graduate School of Social Work, which he believed would serve a pressing need. Unfortunately, this program did not achieve academic respectability, an adequate budget, or stable teaching faculty, although it still functioned when Holland retired.

More significantly, in 1940 programs in business administration and secretarial studies were removed from the College of Sciences

Then, in 1942, with generous financial backing from the United States Public Health Service, Washington State College joined with Deaconess and St. Luke's hospitals in Spokane to inaugurate a cooperative nurses' training program. The college provided academic studies while the hospitals supplied clinical nursing experience.

and Arts and organized into a separate School of Business Administration. Led by Dean R. B. Heflebower, one of Holland's most
trusted administrators, courses offered through the school were
popular with students in the wake of the economic upturn that came
with the war. The new school's size justified these developments
which, incidentally, left the Department of Economics temporarily
in the College of Sciences and Arts.[77]

President Holland also took a keen interest in academic training
for police administration and services. In developing a curriculum
in this area he relied heavily on advice from the University of
California, the pioneer in academic police training, and modeled
WSC's program on the one offered by that university. In 1941,
Holland brought in V. A. Leonard as chairman of the new department.
Funding proved adequate and a steady flow of undergraduate majors
soon followed, thus insuring the development of a modest but
successful program.[78]

Then, in 1942, with generous financial backing from the United
States Public Health Service, Washington State College joined with
Deaconess and St. Luke's hospitals in Spokane to inaugurate a
cooperative nurses' training program. The college provided academic studies while the hospitals supplied clinical nursing experience. Actually, this Bachelor of Science curriculum provided a
capstone to a far-flung set of extension nursing programs established in Walla Walla, Wenatchee, Spokane, and in psychiatric
nursing at the State Hospital in Medical Lake.[79]

Holland's efforts to remodel programs and add new curricula did
not enable the State College to contribute significantly to the
advancement of scholarship or to expand the frontiers of science.
Of course, the energy and resources drained away by the "war
effort" had already insured the impossibility of placing much
attention on the disinterested search for truth, whether it be in the
natural or social sciences or creative activity in the arts.

Generally, pure and applied research suffered in areas of agricultural research as well, despite the fact that federal monies were
annually available for that purpose. Dean E. C. Johnson, of the
College of Agriculture, pointed out that while declining enrollments
made more time available for research, serious shortages of supplies,
facilities, and equipment nullified any fiscal advantage. Inevitably,
the demands for more food forced agricultural scientists and extension workers to seek practical means of increasing production of
food and fiber and to bolster morale through encouraging the public
to cultivate "victory gardens." Dean Johnson concluded a report of
the war years in 1946 by acknowledging that the research had been
fueled by previously accumulated basic information. Among numerous applications of research to meet wartime needs, Dean Johnson
noted that "research on cereal smuts . . . has reduced the smutty
wheat received on Pacific Northwest terminal markets from approximately 35 percent fifteen years ago to slightly more than 3 percent in
1941-42." In contrast, he had little to state about further additions to
the pool of basic scientific data accumulated during the war.[80]

●

*President Holland also took a
keen interest in academic
training for police
administration and services. In
developing a curriculum in this
area he relied heavily on advice
from the University of
California, the pioneer in
academic police training, and
modeled WSC's program on the
one offered by that university.*

●

Physical science and engineering research offered some opportunities for WSC scientists to make contributions to future peacetime achievements, and even to aid clandestine efforts to create new weapons that might vanquish the enemy. Physicist Paul Anderson and two assistants were employed by the federal government in top secret investigations which President Holland believed would be a great source of pride when, or if, made known. For instance, Homer Dana successfully completed numerous engineering projects designed to further the "war effort." Several staff members worked on a project, begun before the war, to fabricate certain airplane parts from magnesium, a strong, light metal. Boeing's utilization of their discoveries brought unexpected financial rewards and raised hope that research, when combined with the projected cheap power from the Grand Coulee project, might project the State College into scientific leadership and provide Washington with new industries in the postwar years.[81]

Despite the apparent benefits, Dean Clare C. Todd, of the College of Sciences and Arts, recognized the debilitating effect of the war effort on research and scholarship. Of the small staff of professors in Todd's college, fifty-four in number, nineteen took leaves of absence, four to engage in government-sponsored research, six to join federal bureaus or agencies, and nine to serve in the armed forces. Scientists and researchers of equal caliber could not be found during the war to replace them. A crushing blow was felt when it became known that nine absent professors did not plan to return to the State College when hostilities ceased.[82]

It was not surprising, under such circumstances, that in April 1945, Dean Todd acknowledged that research had decreased greatly during the war "and it is not yet on the upgrade." Almost without exception, it seemed, the most productive faculty remaining on the campus had been obliged to take on back-breaking teaching loads. For some, the heavy burden included the exhausting task of teaching extension classes in Spokane. Those inclined to engage in research found yet another obstacle: In most departments it proved impossible to secure graduate assistants. But in spite of heavy loads, several of the most experienced faculty each gave fifty or more public addresses around the state, especially on the meaning of the war.[83]

On June 29, 1942, Holland unwittingly revealed a dilemma regarding research that was largely of his own making. While discussing the performance of the late H. V. Carpenter, Dean of the College of Mechanic Arts and Engineering for twenty-five years, he complained to the Regents that the Carpenter had wanted to be involved with research but had spent his time largely upon administration, a function Holland valued highly. Unfortunately, Carpenter was not particularly good in administration and, as a result, the president could only bemoan his own decision to keep him in the deanship for so long.[84]

But, as Historian Landeen subsequently pointed out, Holland expected his deans to be meticulous administrators and that is what he got. A few years later, at the dedication of Carpenter Hall, Homer J. Dana, Director of the Engineering Experiment Station, praised the late dean for his ingenuity in constructing a campus radio station KFAE (later, KWSC) in 1922 and developing the first programming. Holland had taken great pride in this achievement. Carpenter, like Holland's other deans (and department chairmen) showed a commendable adaptability to sustain programs in the face of poverty-stricken research facilities, a matter not lost on the president at other times.[85]

Holland's complaint about Dean Carpenter carried the peevish ring of an executive exhausted by twenty-six years of trial, confronting the varying fortunes of the State College. He had been considering retirement when the WSC adopted its wartime programs. After Pearl Harbor, Holland steeled himself to serve until the conflict ended, filled with the conviction that WSC—like the nation—needed an experienced leader. But as time passed his energy was consumed more quickly and he no longer possessed the strength to work at all hours, a matter which yielded countless rumors about his poor health. Finally, in April of 1943, the Regents discussed the matter frankly with the president, urging him not to over-exert himself, but also expressing their strong support of his continuing leadership.[86]

But flagging vitality probably had less to do with Holland's administrative difficulties than had the sheer length of his tenure, which encompassed America's entry into World War I, the Roaring Twenties, the Great Depression , and now World War II. Circumstances of the time, including small budgets, a penurious legislature, and a feud with the University of Washington fixed the president and the State College in a cautious, defensive attitude. Whatever plans Holland, the Regents, and the faculty had for improvements often were shattered by public indifference.

Furthermore, pressure groups with specific objectives continued to disrupt WSC's land grant mission. One of the groups highly critical of the school's agricultural program was the Washington Cattleman's Association which, in July 1943, stated that "they thought that the State College should be primarily a College of Agriculture." Holland, in rebuttal, was reduced to arguing in terms of the association's parochial view of higher education, including arguing that agriculture had been treated with relative generosity for many years.[87]

The Regents quickly supported Holland's broader concept of the nature of the institution but had few resources with which to counterattack. The sad condition of the library revealed their dilemma. Over the years, Washington State College had not been able to develop library resources and services that were commensurate with its institutional mission. In lieu of an adequate budget Librarian Foote's formula for success, by means of which he collected and traded for discarded books and documents with other libraries, had not produced a superior quality, up-to-date collection. Much of the material was out of date or bore little relation to student or faculty needs. Furthermore, the diffuse collection could not be

Shortly after the United States entered World War II, CBS war correspondent and WSC Alumnus Edward R. Murrow returned to campus for a visit. After delivering an address to assembled students and faculty Murrow (right) posed for photographs with President Holland. (Historical Photograph Collections, Washington State University Libraries)

supported with necessary research aids, such as reference works and collateral documentation. Finally, countless duplicate volumes served only to "pad" the impressive total volume count announced by Holland and to compound difficulties users faced when trying to find working space in the small library building.[88]

As early as 1937, faculty and students began to clamor for a new library and better services. The November 5, 1937 issue of the student newspaper, the *Evergreen*, ran an editorial describing the limited library services available in the evenings:

> On Monday night approximately 1,000 Washington State students gulped their dinners, hurriedly ran combs through their hair, grabbed their notebooks and fountain pens, and dashed down their front steps in hopes of getting a seat in E. A. Bryan library. As usual, it was a case of 'first come, first served.' On Monday night by actual count 215 students were turned away. Nearly 40 returned to the Bookstore to find booths in which to prepare their next day's assignments— under even worse lighting and study conditions than they found in the library. What of the others? 'Some sat on the cold marble steps of the library to read.' Others returned to the dormitories, without having used library resources. The next night, Tuesday, saw a repetition of Monday, with 198 students failing to find seating in the library. So it went, certainly, in every week of mid-terms and finals.[89]

Librarian Foote revealed some of the library's flaws when, in 1937, he complained that he had missed an opportunity to purchase a valuable collection of Pacific Northwest Americana for want of funds. In fact, he noted that his current budget yielded barely enough money to purchase essential indexes and basic reference works, without considering research materials. Holland appeared to recognize imbalances in the collection when he sought special private contributions to purchase much-needed works. Such collect-ing was carried on through the Friends of the Library, an organization that assiduously cultivated support for special collections. Unfortu-nately, as commendable as these purchases were, they often served as "window dressing" for the institution, either because they were unrelated to other library materials or because appropriate faculty did not have time for research.[90]

Holland and Foote were as anxious as the students and faculty to build a new library and first laid plans for the new structure in 1938. They envisioned a traditional edifice, devoted primarily to custodian-ship rather than easy access to materials. It would be designed to rival the Suzzallo library at the University of Washington which, according to that institution's historian, was a stately "cathedral where the spirit as well as the mind would find strength and stimulus."

The proposed building, would house only a million volumes and omitted many recent innovations designed to increase a library's usefulness to students and faculty. To spend a great amount of creative energy as well as money for such modest increases in capacity and utility suggests that Holland had misplaced priorities. In any event, the time for construction had not arrived. In 1943, Holland

•

On November 12, 1932, the teams played to a scoreless tie on a muddy field in Seattle in what, to the impartial observer, might have seemed the epitome of dullness. A student reporter for the Evergreen, *however, focused on half-time activity and saw it otherwise. He depicted the event as "rivaling the Battle of Bunker Hill or Bull Run in its intensity. . . ."*

•

learned that the State College had lost seven valued librarians from its small staff and he had to concentrate on keeping the remaining fourteen by raising their salaries. The new library would be built in another day.[91]

Students did not long dwell on campus strikes for independence or agasinst inadequate library facilities if exciting activities were at hand. Intercollegiate football and other sports, in the 1930s, held great fascination and were a source of community and collegial pride. Football games with the University of Washington Huskies in 1932 and 1933 provided great opportunities for the State College students to unleash the "Cougar fighting spirit."

On November 12, 1932, the teams played to a scoreless tie on a muddy field in Seattle in what, to the impartial observer, might have seemed the epitome of dullness. A student reporter for the *Evergreen*, however, focused on half-time activity and saw it otherwise. He depicted the event as "rivaling the Battle of Bunker Hill or Bull Run in its intensity. . . ." The two student bodies found themselves tumbling onto the playing field engaged in an "epic struggle" over a trophy of the competition—a stuffed cougar, which some years earlier had been proudly displayed in Pullman until stolen by students from the University of Washington. The battle began when WSC students, in a "daring coup," and a "good piece of work," wrestled with the Husky defenders, finally tearing the Cougar into tatters, but nevertheless taking it home in triumph.[92]

The campus girded for trouble as the 1933 game, to be played in Pullman, approached. A Public Safety Committee, composed of administrators, faculty, and students, prepared for the possibility of a riot if WSC students displayed the "Big Stick" which they had stolen six months earlier from the University of Washington. The Regents, too, urged that precautions be taken and prayed that nothing untoward might happen. Nothing did, as the strength of the Cougars both on and off the playing field was overwhelming. The team won the game, 17-0 and the Big Stick was paraded at halftime without incident. The presence of an honor guard of thirty freshmen football players and the boxing squad successfully discouraged attackers.[93]

The Great Depression mentality and the difficult circumstances of the thirties gave way abruptly to anger and renewed sense of purpose after the Japanese attack on Pearl Harbor on December 7, 1941. Combative and peaceful students alike found their aggressions channeled into war-related activities. Within three months of the Japanese attack students were being pressured to enter shortened, speeded-up, and intensely practical training programs of the War Year curriculum and of the ROTC. Indeed, even before the United States had declared war, the faculty had voted to grant academic credit to students who dropped out of school at mid-term to join the armed forces. Civilian men soon learned that a military presence on campus might disturb them in personal ways, as well. In the Fall of 1942, two men's dormitories, Stimson and Ferry Halls, were taken from them for military use. The civilians had only Waller

The Great Depression mentality and the difficult circumstances of the thirties gave way abruptly to anger and renewed sense of purpose after the Japanese attack on Pearl Harbor on December 7, 1941. Combative and peaceful students alike found their aggressions channeled into war-related activities.

E. O. Holland, fourth president of Washington State College. This formal portrait was taken in 1944, shortly before he retired. (Historical Photograph Collections, Washington State University Libraries)

Hall left. The remaining civilian male students had to move into town.[94]

Changes in campus life struck even more deeply into student consciousness when leaders sought means "whereby students can actively contribute something important to the war effort while still attending school. . . ." Amid patriotic proposals for individuals and classes to purchase war bonds, salvage "strategic" metals, and cultivate "victory" gardens, the Junior class struck a sour note. The class planned the traditional Junior Prom, which met general approval, but voted to spend more than $1,000 to employ a "big name" band, which met with considerable faculty disapproval as frivolous in wartime. In the face of criticism that conditions were serious enough to warrant sacrifices, the Junior Class backed down, deciding to have a "terrific" dance without an expensive band.[95]

The following spring, in the midst of warm April days, students momentarily forgot patriotism when they performed a traditional rite of Spring—they held a water fight. Ranging over the campus, the rioters finally centered their attack upon Stimson and Waller Halls, causing considerable property damage. Dean of Men, Otis McCreery, who had praised the Junior Class a few weeks earlier, now castigated the rioters as "childish" while student leaders deplored the actions of their peers (although they all loved a good fight in less somber times).[96]

Patriotic events on campus moved inexorably to a conclusion in the spring of 1942 when students celebrated "General MacArthur Day," (a national event) by holding a patriotic rally in the stadium and selling a record-breaking $6,000 in war bonds. Students continued their patriotic activity, and three weeks later organized a drive that netted large quantities of rubber, metal, tinfoil, clothing, paper, and other items judged necessary for carrying on the war. The *Evergreen* commented on the work that day by celebrating the students' seizure of the opportunity to do something of value for "their country's war efforts. . . ."[97]

With each passing month, however, the uncertainties of life and studies increased. Salvage drives and bond sales paled in significance as military conscriptions rose in number and rumors of change predicted that the college would close to make way for needed military programs. By the Christmas of 1942, signs of unrest among the students were matched by uneasiness in the faculty ranks about the future.

A nervous Frank T. Barnard, the Registrar, evidently thinking that President Holland was uncharacteristically inactive amid the tumult, sought to prod him into action. Serious issues were at stake. Some students and faculty feared that the second semester might be cancelled while others feared that the Christmas vacation would be canceled. The latter rumor seemed even more plausible after the Southern Pacific Railway announced that it would be unable to accommodate many passengers at the holiday season unless they were servicemen or their families.[98]

President Holland responded, first on December 11, 1942, and on later occasions, to reassure the community through the *Evergreen* that students should remain in school. Character, he defined as following orders and quietly going about one's studies and other duties, patiently waiting until called to the service. To ease the difficulty in obtaining rail transportation home in the critical holiday season, he temporarily lifted the forty-eight hour rule to permit students to leave classes at their own convenience.[99]

The second semester followed without disruption, but collegiate life and studies would be curbed and modified in many ways by the war crisis. The hope for normal campus life awaited the end of the war and the advent of a new college administration.

Chapter Five

Compton and the Faculty: Pivotal Years in Creating the University

PRESIDENT HOLLAND, ON MARCH 20, 1944, FINALLY REQUESTED THAT he be relieved of the duties of his office and reassigned to a lesser post. Certain that the United States and its Allies would defeat Germany and Japan by that date, he saw his commitment to the institution's "war effort" as having been completed. He admitted that he had remained in office two years longer than earlier intended at the urging of "prominent officials at Washington, D.C.," who felt that the experienced college administrators of the nation should, if possible, continue to serve until the conclusion of the war. After twenty-nine years in office, Holland was tired and in poor health, deserving of a pension that neither he nor any of his faculty had been granted. But, his request for another office was not a mercenary gesture. He simply could not conceive of relinquishing all ties with his beloved State College of Washington.[1]

The Regents quickly accepted his resignation from the presidency, but postponed consideration of his request to serve in a lesser office. All attention now focused on the selection of his successor. In an unprecedented gesture, some fifty-nine faculty members volunteered their services to assist in locating a new president, an indication that they expected to play a significant role in administering the college. Deans and department heads also offered their services, noting a precedent established when their predecessors in office had aided in Holland's appointment. But these offers were largely ignored, as the Board sent a committee to the East to search out candidates. Only Registrar F. T. Barnard joined Regents H. W. Goldsworthy and Charles McAllister for the trip.[2] The trio brought back the name of Wilson M. Compton, of Washington, D.C., as its nominee. On August 12, 1944, the Board of Regents and three members of the College Advisory Committee—two professors and the registrar—interviewed Compton. Nine days later, Dean C. C. Todd reported that the committee unanimously supported Compton, and the Board, in the same mood, cast its vote for the nominee.[3]

OPPOSITE: *This photograph, taken from the top of Wilson Hall in 1953, shows Bryan Tower in the background and E. O. Holland Library is in the center. In the middle right stands the old Gymnasium (TUB), and in the lower right corner a portion of the newly completed Compton Union Building can be seen.* (Washington State University News Service)

Wilson Compton, fifth President of Washington State College. (Washington State University News Service)

The choice of Wilson Martindale Compton, a lobbyist for lumber interests in the national capitol, surprised many people for he had no experience in educational administration. The Compton family, however, had been steeped in intellectual and academic traditions for at least two generations. Wilson Compton's father, Elias, had served long and faithfully as a professor and administrator at Wooster College, in Ohio, and his two brothers were not only prominent physicists but preceded Wilson into educational administration, Karl at the Massachusetts Institute of Technology and Arthur at Washington University, St. Louis. Wilson had earned a Ph.D. in economics at Princeton University in 1915 and a Bachelor of Laws degree from Chicago's Hamilton College of Law in 1917. He was fifty-four years of age and for a quarter of a century had served as the influential Secretary and General Manager of the National Lumberman's Association.[4]

Inexperienced though he was in educational administration, Wilson Compton believed that he understood the economic needs and potential of the State of Washington. Thus, when he telegraphed his acceptance of office on October 5, 1944, he also outlined briefly a new role for the college. He planned to develop "a great institute of technology . . . adapted to the abundant natural resources of the Pacific Northwest. . . ." He then challenged the Regents to join him. "With your help," he wired, "we can build a great institution for the people of the state and [can provide] a great service to agriculture, industry and commerce in the Northwest."[5]

In a personal gesture revealing his belief that a college or university must be more than a technical school, Compton, while being interviewed, touched his lapel button, which showed that he had two sons and a son-in-law serving in the military. He declared that "I expect I made the decision [to become president of Washington State College] because my boys were in the service. It seemed to me I could do more good in this new capacity than in any other. Education must bear a major share of responsibility for seeing that this war is not repeated."[6]

The speaker was a man of medium height, broad shoulders, and a stocky build. He would not have gone unnoticed in a crowd, as a report of the New York *Post* explained, because of his "crest of white hair, deep-set blue eyes, and a bronze complexion." His eyes were arresting, being so deep-seated that they sometimes appeared to have been recovering from a bruising fight, according to one professor. Nevertheless, when curiosity arose regarding the new president, it had less to do with his physical appearance than with the circumstances of his election and change of profession in mid-career.[7]

United States Senator Mon C. Wallgren, the Democratic Party's candidate for the governorship of Washington in 1944, threatened to involve Compton's appointment in a political squabble during his gubernatorial campaign. As a pretext, he seized upon an affront posed when WSU officials failed to invite him promptly to share the speaker's platform with Governor Arthur Langlie, his Republican opponent, at an agricultural meeting in Yakima. Wallgren reacted angrily by criticizing Compton's appointment and questioning his ability to serve the farmers when his total experience had been with lumber barons. Wallgren also accused the Board of Regents of making a political deal with the Master of the State Grange to give him a veto over the choice of the State College president.

The issue might have become serious since Wallgren, once elected, might drastically change the membership on the Board of Regents to rid himself of Compton, and he might adversely reshape the budget of the institution. Compton, a Republican, earnestly assured Wallgren that he had no ulterior motives and, indeed, had not sought office nor had he known any of the Regents before they approached him. More than that, he testified that he, "a hale man in his fifties and in his right mind," had given up security to take a position at one-third his former salary because he believed that "as head of a great educational, research, and public service institution, I can make a larger contribution to a number of things which I think need to be done in this country." A conference between the two, held after Wallgren had been elected, had been inconclusive, but Wallgren subsequently worked in relative harmony with the State College and with Compton.[8]

Compton rode the crest of the small tempest with equanimity, assuring Regent H. E. Goldsworthy that he was optimistic about the outcome. Judging from newspaper editorials and stories pouring in from all parts of the state, he had good reason to feel content. Indeed, except for the Grange, farmers' newspapers and organizations saw nothing but good arising from Compton's appointment. The Spokane *Spokesman-Review* took the lead in reporting favorably on Compton, quoting the Regents' statement he "will be able to make a great contribution to the scientific growth and expansion of the Pullman institution."[9]

The Wenatchee *Daily World* also spoke favorably of Compton for his recognition that the depressed economic status of the state and region had to be attacked by technological development to include, among other matters, refining raw materials locally, not out-of-state. The *Daily World*, long a champion of the Columbia Basin Reclamation Project, noted that the vast hydro-electric potential of the state required "a school as fine as MIT, which Dr. Compton's brother [Karl] heads" to provide the means of harnessing the energy to develop new industries and farms. The editor concluded with the benediction that "there is every indication that Washington State will have such a school."[10]

Compton's honeymoon with the press continued well into 1945, permitting him to enlarge upon his idea of mission. He "electrified a capacity audience" of businessmen in Spokane in early March 1945, with "a dramatic picture of the industrial development ahead" in the region. Refurbishing a myth, forgotten because it had not materialized, Compton "predicted that our trans-Pacific relations will eventually become as important as our trans-Atlantic relations,

•

Inexperienced though he was in educational administration, Wilson Compton believed that he understood the economic needs and potential of the State of Washington. Thus, when he telegraphed his acceptance of office on October 5, 1944, he also outlined briefly a new role for the college.

•

and if I know my economics as well as my geography this state will become the chief gateway [to the Orient]." Two weeks later, he assured another audience that Washington State College would become the intellectual center of the Inland Empire, preparing young people to grapple successfully with the new challenges society would face, not merely to train them narrowly in their professions. The impartial observer, however, might have noted the lack of details about intellectualism and cultural education as opposed to the amount of time Compton spent discussing agriculture and technology.[11]

Compton entered office somewhat handicapped for executing the great mission he envisioned. He was, in the recollections of some faculty and staff, a rather reserved and formal individual who often did not communicate easily and effectively. Had he been an impatient man, his burning ambition might have compounded his difficulty in winning the sympathetic support of the Board of Regents, the faculty, and of course, the legislature. As it was, he quickly perceived that the primary need was to overturn the traditional autocratic organization which might impede his efforts to establish a new program. The president took the first step on his second day in office, obtaining from the Board authority to establish a President's Committee of faculty to review the entire State College program. Since the committee consisted of forty members, the title "Committee of Forty" became its popular designation.[12]

Compton appointed John A. Guthrie, Associate Professor of Economics, to chair the group, a step that signalled his desire to involve the younger scholars in the most important affairs of the institution. Guthrie was relatively young at thirty-eight years of age and had been at the State College only five years. Indeed, younger members dominated the committee, although a number of senior faculty played important roles. Compton desired chiefly, however, to "mobilize the wits and wisdom" of the entire faculty in planning modernization of the program, administration, and faculty of the institution. Within a few and flexible constraints, the Committee of Forty organized and began vigorously to study its problems. It met a Commencement deadline, submitting thirty reports to the president, which he then handed on with his approval to the Board of Regents.[13]

The Board contented itself with approving "in principle" the numerous propositions placed before it. In the first instance, it agreed that faculty, staff, and students should have opportunities to organize without administrative interference and, hence, to function independently in college affairs. To guarantee vigorous exercise of the faculty's prerogatives, a standing committee of the that body would oversee affairs and make appropriate recommendations to the administration as well as to the faculty as a whole.

The Regents also agreed to require the administration to codify and publish all regulations involving the faculty and staff, rather than to permit continuance of the traditional unpublished standards that had given license to arbitrary and highly biased actions. The published code would extend to governing off-campus consulting or other professional work and to encouraging participation in research by assuring financial aid. Above all, the Regents decreed that there must be uniform procedures to equalize and raise salaries and for granting tenure and promotion. Teaching loads, too, were to be equalized across the campus, and lightened to provide time for scholarly, creative, research, and leisure activities.

In curricular matters, the Committee of Forty limited its work to a consideration of two topics heavily freighted with campus politics—duplication of courses in various departments and a practise whereby many freshmen declare majors. It agreed that duplicate courses should be eliminated. Redundancy among departments represented an unresolved problem of long standing, one that revealed jealousies that led some units to monopolize the time of their majors. The Committee also recommended installing a deferred major principle, thereby freeing freshmen from the necessity to establish majors, thus granting them more opportunities to obtain a general education. To render curricular choices by freshmen and other students more satisfactory, the Committee proposed to increase dramatically the counselling services available. The Regents accepted these proposals, once again, "in principle," expecting faculty committees and the administration to develop them in detail and put them into operation.

The final proposition called for by the Committee of Forty and adopted by the Regents specified that budgets, accounting, and fiscal controls should be centralized and developed along modern business lines. This proposal suggested that faculty leaders recognized that if future developments promised to bestow more ample research funds on the college than in the past, the public might require (and the college would need) greater accountability. Other provisions were to be presented later for consideration by the Regents, but the basic proposals were offered in the meeting of June 19, 1945 and were to be put into practice piecemeal.[14]

World War II ended with Japan's surrender on September 2, 1945, and the festive and even euphoric mood of Compton's inaugural as president on December 11 provided the inspiration for his most ardent and expansive statement of faith in American society, higher education, and the State College of Washington. Mindful of the title of his address, "Frontiers Unlimited," he asserted regarding his institution that "we are the guardians of a great tradition, but even more, we are the marshalls of a great duty to help pave the way to a March of Progress and of Peace, in the Pacific Northwest, in the Nation, and throughout the world." That Compton personally felt a great responsibility is evident from his declaration that "No man will undertake the Presidency of this Institution [sic] except as a public trust and as a gateway to great public service." At its zenith, he emphasized, public service required the training of men and women as citizens not only of their own community and the nation, but also of the world. Graduates, he believed, must go forth from the college with an understanding of the peoples of the world and with a desire that all of mankind should share in the opportunities provided by liberal values.

Stepping down from rhetorical heights, the president once again reminded the public that Washington's high role in the unfolding drama could only be played if, first, its citizens pulled themselves into positions of economic security and leadership—climbing out of economic servitude to other regions by controlling the development, processing, and marketing of their resources. Thus, while he respected disinterested scholarship and protected "effective individualism," he made it clear that Washington State College would support economic development as its great service.[15]

To provide mechanisms for that public service, Compton announced that the Regents had authorized creation of an Institute of Agricultural Sciences and an Institute of Technology. Actually, in the first days after he had taken office, the president had invited business and agricultural leaders to set up committees to review the teaching, research, and extension services needed to promote development of the various industrial and farm activities. Serious planning became possible after Governor Wallgren approved a law on March 19, 1945, that provided funding. The Institutes began functioning on January 2, 1946, after the Regents had taken the necessary steps to open them.

The Institute of Agricultural Sciences included the College of Agriculture, the College of Veterinary Medicine, the Agricultural Experiment Stations, and the Agricultural Extension Service. Its principal mission was to coordinate all the farm services found in the individual units and to entertain the requests and recommendations of farm leaders for the state's agricultural development. The Institute of Technology included the College of Engineering, School of Mines, Division of Industrial Research, and Division of Industrial Services, which were to be coordinated to meet the needs of industry. It had fewer advisory boards, a fact suggesting that Compton had accurately assessed the limited industrial growth in the state. In that connection, the Institute of Technology was commanded to promote development of fledgling, light metal industries and new technologies connected with the introduction of hydro-electric power and irrigation provided by the Grand Coulee and the other dams on the Snake and Columbia rivers.[16]

But Compton and the faculty had far more urgent problems than speculating on distant goals or seeking ways to cooperate with farming and industrial interests. There were students to house, feed, and educate, and the campus had to be prepared for their influx in unprecedented numbers. Since 1939, when the State College had accommodated a record number of 4,015 students, no new construction had taken place on campus or in Pullman. Indeed, Compton feared that town housing had deteriorated badly in the meantime. Teaching and laboratory facilities had not changed, yet the administration would have to take care of a much greater number of students. The college, it was freely predicted, would be swamped at an early date by war veterans who would come handsomely supported by the federal government.[17]

Two thousand seven hundred and eight students actually enrolled in September 1945, not an overwhelming number, but records were set in the Fall of 1946 with 5,907 students and, once again the following year with 6,770. The number of veterans rose to a high point at 3,725 for 1947-1948, representing approximately fifty-five percent of the total student body. Total enrollments remained above 6,000 until the Spring of 1950, the decline thereafter reflecting the departure of veterans. The number of former service personnel attending WSC dropped to 848 in September 1952, and then to 400 the following fall.

The small size of the faculty, numbering approximately 348 in 1949, added to the congestion in classrooms and laboratories and to heavy teaching loads. The faculty-student ratio rose to more than 1:21, whereas the ideal posed by educational experts called for one teacher for every ten students. In its biennial report for 1945-1947, the Board of Regents put the best face on the matter, reporting cheerily that everyone endured with equanimity the long hours and substandard conditions—"inconveniences were many, and 'temporary' was an elastic word. . . . One day, only the pleasant part of the story will be remembered—that the students were here for business, that they did get an education if they really wanted it. Veterans became known to their classmates as 'D.A.R.s' (darned average raisers), and few of them dropped out of school except for obvious reasons such as health."[18]

As early as September, 1945, the State College began searching for "demountable temporary housing" for both student and faculty use. Soon, the federal government—in a kind of lend-lease program, in effect paying back institutions for the use of their facilities during the war—offered to colleges and universities housing, furniture, equipment, machinery, and tools of all kinds for classrooms, laboratories, and dwellings. The State College profited immensely from this generosity, since it obtained more than a hundred truck and trailer loads of housing and educational facilities for the mere payment of shipping and installing costs.[19]

Then, the Veterans Administration involved the federal government further in the affairs of the State College. On February 1, 1946, A. L. Brown, Chief of the Seattle office, suggested that the college might solve its problem of housing veterans by seeking to obtain the Army's Baxter General Hospital, in Spokane, after it had been decommissioned. Brown argued that the installation would provide facilities for technical instruction for the students and housing for their families.

Compton ran into severe opposition when he broached the possibility of using Baxter as a "temporary College instructional center" to the Faculty Executive Committee. Chairman Stewart E. Hazlet, Professor of Chemistry, speaking for the committee, doubted the possibility of hiring a good faculty for a branch campus and called the proposition economically unsound. Moreover, the committee asked that efforts be concentrated on improving the institution's image and reputation by developing additional facilities

Professor of Sociology T. H. Kennedy came to WSC in 1944. Among his many areas of interest was research in the mid-1950s on social institutions as they related to family relations in South Africa. In 1964 Kennedy became senior dean of the College of Sciences and Arts. (Washington State University News Service)

*When military authorities
reduced space available to WSC
to proportions inadequate for
instructional use, Compton
turned again to the campus in
Pullman to resolve his problems.*

on the Pullman campus. To that end, the committee asked that more temporary structures be set up in Pullman. The matter of Spokane facility became academic, however, in April when negotiations were dropped and labeled "inconclusive."[20]

Attention shifted to an attempt to obtain Fort George Wright, another military facility in Spokane that appeared on the verge of being decommissioned. On July 23, 1946, the Board of Regents approved in principle Compton's proposal to establish an extension branch for 2,000 students if the Fort became available. While problems caused by meeting veterans' needs might be of short duration, Compton had in mind a permanent facility in Spokane to house a greatly enlarged general extension program.[21]

When military authorities reduced space available to WSC to proportions inadequate for instructional use, Compton turned again to the campus in Pullman to resolve his problems. Although it is possible that the president might have thought, early on, of relocating a major portion of the institution (except possibly for engineering and, of course, agriculture), by 1947 he had concluded there was no justification for moving to Spokane or anywhere else. Perhaps he was admitting to a sense of frustration, as well as to an ignorance of the school's history, when he claimed that he "sometimes marveled at the lack of imagination of those who some fifty or sixty years ago located W.S.C. where it is now located." He was absolutely clear, however, about the simple pragmatic truth which he faced: "Each course of brick that we lay and each stroke of the hammer further commits W.S.C. as an institution to its traditional location."[22]

Arrival of three wartime dormitories in early 1946 reduced the gravity of the housing shortage. Soon, "truckloads of demounted war housing units" promised further relief, as did carload lots of furniture and equipment. The shipments, taken together, provided shelter for 1,800 single students and 290 student and faculty families. Delays in erecting the buildings brought discomfort and even deprivation to both students and faculty, despite administration efforts to avert hardships by postponing the opening of the Fall semester for two weeks. Even then, the workers could not finish all of the housing for the opening of the term. As a further complication, some 300 construction workers had to be housed in Ferry Hall, displacing a like number of students and reducing the proposed enrollment from 5,600 to 5,300 at one point. Since ultimately 5,907 students registered in that semester, it is likely that all available living space in town as well as on the campus was utilized.[23]

Much of the new, temporary housing dotted the perimeter of the college golf course, inspiring the names of three such clusters that grew up: East, North, and South Fairways. Student and faculty families occupied these apartments. Several large single-student dormitories, and a huge army mess hall, termed Stadium Commons, arose along Stadium Way, the new loop highway under construction. Victory Square, a cluster of single family dwellings, occupied largely by faculty and staff, appeared on the western slopes of College Hill, leading down to the Palouse River. While walking over much of the campus, an ex-GI might find it hard to believe he had left army cantonment life behind.[24]

The college reluctantly became landlord to faculty and staff, doing so only because no viable alternative existed. Little suitable housing could be found in Pullman nor were private commercial builders attracted to the community. Many junior faculty and staff, under these circumstances, were in no position to finance housing. The college, in short, had to supply dwellings in order to attract needed personnel.[25] Briefly, in 1946, the Regents may have been optimistic that private enterprise would solve their problem. An out-of-town firm began building sixty-four houses on Military Hill, thirty-four with basements to be rented out. Unfortunately, the builder could not complete the structures. In June 1947, as a result, the State College acquired the houses and proceeded to finish and rent them to faculty and staff. Beginning in 1950, the houses were sold to State College employees. As faculty and staff moved out of temporary housing, student families moved in.[26]

Restrictive college entrance requirements became a reality for the first time because of limited available housing. On April 12, 1946, the Board of Regents approved recommendations from the College Senate that in-state and Alaskan applicants would be required only to have earned a C (2.00) average in previous work, high school or college, while out-of-staters were required to have achieved at least a B minus (2.75) grade average. Preferences were further refined to favor upper-class students enrolling in engineering, agriculture, or other departments with facilities for handling large numbers of students. In June, Compton not only acknowledged that housing shortages made these restrictions necessary but, as if to compensate for the imposition of such standards, declared that scholarship would be given the highest preference, with Washington State residence second. In the following month, however, first preference swung to resident veterans and, as if to make certain of the admission of ex-GIs, all foreign students were barred, except for those to whom the college had "moral obligations."[27]

Despite these confusing priorities, Claude Simpson, the new Director of Admissions that year, looked back on that summer and found his job "tremendous. Hundreds of applications were being filed every day and letters of inquiry by the thousands were being received. . . ." A largely inexperienced staff greatly complicated the process of admission, while the use of an elaborate check-off list of priorities contributed to numerous errors. These required the whole summer to untangle.[28]

Reflecting the rising tide of veterans' applications, in 1947, the Regents granted all returning servicemen and women first priority, regardless of whether or not they were Washingtonians. After veterans came high scholarship. Location in Washington and Alaska now ranked third, not a very meaningful demotion, since enrollment figures for the period 1939-1949 show no significant increases in percentages of out-of-state students in the decade. Pronouncements by the administration and the faculty suggesting preferences

•

Restrictive college entrance requirements became a reality for the first time because of limited available housing. On April 12, 1946, the Board of Regents approved recommendations from the College Senate that in-state and Alaskan applicants would be required only to have earned a C (2.00) average in previous work, high school or college, while out-of-staters were required to have achieved at least a B minus (2.75) grade average.

•

Professor Claudius O. Johnson came to WSC in 1928 as chairman of the newly formed Department of History and Political Science. Colleagues and students described Johnson as one of the most stimulating people who ever entered the classroom at the University. The author of many books including Borah of Idaho, *Johnson also served on the Advisory Constitutional Revision Commission in 1934-1935 and was a Fulbright Lecturer.* (Washington State University News Service)

for technologies or agriculture over other fields probably had little influence upon student choices of major.[29]

To students and faculty it seemed that the campus was continuously under construction. In November 1946, the Regents noted that twelve buildings were undergoing remodelling and that work on one required doubling the activities in another. Inconveniences spared no one. Even President and Mrs. Compton endured hardships of "camping out." As the president wrote to the students on November 15, 1946, "In my own home during the past year we have had temporarily at one time as many as twenty-seven students and faculty members and their families, including my own household."[30]

The task of feeding 6,000 students took on heroic proportions in that fall season as dining facilities were strained to the limit. The brick Commons, the main dining hall, had been enlarged from a capacity of 600 to 2,000 in anticipation of the need and the home economists opeated a dining room to serve faculty and staff. Students also ate regular meals at the Temporary Union Building. If, as the Regents reported laconically, "there were long lines and a few 'gripes,' but everybody was fed wholesome, balanced meals," it is understandable that President Compton felt impelled to counsel "good humored patience" to students.[31]

Students and faculty sometimes needed all the patience they could muster while attending classes and working in laboratories. Providing adequate housing had been an easy task in comparison with arranging for sufficient teaching facilities and equipment. Social scientists and business professors found that many of their classes were located far from their offices. They particularly deplored the inadequate accommodations for counseling students. Classrooms, they noted, lacked equipment necessary to accommodate modern teaching methods and were "poorly lighted and outmoded in arrangement and appearance."[32] At the same time, inadequate space and facilities in the College of Engineering forced a self-examination and critical judgment that the facilities available might be more appropriately used if courses bordering on trade school training were eliminated.[33]

The Department of Geology, closely associated with engineering at that time, suffered perhaps more than any other discipline from deprivation and neglect. In the Fall of 1946, it was scheduled to be transferred to Morrill Hall, which was in a deplorable condition. Necessary repairs and remodelling, though promised, had not been accomplished two months after school opened. At that time, Chairman Harold Culver complained to Vice President E. H. Hopkins "we have no rocks, no minerals, no fossils, no maps, no charts, or, in brief, no teaching equipment." In what might be regarded as a mild conclusion after that recital of poverty, Culver declared that "there is a limit beyond which this procedure [teaching] is not only inefficient but futile." Perhaps Culver's exasperation stemmed in part from the fact that he had been forced to take charge temporarily of the School of Mines, which also was operating at a low level of efficiency and was squeezed, along with Geology, into the limited Morrill Hall space.[34]

The College of Agriculture suffered when a considerable portion of its office, teaching, and research space was demolished to make way for improvements to other units and to the amenities of the campus as a whole. Authorities tore down an old horse barn to make space for dormitories and the right of way for the new Stadium Loop Highway (soon to be called Stadium Way). The latter would provide better access to the campus and, together with new parking lots, would make football game attendance easier and more attractive to the public. The College of Agriculture also had to shift orchards to new locations, thus delaying experimental work. It also had to find new lands to which it might move dairy pastures eliminated by the march of progress.

The Regents purchased additional lands and erected minor agricultural installations but no large farm buildings were finished during the 1945-1947 biennium. Indeed, no major structures were completed anywhere on the campus during that time. But, to relieve congestion and inefficiency in agriculture and engineering, construction work was started on new laboratory buildings. In addition, a large classroom building (subsequently named Todd Hall) desired by the social sciences and business was started. Plans for a new library were under consideration but construction dates had not yet been set.[35]

Compton recognized that while buildings and books were necessary, students and faculty were the heart of the institution. In January 1946, he called on the deans and directors to assist him in keeping attention focussed on this central fact. He already had experienced difficulties when he tried to hire additional qualified teachers to meet the needs of the burgeoning student body. He had observed, in addition, that the State College faculty suffered not only from deprivation of funds but also from time to develop breadth and depth of scholarship and research. He understood that they also required leisure time to experience the cultural diversity needed to become fully mature teachers. He proposed to meet these needs in order to strengthen the existing faculty and attract the most promising new candidates.[36]

In December 1945, the Regents, at Compton's request, and with funds made available by the governor, granted salary increases which were designed at least as a first step to match the salary scale of the University of Washington. How close they were to equalling the Seattle institution is not known, but Compton further improved his faculty's condition by reducing the work year of most individuals from eleven to nine-and-one-half months; exceptions to this rule were research, extension, and administrative staffs. In doing so, Compton acceded to recommendations of the Faculty Executive Committee. The president also agreed to the committee's request that the average work week should include no more than forty-five hours and that contact hours in the classroom be limited to twelve— a substantial reduction for most faculty. On one point Compton rebuffed the committee. When it asked that research be recognized up to the equivalent of three hours per week on a fifteen-hour schedule,

Compton bluntly refused. The presence of a large number of temporary faculty, he felt, made much faculty research sub-standard.[37]

Compton took an additional step to improve faculty morale and a sense of security when he announced to the deans and directors that he would not countenance "cronyism," or playing favorites, in personnel matters. There would be no extraordinary or biased hirings, firings, or promotions. Instead, he demanded strict adherence to established schedules and to a systematic review of all faculty. Merit would prevail. He noted that in the past "there had been a number of individual cases where there has been no consideration of advancement in the absence of special circumstances, other instances of rapid advancement under pressure of special factors, presumably outside offers." He deplored the circumstances which forced good faculty members to seek salary increases by bargaining with outside institutions and believed frank and open evaluations would improve the climate of opinion on the campus. Out of this new policy there emerged the *Faculty Manual.* First published in 1949, it was an extensive code of regulations to which the faculty made a major contribution.[38]

Within a year after the salary increases, on February 8, 1947, the Faculty Executive Committee revealed the Faculty's strengthened sense of its own worth. At that time the committee issued a report "On the Problems of an Institution of Higher Education, or more specifically: The Program of the State College of Washington." The Committee sought to evaluate the program at "a moment full of promise for the College," asserting its wish to determine whether the institution had "all the ingredients of greatness or whether lacking some, it may bring us only enlightened mediocrity." To rise above the latter condition, the "philosophy of scarcity" must be replaced by, at least, "adequacy," in the budget, the committee decided.[39]

The College Senate took a bolder step when, in 1946, it adopted a program recommended by the Committee of Forty designed to strengthen greatly the general education of all students. Approximately 140 courses selected from among the humanities, social sciences, and natural sciences, judged to be useful for breadth of interest or stimulating to the individual's cultural development, were included in a panel from which students would select some thirty semester hours of work, including six hours of English composition. Each student would take a minimum of twelve hours in humanities and social sciences (at least three hours in each) and twelve hours in the natural sciences (with at least two hours of laboratory credit and at least three hours taken in the biological sciences and three in the physical sciences). Further stimulus to improved general education arose from the introduction of the academic distinction of graduation with honors and the adoption of a general studies degree program.[40]

The potpourri of courses carrying general education credit might satisfy the majority of conservative students and faculty, but offered many obstacles to the well-rounded learning experiences presupposed in the philosophical justification for the program announced in 1950: The purpose of General Education was "to the end that the student may have the opportunity to increase his knowledge and develop his abilities for the common, unifying experiences of mankind, and at the same time further the unfoldment of the potentialities that are peculiarly his own. . . ." In an effort to approach closer to the ideal, the Faculty introduced integrated courses in the humanities, social sciences, biological sciences, and physical sciences, all of which had appeared for the first time in the 1946 catalog. Their sponsors hoped that these courses might be made mandatory for graduation, giving the student body a common store of knowledge and experience.[41] The matter seemed urgent to the president, probably because he had coupled the general education program with the inauguration of the Institutes of Agricultural Science and Technology, which represented another set of societal needs—in this case, the advance of agriculture and new industry in the State of Washington. He did not wish to sacrifice general to technical education, or vice versa, stating on one occasion: "It is as important that trained men be educated as that educated men be trained."[42]

The capstone of Compton's grand scheme of reorganization involved the conversion of the College of Sciences and Arts into four divisions, each representing a single segment of the fundamental core of knowledge—humanities, social sciences, biological sciences, and physical sciences. A chair would head each division and would not only administer the program, but would assume responsibility for developing and integrating courses into the general education program and insure that instruction would be a means of linking a broad liberal education with specialized training.

Also, the chairs were to serve as the principal academic advisors to the vice-president and advise the heads of professional schools and programs appropriate to their divisions. Theoretically, these lines of communication would enable WSC's educational functions to be drawn into a close relationship, whether they be teaching, research, or extension. This rationale, in the planning stage at least, might have seemed convincing, but heads of professional programs feared that lines of communication would become lines of authority, destroying their credibility with outside support groups and diminishing their authority on campus.[43]

Not surprisingly, leaders in the professional schools lost little time in criticizing the new organization. The Dean of the School of Pharmacy angrily opposed outside faculty advising his majors and their programs. He objected also to being placed under the jurisdiction, as he saw it, of the Chairman of the Division of Biological Sciences. Instead, he preferred a line of communication through the Chairman of the Division of Physical Sciences, despite the fact that such a placing would seem to have defeated the purpose of integration, which logically linked Pharmacy with the biological sciences.

Once divisional chairmen took full control of their units upon Clare C. Todd's retirement on January 1, 1949 as dean of the College

●

The capstone of Compton's grand scheme of reorganization involved the conversion of the College of Sciences and Arts into four divisions, each representing a single segment of the fundamental core of knowledge—humanities, social sciences, biological sciences, and physical sciences.

●

Professor Rodney Bertramson came to WSC in 1939 as a faculty member in the College of Agriculture. In 1949 he was appointed chairman of the Agronomy Department and from 1967 to 1979 he served as director of Resident Instruction for the College of Agriculture. (Washington State University News Service)

of Sciences and Arts, criticism intensified. On April 19, twelve scientists, from various fields, protested to the president that under the new arrangement the special requirements of each discipline would be "arbitrarily minimized" and that administration would be unnecessarily "awkward." Moreover, they asserted that there would be an overlapping jurisdiction among divisional chairmen and the directors of the Institutes of Technology and Agricultural Sciences. Later, some fifteen to twenty faculty members from the two institutes protested what Compton termed "misunderstandings" and "farfetched interpretations." Compton acknowledged to Vice President E. H. Hopkins, a strong champion of the reorganization, that "there is genuine resistance to what some think is an "assumption of admin[istrative] authority by Div[ision] Chairmen."[44]

Discussion with the sanguine Hopkins failed to placate opponents, but strengthened Compton's resolve to retain the plan despite the stings of increasing criticism. The president might well have paused to reconsider when some professors in the humanities and liberal arts wondered with some anxiety what their own roles might be under the new organization. Professional schools were further emboldened to criticize the plan as outside support for their autonomy came to the Regents' attention. On September 10, 1949, for example, the Washington State Veterinary Medical Association condemned placing the College of Veterinary Medicine under the Institute of Agricultural Sciences, arguing that medicine was not agriculture and that under the 1917 law veterinary studies had been left independent of any other work. Later in September, Compton and the Regents bowed to increasing criticism by limiting the authority and advisory functions of division chairs to their own units. Communication with the president on the general academic program henceforth would be conducted through a Committee on Academic Programs, a body of the Administrative Council.[45]

Although the grand scheme to integrate educational offerings from top to bottom failed, probably because of complexities and ambiguities of the system as much as anything else, numerous important curricular changes took place in the 1947-1949 biennium. Notably, several previously subordinated sciences and social sciences, offering primarily service courses to technical and professional fields, joined the College of Sciences and Arts. As a result, they were to be permitted to develop fully in both undergraduate and graduate education and each would have an opportunity to promote research programs. Human physiology, for example, became associated with more liberal studies when removed from the College of Veterinary Medicine. Transfer of Mathematics and Physics from the College of Engineering, and Geology from the School of Mines, promised to broaden the scientific pursuit of these disciplines. Psychology, after lengthy service largely to teacher training, left the School of Education to broaden its offering both in teaching and research. The School of Music and Fine Arts also joined the College of Sciences and Arts, probably as a matter of administrative convenience since its liberal education programs were already well developed. On the other hand, economics was removed from the College of Sciences and Arts to join the School of Business Administration (thereafter known as the School of Economics and Business), a change which ultimately raised barriers between it and the other social sciences.[46]

Additional changes to the curriculum strengthened Veterinary Medicine by lengthening its program to six years and that of Pharmacy to five years. The faculty, in addition, improved the fledgling deferred major program by introducing better advising and other techniques to insure that the students chose their major fields of study with greater care. Then, in 1950, chemical engineering was separated from chemistry, proper, creating an additional department emphasizing applied arts. The previous year, the Regents eliminated the Graduate School of Social Work as it failed to meet standards and also because of the competition with similar programs at the University of Washington.[47]

In addition to shifting departments, in April 1947, Compton eliminated the traditional position of the department head who served indefinitely, inaugurating chairs who served one or more four year terms. The president chose the department heads, of course, but normally selected that person from among nominees proposed by departmental faculty. The president expected to eliminate "administration by crony," which he had observed to be a carry over from the Holland administration. Short terms of office and faculty involvement, he hoped, would produce a more cooperative spirit in departments and an unleashing of fresh ideas and more productive activity. Compton also "hoped that the new plan also . . . [would] further encourage and facilitate the consideration of institutional interests as distinguished from departmental viewpoints and departmental interests." Had he been more candid, he might have acknowledged that the appointments for limited terms might give him better control of his administration.[48]

By the opening of the 1947-1949 biennium, the State College had established a comprehensive student counseling and activities program, a matter which the Committee of Forty had recommended in 1945. Numerous specialists, working under the direction of the dean of students, staffed a counseling center, student activities center, resident hall advising, and a veterans' advising staff. They brought psychological guidance to areas, where earlier, only students in obvious difficulty were likely to receive attention—and then perhaps only as punishment after the fact. The many-sided program seemingly shifted the surrogate parental burden from administration and faculty to the ministrations of psychological specialists.[49]

The appearance in 1948 of a pair of courses on English for foreign students heralded the influx of international students in sufficient numbers to affect the curriculum and the counseling needs of the campus.[50] Before World War II foreign students had studied at the State College but in such small in numbers as to be nearly invisible. Indeed, the first foreign students may be traced to a handful in Bryan's administration who, in 1910, were members of the Cosmopolitan

By the opening of the 1947-1949 biennium, the State College had established a comprehensive student counseling and activities program, a matter which the Committee of Forty had recommended in 1945.

The first post-war impetus to foreign student enrollment came when the state legislature, in the spring of 1945, permitted the University of Washington and Washington State College each to grant fifty tuition and fee waiver scholarships to foreign students.

Club. In its first year this organization listed twelve members, including Japanese, Norwegian, Australian, Russian, Mexican students, "and two Hindu princes," as well as several Americans. Though the club became inactive during World War I it resumed meeting later. It had forty-two members in 1926 and twenty-six in the 1941-1942 school year.[51] A 1941 alumna, when depositing Cosmopolitan Club records with the Washington State University Archives many years later, compared her fond memories of undergraduate days with the troubled times of the early 1970s: "In these days of racial turmoil it is interesting to be able to remember that, thirty years ago, we were working and playing together with never a problem." Foreign students were a precious anomaly in the depression years, certainly they were not a threat of any kind to the existing order.[52]

Only two ethnic groups seemed to be large enough to establish exclusive clubs. The Chinese organized in 1923 and maintained their organization until 1935. Filipino students met in a club at least as early as 1922, with fifteen members. Their high point may have been in 1928 when the membership list contained thirty-eight names. No doubt, these clubs and others not detected died out before World War II. The Chinese left only their minutes, which have not been translated. The Filipinos, on the contrary, left a pictorial and written record, in English, which suggests that they found life on the campus good. There is no evidence of a Japanese club, but eleven Japanese-born students enrolled at WSC between 1917 and 1942. In addition, there were fifty-eight others of Japanese ancestry, born in the United States, who studied at the college during that time.[53]

The first post-war impetus to foreign student enrollment came when the state legislature, in the spring of 1945, permitted the University of Washington and Washington State College each to grant fifty tuition and fee waiver scholarships to foreign students. The Committee of Forty urged officials to seize the opportunity to attract "foreign-exchange" students and President Compton needed no special urging to support the idea.

The issue was far from simple, however, as the law prohibited enrollment of students from wartime enemy nations.[54] Thus, Japanese and German youth could not be admitted until peace treaties were signed and until reciprocal arrangements were made to admit American students on scholarships. Foreign students, seeking admission in late 1945 and early 1946, found transportation either not available or quickly learned that the tuition waiver scholarships covered a only a small portion of their total costs. The only response by the legislature occurred in 1949 when it doubled the number of tuition waiver scholarships available.[55]

Foreign enrollments in 1946-1947 totaled only sixty-eight, including thirty-seven Canadians (who were neither subject to quotas nor eligible for tuition-free scholarships) but in 1947-1948, the number reached 151, highest in the Compton years. Canada, except for one year, had the highest enrollment, and students from China ranked second in number during the those years. Remaining students were from areas widely scattered around the world, from Europe, Asia, Africa, and South America.[56]

Many foreign students lacked facility with English, which posed special problems. Neither the college, nor international agencies set up to handle such education, could establish adequate screening or prevent numbers of such students from arriving in Pullman. Another hazard to teaching foreign students arose with the development of the Cold War mentality of the second half of the 1940s. It produced some sentiment that the State College should prepare foreign students with an especially sympathetic attitude for the American way of life so that they might return home as ambassadors of good will. There is, however, little or no evidence that such propagandizing replaced genuine education, or that the wish was more than rhetoric.[57]

Certainly, it could not be said that foreign students received "free rides" or were coddled when they came to Washington State College. Tuition-free scholarships proved to be a disappointment: in 1951, for example, only thirty-nine of the 100 available scholarships were in use. Most, if not all, foreign students found it necessary to draw on family funds to stay in school. In no case (leaving Canadians out of consideration) did the foreign delegations grow to constitute an insular community—a foreign student ghetto. They continued to mingle with the entire campus, to serve as leaven in the lump rather than an indigestible mass, or pressure group.[58]

Fulfilling new as well as traditional State College goals required that academic freedom be safeguarded for teachers, students, and researchers. The Committee of Forty, encouraged by Compton, asserted in 1945 that professors must have "full freedom in research and in the publication of the results." The Committee further stated that the professor "is a citizen, a member of a learned profession, and an officer of an educational institution." He or she must not only "be accurate" but must "respect" the opinions of others. The touchstone of the whole academic process should be that the individual must not presume to speak for the institution, a matter which would threaten the freedom of all.[59]

The Faculty Executive Committee, generally following the creed of the American Association of University Professors, shouldered the responsibility to provide substance for the fine proposals of the Committee of Forty. In 1948, the Faculty Executive Committee, supported by Compton and Hopkins, proposed to the Board of Regents that tenure be granted to faculty to encourage and safeguard free inquiry after truth. Tenure meant granting permanent appointment, with dismissal only for cause, and was thought of as a means of protecting the integrity of the institution as well as the freedom of the professor.[60]

The Regents approved the tenure proposal, making it effective on April 16, 1949. They extended the privilege to all full-time faculty, which included the Resident Instructional Staff (all members of the College who regularly taught courses found in the catalog), the non-instructional research staff, extension staff, and librarians. Under the

•

The Committee of Forty, encouraged by Compton, asserted in 1945 that professors must have "full freedom in research and in the publication of the results." The Committee further stated that the professor "is a citizen, a member of a learned profession, and an officer of an educational institution."

•

regulation, associate and full professors (plus those of equivalent rank on other staffs) would undergo a one year probationary period before consideration for tenure. Assistant professors had a three-year probationary period before becoming eligible while instructors had to wait four years. Although students were not mentioned in tenure regulations, their greater freedom would be a by-product of unfettered inquiry in the classroom and laboratory.[61]

Once tenured, faculty members might not be dismissed except for cause. Normally, they would have little to fear if they remained dedicated to their disciplines and to the institution. Circumstances for dismissal included "deliberate or repeated infraction of the law," incompetence, inefficiency, neglect of duty, dishonesty, immorality, conduct "seriously prejudicial" to the State College or violation of the oath to uphold the government (see next paragraph). Any attempt to dismiss a tenured person would be heavily encumbered with legal procedures. The accused had the right to receive charges in writing, and a reasonable opportunity to reply, he or she might obtain legal counsel, submit evidence, and cross-examine witnesses. The Faculty Executive Committee served as the court of first resort, with appeals being carried to the Board of Regents.[62]

In the Cold War, which coincided with the establishing of tenure principles, professors had to come to terms with the public's demand, expressed in state law, that they affirm their loyalty to the state and the national government by swearing an oath. On October 16, 1948, the Regents declared "that any person who, by his own deliberate act, has associated himself with a group . . . which seeks the overthrow of free political institutions and constitutional government . . . is not eligible to serve on the faculty of the State College of Washington. . . ." The faculty, exhibiting only the deepest loyalty, accepted the necessity to take the oath. To do otherwise, without successfully challenging the law in court, would bring loss of position.[63]

The faculty's desire for promotions and raises in salary, not surprisingly, matched its concern with tenure and oaths. Indeed, at the outset of Compton's administration anticipation must have been great for the possibilities of change in these matters. During Holland's term of office, promotions often reflected the idiosyncrasies of personal and paternalistic government. Professors had been ignored if classes were small, while others had been more adequately compensated for enduring heavy loads without a murmur. Promotions had been made out-of-season and salaries likewise increased, if a favorite professor or administrator threatened to leave the institution. Compton recognized that a systematic and impartial promotional procedure would create better morale, but also saw a golden opportunity to underscore teaching as the State College's highest goal while developing a salary schedule.[64]

The administration instituted an annual review for all faculty members in order to regularize evaluations on a merit basis. Every faculty person, thereafter, would be judged by his or her department head and the administration only at the one season—no promotions

Professor John P. Spielman came to WSC in 1949 to serve as Dean of the School of Mines and later dean of the College of Engineering. In 1957 he was appointed vice-director of the Institute of Technology. (Washington State University News Service)

or salary increases were to be made at other times. At Compton's insistence, four major criteria were used to evaluate faculty members for promotion and salary raises: (1) effectiveness in teaching lower division courses, (2) effectiveness in teaching upper division and graduate courses, (3) success in research and creative activity, and (4) service to the institution and the public. Once more, Compton had placed teaching first and had given less consideration to research. The *Faculty Manual* supported him with a rather lukewarm pledge to research when it declared: "The administration will make every practicable effort to provide some time and facilities for those individuals who have demonstrated genuine research aptitude, and will thus encourage each individual to select research as one of the qualifications for promotion." To make certain no one misunderstood, the manual's statement concluded with a ringing reaffirmation of the chief criterion: "Nevertheless, good teaching and evidence of high scholarship shall be considered the most important qualifications for promotions in academic rank."[65]

Sick leaves and sabbaticals also came to the attention of the Regents in the fall of 1948, but with differing results in the two cases. The Board inquired of the state's attorney-general as to its legal authority in the first matter. Once assured of its power, the Board approved a sick leave policy, thereby relieving the faculty of a serious financial burden in time of illness or injury. Thereafter, faculty might earn sick leave with full pay at the rate of one day per month, or twelve calendar days per year, and could accumulate a maximum of 180 days in fifteen years. But, the Regents turned down the Faculty Executive Committee's proposal that sabbatical leaves be granted to faculty for refreshment and renewal of their skills, scholarship, and knowledge of the world.[66]

When the faculty and administration turned from examining personnel matters to contemplating educational facilities, a new library was seen as essential to the progress of the State College.[67] The existing facility in Bryan Hall had long since become outmoded and much too small to house the burgeoning collection and provide room for study and research. Remote rooms in various buildings around the campus—ranging from the Home Economics Building, to the Women's Gymnasium, and to the Rifle Range—were used to store increasingly large portions of the collection. The claim that any book could be produced at Bryan Hall's charge desk from these depositories within twenty-four hours was highly suspect. Faculty members had long since learned that they had better place assigned books on two hour reserve if they wished to have students read them. The result was that by 1950 the several thousand volumes held in the reserve book cage constituted the core of the undergraduate library.[68]

Holland and W. W. Foote, the librarian, had begun years before to make plans for a magnificent new structure, to be placed at or near the highest elevation on College Hill. It should, they thought, be a monument that was an inspiration to all who trod the campus. And, hardly a small point to Holland, it should rival the grandeur of the cathedral-like, "academic Gothic" Suzzallo Library at the University of Washington.[69]

•

In the Cold War, which coincided with the establishing of tenure principles, professors had to come to terms with the public's demand, expressed in state law, that they affirm their loyalty to the state and the national government by swearing an oath.

•

Holland and Foote with great ingenuity had created a book collection of major proportions. Foote had found considerable riches in a vast grab-bag of discarded volumes obtained from larger and more affluent libraries. Holland, exercising more discretion, had contributed valuable library materials for exhibition and research purposes with the invaluable assistance of the Friends of the Library. That organization, founded in 1938, had obtained for the library more than $50,000 worth of rare books and manuscripts on Abraham Lincoln, Indian history, Pacific Northwest Americana, Hispanic materials, European literature and history, and books and documents on two world wars.[70]

But in the eyes of Compton and many on the faculty, neither the collecting policies nor the architect's plans from the Holland administration would serve the needs of Washington State College in the post-war period. Four days after he took office in January 1945, the new president called for a new library as "indispensable" for making the college "the intellectual center of the Inland Empire." He urged Holland, who remained on the staff as a library consultant, to study the "eminent" libraries of the East, searching for innovative features to put into the new building. But, the plans that Holland already had approved called for an old-fashioned book depository that emphasized outmoded architectural features that wasted space and provided no compensating elements of comfort and utility. Holland's plan also failed to make allowance for the developing new media, such as microfilm, microforms, and cinema. Most important, Holland and Foote failed to anticipate properly expanded reader usage in the coming years.[71]

Meanwhile, a special faculty committee reported that the existing library lacked enough well-trained staff and sufficient space to allow for improving the quality of education. Furthermore, the professional librarians, whose salary was only slightly more than that of the non-professionals, predictably suffered from low morale. In addition, as the special committee noted, there was "a staggering backlog of unprocessed materials."[72]

The situation verged on the desperate when, in the summer of 1946 the Regents appointed G. Donald Smith to the post of librarian, effective on November 1. Smith, a New Englander who had begun his career as an apprentice librarian while working toward a Bachelor's degree in Library Science at Columbia University in 1933, later earned a Master of Arts degree in 1942 and a Ph.D. degree in 1946 in library science at the University of Chicago. He emerged from Chicago fully imbued with the idea that libraries should not simply collect books but should provide educational services of all kinds to students and faculty. Indeed, he believed librarians should be regarded as faculty and should perform all manner of teaching duties and services.[73]

Furthermore, Smith insisted that for efficiency and good service the library collection should be centralized completely in the new building, eliminating traditional departmental and divisional collections. As a compensation for problems caused by centralization,

Smith offered to develop special reading rooms for humanities, social sciences, and natural sciences. Anticipating the rapid development of motion pictures as a learning resource (and, perhaps, television), and microfilm and other microforms for easy communication and condensed storage, Smith planned ducts for electronic connections which could not yet be made and space to house equipment not yet devised. Obviously, the old-fashioned library on the drawing board would not do.[74]

A faculty and staff committee fully supported Smith's demand for a modern, functional building, stating on June 10, 1947, that "The library . . . should be sufficiently adaptable to serve functional demands ranging from simple book storage to active participation in complex programs of instruction, research and extension. Rather than a great architectural monument, the new library will be a sensible workshop. . . ." Old plans were set aside in the summer of 1947 and architect John Maloney, of Spokane, produced new drawings which were thoroughly debated. The severely functional idea for the building met with approval, except, of course, for Holland's opposition. In a last ditch effort, he tried unsuccessfully to obtain elevated ceilings for the first floor.[75]

The new plans, accepted by the Regents, were designed to produce a modular structure of the type advocated by Angus Snead McDonald, a nationally-celebrated architect. By organizing the entire building in units or modules of standard size the structure could easily be modified at any time to fit new needs. Interior walls could be removed, for example, without difficulty since the load was borne by outside walls and interior pillars. Subsequently, the Regents commissioned an artist to sculpt a high relief statute, dubbed "Nature Boy," which was placed on the face of the building to soften lines thought to be too severe.[76]

In spite of his enthusiasm for a new library, early in 1947 Compton had placed the library fourth on his priority list when requesting funds from Governor Mon C. Wallgren. The president dropped the library to sixth place in May, deciding that a union building, an agricultural sciences edifice, and a general classroom building, among others, should come before it. Governor Wallgren, however, working with Holland, had prepared a surprise announcement for Compton and the State College, which he released in the midst of an address at the May 1947 Commencement Exercises in Pullman. At that time, the Governor authorized spending $2,500,000 for the new library without delay. Compton may have learned of the grant a few days in advance but probably had not realized that Holland had worked behind his back to obtain the money. In effect, Holland had thwarted some of Compton's objectives by elevating the ranking of the library ahead of other buildings. In any event, Compton quickly acquiesced and gladly accepted the grant.[77]

Given Holland's history of interference and his persistence in championing the new library, Compton should have suspected his predecessor's continued political activity and thus thwarted it, if

G. Donald Smith served as director of Libraries at Washington State University from 1946 until his retirement in 1976. Construction on E. O. Holland Library was begun in 1950 and on Owen Science and Engineering Library in 1976. Under his leadership WSU Libraries installed its first computer support system in 1965. (Washington State University News Service)

Professor of Zoology Herbert Eastlick joined the Washington State College faculty in 1940 and served as department chair from 1947 until 1964. Eastlick was a demanding scholar and an outstanding teacher. Widely known for his research on the origin of pigment cells in vertebrates, Eastlick was a Fellow of the American Association for the Advancement of Science. (Washington State University News Service)

necessary. Compton also knew that Governor Wallgren had been interested in the library ever since James C. Taylor, his architectural consultant, had praised the plans in a Regent's meeting as "practical in every sense of the word but also beautiful" and predicted that "architects would come from all over the country to study . . . [the library]."[78] When completed in 1950 and named after Holland, this building, had already drawn national attention as "the first important 'modular library' under construction" in *The Architectural Record* for July, 1948. Librarian Smith had gained most of his objectives, although the library was not completely centralized, as he had wished, for a few outlying sub-libraries were permitted to continue. When he moved into the Holland Library with his central office staff in 1950, the books and other librarians stayed behind in Bryan Hall, being held there until the late summer of 1951, when the library shelving and other furniture had arrived.[79]

The planning and construction of the new library was timely if only because its facilities and resources would help underwrite development of a substantial graduate school in the post-war years. Of course, graduate education had existed before World War II but enrollments had been so small as to make it little more than an adjunct to the undergraduate program. In 1939-1940, for example, the post-baccalaureate student body numbered only 253 persons in both semesters, or six per cent of all students registered.

When Dean Paul H. Landis reported on November 5, 1945, that only 101 graduate students had registered, three-and-a-half percent of the total enrollment, he could find only seventeen candidates seeking Ph.D.s and thirty-one striving to earn master's degrees. The remainder included candidates for the degree of Doctor of Veterinary Medicine and lesser degrees and certificates. Far from presenting a cosmopolitan image, graduate students came overwhelmingly from the State of Washington. Foreign graduate students were almost nonexistent, there being five from Canada and two from China. Numbers rose more rapidly in succeeding terms so that in 1948-1949, fifteen percent, or 1,163 students were enrolled in graduate study. But Landis, and his successor, Stewart E. Hazlet, remained dissatisfied with the caliber of students, as well as with the totals.[80]

Landis and other supporters of graduate education felt keenly that the reduction of teaching and research assistantships during the war from 105 to thirty-five prevented attracting a truly gifted graduate student body. Landis urged Compton to raise the stipend from $600 per year to $900 and to increase the number of positions to the postwar maximum of seventy-five. When Compton hesitated, Landis predicted that many fellowships would remain unfilled, since the existing stipend would attract few superior students.[81] The president faced a dilemma. He believed that greatly increasing the number of graduate assistantships without careful screening, would reward both professors and graduate students without regard for intrinsic merit. Behind that fear lay his judgment, already discussed above, that most research was unworthy of the time and money spent upon it. In the end, Compton supported Landis and on April 21, 1945, the Regents raised the stipends for research and teaching assistants to $900 for nine-and-one-half months service, with an increase to $1,000 authorized for second and subsequent years of service.[82]

Encouragement of basic research by professors quite naturally accompanied faculty discussions about graduate education. On April 1, 1946, Stewart E. Hazlet, Chairman of the Educational Policies Committee, voicing his personal opinion, called for generous support for basic research through improved salaries. He also boldly put himself on record as differentiating pure from applied research, declaring that the latter should be paid for by the customers who benefitted from it. The full Educational Policies Committee joined him in declaring that the reputation of the institution bore directly upon the achievements of its graduate program and its fundamental research.[83] Amid the lengthy consideration of the means by which WSC might support research and publication of findings, the Educational Policies Committee emphasized the need for a free and tolerant atmosphere within which individuals might seek truth without fear or the need to justify their work in terms of practical application.[84]

To three skeptical professors from the social sciences, and no doubt to many of their colleagues, the administration's somewhat reluctant affirmations of research seemed to exclude their disciplines. They expressed their concern to Compton by declaring that "The atomic age has emphasized the importance of the [natural] sciences but not the contributions of the social sciences which are equally important." They recognized early in this new age that "strong work in the social sciences . . . [was] necessary to the solution of the problems created by technological advances." Although a sturdy defense of the social sciences, the statement offered a narrow and even parochial view of those social disciplines and of the needs of society. The professors' remarks yielded nothing concerning a role for the humanities nor is there any evidence that humanists entered the discussion. Indeed, Compton reinforced suspicians that the social sciences and the humanities would be neglected when he called exclusively for substantial salary increases for natural scientists.[85]

Meanwhile, the Regents recognized in their 1947-1949 report to the governor that significant increases had taken place in research, noting that "In spite of heavy teaching loads and committee assignments, members of the faculty contributed much significant research. . . ." They reported that government agencies, private corporations, and foundations were providing "many hundreds of thousands of dollars annually" for research and that totals were increasing. These monies not only supported professors' work but made possible hiring more and better graduate student assistants. The presence of these students, in turn, improved faculty research. It was clear that research and graduate education were one in practice, even though they might be divided in college's table of organization.[86]

Encouragement of basic research by professors quite naturally accompanied faculty discussions about graduate education. On April 1, 1946, Stewart E. Hazlet, Chairman of the Educational Policies Committee, voicing his personal opinion, called for generous support for basic research through improved salaries.

●

The idea of the State College of Washington as a "People's University" carried with it the obligation to extend general education to communities that lacked adequate facilities for such activity. Of course, WSC had offered agricultural extension from the opening of the school and since 1919 had provided general college courses regularly in Spokane and intermittently in a host of smaller communities.

●

The idea of the State College of Washington as a "People's University" carried with it the obligation to extend general education to communities that lacked adequate facilities for such activity. Of course, WSC had offered agricultural extension from the opening of the school and since 1919 had provided general college courses regularly in Spokane and intermittently in a host of smaller communities. In the immediate postwar period, the administration gave much attention to enlarging the program in Spokane, giving it a broader perspective and a permanent center.

The mood ran almost to euphoria as State college officials contemplated rich programs in art, music, and other liberal studies which might lend dignity and satisfaction to the middle class of that city. In the postwar world nothing seemed impossible if it fell within the parameters of the land-grant mission and as long as money remained abundant. Glenn Jones, Director of General Extension, wrote on March 21, 1947, that the center must have an "educational statesman" at the helm in Spokane, a person of stature to organize a program "which is a functioning part of the life of Spokane." Jones wanted him "to start with the community where it is and, through educational leadership, help it, and the individuals in it, improve the level of its performance—not by grafting from without but by stimulating from within."

Anticipated competition from the University of Washington did not develop, stimulating confidence that the State College might bring general education to the whole of eastern Washington. It opened a new Spokane Center in 1947, with a full-time director. In the 1947-1949 period twelve cities and towns east of the Cascades hosted extension classes from the State College and the number of students enrolled proved gratifying. Enrollment statistics are revealing, if not complete. In the 1945-1947 biennium 1,508 students enrolled for courses, a total, apparently, for all programs. For 1947-1949, the enrollment figures available include only three large centers at Pullman, Pasco, and Spokane, but they totaled 3,541. Spokane's share of that total was 2,002.[87]

The administration opened the Pasco Center in September of 1947, bent on a major missionary enterprise. Pasco, of course, represented but one-third of the Tri-Cities, of which Kennewick and Richland were the remaining portions. The Tri-Cities was a nuclear engineering community, especially as represented by Richland, center for the secret wartime Manhattan Project. Created in 1942, Richland had few cultural amenities but possessed a relatively large middle class professional population starved, not only for culture, but for advanced engineering training required in the work of the General Electric Corporation and other nuclear-related industries expected to develop there.[88]

Director Glenn Jones, of the general extension service, claimed that the Tri-Cities center made "a profound impression" in its first year, achieving enrollments satisfactory for a new program. But, the center had to be closed in 1949 due to a financial exigency at the State College. Paradoxically, General Extension opened a new center in

Yakima in the same year, which also had to close in two years, victim of money shortages but also of a transportation and communication problem. Yakima, in 1949, remained remote from Pullman. Professors simply could not meet an extension schedule half way across the state.[89]

By 1951, the General Extension Service had been reduced to supplying classes for the Spokane Center and Pullman. Financial stringency did not force closure of the Spokane Center but the curriculum and programs did not give the State College cultural prominence or the city a full-fledged program. In fact, the statements of purpose and claims for achievement at the Spokane Center contained a considerable amount of ambiguity and exaggeration. Assertions that the Center worked with influential intellectuals, artists, alumni, and leaders of service organizations to develop the program are belied by results. There is no evidence that civic leaders influenced the curriculum or Center activities or sought to do so. The claim that the Center served effectively as a public relations agency for the State College also lacks credibility. The most obvious evidence of this point is the failure to garner for the Spokane Center a respectable amount of newspaper space in the form of stories and editorials or a high ranking among the cultural agencies of the city.[90]

The Spokane Center student body included both young and old, professional, blue-collar, and white-collar workers, unskilled young people, housewives, soldiers, airmen and sailors. These students listened to lectures in the evening after a day's work, an experience perhaps as demanding for them as it was for their teachers, many of whom had driven eighty miles from Pullman to teach. Others had spent a full day teaching in Spokane public schools and at night "moonlighted" for the State College. Obtaining a bachelor's degree at the Spokane Center was impossible since no laboratory courses could be offered and relatively few upper division courses were in the curriculum. Probably no more than a small number of the center's students went on to take up residence in Pullman to complete degrees. Since a considerable number of students simply enrolled for no credit, the possibility of completing academic training seems to have been even more remote. Nonetheless, the Center's Director, Richard Bray, claimed that at the first semester for 1948-1949 some 740 students enrolled and in the second semester the number was 722, totals that he regarded as "very satisfactory."[91]

Thereafter, the Director of the General Extension Service listed the enrollments rather than head counts when reporting developments. He found that registration in the first few years was relatively stable, with the high point being reached in 1949-1950 when 3,034 enrollments were achieved. Though that figure was almost matched two years later, the subsequent history emphasized, with only 1,182 enrollments at the end of the decade. It should also be noted that throughout this period the General Extension Service furnished teaching aids, such as movies and other audio-visual devices, for classroom use in public schools as well as the State College and correspondence courses. This outreach activity further enriched

The Student Bookstore, 1949.
(Historical Photograph Collections,
Washington State University Libraries)

student programs at secondary and college levels by providing
opportunities for individual study of standard subjects through correspondence courses.[92]

Extension work in another form was inaugurated in 1942 when
the State College joined with Deaconess and St. Luke's Hospitals in
Spokane in a cooperative program to train nurses for the wartime
emergency. This collegiate program had led to the degree of bachelor of science. That agreement came to an end in 1945, being replaced
by a contract with St. Luke's which ran until the middle 1950s. The
college established a Department of Nursing Education located in
the College of Sciences and Arts, offered two years of basic science
training and general college courses in Pullman. The hospital
offered two and one-half years of clinical work. Students who
finished the combined program earned a B.S. in Nursing.[93]

The cooperative program continued with strong support from the
Board of Regents and the dutiful discharge of obligations by both
institutions. Enrollments, however, never rose sufficiently to make
the State College a major contributor to the pool of nurses available.
In December 1954, the WSC program ranked fourth among the five
collegiate programs in the state in numbers of students, falling
behind the University of Washington, Walla Walla College, and
Seattle University. The University of Washington could boast of 395
enrolled students, while Washington State College had but seventy-
eight. If enrollments seemed low, they nevertheless were taxing the
fiscal resources heavily, making improvements difficult to achieve.
Moreover, St. Luke's in 1956 eliminated its psychiatric work, forcing
students to travel to Seattle for that specialty. Both institutions began
looking for a way out of this fiscally debilitating program. Finally, in
June 1956, new enrollments were stopped by mutual agreement and
a phasing out began, a matter not complete until the first semester of

1957-1958. Thus, the State College's first experiences in nursing education came to an end.[94]

Compton expected the Institutes of Agricultural Sciences and Technology, created in January 1946, to bring innovation needed to lift Washington's economy out of debtor, or colonial status, and improve the lives of the people. Each Institute, in its own sphere, it was proposed, would bring teaching, research, and extension services into line to serve the purposes of particular industries or farming activities, the work to be under the watchful eyes of industry and farm leaders, organized into advisory committees.

The president did not have to wait long for a challenge. Leaders in the horticulture industry soon found good intentions to be inadequate. The chief operators of this important industry severely criticized the college for what it conceived to be a poor research program, headed by an incompetent professor. Compton sympathized with the professor, who had taken abuse no one should have had to take, he said. But he then conferred with colleagues in agriculture to find out what they might do to provide practical marketing information, which had seemed to be lacking, while at the same time continuing to develop the basic scientific and technical knowledge essential to future development of the fruit industry. Compton soon took the measure of the critics, becoming disturbed by their unabashed belief that the college should serve the fruit industry before all else. Nevertheless, the president anxiously sought to respond constructively to the demands of the entrepreneurs, rejoicing that the State College seemed to be at the center of activity.[95] In February 1946, probably because Compton acceded to some of their demands, including improving the facilities for research and providing new personnel, the Horticulture Advisory Committee changed its tune to praise of the College.[96]

The Animal Husbandry Advisory Committee bolstered Compton's confidence in his new organization by praising the progress made in animal sciences work. The Committee noted with approval the enlarging of farm yards, construction of new buildings, and acquiring of superior flocks and herds. Compton, thereafter, reported happily to the deans and directors that "The public response to the Washington State Institute of Technology and the Institute of Agricultural Sciences has been prompt, generous, and favorable." He struck an off-key note, however, though one quite understandable, when he stated that the purpose of the Institutes would be lost unless means were provided whereby "they enable the included department heads and faculties more completely than heretofore to devote their energies to their primary teaching and research functions."[97]

The new organization offered poor prospects for protecting the teaching and research time of chairmen and other faculty, however, since the number and diversity of utilitarian experiments and commercial adaptations of products greatly increased. Such developments required more administration than before and less attention to individual creativity. In the 1945-1947 biennium, for example, the agricultural experiment stations found much more state money in

The Agricultural Extension Service mirrored the research activities and findings of the experiment stations by seeking to educate the public in rural living and in the latest techniques in cultivation and sale of commodities. It paid particular attention to the social and recreational needs of the new farm families in the Columbia Basin and to applications of irrigation to crops.

their hands than was usual. The result was that the stations undertook some 250 projects in the biennium at the eight stations, tasks dealing with agricultural production and improving rural and small town life. The opening of the Columbia Basin Irrigation Project made necessary a great deal of research in irrigation agriculture at the Irrigation Branch Experiment Station in Prosser and at the Main Station in Pullman. Developing new plans for putting water on the land remained a major activity absorbing manpower, time, and money for the next few years.[98]

The Agricultural Extension Service mirrored the research activities and findings of the experiment stations by seeking to educate the public in rural living and in the latest techniques in cultivation and sale of commodities. It paid particular attention to the social and recreational needs of the new farm families in the Columbia Basin and to applications of irrigation to crops. The Service supplied countless bulletins on farming and living and even trained agents who demonstrated improved functioning of the home, dealing with family problems and development of youth.[99]

At the Main Experiment Station in Pullman, scientists "played an important role in the discovery of Vitamin B-12," useful as a poultry diet supplement and as an agent for combatting pernicious anemia in humans. Two more in a long line of wheat strains were released, the Elmar and Brevor, and there were numerous other plant and animal investigations of importance. Scientists at the Irrigation Experiment Station pursued research on irrigation agriculture, essential to completing the extension work on living in the Columbia Basin, mentioned above.[100]

Accreditation of the Department of Agricultural Engineering in 1950 increased the prospect of offering improved services in agriculture. The College farm by 1951, had been completely mechanized and was selling all its horses, the latter a cause for concern about the future of the College of Veterinary Medicine, perhaps, but hardly noticed as a problem by agriculturalists. A goal of eighty milking cows had been reached, a number which made possible a creamery business which earned $60,000 for 1950-1951. Agriculture in the outside world had changed as greatly as campus programs suggested it would, but agrarian life had also changed in a ways that were disquieting to both the campus and the outside world. A survey of agricultural graduates at the State College showed that while ninety-one percent of the graduates had settled into agricultural occupations, only sixteen percent of that group actually farmed. The technology of marketing and the mechanization of production seemed to be rendering farming obsolete as a way of life. The Institute of Agricultural Sciences, as it were, seemed to be coalescing with the Institute of Technology.[101]

The Institute of Technology brought together instruction, research, and extension services in engineering, all of which represented attempts to broaden the narrow industrial base of Washington's economy. "Clay into Alumina," a much discussed project of the pre-war years for developing an aluminum industry, continued with the same dedication but yielded nothing of commercial value. Various light metals researches also continued and as before, reflected Boeing's interest in airplane parts but found no other major corporations rising within the region to widen the market.

In 1949, Institute officials reported that forty-nine important projects in ten different major fields of activity were under way, many of which were sponsored by the United States Army, the Office of Naval Research, and the United States Department of Commerce. As evidence of stepped-up activity, it was reported that the Engineering Experiment Station completed four times the number of projects as in any previous two-year period. These ventures ranged from examining problems in radio communication, transmission of maps, pictures, and documents to and from aircraft by facsimile reproduction, to developing a light weight pumice building block, and creating boards and pulp from wood chips in a wood technology laboratory. The latter investigations were particularly close to the needs of the Washington economy, for success in fabricating new wood products would create more efficient use of the state's forests.[102]

Progress in engineering research had its counterpart in extension services offered by a new Division of Industrial Services, notably the latter's sponsorship of a light metals clinic in Pullman and a wood products clinic in Spokane. Enthusiastic receptions accorded these gatherings encouraged the leaders to plan regular meetings concerning their projects. The Division, in fact, found no practical industrial problem too great or too small, as it provided for individual consultation and established a host of clinics, conferences, and demonstrations. Its leaders tirelessly preached the message that industries must use science and the scientific method to solve their problems. Its work closed the circle between the academic studies of the College of Engineering and the creation of new products, devices and improved techniques and processes in order to elevate the economy and the state and region.[103]

Chapter Six

The 1950s and Early 1960s: An Enlarging Campus Amid the Cold War

RESEARCH AND PUBLIC SERVICE HARDLY SEEMED AS IMPORTANT TO undergraduates as did teaching and pursuit of extra-curricular activities and social life. Social scientists investigating ways to aid an ailing economy or geneticists laboring to introduce new strains of wheat were not engaged in activities that appeared to touch their lives. In this light, the ceremonies celebrating Compton's formal induction as president and its attendant inaugural rituals, held on December 11, 1945, almost a year after his arrival, contained little that was of interest to students. The presence of thirty college and university presidents and the outpouring of congratulatory messages from celebrities, held a great share of the attention of the students' elders. Flights of prophecy, congratulation, and hyperbole dominated events.

Then suddenly, late in the program, the undergraduates had their moment which briefly but significantly illuminated the scene. Doris Pierson, president of the student body, described by the *Evergreen* as a "charming" young woman, rose to deliver greetings to the assemblage. She spoke for only one minute and forty seconds, according to her notes, but one professor recalled twenty-seven years later that she enthralled the audience.[1]

She directed attention to the students in the audience, saying that the ceremonies of the day "are really for us. This we feel because in the life of any educational institution and any college president the student body is the essential unit. Today, then, when we honor the man who is to preside over our education we are especially gratified to honor a man who we can truthfully say is our friend." The professor recalled that "she got more applause than anyone else." The *Evergreen* concluded that she was the "unscheduled star of the show."[2]

Doris Pierson's remarks may have startled, or, perhaps, enchanted, many people but, on reflection, campus dwellers could not

OPPOSITE: *A student campaign rally in the mid-1950s.* (Historical Photograph Collections, Washington State University Libraries)

Compton, of course, had brought no experience in student affairs to the office of the president, but he had been wise in choosing Vice President E. H. Hopkins to develop a comprehensive student personnel and counseling program.

have been ignorant of the source of her "deep satisfaction." For a year, she asserted, students had enjoyed a president who had patiently and sympathetically concerned himself with student life.

Compton, of course, had brought no experience in student affairs to the office of the president, but he had been wise in choosing Vice President E. H. Hopkins to develop a comprehensive student personnel and counseling program. Hopkins worked so rapidly that on May 29, 1948, he could report at a national meeting that much of the faculty supported his work and that he had made long strides toward a comprehensive program. The objectives were all encompassing. Students were being counselled and guided in their educational, physical, and psychological needs from their earliest collegiate days through graduation. Hopkins, too, had begun to think ambitiously of keeping in close touch with alumni as well. Professional advisors and faculty from all ranks had been enlisted to help students fill legitimate needs and realize objectives. Hopkins, in addition, expected "continuous appraisal and evaluation" not only to develop individualism, but "to save civilization and democracy," a matter of great urgency in the opening days of the Cold War. A further admonition that a "college campus . . . must be made an efficient laboratory in democratic living" suggested that Hopkins might advocate new freedom for students. In spite of brave new words and ideas, however, the traditional parental role of the administration continued in the observance of a double standard enforced in male-female relationships. Women students still had to observe traditional closing hours in their living quarters while men had to be cognizant only of women's hours.[3]

It is true that on February 25, 1946, the College Senate had taken what it hoped would be a salutary step toward increasing the responsibility as well as independence of the students by abolishing the Forty-eight Hour Rule. Thereafter, they were not punished for failure to attend classes in the two days prior to and following the Thanksgiving and Christmas holidays. For a term or two, good will prevailed, with few students or professors violating the honor system, which succeeded the rule, but subsequently violations of the new code by students and their teachers became rife. In 1949, the faculty's Educational Policies Committee thought briefly of restoring the old rule but apparently never seriously debated the matter.[4]

Even earlier, in 1945, Compton had proposed another policy, one which he hoped might improve student behavior. He urged deferment of fraternity and sorority "rushes" from early September until the beginning of the second semester. But the leaders of Greek houses regarded the September date as crucial to obtaining new members and, hence, to the existence of their organizations. Debate proceeded slowly. Finally, in 1948 the Regents, agreed with Compton and called for postponement of rush until second semester. To the administration the change seemed compelling. Students who participated in "rush" required dormitory space on arrival, greatly upsetting the comfort and routine of regular dormitory dwellers. In addition, on more than one occasion, "rushees" damaged property when the

Greek Houses failed to cooperate in maintaining good order among their pledges.[5]

Though Compton steadfastly supported deferred rushing, it never came about. Much opposition arose from Greek Row but, in addition, faculty and administration clouded the issue by debating its many sides. Claude Simpson, the Registrar, for example, predicted in 1949 that deferred rushing would cause a decline in enrollment of 400 women in the following year. He had already noted in 1948 that freshman women's enrollment had declined 115 and 122, respectively, in the two preceding years. Simpson attributed the losses to the fact that many first year women lived in substandard housing, isolated from the campus center, and had to endure poor dining facilities in the even more remote, temporary Stadium Commons. Deferred invitations to join sororities, in his estimation, would be a crowning blow to many women. But, Simpson also voiced another fear when he pointed out that heavy emphasis in college publicity about the agricultural and engineering programs greatly reduced the appeal of the entire institution to women, sorority sisters or not.[6]

The administration set up a special committee to study the problem. Its report called for construction of 600 units of housing for women, even though none could be started in the near future. In fact, all available construction facilities, equipment, and manpower were in use and would remain unavailable for more than a biennium, erecting the library, the student union, a technology building, a classroom building, and other academic structures. Nevertheless, recruiting women seemed even more urgent at the end of the decade, as World War II veterans, mostly males, graduated faster than high school senior men could replace them.[7]

Another pressing need was a student union to serve as a magnet for activities and as a center for the entire campus community. Compton recognized the need for such a facility as early as July 1945, while making a lengthy report to the Regents on the need for housing. He found the student union to be perhaps a more critical need for student morale than dormitories. A union building would, he believed, attract "the high type of boys and girls whom we ought to aim to get." Once arrived, he wanted them to have a social center of the first order and of great aesthetic appeal. The dormitories, if necessary, could be of lesser appeal and cost.[8]

Joe Matsen, student body president in 1949, agreed completely with Compton, as did many students, but Matsen also believed that the administration had moved too slowly on the project. The students had been paying fees into a building fund since 1925 and had raised nearly $500,000. Impatient of further delay, Matsen called upon the Regents to float a bond issue to make up the difference in cost of several million dollars.[9]

Characterizing the need for a student union as "desperate," Matsen vividly depicted social life in Pullman as poverty stricken. On campus, students had the decrepit Temporary Union Building (the TUB, the women's old gymnasium), soon to be torn down to

●

Simpson attributed the losses to the fact that many first year women lived in substandard housing, isolated from the campus center, and had to endure poor dining facilities in the even more remote, temporary Stadium Commons.

●

Permission for bringing political speakers on campus, according to the Regents' statement in July 1946, required sponsorship by a recognized college organization—not the State College itself—and provision for equal hearing for both sides of any issue and by speakers holding opposing points of view.

make way for the new library. The small town of Pullman could hardly accommodate student needs, he reported. Long lines of patrons—often blocks long—waited to get into the two movie theaters. Pool rooms accommodated others, but offered a poor environment, so "our students can be seen wandering around the streets looking for anything to break the monotony of our closed-in campus living." The Regents were duly impressed with the report. On April 13, 1949, they agreed to provide the needed finances by issuing bonds. Two years later, in April 1951, the structure was completed and dedicated to Compton.[10]

Another sign of the growing regard the faculty and administration held for students came in 1947 when a number of undergraduates were appointed to committees once staffed only by professors. Vice-President Hopkins reported two years later that student members had performed well but that some of their number had suffered rebuffs from committee chairmen who tended to ignore them. On the other hand, Professor Herbert J. Wood recalled years later that students had served with distinction on the Educational Policies Committee "and were often more anxious for higher academic standards than some of the faculty members were."[11]

In spite of the increased regard for students, they suffered the same constraints placed on freedom of thought and expression imposed by the Cold War with Russia as did the faculty. In other words, whether students or faculty sought to bring controversial political speakers to the campus the result was the same. State laws and administrative regulations against communists were enforced. Permission for bringing political speakers on campus, according to the Regents' statement in July 1946, required sponsorship by a recognized college organization—not the State College itself—and provision for equal hearing for both sides of any issue and by speakers holding opposing points of view.[12]

In the Fall of 1948, as the Cold War intensified and as accusations surfaced concerning the presence of Communists in public life and in colleges and universities, the Regents reviewed stated policy. They reminded the campus that by state law of 1931 professors were required to swear to uphold the United States Constitution and state and federal laws. By another statute, passed in 1947, teachers were disqualified if they advocated overthrow of constituted government or if, as state employees, they went on strike. The message was clear and the spirit behind enforcing it was put in uncompromising terms by Compton on October 22, 1948, when he said, "In my judgement, no state is warranted in putting any part of the 'Ship of State' in the hands of any person who has committed himself to sinking the ship."[13]

Neither subversive activities nor challenges to governments and constitutions arose at the State College to test laws, regulations, or Compton's resolve. The Canwell Committee, a joint committee of the Washington legislature established to investigate un-American activities, did not inspect the State College as it did the University of Washington, rendering plans to protect academic and personal freedom moot. On one occasion some 200 faculty and allies congregated off-campus to listen to Dr. E. H. Phillips, an avowed theoretical Marxist of long standing, explain his dismissal from the University of Washington. The local chapter of the American Association of University Professors, a strong defender of academic freedom, refused to send a speaker on academic freedom because Phillips was not permitted to appear on campus.

A minor tempest arose when the Young Progressives, a student organization, which apparently supported Henry Wallace's radical progressive party, violated rules governing the appearance of political candidates on campus. After deliberation, however, the Regents approved the student government's contention that an honest mistake had been made and that the perpetrators should be given only a suspended fine of $50. But, the Board also felt the heavy hand of critics opposed to nonconformity. The following September it reminded the student leaders that the *Evergreen* and other student publications were not to "injure" the college or to "belittle" the Board's policies without running the risk of being closed down.[14]

Nature also provided a severe challenge to life on campus in the early weeks of 1948. Pullman experienced a flooding from the South Fork of the Palouse River which runs through the town. It was neither the first nor the last time Pullman and the campus would be disrupted by a raging torrent, but it was notable in that it provided a special opportunity for testing town and gown relationships in an emergency. Storm warnings had been readily apparent in the first seven days of the new year when it rained incessantly, establishing a precipitation record. The river finally rose above its banks, flooding the adjacent Palouse Trailer Court. Some 300 students, mostly veterans, together with their wives and children, fled trailers as the flood waters seeped into dwellings, leaving occupants homeless.[15]

Volunteers from campus and town heroically stacked 20,000 sacks of sand, creating a dike to curb the river. Despite these efforts, parts of the downtown streets and stores suffered flooding as well as the trailer court. Meanwhile, President Compton took command of the situation, directing traffic, sand-bagging, and evacuating residents to temporary quarters at the college and elsewhere. His leadership and compassion, together with that of his wife Helen, greatly impressed the students who referred to the president, according to the Evergreen as "a regular Joe." Helen Compton, who directed the emergency food and housing operations, also came in for praise, which led her to remark that "Pullman people are wonderful. I think if the entire college had been flooded the people here would still have taken care of it."[16]

The people would have their opportunities for further close relations. On February 21, the dike broke and flood waters spread out again. This time even the Cougar basketball team, on the way to play in Oregon, felt the strain. It became stranded in Endicott, thirty miles north of Pullman, when a railroad bridge washed out, forcing the players to stay in the town overnight. The dike in Pullman

A minor tempest arose when the Young Progressives, a student organization, which apparently supported Henry Wallace's radical progressive party, violated rules governing the appearance of political candidates on campus.

Budget tensions grew as state support for WSC was reduced and as ex-GI student enrollments declined. New student activities and counseling programs proved expensive, which rendered them vulnerable to public displeasure. A slowing down of progress and even elimination of faculty, staff, and programs were foreshadowed.

yielded again to flooding five days later, when much of Main Street went under water. This time the Compton home served as the clearinghouse for dispensing food and temporary housing for students.[17]

The heroics and tense drama involved in fighting flood waters soon gave way to a crisis in educational funding which threatened the progress and innovation of the Compton administration. Ostensibly, the difficulties arose from legislative moves to reduce the asking budget materially. The first signs of trouble became apparent in the 1947 legislative session when one of the committees "mistakenly" erased $2,246,000 from the operating budget, despite the fact that a sub-committee had unanimously recommended the full amount. The State College, the president's budget report stated, could not rectify the damage to the program "until this additional amount is restored."[18]

Budget tensions grew as state support for WSC was reduced and as ex-GI student enrollments, declined. New student activities and counseling programs proved expensive, which rendered them vulnerable to public displeasure. A slowing down of progress and even elimination of faculty, staff, and programs were foreshadowed. As the legislature considered the budget of January 1949, Compton warned his administrative officers and department heads that "riding the crest of the 'GI bulge'" would soon be but a memory. "High-grade education so far as practicable" would have to be the product of "low-grade costs." Research, Compton advised departmental chairmen, would have to be funded from some of the many private sources "to which W.S.C. is at least eligible to apply."[19]

Additional tension grew when, on March 22, 1949, Governor Arthur Langlie vetoed $750,000 from the operations budget. The building program, including the new library, the classroom building, and the Institute of Technology building was not touched, but plans for proposed facilities for the Institute of Agricultural Sciences were laid aside until the next biennium.[20]

A chorus of advice regarding staff and program reductions descended upon President Compton from deans, directors, and chairmen, which generally called for husbanding resources to promote the strengths of the institution and reward its best professors. Vice-President Hopkins expressed a common sentiment among these leaders when he commented wryly that the State College had tried to be "all things to all men" instead of being "superior" in selected basic programs. Agreement on what constituted superiority proved impossible to obtain, though some consensus arose over programs to be reduced or eliminated. Greatest agreement probably concerned reduction or elimination of the student activities program and staff, with some consensus that the professional counseling service be also reduced or removed, along with the satellite programs of the Community College Service (the general extension service).[21]

In the end, the budget precipitated neither disaster nor chaos, since from it some salary advances could be made, operations could be carried on with slightly more money than previously available, and a handful of new positions could be filled. The Community College Service, which had not been cost effective, lost much of its off-campus program. A notable change, however, foreshadowed the loss of confidence in Compton's administration—the reduction in size and scope of the student counseling and activity centers. The latter, in particular, had not met with general faculty approval, perhaps because many people reacted negatively to the praise which Vice-President Hopkins had bestowed upon it—what he saw as virtue they pictured as the opposite. For example, Hopkins had proclaimed that the Activities Center had been established in the belief that extracurricular activities were as important as a formal education. But, with the loss of the special activities staff anticipated, he asserted that the faculty might have to stand in its stead, for the program "requires good faculty leadership and supervision." An overworked faculty did not find that a great boon. Likely to prove troublesome for Compton in the days ahead, too, was his inability to satisfy agriculturists by constructing a permanent installation for the Institute of Agricultural Sciences.[22]

The demise of the Compton Administration came on the morning of April 13, 1951, when the Board of Regents, meeting in Spokane's Davenport Hotel, went into executive session leaving President Compton and any visitors out in the hall. Once secreted, Regent John Camp, Jr., stated that in his opinion the president should resign, along with the Dean of Students and the Vice-President. After that, the Board passed resolutions that challenged Compton's presidential authority. The Regents required him to declare the Vice-Presidency vacant, to abolish peer evaluation of the faculty, and to terminate the separate student activities program, placing a reduced version under the Dean of Students. In addition, Compton received orders to dismiss 182.5 employees, including fifty-four faculty and ten non-instructional researchers. The Board also voted to reduce, combine, or eliminate numerous programs as soon as possible.[23]

Since Compton had already initiated a plan to reduce the staff drastically to meet budget constraints, he had no difficulty complying with that mandate when the Regents insisted upon it at another meeting on April 27. Agreement ended when the Board overrode Compton's objections to removing the Vice-President, eviscerating the student activities and counseling programs, and eliminating peer review of faculty. The Board then took up Compton's resignation letter (which he had tendered upon taking the office of president) and his authority ended.[24]

Finally, perhaps because they recognized the shocking nature of their decision, the Regents hastened to name the still unfinished student union building in honor of the departing president—the Compton Union Building (CUB). Mending fences and quieting the campus and its clientele, past and present, however, depended more upon restoring confidence in the administration—which at that moment became the Board of Regents—than upon fine words and gestures.[25]

The demise of the Compton Administration came on the morning of April 13, 1951, when the Board of Regents, meeting in Spokane's Davenport Hotel, went into executive session leaving President Compton and any visitors out in the hall. Once secreted, Regent John Camp, Jr., stated that in his opinion the president should resign, along with the Dean of Students and the Vice-President. After that, the Board passed resolutions that challenged Compton's presidential authority.

The process of selecting Compton's successor became intertwined with faculty and student efforts to safeguard the gains made during his tenure and to obtain further advances. Meetings held between special committees of faculty, students, and regents produced an accord as early as May 28, 1951.

Early inquiries as to the reasons for Compton's dismissal yielded only statements of "no comment" by Regents and suggestions by Compton that the Board ought to explain its actions. On April 27, the president had rendered a somber report and "farewell address" to the Regents about their responsibilities. Gestures of that kind and the seeming disorder suggested by evasive comments by Regents stirred Phil Patterson, editor of the *Evergreen,* and others to analyze the events and policies resulting in Compton's dismissal and the termination of a brief but exciting era in which the institution moved rapidly toward university status.[26]

Editor Patterson found "a rapid fire string" of resignations following that of Compton, including William G. Craig, Acting Dean of Students, whose position became untenable following the dismantling of the student activities program. Craig was joined by Robert G. Brumblay, Director of Athletics, who complained of divided authority, a product, in part at least, of Compton's restructuring of the administration of athletics.[27]

The Faculty Executive Committee, using its prerogative, called a meeting of the faculty on May 3, 1951, in which the assembled professors expressed themselves "profoundly shocked" by the dismissal of the president and vice-president and stated that they deeply regretted "that the College is to lose his strong and constructive leadership." There was more, all of which revealed a deep sense of loss, especially of Compton's integrity and his democratic handling of the faculty. Further resolutions deplored the removal of Vice-President Hopkins and abandonment of that office and pledged support for the welfare of the college. Explanations were demanded of the Board of Regents and, finally, the faculty directed the Executive Committee to negotiate a role for it in the selection of a new president.[28]

Though Compton later asserted that he never had learned why he had been dismissed, at the time he sought to lay the blame, somewhat obtusely, to politics. He pointed out, inaccurately as to substance, that during 1950 and 1951 some six of seven members of the Board of Regents had been replaced, much to his detriment: Actually, only four new Regents had been added to the seven-member Board during those years. They, of course, were enough to constitute an unfavorable majority when the situation arose, but the leader of the opposition to Compton had served for some time and had hardly concealed his desire to control the college's administration.[29]

Robert Sandberg, Compton's Executive Assistant, corroborated the president's supposition that he had been dealt an unfavorable majority when he recalled years later that Regents' meetings sometimes became disorderly, with one or another of the members quarreling with the president. Compton must have recognized, too, that members of the Board as well as individuals on the campus and in town sometimes criticized the administration when they complained of Helen Compton's real estate activities, her attempts to beautify the town and campus, and her personal attention to the affairs and needs of married students and new faculty and staff.[30]

Compton's nemesis on the Board was the Very Reverend Charles E. McAllister, Dean of the Episcopal Cathedral of St. John the Evangelist in Spokane, who laid claim to considerable expertise in administering colleges and universities. Not only had he inspected many institutions, but he had published a book entitled *Inside the Campus; Mr. Citizen Looks at his Universities,* for the Association of Governing Boards of State Universities and Allied Institutions. He also had served longer on the Board of Regents than had Compton or any other member. By 1950, McAllister had found an ally in new member John Camp, Jr., and in the Spring of 1951 McAllister found a majority supporting Compton's resignation.[31]

Compton must have been greatly pleased that the students never seemed to waver in their support for him. If, however, he had looked critically at the faculty he would have noticed that various factions had opposed particular programs, some of which have been discussed above. Indeed, some faculty members chose to undercut the administration on special issues by appealing directly to individual members of the Board of Regents. Alumni disaffection arose over such high profile issues as the governance of intercollegiate athletics. When the president fired Football Coach Phil Sarboe in December 1949, he was accused of "meddling with the athletic program." Thus, when Compton subsequently dismissed the graduate manager, who ran the program on behalf of the Associated Students, and introduced instead a director who was under the president's control, much unhappiness resulted. Then, when Athletic Director Robert G. Brumblay resigned after Compton's dismissals the resignation signified to critics that they had been right all along.[32]

The process of selecting Compton's successor became intertwined with faculty and student efforts to safeguard the gains made during his tenure and to obtain further advances. Meetings held between special committees of faculty, students, and regents produced an accord as early as May 28, 1951. Under its terms, students held the privilege of presenting grievances to the Board of Regents through their own representatives as would the faculty through its agents. The *Faculty Manual* once again gained recognition by the Regents as the official code of regulations guaranteeing privileges and rights.[33]

The accord also stipulated that a student activities center would be consolidated with the office of the Dean of Students, rather than abolished entirely. Also, the faculty might have peer review, a much-debated Hopkins' innovation, if it were still desired. In addition, the faculty might have the privilege of being represented by one of its own members at Regents' meetings. To make that privilege meaningful, the Board agreed to have as many meetings in Pullman as "practicable." Finally, the most important immediate objective was obtained when the Board agreed to seek advice of selecting a new president from a committee or committees which would include faculty, students, and alumni.[34]

Faculty moved with alacrity to participate in selecting the new president. A committee of twenty-five, organized to represent all parts of the campus, prepared a list of nominees from among the vast number of applicants. On June 1, 1951, a committee of students and faculty met with a group of Regents to name a council of eleven to present the final approved list of names to the Board for election. That elite committee consisted of four Regents, five professors, one student and an alumnus.[35]

A growing rapprochement between the Board of Regents and the faculty emerged during the hiatus between old and new presidents. Subsequently, it could be measured by the number of important new programs that were instituted. The Regents readily accepted faculty advocacy of progressive reform and innovation which, in some cases, had begun under Compton. An example occurred at a Board meeting on October 26, 1951, when McAllister moved and Rogers seconded a motion " that a restricted policy of sabbatical leaves be set up for the faculty. . . ." It was a modest step, "not a right . . . but rather a privilege extended to a selected few in recognition of excellence in teaching or research." There would be no more than three awards for the 1951-1953 biennium but the faculty eagerly watched for more generous terms in the future.[36]

The Graduate Studies Committee, on November 9, 1951, recommended to the Resident Instructional Staff (the teaching faculty) that a new type of advanced degree be instituted—the "Master of Arts in Teaching" (M.A.T.) a particular subject. The purpose was to increase the subject matter competence of public school teachers, mandated by new state regulations, and to that end a thesis was dropped in favor of several seminar papers. The Resident Instructional Staff and the Board of Regents approved M.A.T. degrees in twenty subjects, ranging from Agriculture and Biological Science to English, Fine Arts, and History. The State College also modified an existing degree, the Master of Education, to make it less theoretical and more related to practical application of public school administration.[37]

Selection of a new president proceeded slowly through the fall of 1951 and into the winter of 1951-1952 Then, at a meeting in Chicago on February 24, C. Clement French, Vice-President of Texas Agricultural and Mechanical College, accepted the position as it had been offered to him by the Board of Regents. The final obstacle to the Board's action had been cleared when the agricultural interests of the state (and on the campus) fell into line, giving French's candidacy hearty approval. The new president, fifty-one years of age and a native of Philadelphia, had earned three degrees in chemistry from the University of Pennsylvania, where he did his first teaching. He next spent nineteen years at Randolph-Macon College, Lynchburg, Virginia, teaching chemistry and serving as chairman and later as the dean of the college. He had followed that tour of duty with one year in administration at Virginia Polytechnic Institute and approximately a year as vice-president at Texas Agricultural and Mechanical College.[38]

Selection of a new president proceeded slowly through the fall of 1951 and into the winter of 1951-1952. Then, at a meeting in Chicago on February 24, C. Clement French, Vice-President of Texas Agricultural and Mechanical College, accepted the position as it had been offered to him by the Board of Regents.

Virginia Polytechnic Institute and Texas A & M provided President French with experience in administering land-grant schools and learning their mission. The brevity of the experience in each case, however, hardly qualified him as an expert on the special tasks of such an institution in the Pacific Northwest. Indeed, neither he nor his wife had been interested in the State college position when first contacted, but were strongly urged by the Board to make an inspection trip to the Pacific Northwest. Once on the campus grounds, they captivated the Regents and in turn were intrigued by the position, the campus, and the community. In the end, French accepted election and promised to report for the job in early April 1, 1952. He was voted a salary of $18,000 per year.[39]

C. Clement French, sixth president of Washington State College. (Historical Photograph Collections, Washington State University Libraries)

French claimed then, and later in his recollections, that he had known nothing of the problems that had led to Compton's dismissal. When he arrived in Spokane just before Easter he exhibited a charm and dignified presence not lost on a reporter for the *Spokesman-Review* who described him as having "a radiant personality that seems to be bursting with energy and a friendliness that is completely disarming. One handshake and he makes you a friend." He was, in addition, "a fine looking man 6 feet 2, straight as an arrow . . . and has a forehead that has swept a long way back." He proved also to have a sense of humor. When reading that description, he chuckled over the characterization of a high forehead instead of a bald head.[40]

French had intended, before departing for Pullman, to attend Easter services with Regent Charles E. McAllister at the Cathedral of St. John the Evangelist, but the Dean became ill, forcing a change in schedule. Early in the presidential search, the two men had discovered a common bond of no mean proportions. Each played a significant role in the Episcopal church, McAllister as a priest who had once served in Virginia, where French had been a prominent lay leader. French gave McAllister a great deal of credit for his election, an idea with which McAllister fully concurred. When McAllister died shortly after becoming ill, that event changed the composition of the Board of Regents materially and rapidly advanced French's education for office. He remarked, years later, regarding McAllister, "As I found out subsequently, [he was] a very active participant in some of the [late] troubles."[41]

Once in office, French demonstrated a cautious approach to problems old and new as well as keen sense of diplomacy. One of the first letters he received contained a protest from the Alumni Association against naming the student union in honor of Compton. Ivy Lewellen, secretary to President Holland, sent a page from a petition opposing Compton's name and explained that it had long been the students' intention to dedicate the structure as a memorial to classmates and alumni who had fallen in war. Greatly surprised by the furor, French made some "discreet inquiries" about campus affairs that proved to be unsettling. He concluded that his major problem was a "totally divided faculty" and that his first task would be to reunite that group, before undertaking to improve relations

Professor Raymond Muse was appointed the first Chairman of the Department of History by President French when the old Department of Political Science and History was dissolved in 1956. Muse served in that capacity until he retired in 1979. By the end of his tenure, the department had experienced dramatic growth and, by 1977, was ranked among the top fifteen percent of all history programs in the United States. (Washington State University News Service)

with outside communities. He realized further, that he did not know the State of Washington any better than he knew the campus—and the latter problem might be overcome by enlisting alumni support.[42]

French found it easy to blend pragmatic solutions with his philosophy of administration. Years later, he recalled that he had not been a "big plan ahead planner." Rather, he had thought of himself as "really a manager of it as it was." Regarding his previous experience he said, "all the situations I'd been in had been entirely operating, or operable situations. . . . Not ones that unexpectedly showed complete chaos, complete division into two warring factions." The split in the faculty and the unknown State of Washington did not merely challenge him—they provided great stimuli to solving the college's problems.[43]

If French's recollection of problems seems exaggerated and melodramatic, his immediate response reflected his brand of pragmatism. He tackled the question of campus divisions squarely, asking the faculty to accept him and his wife as out-of-staters who knew nothing of past problems and as people interested only in promoting the welfare of the institution by facing the future and not dwelling on the past.[44]

Dedication of the student union, he feared, would prolong, and might even deepen, divisions represented in Compton's dismissal. Once again, French employed pragmatic tactics. He decided not to indulge in a lengthy, formal presidential inaugural, the effect of which might be to sharpen the personality clashes on campus and off. Instead, at his first Commencement in June 1952, he had the Regents induct him into office in a casual, almost incidental, ceremony which required only a few minutes. Then, at the dedication of the union in honor of Compton, which came on Homecoming weekend in October 1952, he employed the opposite tactic. Involved in the ceremony, were more than five hundred students, faculty, alumni, and others keenly interested in the college's welfare. Their participation provided a visible sign of unity. Wilson Compton was not only present, but his speech of acceptance carried a strong conciliatory note and provided a kind of benediction when he re-dedicated the union to the welfare of the students who would use it in the future.[45]

The issue of faculty peer evaluation continued to interest many and thereby caused President French some anxiety about faculty cohesion and morale. In December 1951, even before his arrival, the Faculty Executive Committee conducted a poll that indicated that most of the professors favored some kind of evaluation.[46] When in June 1952, the committee asked French when it might submit to the Board of Regents a new statement on the broader issue of academic freedom, French revealed his deliberate approach to administration. He did not wish to raise such a controversial matter with the Board, he replied, until he had established "a good, sound working relationship" with it, as well as with other administrators and the faculty.[47]

The matter of peer review remained in abeyance until December 1953, when the Faculty Executive committee once again sought to bring the issue to the fore. When, in February 1954, the committee pressed French for restoration of evaluation, the president demurred. The faculty minutes for February 18 describe his response: "The president will do everything in his power to assure a fair hearing for any individual, but will not restore a plan for colleague evaluation at this time." Indeed, he never sought reinstatement of peer evaluation, nor did succeeding presidents.[48]

Improved salaries, of course, offered another means for raising faculty morale and productivity. The first advances, reported to the Board of Regents on May 30, 1952, "have been very well received," according to Dean S. T. Stephenson. Celebration was muted, however, since raises had been made possible, in part, by drastic reduction of faculty and staff positions rather than by prosperity. Nevertheless, the glimpse at improved salaries sparked hope that the State College might soon gain equality with the University of Washington in that matter. The Faculty Executive Committee, watch dog of faculty welfare, investigated comparative salaries that Spring and reported that University of Washington professors and associate professors were being paid salaries that exceeded those of their WSC counterparts by $626 and $240 respectively. The task of improvement was formidable, but perhaps State College hopes might have been buoyed by the fact that assistant professors at two institutions were virtually equal in average pay while the State College instructors already exceeded their University of Washington counterparts by $248. The latter distinction was a mixed blessing, however, for twenty-eight percent of the WSC faculty were at the beginning level as opposed to only twenty-two and one-half percent at the Seattle school.[49]

Administrators and faculty members knew that increased salaries might bring a more distinguished faculty to the State College but first priority remained that of increasing the size of the teaching corps because of a surprising development—the student body was experiencing unexpected growth. The sharp reductions of enrollment in the fall of 1951, a result of the exodus of the last of the ex-GIs, had been expected to cause the student body to decline in size for several more years. Indeed, S. Town Stephenson, Dean of the Faculty, ventured the opinion to the Board of Regents on May 30, 1952, that faculty reduction had not brought any losses "vital to our program." Yet, only five months later he reported—perhaps ruefully—that the State College was the only major institution on the Pacific Coast that enjoyed an enrollment increase that year. Five thousand and eighty-one students had enrolled, 191 more than the previous year. These figures included a twenty-four percent increase of freshmen and other new students, nine percent more than the national average. The period of low and decreasing enrollment, it was apparent, had ended almost as soon as it had been recognized.[50]

After further ruminating about new developments, Dean Stephenson wrote privately to Carl A. Pettibone, Business Manager and Comptroller, on November 12, 1952, that the financial and staff reductions of 1951 had been much too severe. The loss of fifty-four

French recognized even before he arrived on the campus that one of his greatest administrative problems would be to improve relations with the University of Washington. While still president-elect, he established the beginnings of a firm friendship with his counterpart to be in Seattle, President-elect Henry Schmitz, who had not yet moved from the University of Minnesota.

faculty positions (involving sixty-three persons) and more than $1,277,000 in general funds had overloaded the remaining faculty and facilities, a matter that could not be remedied at the time. Some needed classes had to be eliminated and others became badly overcrowded, while student counseling suffered from lack of experienced practitioners. Graduate program revisions were postponed. The bright promise of the new Holland Library dimmed because the reductions in staff impaired services and reduced hours for use by the facility.[51]

By June of 1953, however, Dean Stephenson adopted an ebullient tone when, upon reviewing the prospects for further enrollment increases, he declared that "We are no longer on the defensive, but on the offensive with increasing enrollments." Although figures for the fall semester of 1953 fell to thirty fewer students than in September 1952, Stephenson called on all major faculty committees to consider problems that might arise if projected heavy enrollment increases in the next decade became a reality. With two exceptions thereafter, enrollment rose steadily to an unprecedented 8,325 students ten years later in 1963. By 1966, the student body had doubled over 1953, with 10,662 students.[52]

If salary increases were an accurate barometer of improvements taking place, the faculty should have become strongly motivated to prepare for a student body of unprecedented size. In 1953, President French obtained an extra $100,000 to distribute to faculty in the second year of the biennium, which he proceeded to use to rectify inequities and to move toward parity with the University of Washington. Then, again in 1955, he had a sum which he estimated at $450,000 for distribution in salary advances in the next biennium. Again, he emphasized that the salary package would be used to work toward parity with the University of Washington. More than that, he planned to use the money to materially improve the salaries of eleven month faculty (who had suffered from a salary scale which favored nine months appointees) and of the deans, as the latter had lagged far behind their counterparts at the University of Washington.[53]

Improved salaries kindled interest in comparing the State College with the University of Washington and other institutions. In November 1953, Dean Stephenson reported to President French that their institution was "essentially on the same salary scale as the University of Washington, with the exception of [full] professors, department chairmen and deans." Neither French's response nor that of the faculty are known to this optimistic statement, but it must have been evident to all but the most sanguine of professors, that parity at the upper levels, would be difficult to attain.[54] Nevertheless, Stephenson's April 12, 1955 report to the Faculty Executive committee, showed major advances by the State College at all professional ranks. The college led in median and average salaries at all levels. But since the University of Washington possessed a significant advantage in the higher ranks, it must have been evident that the Seattle institution had a distinct advantage in attracting the higher caliber of professors.[55]

Almost a decade later on September 15, 1964, French remarked that twelve years earlier the school had been at a salary disadvantage with comparable institutions amounting to almost a full rank difference-i.e., full professors at Pullman received approximately the salary of associate professors at comparable institutions. In 1964, he was pleased to report, the American Association of University Professors found only twenty-eight institutions of some 730 reporting, that exceeded Washington State University's salary scale. WSU was on a par with the University of Washington and virtually so with other institutions of a comparable group, which included the universities of California, Illinois, Michigan, Indiana, Oregon, Minnesota, and Wisconsin. Looking forward, French concluded happily that "we should go out of this biennium at an average figure which should be equal to or slightly higher than the average of this comparable group."[56]

Increases in salary funds were only one part of the improved budgets for the school. In March, 1957, the legislature approved a budget which Dean Stephenson termed the best it had ever secured. It provided a thirty percent increase over the previous biennium. The State College, according to President French, received "almost our asking [budget] in salaries and wages." It included $4,500,000 in capital funds and almost $2,000,000 in reappropriated items. In addition, the legislature passed a referendum bill which the voters in the following general election approved. This decision permitted the state to float bonds for capital construction, $7,000,000 of the total being allocated to the State College.[57]

Administrative issues in French's early years often centered around questions of increased productivity and economical use of facilities and staff. He had, first, on January 26, 1953, removed any lingering doubts that he would abandon Compton's scheme to align all educational functions on the campus under the chairmen of the four divisions of the College of the Sciences and Arts—Biological Sciences, Physical Sciences, Social Sciences, and Humanities. However logical such an organization might appear on paper, in practice it disrupted and divided the campus, a condition that was an anathema to French. The functions of the four chairmen of the basic divisions of liberal and scientific knowledge were confirmed for the College of Sciences and Arts but, their duties were specifically limited to that College. As an added assurance, perhaps, their titles were changed to the traditional deanships.[58]

French recognized even before he arrived on the campus that one of his greatest administrative problems would be to improve relations with the University of Washington. While still president-elect, he established the beginnings of a firm friendship with his counterpart to be in Seattle, President-elect Henry Schmitz, who had not yet moved from the University of Minnesota. Writing to Schmitz on March 27, 1952, French proposed that they work cooperatively for the benefit of both schools. Schmitz accepted the warm invitation and within a few months they were discussing common budgetary problems and ways and means of satisfying the legislature, as well as how to improve relations with the public.[59]

William McDougall, a member of the College of Education faculty since 1955, became Director of the University's Summer Programs in 1980. For the next decade he expanded the operation to the point that, in 1988, enrollment reached 4,412. (Washington State University News Service)

Professor of Psychology William A. Cass was a member of the WSC faculty from 1953 to 1979. During that period he served as director of the Counseling Center and taught numerous courses in clinical psychology. (Washington State University News Service)

In addition, French and Schmitz negotiated claims of duplication of courses and programs, issues raised by partisans at both institutions and in the public. In actuality, significant duplication had resulted from the ambitions and need of the State College to provide a full curriculum to meet its obligation as a land-grant college, providing an education for all who wished to attend. Frank discussions between French and Schmitz prepared them to convince legislators in 1954 that the two schools might resolve the issues themselves. Several programs continued, as a result, without either legislative interference or attack from the University of Washington.[60]

Two major problems remained: duplication in journalism and forestry. Neither discipline had been granted to the State College as a major line in the law of 1917, being delegated to the University of Washington. Both, however, had developed on the Pullman campus, although without full standing. Journalism evolved into a program conducted under the banner of the Department of English, its graduates receiving the B.A. in English. This duplication provided a sensitive issue for both presidents but they solved the problems after candid discussion by permitting the State College to maintain the full program but without departmental status or a separate bachelor's degree. The students lost little or nothing in the bargain, being fully prepared to pursue careers in journalism.[61]

Duplication of forestry courses at the State College came to French's attention as a debatable matter in November, 1953. When he inquired as to its justification on the campus, Professor John P. Nagle replied that forestry served as an important part of the curriculum for agriculture majors. The matter languished until 1960 when French and President Charles Odegard of the University of Washington agreed to a compromise which recognized the claims of Washington State University, the new name granted the State College in 1959. The presidents subsequently persuaded the legislature of 1961 to modify the 1917 law to permit both universities to offer forest management as a major line. Logging engineering and forest products, were never offered as courses of study by Washington State University, but remained with the University of Washington as exclusive lines, a matter French had no desire to dispute.[62]

Successes in dealing with these controversial institutional policies were not as easily matched when third-party interests were involved. Thus, when on January 25, 1952, Editor Paul Stoffel, Jr., of the Pullman *Herald,* published an open letter critical of what he discerned to be liberal and radical developments at the State College, he disturbed the fictitious calm that had prevailed since the state's Un-American Activities Committee (the Canwell Committee) had failed to investigate the campus for subversive activity. Stoffel's letter, published shortly before French was elected to the presidency, championed Acting President William Pearl for the permanent post.

At the same time, Stoffel decried the presence of some professors at the college who, in his view, were not "in sympathy with nor were they teaching the American philosophy of individual opportunity" and free enterprise. Indeed, the hour was late, he contended, for the nation was almost at "the crossroads" at which it must choose between state socialism and free enterprise. Denying that he called for a "witch-hunt," Stoffel nevertheless claimed that there were "some bad apples in the barrel" which were "unhealthy influences." To strengthen his claims, the editor revealed that a "score" of local businessmen and farmers had endorsed his statements, presumably his advocacy of Dr. Pearl for president, as well as his support for the indoctrination of students with a particular point of view. Four days later, in response to Stoffel's letter, the Faculty Executive Committee asked the administration, headed by Dr. Pearl, to "clarify to the faculty its position in regard to the matter of academic freedom."[63]

The Committee's blunt request seems not to have been answered—at least not in such a way as to evoke immediate rejoinder. A year later, however, the Faculty Executive Committee once again expressed great concern about the threat of loyalty investigations and so considered ways and means preparing to deal with it. The Committee drew up a memorandum on "Conducting Loyalty Investigations," in which it revealed deep concerns about protecting academic freedom and the civil rights and reputations of those who might be accused of subversion. Their involved efforts to protect the accused reckoned without the motives and actions of investigators, as they assumed that all might sit down at the table to cooperate in developing a means of protection. When French saw the memo he responded only briefly and abruptly, reminding the Committee that the good will of an outside investigating party could not be established in its absence.[64]

French and the Board of Regents had been forced to take a hard, realistic view of their position after the 1951 legislature adopted a "Subversive Activities Act," making it a felony to attempt to overthrow constituted government. College authorities had been required to remove persons who could not swear an oath denying membership in such an organization.[65] Legislation on subversion became more sharply focussed in March 1955, when law makers identified membership in the Communist Party as subversive and placed all organizations on the United States Attorney-General's list in the same category. The college administration had no alternative under law but to require employees to execute an oath denying membership in these organizations. No full scale investigation ever took place at Washington State College, however, and no faculty or staff were removed for subversion. The 1955 law remained on the books until 1963 when, in a case brought by two University of Washington faculty, the United States Supreme Court found it unconstitutional.[66]

A less startling but more persistent challenge to academic freedom was a steady barrage of criticism that the State College failed to teach Americanism. In addition, individuals, newspaper editors, and special interest groups accused the college of harboring professors who held unpopular and even threatening views. Critical or unpopular judgments concerning politics or regarding the economy brought forth threats to withhold financial and other

•

French and the Board of Regents had been forced to take a hard, realistic view of their position after the 1951 legislature adopted a "Subversive Activities Act," making it a felony to attempt to overthrow constituted government. College authorities had been required to remove persons who could not swear an oath denying membership in such an organization.

•

Sidney G. Hacker served as chairman of the Department of Mathematics from 1955 through 1966. In 1961 Hacker initiated a program for improving the instruction for public school math teachers that was subsequently adopted for use by the states of Idaho, California, and Massachusetts. He was originally hired by President Holland in 1936 to develop WSC's programs in Mathematics and Astronomy. Hacker also served as the first Director of Jewett Observatory after the facility was opened in 1953. (Washington State University News Service)

support. Notably, in 1951 and 1952, the State College presented institutes of international affairs in Spokane. The second institute, according to the Spokane *Spokesman-Review,* attacked the McCarran Act, loyalty oaths, and the American system of free enterprise. Attention had been given to protecting civil rights, according to the newspaper, but not to protecting America from subversion. President French, after reviewing a recording of the institute's proceedings and reading the scripts, defended Professor C. O. Johnson, the college's principal participant as having been scrupulously impartial and scholarly in discussing international politics. French went beyond the bounds of the institute, moreover, to point out that the college was a sounding board for all points of view, not committed to one.[67]

Extremists, such as communist speakers, remained an impediment to the hope of making the State college a universal sounding board. In 1959, for example, a Mr. Jacek Machowski asked for an opportunity to speak on the campus, thereby presenting a unique challenge to the Regents' 1948 rule denying a public platform to Communist speakers. The rule had in the past always seemed unambiguous, but Machowski was not a candidate for office or even a member of the American Communist Party. He was, instead, an official of the Permanent Mission of Poland to the United Nations. Since some interest existed in permitting him to speak, the Board of Regents modified its rule so that, by implication, it would not cover United Nations officials. There is not, however, any evidence that Machowski came to the State College.[68]

Gus Hall, the well-traveled secretary and presidential candidate of the American Communist Party, presented a more serious challenge to the 1948 rule when, in early 1962, he sought an opportunity to speak on the campus. The Board of Control, the undergraduate assembly, suddenly entered the political arena, debating the advisability of modifying the rule. By a vote of 7 to 4, the student representatives requested that the Board of Regents take a more liberal view regarding speakers, permitting all to come who might contribute to the education of students. Three student leaders, headed by Timothy Manring, stated their case to the Regents on May 1, 1962. Although Mrs. Frances P. Owen expressed a willingness to consider a change, William N. Goodwin, the President of the Board, joined French in opposing any alteration, their view prevailing. On a later occasion, in 1964, the Regents once again reviewed their established policy without making a change.[69]

Earlier in this chapter, satisfying faculty salary advances were discussed as evidence of successes achieved by the French administration. Those advances need to be judged against a report of 1952 which revealed that gains had come only after steady declines in purchasing power since 1939, an average of thirteen percent at all ranks. Deans and directors had suffered the most, experiencing a decline of thirty-two percent while professors' purchasing power had fallen nineteen percent. Associate and assistant professors suffered less while instructors had, by 1952, achieved a one percent gain.[70]

It was obvious that more than the stated salary increases would be required in order to improve morale and create a sense of security necessary for improved productivity in teaching and research. Further advances in salaries would be needed, the chairman of the Department of Business Administration, insisted, in June, 1952, if heavy losses of his staff to more lucrative employment in business and government were to be avoided. That was a familiar cry, heard more and more on the campus. On August 6, 1956, for example, Dean Stephenson reported a number of faculty resignations which revealed strong competition for professors from other colleges as well as business and government. His immediate solution? It was to increase faculty salaries by twenty percent as soon as possible.[71]

In response to another "imperative," in 1957, President French raised the compensation of professors for service as department chairmen from a flat $300 per year to as much as one full month of extra pay. For the faculty as a whole, a revision of the retirement system, effected in 1955, permitted members of TIAA and the Aetna retirement programs to join the Federal Old Age and Survivors System as well.[72]

Consideration of improved faculty morale did not invariably spring from monetary considerations, as staff on annual appointment (eleven months) might suggest. The requirement that they work half-days on Saturdays came to an end through President French's order, issued on September, 16, 1953. They would, henceforth, work the same weekly schedule as academic year appointees. When, a year later, the college announced its intention to get out of the real estate business it meant, among other things, that the rental of cheap, wartime demountable housing to staff and faculty would be discontinued after another year. Paternalism of that sort would be transferred from faculty to students, who might now occupy the vacated inexpensive housing, except that new faculty might utilize such dwellings for a year while making plans for permanent homes.[73]

The State College continued to be a tightly-knit campus, offering the advantages and draw-backs of close quarters in a small town, surrounded by vast wheat fields. In fact, a study submitted to President French in September 1964, noted that Washington State University had a 31.3 percent of its students housed in "college operated residence halls," making it the fourth largest among a selected list of Midwestern and Pacific Coast residence institutions. The University of Washington, by contrast, fell below the first ten institutions, since it had but 9.2 percent of its students in university-owned housing.[74]

The relatively closed community in Pullman still offered opportunities for the faculty and administration to focus their concerns on student behavior, despite a growing permissiveness in society. This concern might take the form of an overbearing solicitude of a celebrity's children, such as the time President French promised Bing Crosby that the singer's twin sons would be looked after on campus as the president would look after his own student son. Sometimes, concern for students followed on the heels of a tragic accident, such

The relatively closed community in Pullman still offered opportunities for the faculty and administration to focus their concerns on student behavior, despite a growing permissiveness in society.

Until his death in 1969, Czechoslovakian-born artist and sculptor George A. Laisner spent nearly forty years as a member of the WSU faculty. Winner of the Governor's Arts Award in 1976, Laisner's work has been shown throughout the United States and in Japan. He inaugurated numerous courses in the graphic arts at the University including etching, lithography, silk screening, Styrofoam casting, welding, vitreous enameling, and techniques in wood and metal sculpture and glass blowing. (Washington State University News Service)

as the one that occurred on October 17, 1952, after a beer party in Moscow, when a car carrying seven students rolled over, killing one and injuring the others.

The inevitable question followed: "Is WSC a drinking school?" President French did not think it was, but called a closed-door conference of student leaders and administrators to discuss the subject. It produced no published report or plans. The *Evergreen* ran one editorial on the accident but offered no solutions. The writer thought it necessary only to admonish readers to "think a little" and practice caution—presumably while driving. A two-column picture of the smashed up vehicle did not inspire him or anyone else to take action. On the question of student behavior in general, J. D. Clevenger, Dean of Students, assured the faculty in 1953 that the great majority of those attending WSC were as "orderly and well-adjusted and seriously devoted to the object of gaining as much as possible from all the institution has to offer." The exception, less than one-half of one percent, were identified and disciplined—expelled, suspended, or placed on probation.[75]

Professor John D. Lillywhite, Chairman of the Discipline Committee (which had four faculty and four student members), was less sanguine than Clevenger about the dispensing of justice and its effect on the campus community. Lillywhite, a sociologist, concluded that "consensus is weak in the college community regarding a working code of acceptable conduct." As a result, reactions to his committee's decisions often varied from one extreme to the other. Some critics thought a particular judgment too harsh, while many others thought the decision too lenient. In discussing behavioral controls in living groups, Lillywhite found dormitories and sororities relatively satisfactory, but not fraternities. The differences he ascribed to the remoteness of faculty advisors from the daily life in Greek houses. Dormitories and sororities, on the other hand, received close supervision by house mothers and advisors.[76]

Lillywhite, who was leaving the Discipline Committee after a three-year term, proposed that the committee be given equal responsibility with the Dean of Students in seeking to create a more salutary atmosphere and a greater consensus for a code of behavior on campus. He had been frustrated because his committee could act only upon cases referred to it by the Dean of Students. Although French praised Lillywhite and the committee, he did not consider a larger role for the latter in shaping campus life.[77]

Once again in September 1954 Dean Clevenger, expressed confidence in student behavior. In response to faculty requests about the balance between studies and activities, Clevenger conducted his own survey of the student body. He concluded that eighty-six percent participated in extra-curricular activities, including student government, and that eighty-four percent found such activities satisfactory. Faculty reaction to the claim for such overwhelming approval of the activities might have been surprise, if not skepticism. On the basis of further questioning, Clevenger stated that the ratio between time spent on activities as opposed to studies (including classroom and laboratory time) was 1:7. No word is available on faculty reaction. It is clear, though, that the Dean of Students believed strongly in the value of organized activities. Regardless of the merit of student activities the faculty in general seemed to be less and less eager to serve in traditional supporting roles. such as serving as chaperones at student dances and parties. Professor Victor Dauer and Dean Clevenger, recognizing this flagging interest, wrote an open letter to the faculty in September 1955, appealing to professors to regard their role, not as that of the police force, but as patrons, encouraging students in their social life and taking every opportunity to become better acquainted with them.[78]

Not surprisingly, students seemed more concerned with collegial relations with fellow students than with currying favor with the faculty. An issue which made this feeling evident occurred in early 1959 when the Board of Control, the undergraduate student government, petitioned the Board of Regents to alter radically the traditional plan whereby men's dormitories had been located on the southern edge of the campus, separated from the women's living units on the northern edge. Student officers sought to break the isolation of the sexes by recommending that a 300-unit women's dormitory be built adjacent to Kruegal Hall, a men's dormitory, and a 600-unit men's hall be placed near the existing women's Regent Hill complex. Each dormitory would be exclusively male or female but new, attached dining and social rooms would be used by both sexes. Juxtaposition of dormitories and common usage of dining halls would, it was hoped, improve social relations and graces, especially for the men.[79]

Perhaps the most unrewarding of the difficult tasks President French faced shortly after taking office was that of administering competitive athletics. It seems likely that he had little, if any, experience along that line, since the greater part of his administrative career had been spent in a women's college.

The Board of Regents discussed the issue but in the end, vetoed the plan. From the Board's point of view alteration of the established order "was not in the best interests of the College. Students expressed unhappiness, one leader accused the Board of not offering even one rational argument for its position. Jim Gies, *Evergreen* editor, published an open letter suggesting that the seed had been planted for future change, and, indeed, students, he wrote, would engage in informal cooperative dining more frequently than formerly.[80] Tom Tiede, a colorful and controversial *Evergreen* columnist, had the last word. Asserting that the proposal's object had been "the betterment of the school," he lashed out sarcastically at the Board of Regents by offering his sympathy that they "lack the courage and foresight to [see] the benefits of co-educational dining." The administration had his "condolences" for "an apathetic stand on this most important student issue."[81]

Two years later, in 1961, Dean Clevenger recommended what, in essence, had been the students' plan to mingle men's and women's dormitories to provide for co-educational dining and social activities. He insisted that commingling would not only provide "increased opportunity for men-women friendships in a relaxed manner" but would also increase flexibility in the use of housing units, a matter close to the hearts of administrators. The Board, however, was not to be dissuaded from its position that commingling offered unwanted problems and reaffirmed its separatist policy.[82]

Then, in a bemused editorial on March 11, 1964, the *Evergreen's* editor revealed a breakdown in the Regents' resistance to change. Kruegal and McAllister halls were being changed from men's to women's residences to accommodate an overflow of women students. Student leaders had begged in vain for this transformation for five years, and now it was granted, not on philosophical grounds but because of sheer necessity. The final step in breaking way from the isolationist policy came on April 21, 1964, when the Board of Regents studied the schematic drawings for a $6,400,000 dormitory and dining room complex which purposely was being planned to integrate men's dormitories with those for women. The plans called for three dormitories and social-dining room structure which would be placed on the site of a parking lot west of Rogers Hall on the southern edge of the campus. They were ready for occupancy in the Fall of 1966 (later named Stephenson Complex).[83]

Perhaps the most unrewarding of the difficult tasks President French faced shortly after taking office was that of administering competitive athletics. It seems likely that he had little, if any, experience along that line, since the greater part of his administrative career had been spent in a women's college. But, sometime in 1952, Dean Golden Romeny of the School of Physical Education and Athletics, dropped an embarrassing problem in his lap. Of the approximately 110 athletes, employed in the legitimate work-aid program, a considerable number had been paid in part inappropriately from institutional funds rather than wholly from monies contributed by alumni and other supporting groups.[84]

Romney expressed the hope that the Pacific Coast Conference might change its rules to permit use of college funds. He feared that the State College simply would not be able to raise enough outside funds to remain competitive in recruiting athletes of high quality. French, however, refused to toy with unrealistic hopes. He immediately offered to the Conference an apology for misinterpreting the rules and pledged to correct the errors made. Evidently, the problem could not easily be corrected: much to French's chagrin the Executive Director of the conference again reprimanded the State College in 1954 for failure to correct its violations. French renewed his pledge and directed a new athletic director, Stan Bates, to clear up the matter immediately.[85]

In the midst of these difficulties with the Conference office, Dean Romney asserted to President French that the intercollegiate athletic program would be sound as long as it was administered economically. Washington State College, in his view, had always "been fringe school financially in the field of athletics and probably never will have large sums to spend." Fund-raising among private contributors was limited largely to Spokane and the Palouse area, a very modest base to provide for major competition. On the other hand, French reported that in the preceding nineteen years of sports scheduling, the State College showed profits in athletic income for nine years and losses for ten. Although troubling to French, at that time, such a report might have produced relative satisfaction for a president two decades later.[86]

French must have felt content when he viewed the women's athletic program. Intercollegiate competition was limited to occasional field days with other schools in which competitiveness took a secondary place to other satisfactions. To underscore the philosophy and goals of the women's program, Professor Helen G. Smith, the director, wrote to President French on December 28, 1953, opposing any thought that women's sports be included in a regular competitive program like that of the men. Emphasis, she asserted, should be upon health, good sportsmanship, safety, and enjoyment. French assured Professor Smith that he did not intend to change the program.[87]

There were moments in 1954 when French toyed with the idea of returning football to the students, as he reported to the board of Regents when sending its members a newspaper article, "Football for Students." He would like to see the Pacific Coast Conference play a complete round robin football schedule, he asserted. Other home games might be played with the College of Pacific, since it had equivalent entrance requirements to those of the Conference. French and fellow presidents of conference institutions voted 7-0 (the University of Washington absent) to affirm their "determination to go no further down the road to professionalism and, instead, to undertake definite and rigorous steps to reverse the unhealthy trends of recent years."[88]

Shortly after making idealistic statements French had to return to the tasks of keeping competition honest and ethical under existing

University Editor and Rhodes Scholar Henry Grosshans joined the WSC faculty in 1952. Among his many contributions to campus life, he taught in the Honors Program. Grosshans oversaw the Office of Publication and, beginning in the late fifties, expanded scholarly publishing activity of the WSU Press. He served as editor of Research Studies, *and was the author of numerous scholarly works, including:* To Find Something New, The Search For Europe, *and* Hitler and the Artists. *(Washington State University News Service)*

rules. Indeed, he had no rest, for at the Regents' meeting of May 19 and 20, 1954, he thrust before the Board a notification that the football game scheduled the next season with the University of Texas would be in jeopardy if the Cougars planned to play any Blacks. Nevertheless, neither French nor the Board seemed disturbed by the blatant racism expressed, as they argued from ignorance that little likelihood existed that the Cougars would not be an all white team.[89]

The two schools met in University of Texas Stadium, on October 2, in a game which was more interesting than was indicated by the lopsided score, which favored Texas 40-14. Duke Washington, a Black fullback from Pasco, not only started the game for the Cougars but played sensationally on offense and defense. In perhaps the biggest surprise, the Texas players and fans treated this first Black to play in the University of Texas stadium with fine sportsmanship. Assistant Coach Dale Gentry complimented the hosts for their behavior. When asked if the coaches had any doubts beforehand that Duke Washington would be permitted to play, Gentry said "We wouldn't keep our best player at home, would we?"[90]

Unfortunately, one game did not shatter racism in college athletics. The time had not yet arrived when authorities would deal directly with that issue. The problem that caught the attention of college officials in the middle of the 1950s was the greatly accentuated emphasis on recruiting athletes, a competition which produced a myriad of violations of the conference code of conduct. To combat recruiting practice violations, the Pacific Coast Conference, cheered on by French, raised scholarly requirements for athletic participation and transfer requirements for junior college students, among other restrictions. Four institutions—the University of Washington, University of California, University of California at Los Angeles, and the University of Southern California—suffered heavy penalties for violation of the code. In turn, they proceeded to destroy the Pacific Coast Conference in 1958, replacing it later with a five member (Stanford added) Athletic Association of Western Universities.[91]

Washington State College, an innocent by-stander, suffered financially and in terms of high-level competition, for its exclusion from the conference, along with the University of Oregon and Oregon State College. Specifically, the University of California at Los Angeles and the University of Southern California cancelled their 1958 games with the Cougars, precipitating a serious budgetary problem. Then in 1962, the new Athletic Association of Western Universities invited the now renamed Washington State University to join its ranks. The school came into the new organization not as an unwanted orphan but as an entity needed to give credibility to it. The "fathers" of the Big Five, as the press called the new conference, had learned that the National Collegiate Athletic Association would not recognize a conference with fewer than six members. When, subsequently, the two Oregon institutions joined the Big Six, only the University of Idaho remained excluded by the violent breakup of the Pacific Coast Conference.[92]

From the standpoint of the athlete, his coaches, the student body, and the public, membership in a conference provided a better caliber of sports competition than otherwise would have been available. For the administration, it meant, in addition, that the school would receive a lucrative share of receipts of the Rose Bowl football game as a member of the conference which "owned" the game. In the final analysis, conference affiliation (now the PAC-10) in the 1960s precluded the possibility of turning back to the days of Simon-pure amateurism. Those days had first been somewhat compromised by work-aid programs which were restricted to athletes as athletes and not as students, enabling them to earn subsistence for extra-curricular rather than curricular matters. Those programs, over time, had proven to be unrealistic at Washington State University, as well as elsewhere. The work often proved of little value, especially when measured against an athlete's need for study time. The work, unfortunately, sometimes proved fraudulent, an example the institution hardly should have been perpetrating upon its youth.[93]

It was evident by 1964 that all conference members had recognized the inadequacies of their work-aid programs and had ventured a few steps beyond work relief. On August 27, 1964, Professor Wallis Beasley, the Washington State University Faculty Representative to the Athletic Association of Western Universities, and two men from other campuses, reported that all of the universities had instituted non-service scholarships for athletes. Though Conference officials quaintly dubbed them "Rhodes-type" scholarships, the press and public soon recognized them as what would later be called "free rides." They may have been the best means of combining sports and studies in the minds of the conference leaders, coaches, administrators, and the public (not to mention the athletes themselves), but they clearly marked a path toward professionalism.[94]

Men's intercollegiate athletics had attained a kind of "sacred cow" status in French's administration, if not before, Few openly challenged the relevance of spectator sports to higher education. Military training, a second men's activity, had from the beginning of the institution enjoyed a similar untouchable status, but for different reasons. The Morrill Act of 1862, approved by Congress in the midst of the Civil War, bore the marks of that conflict and determination to save the Union. In a laconic statement of authorized lines of study, the law included the words ". . . and including military tactics." That statement held no further explanation nor was one needed in the war atmosphere in which the law was debated. The land-grant college had been given the twin tasks of educating the industrial masses and protecting their nation with a civilian, nonprofessional army.[95]

President Bryan had strongly embraced the notion that military training for male students properly supported his objective of creating a "people's university." Neither he nor his successors—at the president's or other levels—recognized that the mandate for compulsory training, developed over the years, had only a specific

E. O. Holland Library in the mid-1950s. (Washington State University News Service)

state legal authorization. A myth that a federal law also required compulsory training of all lower division students grew to the point at which, in 1925, the college catalog carried such a false statement. Correction did not come until 1933, at which time the catalog reported that only the State of Washington mandated compulsory training. Myths die hard, however, and the prestige of a federal injunction discouraged questioning the relevance of military training in the university.[96]

By 1917, the program had been divided into basic and advanced training, each of two years duration. All freshmen and sophomore men, not incapacitated, who had not served for a substantial period in a military service, took basic drill and attended strategy and tactics lectures. Thereafter, students seeking officer's commissions for active duty or the reserve, enrolled in advanced military studies. The subsistence received for campus training and summer camp constituted one of the early steps taken toward the professional career as a soldier.[97]

More than a decade after the World War II, in 1957, the Departments of the Army and the Air Force declared that elementary military training in colleges no longer served any useful purpose. Neither students nor faculty offered serious opposition, but the administration moved slowly to abandon the program. The Board of Regents finally petitioned the 1961 legislature to eliminate compulsory training, while retaining voluntary programs. The state legislature responded favorably, removing compulsion and decreeing that an elective program be carried on. The era of massed freshmen and sophomore students parading on athletic fields would be no more, to be replaced by a small coterie of students planning military careers.[98]

When French reviewed the elective program in 1965, almost five years later, he found morale among students and military instructors high, quotas of candidates full, and a general sense of satisfaction prevalent. A report in 1969 on army and air force commissioning of WSU cadets must have pleased him immensely. The army had commissioned 1,411 regular and reserve officers between 1931-1969, excluding the war decade, for which figures are not available. The air force had produced 742 officers since 1951. The University currently easily met annual quotas of candidates—twenty-five for the army and fifteen for the air force.[99]

Important questions remained to be resolved before the future of the program might be assured. Student protestors against the war in Vietnam and racism directed their criticism against ROTC programs across the nation. Not surprisingly, local protesters demanded removal of military training in any form from the Washington State University campus. The question arose in committee circles and faculty meetings. Abolition remained a goal not attained, however, for in a direct consideration of the question, the Resident Instructional Staff voted 212 to eighty-nine against that objective.[100]

Faculty debate generally turned on the question as to whether military programs and curricula were of sufficiently scholarly quality to rank with the regular academic programs. After some study, the Educational Policies Committee proposed that academic credit be continued for most courses but that none be granted for military drill or for the two-week summer camp. The committee and the Resident Instructional Staff approved the resolution, the latter on March 19, 1970. The military programs then had sufficient guarantee that they might remain on campus as desired by higher authorities.[101] The new, elective programs turned the college away from minimal military training of the people for the defense of their rights toward preparing highly specialized career officers. The army and air force began that preparation by signing a contract with each candidate, placing each in a reserve force, and granting financial aid and scholarships for the military training and future military service. The results were salutary in training officers but once again reveal that the land-grant university of Enoch A. Bryan was changing its ways to meet the needs and demands of a changing society.[102]

More than a decade after World War II, in 1957, the Departments of the Army and the Air Force declared that elementary military training in colleges no longer served any useful purpose. Neither students nor faculty offered serious opposition, but the administration moved slowly to abandon the program.

*C*hapter Seven

From French To Terrell: The Explosion of Knowledge and Student Activism

When, in 1954, a faculty member suggested renaming the State College as Washington State University, President C. Clement French merely responded by stating that he had no recommendation for such an action "at this time." Four years later, the Board of Regents only expressed "interest" in similar proposal by a state senator who suggested that he might seek a name change in the next legislative session. Professor Emmett L. Avery, Chairman of the Faculty Executive Committee, on the other hand, saw the name-change issue as a matter of some urgency and proceeded to write letters to numerous legislators in Olympia, encouraging them to support a name change. He pointed out cogently that for some time the institution had been a university in fact if not in name. He need not have concerned himself about the outcome, as once the name change bill went before the legislature, the issue was never in doubt. Even the University of Washington threw its support behind the idea. The title "Washington State University" went into effect on September 1, 1959, having met no opposition in the legislature.[1]

Avery's characterization of the State College as a *de facto* university might have seemed trite to many faculty and administrators, for they were accustomed to thinking of the Pullman institution as a university. To most interested observers, universities were combinations of undergraduate college programs and courses of graduate study, comprehensive teaching and research institutions offering degrees ranging from bachelors to doctorates of philosophy in various subjects. Actually, from the point of view of symbolism and prestige, the timing of the institutional name change was propitious. Washington State University, had not yet taken full advantage of the possibilities of the postwar world, but it had begun to respond to the explosion of knowledge and to seek new financial resources that were available. Administrators and faculty, in other words, had entered the highly competitive search for a means to fund new

OPPOSITE: *Thompson Hall, completed in 1894, served as Washington State University's administration building until 1968.* (Washington State University News Service)

One of the first important steps taken to improve and enlarge research capabilities at the institution came in September 1953, when Dean S. Town Stephenson and a dozen science colleagues undertook planning to acquire a low grade nuclear reactor for research.

curricula and research. Under these circumstances, to continue using the title "college," which implied the absence of graduate study, would have been a misrepresentation of the school's overall program and probably a psychological and financial handicap as well.

One of the first important steps taken to improve and enlarge research capabilities at the institution came in September 1953, when Dean S. Town Stephenson and a dozen science colleagues undertook planning to acquire a low grade nuclear reactor for research. They were successful, obtaining a $300,000 grant to construct a building to hold a swimming pool type reactor. The building and an enhanced scientific research capability became a reality in 1957 when the Atomic Energy Commission granted $105,000 to purchase the equipment.[2]

On March 9, 1961, the reactor went "on line," completing its first chain reaction. It was then the fifth reactor of its size in the nation. Others in its class were located at North Carolina State University, Massachusetts Institute of Technology, University of Michigan, and Pennsylvania State University. Its primary use has been in "neutron activation" for research projects in many fields of physical and biological science. By September of 1963, the reactor was being used by eight classes, thirty graduate students, and forty faculty members.[3]

In recent years the great promise of the nuclear reactor as an aid to research at Washington State University and as a magnet to researchers who might bring their work to Pullman, has faded. Such a decline in interest has been experienced elsewhere, too. The expense of operating the equipment more and more became a university responsibility. When outside funds for research fell off, the staff, once numbering five professors, dwindled in size. The effect was to drive away outside research and raise serious questions about the future of the operation. Nevertheless, the reactor (a part of the Nuclear Radiation Center since 1969) remains an important means of conducting student and faculty research.[4]

Superior graduate education and research required more than "state-of-the-art" apparatus. Dean Stewart E. Hazlet of the Graduate School believed that better and more extensive foreign language training was needed if communication with foreign scientists, scholars, and artists was to be of the greatest usefulness and if Americans were to be able to read the journals appropriate to their fields. Thus, on May 19, 1960, he introduced a motion in the meeting of the Resident Instructional Staff (the teaching faculty) to modify the foreign language requirement for doctor of philosophy candidates. Traditionally, such students had been required to qualify in two modern foreign languages at moderate level of competence. Experience had taught, however, that many successful candidates actually had a poor ability to communicate in foreign tongues.

Hazlett, undoubtedly with the support of the Graduate Studies Committee, called for an alternative plan whereby candidates might choose to qualify in only one language, but at a higher level of competence than formerly. To add to the attractiveness of the proposal, he offered an alternative whereby students might substitute an upper division literature course in a foreign language for the test provided they receive a B grade or better. The Resident Instructional Staff adopted Hazlett's proposals after some debate. This amendment represented almost the last effort of the traditionalists to compel all doctoral candidates to become truly fluent in a foreign language for research purposes. The future promised that mathematics, statistics, and other non-verbal "tools" would supersede foreign languages.[5]

Of course, entrance requirements to graduate school also met the critical eye of the dean and his committee. On December 15, 1960, the new graduate dean, Donald S. Farner, proposed that the category of provisional students be sharply narrowed as a means of raising standards of performance. Farner argued that no students should be admitted to graduate school with less than a B minus (2.75) grade point average. . Up to this time, any applicant possessing a C (2.00) average in previous work might be admitted as a provisional student. The Resident Instructional Staff adopted Farner's amendments, which left intact the B (3.00) average for regular admission to graduate school. Provisionals would, also, be required to produce B-average work before full admission to graduate studies.[6]

Further improvement in graduate studies required the opening of new research fields for doctoral studies. The humanities, in particular, lacked a broad program, except for the Ph.D. degree program in History, a quasi-humanistic, quasi-social science discipline. Indeed, the History degree had been in effect for many years, but in 1960 it still was limited to a few areas of study.

While it was evident that the Department of History would be able to provide a broader Ph.D. offering within its own discipline in a few years as a result of the influx of new and more diversified faculty, it sought new outlets for graduate study. In this search, historians were joined by the Department of English, which had not yet developed advanced graduate studies. The two departments drew up a proposal for an interdisciplinary program in the new field of American Studies. When the proposal arrived at the Regents meeting on May 29, 1961 that body immediately adopted it, effective with the 1961-1962 academic year. It was the first doctoral program in American Studies to be instituted in the Pacific Northwest and, in 1975, was one of only six west of the Mississippi. Later, master's and bachelor's programs were added.[7]

The program offered neither a new philosophy nor new methodology, according to a statement of 1970-1971, but students embarking on the course of study were described as "free to seek assistance through theory classes and seminars in all the relevant disciplines." Presumably, all the humanities and social sciences were included. The object, however, involved more than merely exposing students to vagrant influences they might pick up in a random sort of way. Studies for this degree were to illumine American life by viewing it from new perspectives, historical, critical, and literary. Centrifugal or anarchic forces unleashed by broad

•

While it was evident that the Department of History would be able to provide a broader Ph.D. offering within its own discipline in a few years as a result of the influx of new and more diversified faculty, it sought new outlets for graduate study. In this search, historians were joined by the Department of English, which had not yet developed advanced graduate studies.

•

searching were to be overcome by inter-disciplinary seminars and a heavy concentration on intellectual and cultural subjects found in both in history and literature.[8]

The graduate program flourished almost immediately, greatly stimulated by the award of a number of National Defense Education Act Fellowships to outstanding candidates. In 1969, for instance, fourteen doctoral candidates had just finished dissertations or were on the verge of doing so. Today, the program remains in the domain of the English and History departments although for many years students in Speech have participated. The current enrollment (fall 1989) of thirty-four graduate students testifies to the value of the program, which has produced professors of English, History, and American Studies, as well as professionals in the field of publishing.

The need to increase laboratory, classroom, and library resources for graduate students and faculty that accompanied the change in status from college to university exceeded anything that might have been made available from the state or outside funding. The University of Idaho, only eight miles away, faced similar problems as it tried to expand its own research and graduate programs in the 1960s. Each institution, however, possessed resources in certain fields that were clearly superior to those of the other school. Each, too, had been confronted the problem of small enrollments in some classes, which made instruction an expensive proposition. Might each share its areas of expertise with the other? Cooperation across state lines to share resources had never been tried, perhaps due to inertia or to imagined insurmountable legal and financial difficulties.[9]

In December 1961, the deans of the graduate schools at the two institutions proposed cooperation on a limited scale. A few graduate courses at each university were opened to enrollment by students from the other without the payment of extra fees and with the an informal registration scheme. The only serious accounting problem was long-range: over time, the authorities expected that the total number of graduate students involved in cooperation would roughly balance. As early as 1963, authorities judged the interinstitutional plan a success. Dean S. Town Stephenson reported to the Board of Regents in Pullman that the cooperation with Idaho "was providing adequate graduate courses at less cost."[10]

Unfortunately, such cooperation could not satisfy Washington State University's fundamental need in the field of engineering. The national agenda in the early sixties mandated the rapid development and expansion of engineering research in all fields, a burden Washington State University shared with many institutions of higher learning. Traditionally, the University's College of Engineering had so emphasized undergraduate training that graduate studies attracted relatively few teachers or resources. Nevertheless, the university began to meet its obligations in this area when, on January 21, 1964, the Board of Regents authorized the granting of the degree of Ph.D. in Engineering Science.[11]

Two years later, an engineers' study council reported to President Terrell that development of the doctoral program was slow and unpromising. That program had been thoughtfully constructed with a college-wide curriculum because no single engineering department—mechanical or electrical—had the resources, faculty, or experience needed to provide a high-level degree. The difficulties were serious. No set of criteria had been established for a course of study, a matter baffling to graduate students preparing for examinations preliminary to candidacy for the degree. The various departments could not agree on foreign language requirements, suggesting that a host of heterogeneous and diverse special interests divided them. Furthermore, insufficient resources prevented the development of new courses needed to lend coherence to the program. Fortunately, the pure sciences provided a strong undergirding for basic courses, if not for the specialized studies. Many of the difficulties encountered early gave way with experience and the coherent mobilizing of human and physical resources, which made possible specialized doctoral programs in several of the engineering fields.[12]

A number of scientists served notice in January 1965, that they intended to seek elevation for Washington State University to the top circle of graduate schools when they applied to the National Science Foundation for a University Science Development Program. With this federal support they hoped to raise the University to excellence in fields such as biochemistry, biophysics, environmental biology, chemical physics, and continuum mechanics. These scientists also named in their request certain support programs in genetics, information science, and core biology.[13]

A review team evaluated the University in June but the National Science Foundation postponed a decision until some time in 1966, pending receipt of a self study by the science faculty that answered questions posed by the inspectors. WSU scientists expressed a great deal of confidence in their ability to attract students at all university levels. They reported, for example, the presence of twenty two undergraduate majors and thirteen predoctoral students in biochemistry, in addition to five post doctoral fellows. The faculty also offered a long bibliography of its research publications as proof of the university's fitness for the development program.[14]

The environmental biologists noted an fifty percent increase in new courses in the preceding two years, as well as twenty percent increase in applicants for teaching and research assistantships. The presence of the nuclear reactor, of novel computing equipment, and of a recently developed water research center, together with the Ph.D. program in Engineering Science, also were noted as strengthening the science program.[15] The self-study called attention to the vigor of the university and its initiative as it was expressed in other ways. Notably, they reported that the construction program included new facilities that would serve the animal and physical sciences.[16]

Most impressive, the scientists also recognized that a university could not operate without adequate attention to the liberal arts and humanities, and so also mentioned non-science structures being

The Honors program instituted in 1960, placed Washington State University in an exclusive circle occupied by only a few state universities, according to the scientists' self study. Students admitted to Honors had to complete a strong, integrated curriculum, with a nucleus of core courses.

built. These included the Kimbrough Music Building (recently finished), an enlarged student union, a co-educational gymnasium, and a fine arts structure. Due note was taken of an addition to the education building, a new administration building (French Administration Building but familiarly called "Fort-French"), and Johnson Tower, constructed for the social and behavioral sciences. Pride in the university may have been uppermost in listing these non-science installations but discussion of the Honors Program represented a serious attention to the need for improved teaching across the campus, at least for an elite portion of the student body.[17]

The Honors program instituted in 1960, placed Washington State University in an exclusive circle occupied by only a few state universities, according to the scientists' self study. Students admitted to Honors had to complete a strong, integrated curriculum, with a nucleus of core courses. The program also required independent study and undergraduate research. Only the top ten percent of freshmen were eligible, but the first year seventy-two enrolled. In 1965-1966 some 417 studied under the program and authorities confidently expected 700 or more by 1970. This nucleus of undergraduates, nourished by special courses, an honors center, abundant counseling, and encouragement, suggested that the university might, indeed, support excellence in all fields.[18]

The scientists' high hopes for a comprehensive Science Development Program were dashed when the National Science Foundation did not fund their proposal. They did achieve a highly valued counterpart however, when the Foundation suggested that the University apply for a departmental grant for chemistry. Dr. Harold Dodgen responded in 1967 by seeking $708,842, that would enable chemistry and physics professors to expand research in the critical and highly specialized, interdisciplinary field of chemical physics. He received the grant though the sum was reduced to $550,000. The award allowed Washington State University to take a giant step forward, not only in the two departments directly involved, but in all the biological and physical sciences.[19]

President Terrell, who took office on July 1, 1967, did not wait long before ordering a general evaluation of the university's entire program. He informed the Regents less than four months later, on October 20, that he intended to establish a dozen or more study councils representing major curricula and services in order to plan for the future. The councils, each made up of fifteen to twenty members, students and faculty alike, set to work evaluating goals and performance and recommending future plans. The reports, rendered to the president in June, 1968, represent the broadest self study undertaken since the recommendations of the Committee of Forty in the Compton Administration. They also contain materials for a current history of the institution. Often they are candid and generally more useful than latter-day recollections.[20]

The study council for the biological sciences expressed a strong sense of urgency in a resumé of its report of May 28, 1968. Its members stated "that the biological sciences at Washington State

University are poised in the balance between mediocrity and excellence, and can be moved easily to either class by decisions now to be made." Emotionalism arose, perhaps in part, from the realization that the fortunes of their disciplines affected the condition of numerous allied science programs and even contributed to the work of the social sciences, particularly psychology and anthropology. Quantitatively, they bore a heavy burden, too, in their contribution to the University's prestige for they had awarded one-third of all its doctorates since 1950.[21]

A report for the American Council on Education, the Cartter Report, published in 1966, heightened awareness that the biological sciences at WSU stood only midway on the slippery precipice of graduate education. Four areas in the biological sciences—bacteriology and microbiology, botany, entomology, and zoology—were graded as having "acceptable plus" programs, a rating also given to chemistry. In judging faculties, sociology and psychology were added to the list of five departments, and all received either a "good" or "adequate plus" rating. None of these rankings placed WSU programs at the top circle of their fields.

Whatever the value of the Cartter Report to contemporaries, it also suggests that the biological sciences dominated graduate study at Washington State University in the 1960s. Nevertheless, it should be noted that the modern biological sciences were not far removed from their infancy. In 1957, the modern era for that discipline began when the Regents approved the granting of the Ph.D. degree in genetics, a giant step forward in interdisciplinary work. Laboratories for electron microscope use and for molecular biophysics followed in 1962, promising means for unveiling important scientific discoveries.[22]

There was a general awareness that traditional disciplinary boundaries were rapidly breaking down. Genetics proved to be only one of many special programs that breached traditional boundaries and established new areas of scientific inquiry. In fact, the evolution of genetics marked only an early milepost along the road to more sophisticated research which allowed sciences in general to take full advantage of interdisciplinary alliances As the biological science report stated, somewhat pompously yet with full appreciation for innovation and tradition, the faculty had become dissatisfied with "sequestration and duplication of facilities and curricula by traditional departments," and so opted for interdisciplinary organization and processes. The council did not think of these innovations as permanent but rather "interim solutions that are symptomatic not only of the tides of science, but also of the fact that established alignments and academic structures are not readily changed."[23]

Six members of the study council dissented from the majority on one major point—teaching. This group, made up of two professors and four students, argued that the majority report had not dealt with the need to revise an administrative policy whereby those identified primarily as teachers might be given a major role in making policy. Such participation was needed, it was argued, to avoid errors such

*Glenn Terrell, seventh president of
Washington State University.*
(Washington State University News
Service)

as the assumption by the majority that if research were properly handled teaching would take care of itself. Though research might prove valuable for instruction, they conceded, the majority's oversimplification of the matter did a great disservice in their view. Poor teaching, its members believed, was an obvious cause of the small number of undergraduate majors in biology. Unfortunately, the minority report contained no solution to the problem.[24]

The Physical Science Study Council produced only a thin report in June 1968, but left clear impressions of the graduate and undergraduate studies and research programs. Foremost in the council's document was a discussion of the university's nuclear reactor and its significance as a research tool. Much of their description of the reactor's uses has been discussed above. Of special interest here is the report that "Washington State University was one of the first universities to utilize radioisotopes in research and teaching. Radioactive phosphorus was used here as a tracer in biological research studies prior to 1940." The council also noted a growing demand for nuclear education, to which Washington State University had responded by developing eleven nuclear courses, with the expectation that more would soon be added. There seem, in 1968, to have been a confidence that this university would play a major role in supplying nuclear engineers and scientists and that the cynosure of all eyes and attention would remain on the nuclear reactor and its uses in research, a matter for questioning at a later date, as has been discussed above.[25]

Many of these 1968 reports reveal that individual departments in the physical sciences spent a great deal of their time and effort teaching service courses for students in other majors and lower division students seeking to satisfy general university graduate requirements. Chemists claimed that their department instructed 2000 students, only five percent of whom were majoring in chemistry. Physicists reported that undergraduate majors fell far short of students enrolling simply for auxiliary courses to satisfy the general university graduation requirements. In fact, the physicists took a certain pride in the matter, claiming that "physics has come to be more widely recognized as an essential foundation of the sciences and humanities than it used to be. Requests come from such diverse groups as Home Economics, Music, and the Biological Sciences for elementary Physics courses suited to their majors." The geologists, too, reported serving more courses to non-majors than undergraduate majors in their field. They expressed general satisfaction with their undergraduate program but admitted that graduate study and faculty research fell short of expectation, due to smallness of the staff, lack of space, and inadequate funding.[26]

Indeed, only the chemists, among the physical scientists expressed much confidence about their graduate program. Such an attitude, of course, stemmed from the development biochemistry and chemical physics, discussed above. As a matter of fact, the chemists revealed an overweening confidence when they advocated creation of Graduate School of the Natural Sciences with its own regulations, distinct from the humanities, social sciences, and presumably, the professional schools. To carry the issue one step further, the chemists argued that no "outside person" should sit on a chemistry thesis committee. Such developments never came about, perhaps because interdisciplinary methods increasingly came to dominate all lines of scientific investigation.[27]

Social scientists gathered in council, expressed general satisfaction with the condition of their disciplines. In the wake of World War II, the Civil Rights Movement, and Sputnik, the social sciences "experienced one of the fastest growth rates in the University and in student enrollments," the members reported. They reminded their readers that the Division of Social Sciences possessed six doctoral programs. Those in History, Psychology, and Sociology had been in operation long enough to be well established, even if they had not turned out a great many doctors. In addition, three relatively new doctoral programs in American Studies, Anthropology, and Political Science seemed promising. New facilities such as the Laboratory of Anthropology, the Division of Governmental Studies and Services, and a new Police Science court room gave indications that research opportunities were constantly being increased. Furthermore, a large segment of the Division of Social Sciences found itself under one roof when the Johnson Tower (named for Professor Claudius O. Johnson), opened in the fall of 1966.[28]

Perhaps the Department of Psychology benefitted most from occupancy in this new wing of Todd Hall. Certainly, that department had a long history of being scattered at odd places about campus, housed in improbable structures, sometimes remodelled by ingenious psychology professors themselves. After a long service to teacher training, in 1946-1947 the Regents established a full-fledged department of psychology, but left it (and the Department of Education) occupying an old U.S. Navy dispensary building brought from the Farragut, Idaho, Naval Station after World War II.

The Department of Education moved out in 1962 to its new Cleveland Hall facility, but Psychology remained in the antiquated structure until 1966, professors and students treading its uneven floors and utilizing its beaten-up chairs and tables. Soon, the building's nooks, crannies, and hallways came to house a plethora of research specimens, such as turtles, meal worms, and salmon, together with photographic equipment and space for human research. Over the years, research came to occupy the old post office building, notably with an experimental vision tunnel. In addition, a salvaged trailer was used for large animal studies. Research was carried on wherever a vacant laboratory could be borrowed. Indeed, undergraduate courses which included laboratory work ordinarily had to be held to sixteen or fewer students, due to limited experimental space.

The Johnson Tower opening changed all that. Most researchers in the department moved into this new, spacious and well-equipped wing of Todd Hall, except for those involved in primate research, for whom a new building was opened on the eastern edge of the

•

Social scientists gathered in council, expressed general satisfaction with the condition of their disciplines. In the wake of World War II, the Civil Rights Movement, and Sputnik, the social sciences "experienced one of the fastest growth rates in the University and in student enrollments," the members reported.

•

campus. It is not surprising that significant enhancements to the doctoral level could be made once the new buildings were occupied, since faculty caliber matched apparatus and space. It should be noted, however that degrees in experimental psychology date from 1952 and the program in clinical psychology became important after Dr. Clare Thompson arrived in 1958.[29]

The Social Science Division included not only Psychology, Anthropology, History, and Sociology, but Police Science, Political Science, and Nursing Education as well. Economics and Geography were missing from this group, due more to historical circumstance than any philosophy or logic. The Division handled approximately eighteen percent of the University's teaching load, its enrollment growing in direct proportion to the growth of the study body. The authors of the Study Council report remarked that: "in summary, the social sciences are rapidly growing. Graduate programs and research activities are expanding." Then followed a remark universally found in academic reports. They wrote that further development required: "additional resources in faculty, finances, physical space, and other support areas will be needed."[30]

The Social Sciences Study Council did not take a complacent attitude when considering undergraduate education. A people's university the council reported, had an obligation to assist students to cope with personal and social problems and goals while also searching impartially for truth. As the council understood the matter, students increasingly sought solutions to present problems, basing their decisions on historical perspective and careful social analysis. Faculty members on the Council, and perhaps generally in the social sciences, viewed student attitudes somewhat skeptically, but with a resolve to pursue student demands vigorously. They concluded that student demand for improved teaching quality "may be . . . quixotic. . . but it would be a mistake if educators regard it as completely so."[31]

Skeptics may have retreated at least momentarily when the Council repeated a traditional article of faith that "the social sciences are in a unique and to some extent privileged position to provide some answers." Vice-President Wallis Beasley, studying the same issues, and perhaps the exact words of the Council, drew the problems encountered by students and education in general into sharper focus. He noted that integration might provide "an intellectual focus of a liberal education rather than a detailed specialization, and may provide the coherent undergraduate education demanded by the contemporary student."[32]

As an illustration of a pressing social problem and a social scientific approach to it, the Study Council suggested that an entire bachelor's degree program in race relations be established. Anthropologists, the group envisioned, would present "the idea of race and genetic implications." Sociologists might offer consideration of the nature of "the Negro communities." Other social scientists might present the Negro in politics, his psychology, and so forth. This comprehensive and scholarly approach to race relations was swept off the boards within a few months as student unrest erupted around the nation and, finally, on the Pullman campus. Student demands had been misread as being purely intellectual. Now students reacted aggressively and sometimes violently in opposition to war and racial prejudice (discussed below), demanding immediate and simplistic solutions to festering social problems and fears. Integration became a matter of civil rights, equality, and politics rather than leisurely study and impartial analysis.[33]

On another issue, the advocacy of more foreign languages in the curriculum, the Social Sciences Study Council provided decisive opinions. It called for the introduction of Japanese and Chinese, one to be offered immediately, and the second when "practicable." These tongues would strengthen the Asian Studies already being offered. Such language courses, the council insisted, were as necessary in the social sciences as mathematics was to a host of scientific and technical disciplines. In this matter, several departments individually endorsed the proposal, including the Department of Foreign Languages.[34]

Nevertheless, Dr. Tolbert H. Kennedy, Senior Dean of the College of Sciences and Arts, refused to support the proposal, claiming that one professor had swayed his colleagues in the social sciences and humanities to support the proposal. Kennedy, furthermore, expressed serious doubts that offering Japanese and Chinese would cause them to flourish, a claim made by the Department of Foreign Languages. Nevertheless, the two languages appeared in the WSU Catalog four years later, though hardly with generous support, for only two years of Chinese were offered and one year of Japanese.[35]

The Humanities Study Council agreed with Dean Kennedy's opinion that among Pacific Coast institutions the study of foreign languages had not flourished. Indeed, the Council pointed out that at Washington State University the foreign language requirement for graduation in the College of Sciences and Arts—the remainder of the University having one—was "grossly inadequate," a source of embarrassment. Council members resurrected the Beckett Report of 1964 in which a faculty committee had investigated statistics compiled by the Modern Languages Association. The members concluded that "only seven major universities and colleges in the nation had graduation requirements as low as, or lower than, those of Washington State University. And four of those seven were in the State of Washington, namely W.S.U. and the three state colleges!" The Council recommended that additional Latin be introduced and that classes in Greek be made available in order to improve advanced studies in the humanities. None of this took place, however.[36]

The malaise in the University's humanities program was hardly limited to local attitudes and developments, however. The Council believed that since World War II scientific and technological fields had prospered at the expense of the humanities. Humanity had lost ground to the machine, the Council emphasized. The "sustaining vision" of the humanist, according to the report, was that "man" was "the maker—not the naked ape, but the unique, paradoxical

In 1964 Professor of Pharmacy V. N. Bhatia became head of WSU's four-year-old Honors Program. Under his guidance the Honors Program became noted for the high percentage of its graduates that continued on to graduate and professional school. (Washington State University News Service)

creature who makes poems and civilizations, pictures, languages, and wars, who makes himself into what he has become and who is abundantly capable of destroying himself."[37]

The Council acknowledged that humanities programs often failed to capture the essence of humanness described above. The curriculum at Washington State University dwelt too much on past works and suffered from fragmentation and a lack of coherence. Humanities departments, too, sometimes were internally divided by physical isolation or substandard or ill-adapted quarters. Morale seemed low, a matter expressed not only in the physical and related inadequacies discussed above, but because salaries seemed always to lag behind those of other areas.

The council members desired to exorcise "the myth of the dedicated humanist burning with the gem-like flame in his secluded cloister." Some turned to pathos, away from the fatigue of combatting myths to viewing rural Pullman with distaste, heaping unhappiness upon unhappiness. "The horizons of this University are rather severely limited for the humanist, and Pullman is a very parochial place. *Given a few, unrelieved years in Pullman, the humanist can, and does, become just as parochial as anyone else.*"[38]

If a few superior graduate programs had been present to engage their attention, perhaps the members of the Study Council and other humanists might have been less prone to self-defeating introspection. The first assistance along that line came in 1962 with the inaugural of the doctoral degree program in American Studies. Though not mentioned in the Humanities Study Council Report, this interdisciplinary program in American cultural development featured a combination of American history and literature and a partnership of the departments of English and History in administering it.[39]

The program became widely known at an early date since it was only the second American Studies doctoral program west of Iowa and Minnesota (The University of New Mexico had the other program) and received valuable support early in the form of attractive fellowships from the National Defense Education Act. The program, thus flourished from the start, graduating five doctors as early as 1968. The program received an additional recognition in 1981 when WICHE, the Western Interstate Commission for Higher Eduction, named it a regional higher education program for nine western states. Students from those states might matriculate in the program by paying only in-state fees. At the time, only three other Washington State University programs were in this distinguished list. By the late 1980s the WICHE list included seven local programs, but with only American Studies and one other program outside the sciences and engineering. Since the inauguration of American Studies, the English department has introduced a Ph.D. degree in English and, together with the Department of Foreign Languages and Literatures has offered a Doctorate of Philosophy in Literary Studies.[40]

Mathematicians approached self-study by sharing their platform with professors from other disciplines to a greater extent than was true among the other academic Study Councils. Five members out of the twelve were professors of Economics, Physics, Zoology, Electrical Engineering, and Agricultural Economics. Only four were mathematicians and the remaining three probably were students. This roster was a tribute to the service provided by mathematicians to a great variety of departments all over the campus. Minority representation on their own Council did not hamper the mathematicians, however, in expressing their views and venting frustrations. In sum, it became clear that mathematicians not only provided service and general education courses for a vast body of undergraduates, but also offered sophisticated classes for engineers, physical scientists, and statisticians, as well as lower level courses for other fields, including economics and psychology. In addition, they supplied remedial work to correct deficiencies in high school training.[41]

All of this service raised the level of frustration when the mathematicians sought time and energy for high level mathematics teaching and research. The report contains one paragraph teeming with aggravation. It begins as follows: "The problem of poor preparation is one of the most important and far reaching . . . we have encountered. Continued use of the mathematics department and, indeed, of other departments with very large service responsibilities to teach what should have been learned in high school cannot fail to reduce its effectiveness in teaching what must be learned in the university." Short range solutions which involved use of graduate teaching assistants and part-time or full-time instructors, did not offer a satisfactory resolution of the dilemma.[42]

From some quarter within the Department of Mathematics there arose a plan to establish "tenured lecturers," who could eschew advanced teaching and research to devote themselves wholly to service and remedial courses. The professorate, clearly distinguished from the lecturers, would teach upper division and graduate courses and devote a significant amount of time to the creation of new mathematics. This plan met with significant opposition within the Council, especially from the pen of Professor H. B. Knowles, physicist, who viewed the "tenured lectureship" as a "step backward." It would, in his view, have abridged academic freedom and, most damning of all, excuse such faculty from original research. He recommended the obvious: hire more promising mathematicians.[43]

The problem of teaching continued to be handled in the traditional manner, despite growing anxiety. Closely related to it was a conviction that the Doctor of Philosophy program failed to properly prepare instructors for all four year colleges and community colleges. The Ph.D. program required that students create new mathematics at the dissertation level and, of course, gave great attention to the more theoretical aspects of the discipline. The needs of the colleges were for teachers who would skillfully elucidate astandard mathematics. More attention, in other words, to teaching techniques and practices were needed than were provided in the Ph.D. program.

●

From some quarter within the Department of Mathematics there arose a plan to establish "tenured lecturers," who could eschew advanced teaching and research to devote themselves wholly to service and remedial courses. The professorate, clearly distinguished from the lecturers, would teach upper division and graduate courses and devote a significant amount of time to the creation of new mathematics.

●

Since the mid-sixties, artist Jack Dollhausen has developed unique forms of "interactive, electronic art." In the process he has become well known as a creator of complex and intricately sculpted works that respond to human observation. His pieces have been displayed widely throughout the Pacific Northwest and have been included in exhibits that have toured nationally. (Washington State University News Service)

To meet these needs, the Study Council recommended introducing a new doctoral degree, the Doctor of Arts. Strongly supported by the Carnegie Corporation of New York, this doctoral program emphasized teaching, with less attention being paid to traditional scholarly and research approaches to the various disciplines. A sense of urgency prevailed, as many authorities believed that a shortage of college teachers would follow the predicted enrollment growths. Locally, the proposed new degree seemed to answer the need for undergraduate course instructorships discussed in the Study Council Report. In any event, the Department of Mathematics launched its Doctor of Arts program in January of 1973.[44]

Both the Economics and Business Administration Departments of the College of Economics and Business felt strong waves of change in the middle of the 1960s. In fact, when economists responded to the call for Study Council deliberations they pushed aside their recent Ten Year Report in order to explore greatly increased use of mathematics and statistics. They also pondered elimination of foreign languages for the Ph.D. degree, in order to add mathematics and informational science. Policy studies, too, they thought might be reduced to mathematical formulations and econometric concepts. In addition, they suggested that micro and macro-economics would occupy prominent places in advanced studies. The fate of these proposals awaited future developments but suffice it to say, many became policy and practice in succeeding years.[45]

While economists were moving from historical and empirical studies to mathematical work, professors of business administration talked of transforming their curricula from its emphasis on vocationalism to professionalism. The great criticism of business schools in the 1950s had been that they were simply repeating old truths and principles in a routine way without regard for the fact that American business was changing rapidly. A strong sense of urgency was clear in the following statement: "They [the business schools] were not meeting the needs of business . . . for competent, imaginative, flexible and creative managers, prepared to deal with the unsolved problems of tomorrow, rather than the routines of yesterday." according to the Business Administration sub-committee of the Study Council. Business education, in Pullman as elsewhere, "must contribute to the interests of business by providing a 'usefully' trained supply of young men and women for positions in accounting, finance, marketing, personnel and industrial relations, production and general management and thereby to satisfy as well the ambitions of young people to get ahead in the world."[46]

The College of Agriculture's Study Council saw the State of Washington as unique in its land and people and urged the university to seize its special opportunity to plan for the future in its low-density Palouse location and eastern Washington hinterland. Far from viewing the Palouse as a cultural wasteland as had some humanists, members of the Agricultural Council called on the entire institution to plan the agricultural, industrial, and social future from this center. Washington's geographic diversity might provide opportunities for research that would lead to improvements in agricultural production, the rational utilization natural resources, and bring about change that would benefit the region's urban environment, as well. In fact, research in the Palouse region would yield results suitable for improving life in other parts of the world, such as the international programs in Pakistan, which will be discussed below.[47]

The Study Council's report was, in some ways, defensive stating that, despite impressive achievements in fostering food production, the tasks ahead were almost overwhelming. They pleaded that agricultural experimental work would need maximum support for continued success. Members of the Council also expressed fears regarding a possible scenario—which some took seriously—that the College of Agriculture might be dissolved and its researchers placed in various hard science departments. The Council argued the question, "Would they continue to contribute to agriculture in the vital ways that we take for granted under the present structure?" The answer: Very probably not![48]

Perhaps this troubling matter arose from the fact that many appointees to the College of Agriculture had come from the so-called hard or pure sciences. Many feared that some of their colleagues might be easily attracted to pure science, instead of pursuing the vitally-needed applied agricultural investigations ("economic" as opposed to "pure investigations"). There appears to have been a suspicion that only College of Agriculture policy held them to their appointed tasks.[49]

The Council expressed an added anxiety when it acknowledged that the College of Agriculture had met with difficulty when competing for students with other campus units. Furthermore, the report asserted, the faculty communicated poorly with hard scientists, partly a result of course duplication that prevented their students from taking classes in other departments, and, thus, overburdening them with too many credits in their major fields of study. Student members on the Council criticized program inflexibility and repeated "the most widely heard complaint from students . . . that teachers don't want to teach." They were joined by faculty who agreed with them. But, a solution to these teaching and curricular problems did not seem destined for the near future.[50]

By the middle of the 1960s Home Economists saw their profession at a major turning point, so deep seated were their problems. Their Study Council report asserted that they had made great strides since the early days when their curriculum was designed to produce "practical skills in manipulation by constant practice," the means utilized for teaching cooking, sewing, and handling laundry. They were very much concerned, in 1968, with a recent declaration by the National Association of State Universities and Land-Grant Colleges that the discipline of home economics had lagged alarmingly behind social and educational needs. Their narrow focus on the middle class—and in that class, overwhelmingly on white women—meant that problems common to vast segments of American society were ignored.[51]

The National Association, in effect, issued an ultimatum admonishing home economists to broaden their course offerings and make them more socially relevant. Actually, the College of Home Economics at Washington State University, had some five years earlier taken steps toward achieving greater relevance. It had done so by linking social, natural, and behavioral sciences to family problems and child studies. The College had also vowed to engage in research on a large scale and to raise the level of professional competence of its practitioners and students.[52]

The revised program, by 1968, centered around three departments in a strengthened undergraduate program, each concerned with current social issues and infused with scientific data and methodology. . These departments included (1) Child and Family Studies, (2) Clothing, Interior Design, and Textiles and (3) Foods, Nutrition, and Institutional Management. Some promise was held out that a strong graduate program might be developed, especially because of the availability of excellent supporting courses in the social and natural sciences. The Home Economics faculty by itself could not, however, put together a viable graduate program.[53]

Veterinary Medicine, like home economics, came to its own crossroads in the 1960s. Although one of the oldest professional programs on campus, having provided training and service since 1896, the College of Veterinary Medicine had never been considered as among the top circle of such colleges in the United States. It had been accredited with reservations and probations since 1932, when the American Veterinary Medical Association began the practice of judging the fitness of faculty, facilities, and teaching. Subsequently, however, the College could not escape probation, an indication of dissatisfaction with one or more parts of its program. Probation continued in one form or another until 1965, when full accreditation was finally accorded.[54]

"Full accreditation" came with strings attached, however. The University had to overcome, or at least minimize, its "intellectual isolation" by seriously considering moving the entire College of Veterinary Medicine elsewhere, preferably to Seattle. There, its staff would then be able to work closely with University of Washington's medical school to find cures for diseases to which both people and animals were subject. Such a location, it was argued, would overcome the chronic shortage of large animal cases in Pullman, thus improving the student clinical experiences. The Veterinary Medical self study, which appeared as a sub-committee report of the Professional Education Study Council's report, acknowledged certain deficiencies in the College's program. But the idea of moving to Seattle proved totally unacceptable. The veterinarians pointed to substantial progress in overcoming weaknesses in the program, a process they expected to continue. They also pointed to the high cost of a move to Seattle.[55]

Certainly, the confidence the veterinarians exuded about their progress had to be placed in a perspective in which the college appeared as a small and less than prestigious institution. In 1966-1967, it rested in sixteenth position out of the twenty-one colleges of veterinary medicine in the United States and Canada, with a total enrollment of 185 candidates seeking Doctorates in Veterinary Medicine. In addition, there were only twelve graduate students. Small size, furthermore, did not improve classroom or laboratory atmosphere, since the equally small faculty faced a ratio of students to teacher fourth highest among the twenty-one colleges.[56]

The faculty, which must have felt beleaguered at times, recognized the need for major alterations of the curriculum to eliminate out of date, peripheral, and irrelevant materials. Curricular revision and introduction of new scientific knowledge became especially urgent since veterinarians had to deal with the rising popularity of animals as pets and horses for recreational purposes. In consequence, the practice of veterinary medicine had become vastly expanded and more greatly varied than ever before. Conversely, the veterinarians found that the customary "fire engine" practice in dealing with economic animals changed to an emphasis on wellness programs, especially with large herds of dairy cattle.

The solution to coping with the dynamic veterinary medical field of study, according to the report, should begin with requiring all students to pass basic courses in the sciences, medicine, and surgery, after which each student might select two specialties for advanced training. "The result should be, " the Council report stated, "graduates who have more in-depth training in their particular areas of interest such as large animal medicine, etc., but who [also] have a broad general knowledge of Veterinary Medicine."[57]

The College of Pharmacy, like that of Veterinary Medicine, had a long history by the time some of its members formed the their sub-committee of the Professional Education Study Council. Most of that time the Faculty hardly had a major voice, the program being dominated by the dean from 1923 to 1952. The studies during that time emphasized vocationalism—the operation of a drug store or pharmacy. As the sub-committee put it: In the 1920s and 1930s "the learning of the manual skills necessary in compounding [pills] occupied most of the pharmacy student's time."[58]

The faculty's influence on the program became more pronounced in the 1950s, but the shift from vocationalism to professionalism received major impetus only after 1960, under the leadership of Dean Allen I. White. Since then, according to the sub-committee, "the curriculum has moved from the laboratory orientation it once had to a greater emphasis on the students' understanding and increased knowledge of the theory and scientific growth of his profession. Courses have evolved toward giving a deeper understanding of drugs and drug action and interaction." The role of the faculty was plain to see: It had to prepare students to offer professional service, especially advice on the use of drugs and the role of drugs in contemporary society.

But, the faculty of seven full-time professors, three half-time members, and the dean (who taught no more than one course) remained inadequate for the new responsibilities assumed by the

Professor Margaret Hard, chair of the Home Economics Research Center, was the first home economist and first woman to be appointed as head of the Secretary of Agriculture's Committee of Nine of the Cooperative State Research Service. Professor Hard joined the WSC faculty in 1942 and has been nationally recognized for her research in home economics. (Washington State University News Service)

In the post-World War II period the University began responding to the challenge by introducing new programs of technical assistance to Third World and under-developed nations. It soon became apparent that Washington State University's location in semi-arid eastern Washington prepared it to cope with dry land agriculture found in other parts of the world.

college. In fact, the program was so understaffed that "incapacitation of any one person could almost paralyze instruction in that area." Rising enrollments complicated matters further, as became apparent when 176 students enrolled in 1967. The resulting student-faculty ratio rose to an unsatisfactory 21:1. As a result, the College of Pharmacy could not add greatly desired elective courses, nor could graduate work be carried on without major restrictions. Nevertheless, on that point the faculty could have been of a divided mind. Just a few months before the Study Council's report was issued, an accreditation team wrote of the graduate program that though "modest," it appeared to be "sound, and there is a notable increase in the amount of research during recent years."[59]

In the post-World War II period the University began responding to the challenge by introducing new programs of technical assistance to Third World and under-developed nations. It soon became apparent that Washington State University's location in semi-arid eastern Washington prepared it to cope with dry land agricultural found in other parts of the world. Furthermore, the proximity of the Grand Coulee Dam and the Columbia Basin Irrigation Project made it a logical university to provide service to new nations like Pakistan.[60]

In fact, discussions with federal officials in Washington, D.C., and with Pakistani authorities began in 1952 and led to the signing of a contract in 1954 for overseas educational work. Washington State University assumed responsible leadership of a party of experts—most from Pullman—who sought to improve Pakistan's university system. Their work encompassed developing programs in agriculture, business, teacher training, social science, and the creation of library resources for the educational system. The university's party undertook a staggering twenty-nine projects, only two of which had to be aborted. Results varied greatly but the most successful were in soil science, food technology, artificial insemination of cattle, and the improvement of one college library.[61]

The contract provided for reciprocity, so a number of faculty members and technicians from Pakistan studied in Pullman. In a real sense, members of the Washington State University's party benefitted from learning experiences in Pakistan. Before the first phase of the project ended in 1961, thirty-seven Americans, most of whom came from Pullman, had spend a tour of duty in Pakistan. Although the original contract had called for a three year project, the agreement was extended. By June 1959, however, President C. Clement French decided that they had "reached the point of diminishing returns, unless we are prepared to support a program there on a continuing basis." The program actually did not stop before 1961.[62]

A second phase, no doubt arising from the initial successes, emerged when President French, on April 18, 1961, signed a contract to develop a land-grant type institution to be known as the West Pakistan Agricultural University. Once again, a WSU Party embarked on a major project. This venture was filled with more difficulties than the first, as its leaders sought to introduce a purely American institution into a foreign land.[63]

Agricultural Dean Stanley P. Swenson, a man who had played an important role in Pakistan from an early day, became Dean of the new university as it got under way. Under his leadership, the WSU Party introduced American teaching, research, and extension methods and techniques. Once again, Pakistanis traveled to Pullman for advanced training in agricultural and related subjects. The undertaking continued until 1969 and has been described by a recent historian as "remarkably successful." Standard departments of agricultural subjects were established, along with veterinary medicine and rural sociology. In one sense, the project could not be regarded as successful—the failure to develop standard extension service to cover the country, bringing news and demonstrations of agricultural innovation and catering to the needs of farmers. The extension service never reached beyond the immediate vicinity of the campus.[64]

Reflecting on the exciting early days of the Pakistan projects, another historian has noted that they represented "an era of naive good will in an age which thought the transfer of technology would be easy and [would] solve the problems of the world." The projects also represented a Cold War gesture on the part of the nation that hoped to exorcise the Soviet menace by removing poverty and frustration from Third World peoples. Regardless of the degree of success, the creation of an American agricultural university on foreign soil was one of the most idealistic tasks ever undertaken by Washington State University.[65]

The projects in Pakistan proved to be only the beginning of the school's international development work. In 1975, the government of Jordan asked Washington State University to assist in improving and enlarging its agricultural faculty, along the familiar lines of the American land-grant model—teaching, research, and extension. By September, 12 staff members (all but one from Pullman) had arrived in Jordan and were at work in animal science, plant pathology, irrigation, agricultural marketing, and other areas of study. Members of the party trained local students and faculty to carry on the work of a strengthened curriculum and research projects. The renovated institution issued its first degrees in 1977.[66]

The Jordanian higher education project ended in 1986, but work in other areas had been undertaken there in the meantime. In 1982, for instance, Washington State University sent a team to assist in the development of irrigation agriculture in the Jordan River Valley. Then, in 1986, Jordan asked for assistance in dry-land farming. Washington State University responded by sending a group of experts that has continued to work with Jordanian authorities to increase food production and exports to neighboring countries.[67]

All international projects undertaken by Washington State University were funded by agencies of the federal government. This support included money granted under the Foreign Assistance Act of 1961, amended by Congress with Title XII under terms of the

The projects in Pakistan proved to be only the beginning of the school's international development work. In 1975, the government of Jordan asked Washington State University to assist in improving and enlarging its agricultural faculty, along the familiar lines of the American land-grant model—teaching, research, and extension.

Humphrey-Findlay Bill. Indeed, this measure greatly increased the capacity of land-grant schools to provide aid to the very poorest societies. Washington State University became one of 140 American universities involved. In 1979, WSU began to upgrade teaching, research, and library resources and training more than thirty specialists and administrators in Indonesia. The University also provided assistance in Zimbabwe, Yemen, Morocco, Mali, Lesotho, Egypt, and the Sudan.[68]

Theodore Doty, in a 1971 study of the Pakistan project, concluded that, it "never really touched the lives of any but a small handful of the home campus staff who were directly involved. It made more of an impact in Pakistan." It is possible, of course, that Doty may have accurately represented a confidence (and naivete) of participants that caused them to believe theirs was a one-way process, with no useful "feed-back." But, he wrote on the heels of events, not having the luxury of perspective.[69]

On the other hand, Evelyn Rodewald, wrote years later, that benefits to Washington State University from the beginning included "strengthening of the programs [the University] offers its students to give them the ability to operate in an international [sic] world." She also pointed out that these programs introduced "new types of research and new genetic materials" for research. Furthermore, Title XII provided financing which enabled both more faculty and graduate students to participate in overseas experiences than otherwise would have been possible. Such opportunities increased the expertise of entire departments.[70]

When President French called for a termination of the first phase of the Pakistan project in 1959 he undoubtedly feared that founding overseas programs might imperil the creation of new campus programs. As a matter of fact, such a program was launched on October 15, 1959, when the Resident Instructional Staff created an Honors Council. This new body was given the charge to develop a program and curriculum for superior students and to report its progress at a later date. Led by Sidney Hacker, Professor of Mathematics, the Council studied existing programs carefully and painstakingly sought the advice of interested faculty. Their proposal, adopted as policy on May 17, 1960, stated that "the primary objective [of the Honors Program] will be the promotion of the educational well-being of the superior student and the encouragement of a broad, appreciative, and understanding scholarship, with intensive education of the superior student in his chosen major field of study."[71]

The students judged eligible constituted the top ten percent of the freshman class, with the same ratio for sophomores and transfers. Individuals were required to maintain a B average to remain in the program. Curricular requirements included a series of honors courses, including "Man and His Environment," the "Domain of the Arts," and courses on Eastern and Western civilizations. Newly developed honors classes in the sciences, social sciences, and humanities replaced the regular requirements for graduation. The most suitable instructors from the various departments were detailed to teach the honors courses.[72]

The program began informally in 1960 on a relatively modest scale and without fanfare. The following September saw a full-fledged offering, with sixty-three percent of eligible freshmen and fifty-eight percent of eligible sophomores enrolled. When the first class graduated in 1964, Professor Hacker resigned as director of the Honors Program. He was replaced by V. N. Bhatia, Professor of Pharmacy. The program continued to flourish, enrolling 565 students in 1969 and 667 by the fall of 1988.

The Honors Program quickly became noted for its high percentage of graduates but, of course, such successes were expected of such a group. What is more significant, however, is that the director was able to announce in 1970, for example, that seventy-five percent of the Honors graduates continued on to graduate and professional school. In addition, many others became public school teachers.[73]

If the Honors Program was exclusive it was not exclusionary, since students from all areas of study were eligible, a matter of importance at a people's university. Moreover, it was argued that the Honors studies "fed-back" to other students attitudes toward learning that measurably improved their education. With "feed-back" in mind, Vice-President Wallis Beasley, in the Fall of 1966, asked the director of the program for information on the influence of Honors on the rest of the campus.[74]

Abundant testimony came from professors who had taught honors classes, of influences of that program, not only on students, but upon themselves and the ways in which they taught all their classes. A professor from the sciences explained that Honors students induced him to modify his experiments, a matter which he transferred to his non-honors classes. Further experience led him to write: "It is a greater challenge to formulate the factual and conceptual material to present to honors students, but once this has been done, I found with slight modifications, much of this could also be used effectively with non-honors students, thereby presenting them with more interesting and more advanced material than they would otherwise have received. I have also learned better methods for presenting certain concepts to non-honors students."[75]

Additional comment substantiated that satisfaction with teaching honors classes was wide spread and that the program had a positive influence on the total educational process. About honors students, many might have used the words of one professor who wrote: "They do not accept the easy, and generally inadequate, answer. In short, they insist that I remain alive and a working scholar."

Nevertheless, the limits to adaptation of experiences in small honors classes to large—often much larger—regular classes remained severe, as more than one professor stated. Along this line, a veteran of four honors classes wrote: "I think every class I teach would be better if I could adopt the discussion method and dispense with tests; however, my non-honors classes are so large that this is impossible." The Honors Program remained elitist if for no other

●

Ingenious new programming at the graduate level occurred when the deans of graduate studies at the University of Idaho and Washington State University proposed that they be permitted to establish a system of cooperative courses.

●

reason than that its students received more individual attention than did others.[76]

Ingenious new programming at the graduate level occurred when the deans of graduate studies at the University of Idaho and Washington State University proposed that they be permitted to establish a system of cooperative courses. Cooperation in this instance meant that one school would be designated as host for a particular course, which would not be taught at the other institution. Instead, students from the second institution would attend the first, taking that course without extra fees. The number of such courses would not be large but the arrangement would offer special advantages to both schools, particularly in reducing manpower and equipment expenses, especially for small courses. The cooperative offerings, largely in the areas of science and technology, would approximately balance at the schools, over an unspecified period of time. The same situation would prevail in student enrollments in cooperative courses.[77]

The program began in 1963, with the stipulation that the program course grades would be handled with a minimum of bureaucracy. The home institution of such students would record grades in its records, obviating the necessity of treating them punctiliously as transferred grades, to be kept first by the university giving the course. Originally, Master's degree candidates at Washington State University were permitted to earn six semester hours of work in cooperative courses while doctoral candidates might take twelve hours. Subsequently, individual departments assumed the responsibility for determining the number of credits that could be transfered.[78]

Cooperative course scheduling began modestly in the fall of 1963 with four students from each institution taking cooperative courses at the other. Enrollments grew slowly so that by 1967-1968 thirty-six students from Washington State University had enrolled as opposed to fifty from the University of Idaho. In recent years the numbers have climbed more steeply; by 1985-1986, 218 students from Pullman and 240 from Moscow were studying in cooperative courses. Extension of cooperation to the undergraduate level came in 1972 on the heels of a report supporting such programs by the Carnegie Commission on Higher Education. At the same time, a legislative committee urged further cooperation as a means of saving money. The two universities responded in 1973 by creating an undergraduate cooperative courses program in the sciences.[79]

Even in the last years of the French administration a variety of administrative decisions significantly modified educational policies, organization, and programs, especially for undergraduates. As has been discussed earlier in this history, the 1917 state law defining scope of studies at the University of Washington and Washington State University had denied to the latter the possibility of granting degrees in forestry and communications, among other matters. Restrictions on forestry were removed on April 5, 1961, when the Regents approved a bachelor's degree in forest management.[80]

Journalism, too, had been given almost exclusively to the University of Washington (except for agricultural journalism). It had, however, been taught in Pullman under the sponsorship of the Department of English and, later, as a special program. Accreditation of that program had been denied, forcing a decisive policy change. Journalism, in conjunction with studies in radio, television, and parts of the Department of Speech having to do with radio and television combined to become the Department of Communications, destined in the next two decades to be one of the most popular majors on campus. The Journalism credential, a pale substitute for a journalism degree, could now be forgotten as the Bachelor of Arts degree in Communications raised the level of the whole program. The Communications program went into operation on July 1, 1964.[81]

A notable change in academic organization came on March 22, 1965, when the Regents divided the Department of Sociology and Anthropology into two departments. This decision recognized, not only the difficulty of governing two complex disciplines under one head, it also offered a tribute to the emergence of anthropology as a major study on the campus, contributing greatly to the understanding of humanity and culture but also to well-publicized archaeological digs and findings in Washington. Sociology, too, had some time earlier grown in stature, with numerous specialties.[82]

In a reform of another kind, the English Department sought to cope with the perennial problem of teaching compulsory composition courses. A radical change seemed urgent in 1962, due to anticipated sharply rising freshmen enrollments. What might have seemed like a simple matter of logistics—where do you get the funding to instruct so many more freshmen?—received a philosophical gloss when Nelson Ault reported to the Educational Policies Committee a general opinion of English professors that "the entering freshmen are much better prepared than five years ago." To that heartening news the English Department added the notation that annually they were advancing one-fifth of each freshman class to advanced standing, being satisfied that it possessed the writing skills taught in freshman English.[83]

With no apparent dissent, the Educational Policies Committee endorsed a petition to reduce required English composition from six semester hours to three. The committee also endorsed a codicil providing for additional advanced undergraduate English composition courses for those wishing more specialized training. The Resident Instructional Staff, with no apparent opposition or even skepticism about the improved high school training, put the reduced requirement into effect. This program remained as the principal bulwark against what appeared to be an encroaching illiteracy which neither high schools nor universities have managed to prevent.[84]

The administration faced not only modification of academic policies but also curbs on enrollment and major shifts in campus housing arrangements. On October 20, 1961, President French reported to the Regents that great overcrowding existed in Univer-

Professor of English, poet, and writer Ruth Slonim has been widely recognized for her contributions to poetry scholarship. She is the author of San Francisco "The City" in Verse *and was nominated for the Pulitzer Prize in 1982 for* Outer Traces, Inner Places. *Slonim was the first woman to present WSU's Distinguished Faculty Address. In 1988 she was the recipient of one of the prestigious Governor's Arts Awards.* (Washington State University News Service)

The enlarging student body, which would grow to 9,035 by September of 1964 and 10,662, in 1966, forced President French to begin reorganizing his administration. On August 28, 1964, the Board of Regents approved his proposal for elevating the office of Dean of the Faculty to Vice-President for Academic Affairs.

sity housing. He wanted more control over enrollments to help ease matters. French and Dean of Students J. C. Clevenger decided to abandon segregated dormitories in the interest of flexibility in placing students and in order to find additional housing for an increasing number of women. They proposed mixing men's and women's dormitories in the same neighborhood.[85] The Regents immediately approved French's proposal to slow the growth of enrollment by requiring $50 deposits on reserving housing and an additional $50 non-refundable portion of admissions fees.[86]

One year later, the Regents approved French's plan to institute flexible dormitory arrangements. Mrs. Francis P. Owen, a Regent, proposed and the Board approved a plan whereby the next dormitory, Orton Hall, would be exclusively for women but thereafter dormitories would be designed for both men and women. The Regents also called for inter-changeable use of existing smaller units. Again, in September, 1964, French recited census figures that revealed flexibility in housing use had become absolutely essential. Since 1952, he reported, the student body had increased in size sixty-four percent. More striking: Women during the same time span, increased from thirty-two percent to nearly thirty-eight percent of the student body, once again testifying to the acumen of President French calling for flexible housing.[87]

French also presented statistics concerning the popularity of various majors over the past decade, which may have surprised people accustomed to the stereotype that agriculture and engineering were the hallmark of the land-grant institution. Education had gained the highest percentage, more than ninety-eight percent. The sciences and arts were next with an eighty-three percent increase. Within that group, the social sciences gained 114 percent, the humanities gained sixty-eight percent, and the natural sciences increased seventy-eight percent. Economics and Business experienced a fifty-five percent growth, while Engineering had a fifty-four percent increase. Agriculture suffered a five percent decline, while students with majors in Pharmacy were down thirty-two percent by 1962. Veterinary medicine and home economics gained only seven and eight percent, respectively, percentages which might have reflected lack of facilities. Although French offered these figures without comment—at least none recorded—it seems clear that the land-grant school in Pullman was, more and more, emphasizing the broadest conception of the Morrill Act.[88]

The enlarging student body, which would grow to 9,035 by September of 1964 and 10,662, in 1966, forced President French to begin reorganizing his administration. On August 28, 1964, the Board of Regents approved his proposal for elevating the office of Dean of the Faculty to Vice-President for Academic Affairs. The Business Manager now became Vice-President for Business. In addition, the Regents created the post of Assistant to the President. With this top administration, French now was ready to create the larger bureaucracy needed to carry on the daily functions of an institution which were growing more complex by the year. The

Assistant to the President, in particular, would fill a need to aid the president to carry on the ever-present public relations.[89]

A few months later, on March 22, 1965, French expressed "continuing dissatisfaction" with the Institutes of Agricultural Sciences and Technology. President Compton had organized the institutes to administer teaching, research, and extension. French found a feature of their organization troublesome—the existence of committees made up of representatives of business, engineering, and agriculture to advise the director of each institute. The president's greatest displeasure probably arose from the duplication in administration of agriculture and engineering, since each sector had a dean and director. The Regents were sympathetic, approving the termination of the institutes on April 16, 1965, permitting the Dean of Agriculture to take undisputed control of functions within the agricultural institute and the Dean of Engineering the other.

Another change came to agriculture at this time. President French overhauled the state-wide agricultural experiment station system. Thereafter, Pullman was to have the College of Agriculture Research center and three regional centers were specified: an Irrigated Agricultural Research and Extension Center in Prosser, a Tree Fruit Research Center in Wenatchee, and the Western Washington Research and Extension Center at Puyallup. The remaining stations were subordinated under the regional centers.[90]

Even as French busily reorganized the Colleges of Engineering and Agriculture he prepared for a final policy statement—that of his retirement. He first wrote to Dr. Milton Durham, President of the Board of Regents, offering a glint of humor that "certainly a man should try to judge the timing so well that, when he goes, a majority of his colleagues will ask why he went so soon rather than bewail the fact that he stayed so long." More soberly, he acknowledged that his had been a good tour of duty in higher education for twenty-nine years. "But pressures have become steadily greater and the days more tense, even in a good situation as we have here." He concluded by determining to retire on October 24, 1966, at exactly 65 years of age.[91]

When the Regents next assembled, on May 31, 1965, they accepted the president's resignation, gratified that French would continue to serve temporarily and that he had given them many months to find his successor. The Board immediately appointed three of its members to form an advisory committee to aid it in selecting a new president. It then asked the Faculty Executive Committee to add three faculty to the committee. In addition, the Board requested the Board of Control to choose a student and the Alumni Board of Directors to add an alumnus. Later, at the 1966 Commencement, the Faculty and Board of Regents bestowed an honorary Doctor of Laws degree upon the retiring president. That fall, on November 1, 1966, the Board appointed Vice-President Wallis Beasley to serve as Acting President.[92]

The advisory committee grappled with a list of 270 names, paring it down to ten for interviews by February 25, 1966. Once the advisors

•

When the Regents next assembled, on May 31, 1965, they accepted the president's resignation, gratified that French would continue to serve temporarily and that he had given them many months to find his successor.

•

concluded the interviews, the list was turned over to the Regents. Interviews by the Board continued until November 30, 1966, but the Regents did not come forth with a new president. Then, in a meeting in Spokane on February 24, 1967, the Board announced that Glenn Terrell, Dean of Faculties at the University of Illinois, Chicago Circle, who had first been interviewed on April 2, 1966, had accepted the presidency. Mr. and Mrs. Terrell then drove to the campus to confer with architects concerning the remodelling of the executive mansion to accommodate two young children in the family as well as to make the lower quarters and gardens more useful for public events. The remodelling proved so extensive that the family lived in a rented home for some months after President Terrell took office on July 1, 1967.[93]

The new president soon established cordial relations with the faculty but even more rapidly acquired the reputation as a "student's president." A reporter of the Spokane *Spokesman-Review,* on October 1, 1967, provided an anecdote that characterized the president as a friendly "Samaritan." He had discovered two students and a parent whose automobile was "hopelessly stalled on one of the steep streets of the . . . campus. . . . Suddenly a sizeable chunk of help six feet, two inches tall appeared behind them and started pushing.

He pushed them all the way to down-town Pullman.

Then, with a good-natured wave, [he] drove off again to pursue his own errands. The students did not know who he was; they still don't. But they had just received an 'academic assist' from Dr. Glenn Terrell, new president—at only 47—at Washington State University."

The demands of office did not deter Terrell from taking great pains to understand university events from the students' point of view. He exuded a firm confidence in the maturity and integrity of youth. "He's (or she's) brighter, better informed, more sophisticated [then past generations]. He knows more about general issues, political questions, and social problems." Furthermore, Terrell did not find a growing generation gap. Indeed, he concluded that "today's university student comes much closer to knowing as much as his elders than did those of several years ago."[94]

The possessor of this optimistic attitude, W. Glenn Terrell, was born in Tallahassee, Florida, on May 24, 1920. He received a Bachelor Arts degree in 1942 from Davidson College in North Carolina. After graduation he entered the U.S. Army, serving as a lieutenant in the European theater during World War II. Subsequently he entered graduate study in psychology, earning a M.S. degree from Florida State University in 1948 and a Ph.D. degree in the same subject at the University of Iowa in 1952. Terrell taught psychology at Florida State University from 1948 to 1955, with time out for graduate studies, and served in the same department at the University of Colorado from 1955 to 1959. After that, he taught and served in administrative capacities at the University of Colorado and at the University of Illinois, Chicago Circle, from 1959 to 1967, the last two years as Dean of Faculties at Chicago.[95]

Terrell's formal inauguration as President took place on March 15, 1968, more than nine months after he had taken up the tasks of office.

●

Terrell's formal inauguration as President took place on March 15, 1968, more than nine months after he had taken up the tasks of office. Two days before the ceremonies, the Daily Evergreen *ran an editorial suggesting that Terrell had been correct in judging students of that day to be more politically and socially mature than students of a few years earlier.*

●

Two days before the ceremonies, the *Daily Evergreen* ran an editorial suggesting that Terrell had been correct in judging students of that day to be more politically and socially mature than students of a few years earlier. The title read, "We ask you Mr. President." What followed was a provocative advocacy of a charter of freedom and responsibility for students, as they understood the matter. While the writer challenged Terrell to improve the university, his expectations were different from those associated with students from earlier eras. The graduates of 1968, the editorialist continued, should be prepared "to take an active role in society." Indeed, he wrote that "these people must be ready to face and help resolve the public issues and problems [and] to place their narrow and personal interests aside in favor of the public welfare." Toward that end, "the university must foster independence and individualism," so that students might decide for themselves what and how to study."[96]

In his inaugural address, Terrell praised the founders for starting the college in 1890, so it might grow in usefulness to the fledgling State of Washington. He also indulged in a bit of fantasy by noting that Pullman's small town atmosphere solidified collegiality and removed distractions from study. His hope that such a community of scholars might be perpetuated was destroyed in a few years when Pullman proved as vulnerable as any large city to the unrest associated with the antiwar, anti-racism and women's rights movements. The cozy, small-town atmosphere would prove to be a myth.[97]

Indeed, Terrell could not have taken the myth very seriously, for he readily agreed with the *Evergreen* editorial that the University must foster leadership in world affairs to eliminate hunger, racial strife, warfare, pollution, and other problems. At the same time, the new president pledged that his university would not champion a particular school of thought. In this matter, he agreed with President Howard R. Bowen of the University of Iowa, and an alumnus of Washington State University. President Bowen, also speaking at the inauguration, insisted that universities must pull back from over-indulgence on applied research and consulting work to concentrate upon the slow, disinterested search for truth. Terrell also agreed when Bowen expressed the fear that continued dominance of a Cold War mentality, which stressed producing vast amounts of technology," would limit ability to carry out the true functions of universities.[98]

Terrell recognized the strong role of the liberal arts and sciences at the university in the past and pledged to support them in the future. His own preferences included strengthening undergraduate research and striving to raise Washington State University to the top rank of graduate and research institutions, particularly in the environmental, biological, and physical sciences and in engineering and the behavioral sciences. To those who always asked the new president about the future of the College of Agriculture, Terrell had ready reply. Hunger, he stated, was the number one world problem. Until that issue was revolved, "food production technology would have high priority at his institution."[99]

●

Terrell recognized the strong role of the liberal arts and sciences at the university in the past and pledged to support them in the future. His own preferences included strengthening undergraduate research and striving to raise Washington State University to the top rank of graduate and research institutions . . .

●

Professor Loran Olsen, left, is noted for his research in and preservation of the musical heritage of Pacific Northwest Native Americans. In this 1972 photograph, he is shown checking proofs for the publication Nez Perce Songs *with Ron Halfmoon of the Nez Perce Tribe.* (Washington State University News Service)

At the first meeting of the Board of Regents the next Fall, September 1968, President Terrell revealed his dedication to the words he uttered at his inauguration. In his asking budget for the biennium, he stressed the need for continuing "heavy commitment" to undergraduate education. In addition, he also stated that there must be increased support for graduate studies. Although at least four to five times more expensive than undergraduate education, a bolstered graduate offering was needed to "increase the stature of WSU . . . to that of a second first-rate institution in the state." The programs he particularly desired to improve included veterinary medicine (to be located in Pullman, not elsewhere), biological science, humanities, the library, nursing education, and a new unit, the Center for Applied Research in the Social Sciences.[100]

New programs and expansion in certain critical areas required support from the public in the form of budgets and good will. Therefore, at the September meeting, the president announced creation of a new position—Vice-President for University Development. He appointed to the post Warren Bishop already Vice-President for Business. In the following month, Terrell elevated Wallis Beasley, then Academic Vice-President, to the new post of Executive Vice-President. The appointment of Bishop signalled the growing necessity to systematically seek outside funding for research and creation of new research facilities. Beasley's elevation indicated a measure of the growing administrative complexity accompanying new programming and a rising enrollment.[101]

Perhaps the most surprising development in Terrell's early days in Pullman was neither a policy statement nor a crisis but the 1968 discovery of the 10,000 year old "Marmes Man." Roald Fryxell, a member of a WSU archaeological team led by Professor Richard D. Daugherty, made the discovery. Announcement of finding the oldest living human remains in Washington's history came at an elaborate news conference in the offices of U.S. Senator Warren G. Magnuson, overflowing with numerous dignitaries.[102]

The archaeological work had begun much earlier, in 1953, when Daugherty and a private citizen, John McGregor, of Hooper, in Whitman County, had first reported the possibilities of the Marmes site. Nine years later, in 1962, Daugherty directed the first archaeological salvage operation at the remote site, a rocky, desiccated landscape on the west bank of the Palouse River, one and one-half miles from its confluence with the Snake. At that time, Fryxell also began geological investigations of the site.[103]

The discovery of human remains and dating them by the radio carbon method were triumphs for the archaeologists and for science at the University. Unfortunately, little time remained for careful planning or long-term excavations. The flood plain and rocky shelter of "Marmes Man" were scheduled to be inundated by impounded waters from the Snake River, upon completion of the Lower Monumental Dam. In October 1968, Senator Magnuson, President Terrell, and others petitioned U.S. President Lyndon B. Johnson to authorize construction of a coffer dam to prevent flood waters from enveloping the rock shelter. Johnson assented and the dam was constructed. Unfortunately, water seeped under the dam, threatening disaster. Archaeologists turned laborers, worked in mud and snow for six weeks without pay. Nevertheless, by late February of 1969 the entire site had been flooded and all work halted. Fryxell put on a brave face, declaring that "this project is moth-balled—not ended." Daugherty estimated that only one-third of the site had been excavated, but resuming work became an impossibility. Much had been learned about primitive forebears but the mysteries loomed as intriguing as before.

Chapter Eight

From Student Unrest to New Professional Programs, 1967-1988

THREE MONTHS AFTER PRESIDENT TERRELL, AT HIS INAUGURAL, HAD praised students of the sixties as being brighter and more sophisticated than those of previous generations, he received a report that revealed a potential problem with the attitudes of many white students, the overwhelming majority on the campus. Prepared by the Study Council on Student Life, and issued on June 7, 1968, the document conveyed a somber notation that students generally tended to become cynical or alienated as institutions of higher learning became larger and more complex—a situation that was occurring at Washington State University. Lack of communication, the Council report continued, often triggered unhappy and destructive responses on campus. In short, members of this Study Council feared that many students had become merely "course takers," clinging to conventional values and avoiding the broadening cultural influences of the humanities.[1]

These disturbing observations had become matters of debate earlier, on September 22, 1967, when the *Evergreen* had published an open letter submitted by seventeen ASWSU officers of the 1960s. Their spokesman, Timothy Manring, student body president in 1961-1962, had recently observed the campus with some care, and called for relevance in education to be determined by student convictions on issues and objectives. A few days later, Manring pointed out critical and dissenting experiences on other campuses, many of which could be adapted at WSU: creation of a free university for unorthodox learning, teach-ins, and perhaps, strikes. In all this discussion, attention remained focused on individuals and their desires. Apparently, "irrelevant" or dispassionate research and investigative studies were not considered as alternatives.[2]

The Study Council's eight faculty and nine student members strongly urged the university community to meet the demand for "relevance," a popular catch phrase, by responding to student criticism of the Vietnam War, the draft, racism, and the like. Communi-

OPPOSITE: *Washington State University Agronomy Professor Thomas Lumpkin and his assistant, Charlene Chan, examine the leaves of upstanding milkvetch, a legume that Lumpkin believes has a potential as a rotation crop in the State of Washington.* (Washington State University News Service)

cation and understanding were deficient, they recognized, because, as it was stated, "WSU is strikingly lacking in representation of members of minority groups, judged either on physical or cultural grounds." Admittedly, the State of Washington was a predominantly middle-class, white society, but the Study Council argued that the university had an obligation to change that situation within its campus population: "In order to provide all of our students with an adequate variety of experiences, the University should undertake vigorous programs to alter the present balance of types of students." In other words, the council stated that Washington State University had a responsibility to establish its own *de facto* desegregation.[3]

This council also came close to answering the popular clamor for relevance when it excoriated the general university requirements for graduation. In 1968, the program consisted of more than 300 courses, ranging from technical studies to liberal arts and sciences. Students completed a certain minimum number of hours in each of the major fields of learning were represented on this polyglot list. The Council contended that neither a humane philosophy nor a common core of learning could be obtained from the program. In fact, general university requirements seemed so unproductive as to make the schedule of studies in students' major fields seem models of clarity and articulation by comparison. To make amends, the Study Council recommended a required core of broad courses which would introduce all students to a philosophy of life and a common culture.[4]

But, the need for improved communication to overcome adverse student reactions to campus life did not end with suggesting changes to courses of study and the curriculum. An impersonal, hotel-like atmosphere of numerous dormitories detracted from a sense of security, furthering isolation for some and, possibly, contributing to a sense of alienation.

But, the need for improved communication to overcome adverse student reactions to campus life did not end with suggesting changes to courses of study and the curriculum. An impersonal, hotel-like atmosphere of numerous dormitories detracted from a sense of security, furthering isolation for some and, possibly, contributing to a sense of alienation. Negative feelings, the Council feared, were being deepened by "more striking events on other campuses reported almost daily in Pullman in the public press." Yet, its members felt, "such open strife need not occur at Washington State University, but could well occur in the absence of concerted efforts on the part of all members of the academic community."[5]

All student groups interviewed by the Study Council "demanded a sympathetic, responsive hearing from the faculty and the administration" on many aspects of student-faculty relationships, including teaching and grading. Numerous students reported that they were "favorably impressed" with an experimental pass-fail alternative to letter grading which the Resident Instructional Staff placed into operation on May 16, 1968. Under the plan, each student might choose to take eighteen semester hours of work toward a bachelor's degree under the pass-fail system with no effect on the grade-point average. The purpose was to encourage students to extend their studies to a great variety of fields in order to broaden their learning experience as much as possible. The Study Council in an ebullient mood, thought that young scholars "may not be satisfied for long with an opportunity to elect only 18 hours of course work to be graded on this basis."[6]

If the Study Council's sense of urgency seemed overly dramatic, critics needed only to be reminded of a statement emanating from the Educational Policies Committee on March 7, 1968. At that time, while presenting a twelve page report on the pass-fail plan, a sub-committee chairman said that "It is important that our students be given tangible evidence that reasonable requests for program reforms will be granted prompt and serious attention. The apparent docility of students in a given institutional setting can be highly deceptive: *"it may be later than some of us would prefer to believe."*[7]

The plan finally approved by the Resident Instructional Staff, on May 16, 1968, permitted students to take a maximum of six semester hours of course work pass-fail per semester and a total of eighteen hours for a bachelor's degree. The faculty would evaluate this experiment at the end of three years. Professors were denied the opportunity to identify students enrolled on a pass-fail basis, evidence that they were trusted neither by their peers nor their students to judge without bias. This lack of trust flawed the new arrangement for grading reform right from the start.[8]

An examination of the operation of pass-fail in 1971 revealed that it had relieved much anxiety over grades, but the idealistic vision of students exploring new and exciting fields of knowledge had not become a reality. The Resident Instructional Staff made pass-fail a permanent option in 1971, but because so many students had used it to meet general university requirements, all 100-level courses of that nature were removed from such grading. Further investigation in 1976 and 1977 produced recommendations that the pass-fail option be continued, but in the latter year all courses satisfying general university requirements were removed from the program. Pass-fail study remains an option at WSU, but with small enrollments, possessing little popularity, and none of the idealistic hopes of 1968.[9]

The criticism by the Study Council that the student body "is strikingly lacking in . . . members of minority groups" and suggestions that it should actively recruit them "in order to provide all of our students with an adequate variety of experiences" struck a responsive chord. In fact, before that statement was made President Terrell's Committee on Social Responsibility, a faculty group, had laid plans for such recruitment. In a program, which came to be known as the Experimental Educational Program, the administration recruited twenty-four disadvantaged students, many of whom belonged to racial minorities. These students had the skills required for academic success but not the financial means. The University provided scholarships and expenses.[10]

In February, 1969, the Board of Control, the undergraduate student government, endorsed expansion of Experimental Education Programs and offered assistance and moral support. That body also endorsed a proposal of the Social Responsibility Committee that additional Black faculty and staff be hired in order to provide an environment more conducive to academic success for minority students. The Board of Control went beyond statements made in the Social Responsibility Committee's document, asserting that "increasing

The plan finally approved by the Resident Instructional Staff, on May 16, 1968, permitted students to take a maximum of six semester hours of course work pass-fail per semester and a total of eighteen hours for a bachelor's degree.

the number of Black faculty and staff would improve the general educational environment of the University. It could well provide in the most basic sense, a broadening experience for many students."[11]

The university started a complementary training program in September 1967, entitled High School Equivalency, in essence another program for minorities. A generous grant from the federal Office of Economic Opportunity permitted the institution to recruit migratory and seasonal farm workers, age seventeen to twenty-two years whose families lived at the poverty level, to attend special classes for one year, preparing themselves for college or for a higher caliber of employment. Chicanos and Native Americans were the chief groups sought. Numerous adjustment problems, similar to those encountered by students in the Experimental Education Program, were anticipated. The equivalency program prospered, however, as evidenced by continuing federal support in succeeding years. Recently, program enrollment has reached approximately 100 students per year.[12]

The new programs admittedly were minor responses to campus needs, pale reflections of social problems that threatened to engulf the Pullman university at the end of the 1960s. The Board of Control also tried to quiet grumbling about such mundane matters as mandatory class attendance and "pop quizzes." It also tried to assure students that they had a voice in their own destiny by issuing a Student Bill of Rights and Responsibilities. The document declared "the student in the university should be granted the right to make vital decisions concerning his academic life and accept responsibility for those decisions." Undergraduates adopted the statement in a general election in March 1968 by a vote of 3,873 to 522. Mark Reese, editorialized in the *Evergreen* that it was "the greatest single achievement of the Board of Control during the year."[13]

Reese may have been correct in his estimation of events, for the debate over rights and responsibilities stimulated further criticism of the *status quo* and of efforts to implement change. As a matter of fact, the Associated Students contributed its potentially most important assistance toward building a new curriculum when it published a *Course and Instructor Critique* (1968), a student evaluation of 225 courses and instructors teaching them. Although lack of time and a shortage of funds forced a reduction of the scale of evaluation from a projected 500 courses, the objective was noteworthy: The *Critique's* intended purpose was to assist students in selecting classes, as well as "to create a deeper interest in, and perhaps later, monetary rewards for good teaching."[14]

As early as March 1968 the Board of Control also sought out student attitudes toward the military draft and the Vietnam War with a referendum. A ballot with eight possible responses, the poll attracted 4,494 respondents, a number perhaps twice as large as a normal turnout for student-body elections. Great interest did not produce a clear-cut campus opinion, however. A majority favored continued fighting but support for unconditional escalation found only 453 adherents. On the other hand, 672 demanded immediate and uncon-

As early as March 1968 the Board of Control also sought out student attitudes toward the military draft and the Vietnam War with a referendum. A ballot with eight possible responses, the poll attracted 4,494 respondents, a number perhaps twice as large as a normal turnout for student-body elections.

ditional withdrawal from Southeast Asia. Some 133 ventured no opinion at all. The *Evergreen* staff, surveying the widely scattered voting, still found one category omitted—the decision to make a slow and safe withdrawal.[15]

Washington State University's response to a National Student Strike set for April 26, 1968 revealed nothing but apathy for a distant event as only one class was cancelled for the occasion. In fact, a university official reported that class absences for the day seemed normal. However, developments within the national protest movement would soon alter this situation. A few days after the aborted strike, Student Body President Steve Kikuchi joined 500 other student-body officers across the nation in sponsoring a four-page advertisement in the New York *Times* decrying the Vietnam War as unjust and immoral and asserting that they (and their constituents) should not be forced to fight in it. About the same time, a number of white and minority faculty members and Black students joined together in calling for a more active policy for Black student recruitment and funding for scholarships for minorities. Slowly, the campus was becoming politicized.[16]

Then an unfortunate incident occurred, triggered by misunderstanding, insensitive gestures, and racial slurs, which brought home to the campus community the immediacy of racism. On the evening of Thursday, May 9, 1968, fifty-four Black students from Seattle's Garfield High School arrived in Pullman for a campus visit. Expecting to find hospitality they were greeted instead with insults.

Due to an oversight, residence hall officials were not prepared to receive the visitors. The ensuing confusion understandably disturbed the young Blacks who were forced to stand around and wait. The situation worsened when a few WSU students began taunting the them with racial slurs. Then, at 2:30 in the morning, the students boarded a bus to return to Seattle. President Terrell promptly issued a public apology and a lament for this ill-treatment. On the other hand, the *Evergreen* editor may have expressed a more prevalent attitude when he turned a blind eye to racism and wrote of the incident that "a ridiculous mountain is born [out of a molehill?]."[17]

The campus experienced sharp escalation of racial tensions on January 15, 1969, in the aftermath of an intramural basketball game between a white fraternity and a Black dormitory team. Misunderstanding led to violence when the Black players from Goldsworthy Hall visited the fraternity, Alpha Gamma Rho, uninvited. In a scuffle that followed, two shots were fired, fortunately striking only the building. Subsequently, two Black students admitted firing the shots and were taken to Colfax, the county seat, charged with second degree assault. Three other Blacks later joined them, charged with third degree assault. All five were found guilty.[18] Those convicted of third-degree assault were sentenced to thirty days, the others to ninety days incarceration, much of which they served on weekends so that they might continue their studies.

A number of students, white as well as minority, journeyed seventeen miles north to Colfax to intercede bodily against jailing the

Washington State University's response to a National Student Strike set for April 26, 1968 revealed nothing but apathy for a distant event as only one class was cancelled for the occasion.

President Terrell placed great faith in the ability of men and women of good will to prevent escalation of tensions and incidents into action which would "seriously impair . . . efforts to create at WSU an environment conducive to learning for all members of the campus community."

convicted. Forty-one students and one faculty member were incarcerated briefly, amid rumors that local citizens were driving around town with loaded guns. Later, Leonard Kirschner, chair of the University's Human Relations Committee, denied the that the threat of vigilantism was serious when he reported that "the residents of Colfax acted better than we expected residents of a small rural town should in such a situation." Forty-two people were fined twenty-five dollars each for obstructing the judicial process and were placed on probation until January 1, 1970. President Terrell defused tensions by suspending University discipline against the activists and the convicted on the grounds that the legal punishments had been enough.[19]

President Terrell placed great faith in the ability of men and women of good will to prevent escalation of tensions and incidents into action which would "seriously impair . . . efforts to create at WSU an environment conducive to learning for all members of the campus community." Looking about the campus Terrell might well have felt some security in his position. When pressured by an ad hoc committee in early October, 1969, to prohibit military recruiting on campus he argued that students had the right to consider serving in the military forces. He soon found that the "Young Americans for Freedom," the Student Senate, and a special blue ribbon faculty and administrator's committee agreed with his decision to permit such recruiting.[20]

When the student body participated in a nationwide moratorium of the Vietnam War on October 15, 1969, an *Evergreen* reporter guessed that several thousand" people were present to protest war or simply to watch the activities. Interestingly, Governor Dan Evans lent his presence. Later, he wrote to President Nixon that the 2500 students he estimated as present represented a cross-section of the University. But despite representing all political factions, "they all shared one thing in common, a deepening dismay over a seemingly endless war in Southeast Asia." Their voices needed to be heard, he concluded "if we are to have any real hope of attaining an honorable peace abroad or solutions to our problems here at home."[21]

Optimism concerning academic reform flared up briefly on campus when, on May 6, 1969, the Resident Instructional Staff approved a joint resolution of the Educational Policies Committee and the Black Studies Committee to establish programs in American Minority Studies. The proposal had the endorsement of twelve department chairs in the humanities, social sciences, and education. Not only would Blacks be part of the group but the Black Studies Program, leading to the Bachelor of Arts degree, would be the first minority curriculum developed. The rationale for beginning with Black Studies was easy to establish. Black Student organizations had worked earliest and hardest for their program and they already had sufficient materials and even had the benefit of a few minority courses established by existing departments. Plans were laid, too, for a Chicano program and one for Native Americans.[22]

The expectation was that Blacks might work toward goals of equality and justice through the program and that sympathetic instructors would be absolutely essential to that end. Hence, the original petition called for recruiting "whenever possible, faculty with an appropriate experience and identification with Black people." Furthermore, the leaders anticipated that white students would flock to these new courses as they had to protest marches and demonstrations and that some would major in Black Studies.[23]

President Terrell, too, joined other campus leaders in expressing gratitude for developing a means for avoiding radical confrontation through wide-spread support of ethnic studies. Shortly after the first classes convened in the fall of 1969, the *Evergreen* revealed support for Terrell's hopes when it announced that four students had declared Black Studies majors and 424 students had enrolled in the six ethnic courses offered. Since it is estimated that no more than 132 Blacks were enrolled at the time, it is obvious that Black Studies had campus-wide support.[24]

The hoped-for peaceful, orderly development of ethnic studies programs was seriously impaired by outside events some months later. President Nixon's decision to sent troops into Cambodia on April 30, 1970, fueled student discontent and triggered rioting and demonstrations at campuses across the nation. Then, on May 4, 1970, National Guardsmen fired on protesting Kent State University students, killing four. That action brought a gathering of 400 students in Pullman who voted to strike by noon the next day if certain demands were not met. Besides introducing a frightening sense of crisis, dissidents tried to push Terrell into the role of peace advocate. They demanded, first, that he telegraph President Nixon deploring the Kent State tragedy. Second, they insisted that Terrell cancel classes and all other official activities for one day to protest sending troops to Cambodia.[25]

President Terrell called off classes after discussions with faculty and student leaders in the belief that it would be better to give students an opportunity to discuss the war constructively rather than to bottle up emotions and anger. He sent his protest letter to Nixon but made it clear that it was a personal statement, thus remaining true to his conviction that the University should not become politicized.[26]

A second day of protest followed in which three faculty members joined students in denouncing the war and the student killings at Kent State. In the afternoon, approximately 700 persons invaded the French Administration Building, a number which rose to 800 or more by nine o'clock in the evening. As the *Evergreen* described the scene, a peaceful atmosphere prevailed, in which "sympathetic faculty wives" served coffee, soft drinks, and sandwiches. Stereo and radio music added to a carnival mood. After discussions between protest leaders and administrators, the invaders cleaned up the mess and left quietly.[27]

Terrell had been wise to couch his objections to the war in personal terms since 1600 persons subsequently signed a petition protesting his action in telegraphing to Nixon. They also made it clear that they opposed the cancelling of classes. A poll of 600 graduate students (about one-half of those active on the campus) found fifty-

The hoped-for peaceful, orderly development of ethnic studies programs was seriously impaired by outside events some months later. President Nixon's decision to send troops into Cambodia on April 30, 1970, fueled student discontent and triggered rioting and demonstrations at campuses across the nation. Then, on May 4, 1970, National Guardsmen fired on protesting Kent State University students, killing four.

*Protest activity reached a
boiling point on May 18, 1970,
when the Black Student Union,
MECHA (the Chicano student
group), and several other
radical organizations, as well as
the Women's Liberation Front,
issued eleven "non-negotiable
demands" to the
administration.*

eight per cent favoring the decision to cancel classes, with thirty-eighty percent opposed. Only four percent offered no opinion, a matter that revealed the prevalence of highly emotional responses to the presidential gesture.[28]

A "teach-in" involving 800 people, held shortly after, denounced war, the plight of the Chicanos, and advocated women's rights. Speakers at one lone rally, with about 250 people in attendance offered "a rational alternative," and deplored the irrationalism stirred up by the protests as detrimental to the fragile teaching and learning process. At noon, there was a memorial service in Bryan Auditorium for the four students killed at Kent State. Finally, despite whatever else might have transpired, the YWCA's Racial Justice Committee continued to insist that students were not fully conscious of the racial prejudice still rampant on the WSU campus.[29]

Protest activity reached a boiling point on May 18, 1970, when the Black Student Union, MECHA (the Chicano student group), and several other radical organizations, as well as the Women's Liberation Front, issued eleven "non-negotiable demands" to the administration. The underlying purpose of those demands was clear. The proponents feared continued denial of full civil rights and perpetuation of poorly developed ethnic studies programs unless ample budgets and skilled assistance in recruiting and counselling could be forced from the administration. A Strike Steering Committee composed of whites supported the minorities. Given the climate of the times, however, minorities felt isolated. They even demanded a kind of "extraterritoriality" on the campus in which "Third World" people would judge and discipline themselves.[30]

Placing great faith in "teach-ins," the protest leaders demanded a mandatory ten-day anti-racism workshop for all staff and faculty at the beginning of each academic year. These programs were to be developed by minority group members. They also made the staggering demand that within three years the University must achieve a racial balance.[31]

Terrell rejected the eleven demands on grounds that they were not constructive, manifestly impossible to fulfill, and because they infringed upon the prerogatives of the president and the Board of Regents. Thereafter, a move to stampede Blacks into withdrawing from school failed. Probably, Terrell's explanation that he remained strongly committed to eliminate racism and his friendly response to a crowd of perhaps 4000 people when they marched to his house pacified them.[32]

May 28th brought a climax to the Strike. Approximately 1,000 students marched around the campus before stopping at French Administration Building, where they expected a confrontation with the president. The meeting did not occur. Failure came when the Black Student Union and MECHA decided, for reasons not clear, to avoid a confrontation.

At that point, attention shifted to an afternoon meeting of the Resident Instructional Staff, which had an extraordinarily large attendance of perhaps 600 members and an unprecedented invasion by students. In numbers large and uncounted, students did not merely congregate in the foyer or along the walls of the auditorium. They sat in members' seats and posed the threat of voting illegally in deliberations. President Terrell, the presiding officer, ignored the student presence as the body approved legislation which the strikers had demanded.[33]

At this May 28 meeting, the Resident Instructional Staff approved a B.A. program in Chicano Studies. It also ratified a liberalized grading program for the often disrupted semester just ending, a matter of equal concern to strikers and non-strikers. In recognition of the recent escalating desire among students to participate in partisan politics, the body approved a plan to permit them to take leave from their studies to campaign in elections, fitting such activities, however awkwardly, into academic programs. Finally, the Resident Instructional Staff authorized two-day, anti-racism workshops for each of the 1970-1971 semesters to prepare faculty and students for life in a new era.

Of the interested minorities, probably only the Blacks, whose ethnic studies program had been functioning for a year, failed to make substantial gains in 1970. Indeed, they suffered a serious loss when Dr. Johnetta Cole, Director of the program, resigned from the university in protest over what she termed the administration's failures. Perhaps her cohorts were mollified when, in mid-summer, President Terrell appointed four minority students, one a Black, to the committee planning the workshops to be held the coming year.[34]

Public reception of the strike and support for the solution of problems by the campus community as a whole are matters difficult to measure. Clearly, the protesters and bystanders represented a small fraction of the 14,520 student enrollment in September 1970. The Black and the newly instituted Chicano Studies courses enrolled

Washington State University's campus in 1971. To the left of center the Fine Arts Center, which was completed in 1972, can be seen under construction. (Washington State University News Service)

The two anti-racism workshops were held in due course, the first on October 7 and 8, 1970, and the second on March 9, and 10, 1971. The October gathering, coupled with dismissal of classes, attracted perhaps as many as 5,000 persons—students, faculty, and townspeople—who were exhorted by one speaker to engage in "the revolutionizing of universities and the rehumanizing of society."

393 and 150 students. These numbers are significant in light of the fact that only 132 Blacks and thirty-eight Chicanos were in enrolled in the University at the time. Thus, the majority of students taking minorities courses were white, a testimony to their considerable sympathy and interest in the minority issues.

In the case of the faculty, the extent of support for, or opposition to, the president's handing of the strike emergency remains debatable, as no formal resolution on the subject came from the Resident Instructional Staff meeting. An informal "rump" session, held immediately after the RIS had adjourned from its May 28 meeting, produced a voiced support for the president from approximately 400 faculty. Letters from the public expressed outrage over the president's failure to expel faculty and students who had struck to support the freedom of discussion on campus. President Terrell uniformly expressed gratitude for such messages and, responded in a quiet manner. Even when permissive behavior was labeled socialism or communism by a legislator, Terrell responded diplomatically, stating "yours is a thoughtful letter." The varied and sometimes outrageous suggestions for dismissing faculty and students must have settled more deeply his conviction that the executive officer could not speak for the university, or permit it to become politicized, if it was to survive.[35]

The two anti-racism workshops were held in due course, the first on October 7 and 8, 1970, and the second on March 9, and 10, 1971. The October gathering, coupled with dismissal of classes, attracted perhaps as many as 5,000 persons—students, faculty, and townspeople—who were exhorted by one speaker to engage in "the revolutionizing of universities and the rehumanizing of society." Numerous speakers excoriated white racism, leaving many Caucasians with a strong sense of guilt. On the other hand, extravagant rhetoric seemingly did nothing to reduce the distance separating the minorities from one another. Indeed, Native American students absented themselves from the workshop, affirming that they had not been consulted regarding the eleven demands and that, in addition, they had special claims which had not been heard.[36]

Speakers at the second workshop once again sought to educate the whites about racism, but also revealed a continuing division among the minority groups themselves, in spite of the fact that two Native Americans now sat on the speaker's platform. The University's Social Research Center polled the campus, reporting "broad approval" of the first workshop by faculty, students, and townspeople. After the second workshop, pollsters reported a "generally favorable" response. But of those questioned, only twelve percent of faculty, staff, and townspeople believed that the second workshop was more valuable than the two days of classes would have been, while sixty-two percent of the students voted for the workshop.[37]

At the approach of the fall semester, Chicanos launched a bachelor's degree program and began to focus attention on their own interpretation of Chicano culture. An easy target for their criticism was a Chicano History course, offered by the Department of History.

Taught by a History graduate student, it met with utter disapproval by Chicanos attending the class. The teaching assistant offered an orthodox treatment of Mexican history, whereas the Chicanos were demanding a new interpretation of their past. As a result, the teaching assistant was forced to resign. The course was dropped by the History Department on the grounds that the teacher's academic freedom had been violated and because there was no other competent instructor available.

Chicano militancy also turned to protests and picketing against the sale of lettuce from California farms that had refused to bargain with Caesar Chavez's United Farm Workers Organizing Committee, representing Chicano field workers. Picketing continued for some time, but the university remained neutral, once again, in a political dispute despite student pressure for it to boycott non-union lettuce. The Chicano program, in the meantime, prospered, as evidenced by the fact that sixty-five new students enrolled in September of 1972, and a number Chicanos had certified majors in a variety of fields from communications to public health.[38]

The Native Americans, who had ignored the Strike and the first workshop, pursued their goals through committee channels. Discussions, begun in the spring of 1971, yielded a curricular proposal similar to those of Blacks and Chicanos In addition, the Native American plan called for special attention to the needs of Indians on reservations and to the social needs of all Native Americans. Lengthy delays in responding to the proposal occurred, due primarily to the university's inability to find a permanent director. On February 27, 1975, the University Senate (successor to the Resident Instructional Staff as a governing body) approved the Native American program and classes met for the first time in the following September.[39]

Japanese American students and faculty apparently first proposed an Asian-American program when, on March 4, 1973, they formed an Asian-American Students Association. There is no evidence that they had participated formally in any protest, strike, or workshop up to that time. Events moved slowly until a startling development on September 18, 1978. At that time the Spokane Japanese American Citizens League sued the University on behalf of four students and one former student for failure to respond to the educational needs of their minority. After amendment in March 1979, the suit included all Asian Americans, not merely Japanese. By coincidence, a university committee had announced a plan for a minor in Asian American Studies on the day the suit was started. While the suit remained pending, the University Senate approved the completed program, which had been developed by a cross-campus committee, headed by Dr. George Brain, Dean of the School of Education. The program included a minor in Asian American studies and courses that reflected the broad spectrum of Asian American cultures involved. Regents approved the program to start in September 1979. The principals in the suit later settled the issue out of court, essentially along the lines of the program already approved and in place.[40]

Chicano militancy also turned to protests and picketing against the sale of lettuce from California farms that had refused to bargain with Caesar Chavez's United Farm Workers Organizing Committee, representing Chicano field workers.

Professor of Anthropology Richard D. Dougherty has been cited as Washington's premier archaeologist. A member of the WSU faculty from 1954 to 1983, he developed innovative new techniques for carrying on archaeological investigation. He is particularly noted for work at the Ozette site on the Washington coast that has led to a better understanding of prehistoric Native American culture in the Pacific Northwest. (Washington State University News Service)

The excitement that accompanied the establishment of the new ethnic studies programs waned after a time. Louis McNew, Director of the Curricular Advisory Program, which served students until they declared majors, recognized the urgency of the matter in January, 1980. At that time he reported to his staff of advisors that "The single strongest argument for these programs was that the University had a responsibility to provide for non-minority students an opportunity for an academic experience in the character and problems of minority groups. This experience was . . . one of the several ways to combat racism on campus and in society. . . ." Ironically, the programs were conceived in the midst of tension and crisis, but the cooling of tempers had brought neither relief from nor the death of racism. McNew now sought to kindle a renewed interest in ethnic studies as therapy for whites by encouraging all lower-division students to enroll in at least one of the minority classes.[41]

Unfortunately, registration at the next fall Semester left the Chicano Studies Program with only seventy-six enrollments in its six classes and special problems work. Fernando Padilla, director of the program, had sent out 1500 copies of the Fall Schedule in Chicano Studies, following the example of McNew the semester before, only to find little success. He was as greatly disturbed as McNew that the anti-racist objective was not being met. He reported for example, that Anglo enrollments in "Introduction to Chicano Studies" had dropped from fifteen in a class of twenty-seven in 1979 to only one of six in 1980. His question to McNew: "Why have CAP advisors suddenly stopped advising students to take our courses" might well have been regarded as simply rhetorical. No one had a solution to the problem of declining enrollment.[42]

Fall registration for 1988 revealed a happier turn of events for Chicano Studies as the introductory course had 216 enrollees. The four other courses added only forty-one enrollees to the program. Black Studies, however, had changed little between 1980 and 1988. It had total enrollments of 194 in 1980 and a rise to 219 eight years later. The Native American Program probably grew fastest in the 1980s, rising from forty-two enrollees in the first year to 356 in 1988. The Asian/Pacific American Studies Program had hardly started in 1980 but had 109 students in 1988. There is nothing to suggest a dramatic increase in the number of white student enrollees or an increased hope of eliminating racism through these curriculum changes. Nevertheless, it seems obvious that exposure of white students to these cultures should improve the cultural tone of the University.[43]

A movement for women's rights, akin to the ethnic studies and minority right developments became a major issue on campus in the 1970s. Traditionally, women, whether faculty, staff, or students, had suffered discrimination and restricted opportunities at Washington State University, as elsewhere.

In the Spring of 1971, however, President Terrell established a Commission on the Status of Women, composed of women faculty, staff, and students. Their task was to investigate and report on gender discrimination, to work with other interested women's groups, and to consider establishing an affirmative action program. This program would seek to enforce equal opportunity for women and minorities in employment. In addition, the commission would investigate possible educational programs for and about women.[44]

In the next ten months the Commission addressed a number of pressing problems. Among their concerns was the development of a coherent maternity leave policy for women (and paternity leave policy for men) that would enable faculty members to serve as role models for students in pursuit of both careers and families. The commission also undertook indoctrination of men, seeking to persuade them to use "inclusionary" rather than "exclusionary" language. That is, it sought to exclude the use of male gender terms in favor of those incorporating men and women or neutral expressions.

The need for new policies became apparent when commission members investigated employment discrimination and found, for example, that there were eight male deans and only one female. Also, of the fifty-three department chairs four were women. They learned too, that only a mere 15.11 percent of the faculty (full and part-time, permanent and temporary) were women, 185 out of a body that numbered 1,224. The percentages of permanent, full-time professors roughly corresponded with the ratios for the entire faculty, since 14.03 percent of that group were women. Perhaps the most glaring example of deprivation in the professional ranks came among researchers, there being but one woman among the ninety-two on that roster. There were, of course, more subtle forms of discrimination. Men tended to be promoted faster than women. In the "trades and custodial" classification, for example, it took women almost five times as long as men to be reclassified to their advantage. Under these circumstances, it could hardly have been surprising that the Commission on the Status of Women called for introducing affirmative action procedures.[45]

Since 1972 the University's gains in the area of female employment have been significant though unspectacular. The 15.11 percent of faculty that were women increased to 24.8 percent in 1986. The greatest gains for women, as found in another ranking made in 1985, have been made at the assistant professor level, where 36.3 percent of the occupants were female. Women associate professors now constituted 18.4 percent of that rank in 1985. At the full professorship, the story had a different twist. There are many fields in which women have not been prepared by training and experience to enter the full professorial rank. In 1979 6.4 percent of the possessors of that rank were women but since then declines have left only 5.2 percent of the positions in the hands of women. An ad hoc committee reporting in 1988 also recognized that minority women—and by implication minority men, though not reported—were in a far less desirable situation than were white women. Thus, though important gains had been made in overcoming sex discrimination in employment, much had still to be accomplished.[46]

Efforts to achieve equality between men and women in intercollegiate athletics remained incomplete at the end of WSU's first century, but much had been achieved. A byproduct has been the merging of women's and men's physical education departments into a single Department of Physical Education, Sport, and Leisure Studies.

Salaries, of course, were another important and sensitive measure by which progress in women's rights might be judged. In 1972, the mean salary for men on permanent appointment at the full professional rank, with doctorate, reached $17,667, a figure which was $1460 higher than that for women. At the associate professor's rank the difference favored men only by twenty dollars but male assistant professors enjoyed a median salary of $900 higher than that of women. The margin widened, at least psychologically, when women noted that in every case but one, they served longer in rank than did men.

In 1988, the mean salaries for men remained greater than for women full and assistant professors. Unlike 1972, however, women associate professors had the higher mean salary figure, it being $666 above that of the men. Such figures do not yield clear evidence of improvement, or the lack of it, since many factors cannot be taken into account by a mere salary study. Intimation of women's progress can be seen, however, in the fact that *more* women are found in each rank than was true in 1972. At that time, only thirty-three women with doctorates were in the three ranks. In 1988, the number of women with doctorates had risen to eighty-two, with the number of women full professors rising from seven to sixteen.[47]

Employing more women on the faculty and making their salaries comparable to those of men had been, in part, responses to mandates by the federal government. The first came in 1965 the form of Executive Order Number 11246 as amended in 1967 by Executive Order Number 11375. These decrees forbade discrimination in employment on the basis of race, color, creed, national origin, or sex at institutions holding federal contracts. Then, in 1972, Congress, under Title IX of the Education Act of 1972, prohibited exclusion of anyone in the nation from the benefits of education programs on the basis of sex. In both cases the federal government possessed ample means of enforcement of the decrees—i.e., withholding federal monies from contracts with educational institutions until compliance was assured.[48]

These thrusts of federal authority precluded the possibility of evading or long postponing steps toward equality in more than employment. In response, the university administration soon appointed an affirmative action officer to monitor employment compliance. Across the campus, affirmative action came to mean that both vernacular and polite language had to be purged of sexist expressions and exclusionary use of male terms when both sexes were involved in events and discussion. The Director of Residence Living pledged to eliminate "beauty queen" contests—of which there were many, apparently—arguing that they singled out one sex for exploitation by the other. Likewise, efforts were made to balance the publicity and news of women's sports with those of the men in university publications.[49]

Indeed, the struggle for equality in women's athletics proceeded slowly, became filled with acrimony, and occupied an inordinate amount of time, energy, and resources. It should be noted, at least in passing, that equality of educational opportunity concerned more than athletics, for it dealt also with student services and employment, admissions, and the like. But athletics received the greatest attention.

In February of 1979, for example, a delegation of women met with the Regents to complain of inequities in funding women's sports. They were strongly seconding a detailed bill of grievances issued by the federal government as it sought compliance with Title IX. That report stipulated that although males at the university represented but 68.1 percent of the total number of athletes, they received all but 8.8 percent of athletic funds. In every category, from locker-room space to athletic scholarships, from travel funds to equipment and uniforms, the University had failed to comply with Title IX. A peremptory command to reply to federal authorities did not solve problems.[50]

Efforts to achieve equality between men and women in intercollegiate athletics remained incomplete at the end of WSU's first century, but much had been achieved. A byproduct has been the merging of women's and men's physical education departments into a single Department of Physical Education, Sport, and Leisure Studies. This development is in keeping with the ideal of equal curricular opportunities. It also worked, at least at first, to the detriment of women's sports, as coaches shared responsibilities in physical education classes.[51]

The ideal of achieving equality between men's and women's athletics, which is inherent in Title IX, came to be exemplified by the Blair case. This well-known piece of litigation came to a head in August 1987, when the appellants, a number of women coaches and athletes, were upheld in their complaint that WSU had not complied with the mandate to guarantee equality in athletics. The university, as a result of the decision in the Blair Case, came under obligation to provide sufficient scholarships for women to overcome the traditional imbalances that had left the men with 140 out of 196 total awards. When the Washington Supreme Court ruled that football, with its large number of scholarships had to be included in consideration, the task of first priority became that of finding enough women's sports and money to provide the balance. Other possibilities not meeting with much support or enthusiasm included reducing the size of the football program or eliminating all men's sports except football and basketball in order to provide a balance.[52]

The Commission on the Status of Women, which began reporting on women's issues in 1972, had by 1975 turned to searching for ways and means to elevate extension work (night classes, off-campus programs) to full recognition for resident, campus credit. Commission members were anxious to meet the needs of those who soon would be called "place-bound women," those who could not participate in standard day-time higher education programs or move to Pullman and study. That idea became eclipsed, as attention shifted to establishing a Women's Resource Center to provide guidance, counseling, and material support to encourage women to come to Pullman to study. The Commission also proposed a women studies program dedicated to offering academic courses concerning women.[53]

A setback to a united women's front arose in 1975 when women in the Chicano Studies Program declined to participate in the proposed Women Studies Program, fearing they would be deprived of effective input. A committee of minority women, on May 5, 1975, also withdrew its support for Women Studies and other special programs, pleading that they had unique needs and values. The Native American women submitted their own rejection on June 5, 1975, noting that they had a greater need for a program involving both men and women. The social distance involved can be judged from their statement that "For Indian women to work with non-Indian women requires drastic changes in our values, which we frequently find frustrating and we will not accept."[54]

Despite these rejections, the Women's Resource Center opened in 1974, on a restricted basis, dispensing advice, and other aid to female students. The Women Studies Program started in 1977, offering a minor in that subject. Included in the curriculum was a new course, "Introduction to Women Studies." According to the WSU Catalog for 1978-1980, it provided "multidisciplinary perspectives on women and on their past, present, and potential contributions." Other courses were borrowed (or "cross-listed") from other departments. In sum, the curriculum was designed ambitiously not only to provide a systematic study of the literature on women but also to prepare the enrollees to better understand "gender related activities" and to promote "sexual equality."[55]

The most facile and easily obtained measure of the program's success are enrollment figures and the number of specialized courses offered. In September of 1980, for instance, total Women Studies enrollment was 112, with only one male enrollee, in two program courses and seven cross-listed offerings from other departments. In September 1988, Women Studies enrollees numbered 136, with nineteen males included. More to the point concerning the growing strength of the program, 1988 saw 112 students enrolled in four Women Studies program courses whereas in 1980 only twenty-two had been in that category, the remainder, of course, having been in cross-listed classes.[56]

Women's gains in academic programming did not resolve all doubts held by women and minorities about student welfare. Anxiety arose in 1977—if not earlier—when it became known that President Terrell planned to abolish the office of Vice-President for Student Affairs upon the retirement of James C. Clevenger in January 1978. Debate arose over two issues. The first concerned the protection of student rights and privileges, which were seen to be dependant on retaining the vice-presidency to insure that students had a spokesman in immediate touch with the president. The second issue centered upon the desire to elevate a woman or a member of an ethnic minority to the office, thus symbolizing the Affirmative Action program's success.[57]

When Terrell "suspended" the vice-presidency in the spring of 1977 (to take effect when Clevenger retired) the *Evergreen* reported that the object was to save $50,000 for educational purposes in a time of budgetary constraint. Severe criticism immediately arose from the student government and other, informed groups. Some critics challenged the president's claim that he would save a substantial sum by abolishing the vice-presidency. Terrell, in a response that would have been uncharacteristic earlier in his administration, reported that he had heard little of the uproar over the position and that he thought reaction was balanced between the pros and cons.

He could hardly have misunderstood the unhappiness over the suspension of the vice-presidency voiced in a somewhat raucous meeting of the Board of Regents on April 29, 1977. At that gathering student and minority leaders expressed their fears over deteriorating student services and the administration's failure to carry out affirmative action procedures. Three weeks later, on May 19, 1977, additional strains were placed on Terrell's customary good relations with students when approximately 100 people crowded into a meeting of the Student Affairs Restructuring Task Force and several speakers accused him of failing to live up to his responsibilities to women and minorities.[58]

Acrimonious discussion continued through the summer and fall of 1977 over Terrell's suspension of the vice-presidency and its implication for affirmative action and equality of opportunity. On October 28, the Regents reviewed affirmative action results on the campus, listening to Executive Vice-President Wallis Beasley state his opinion that the university was living up to its obligations. He reported that the number of ethnic minorities had increased by ninety percent since 1970, "despite complaints to the contrary."[59]

Beasley especially noted that the University had financed seventy-nine minority and women graduate students in a variety of sciences, engineering, and other disciplines, with fifteen Ph.D. degrees awarded, and others in process. He also called attention to the fact that there were 130 minority graduate students currently enrolled, constituting nearly seven percent of the total graduate enrollment. Total ethnic enrollment had risen from 470 in 1970 to 803 in 1977, but more needed to be accomplished since the latter figure represented only 4.8 percent of the total University student body. Most disturbing, however, was a decline in the number of Black students.[60]

The Executive Vice-President acknowledged that employment of women and minorities had lagged behind expectations in all categories—faculty, staff, and administration. Of faculty, for example, only four percent were from the minorities and but twenty percent of that group were women. Beasley hoped to rectify discrepancies in one area at a time instead, presumably, of scattering prominent but "cosmetic" appointments to bring favorable publicity. The result, in any case, was likely to leave an impression, as one critic had put it earlier, that the upper administration was "a white man's club."[61]

While failing to resolve all the issues of discrimination and affirmative action, the administration did not face a repetition of the difficulties of 1969 and 1970. Indeed, Terrell and the Regents, on September 3, 1970, had agreed upon a set of regulations to deal with possible racial and anti-war protests. These regulations were designed to

The Board of Regents approved the University Senate on April 12, 1971, but the issue of undergraduate student membership and adequacy of faculty representation remained in contention.

protect the civil rights of all persons and to guarantee freedom of expression and acceptance of accompanying responsibilities. So armed, Terrell expressed confidence that he would be able to handle the "survival issues." That he did not face more student strikes but instead engaged in more rational debates on how and when to implement programs testifies to his leadership as well as to a return to good sense on the campus as tempers cooled.[62]

Instead of concentrating on "survival," Terrell turned to creating a new vehicle for cooperative faculty-student debate on legislative matters, formerly the prerogative solely of the faculty. In point of fact, faculty committees, at least since 1965, had considered introducing a senate to replace governance by the unwieldy body of the whole, the Resident Instructional Staff. After much debate, that body yielded to enthusiasm for not merely a senate but for an *All-University Senate*, with undergraduate and graduate student representatives as well as faculty. Inclusion of students represented a concession to Terrell's sense of leadership and his desire to draw undergraduates and graduates into the center of his administration. Faculty leaders vacillated between the fear that democratic practices might not survive in a institution that was less than the "whole" and the desire for the greater efficiency in legislative procedures promised by a smaller representative body.[63]

The Board of Regents approved the University Senate on April 12, 1971, but the issue of undergraduate student membership and adequacy of faculty representation remained in contention. Indeed, some faculty leaders remained skeptical of the possibility that the new body might provide adequate representation for their special interests. The Resident Instructional staff conducted inquiries in 1975 and 1978 into its operations. But, despite criticisms and freely expressed frustrations about a perceived loss of faculty power, RIS supported retention of the Senate.[64]

From time to time, Senate chairs tried to inspire leadership within that body and faculty support of it. The results were only partially successful. Chairman Toshio Akamine, Professor of Education, opened the 1978-1979 Senate year by voicing a widespread conviction that the Senate's prestige had declined since its earliest days. Records supported his contention, as average attendance at sessions stood at only 70.5 percent in 1977 whereas it had reached 75.8 percent three years earlier. Akamine proposed to reverse the decline by seeking ways and means to involve senators more intensively in committee work. Two years later, another chair, Extension Economist Bruce Florea, repeated the same complaint when he called for "more broadly based and more serious participation by faculty and students in the Senate and its various committees and sub-committees." The difficulty of attaining such a goal had not escaped his notice, however, for he commented that "Senate service is viewed across this campus as anywhere from moderately desirable . . . to an outright detriment. . . ."[65]

The presence of undergraduate students came to be the most serious obstacle to the Senate's credibility in the eyes of critics among the faculty. To them, student participation in legislative deliberations seemed an affront and a denial of their prerogatives. Finally, on May 26, 1982, the Resident Instructional Staff enjoined its Executive Committee to cooperate with the University Senate's Steering Committee in drawing up plans for an exclusively Faculty Senate. The plans were prepared, endorsed by the Resident Instructional Staff in November, 1982, and by the University Senate on March 31, 1983. The Board of Regents made the change official on June 3 of that year. Thereafter, the faculty senators, along with a few graduate students, could settle down to deliberate in Faculty Senate without having to contend with undergraduates voting *en bloc*, often not in the perceived best interests of the faculty.[66]

Shortly before the demise of the University Senate, Donald Bushaw, its chairman and a Professor of Mathematics, offered a benediction. It had been a good year, for which he thanked the senators, a year in which its members had in effect, refuted the commonly "stylish" criticism that "the Senate was [an] ineffective body." It had, in reality, "covered a good deal of ground . . . in a methodical and constructive way with reasonable despatch."

Then, looking toward the future, he expressed optimism about a growing collegiality and strengthened role in governing the university, a conclusion drawn from the Senate's legislative successes. That body, he stated, had "prevailed or [has] seemed almost certain to prevail" on most issues of importance taken up with the administration. The Senate's task in the future, he thought, must be to maintain and enlarge its role in legislation and in perpetuating good relations with the whole campus community.[67]

The faculty's concern for undergraduate education—apart from its decision to banish undergraduate representatives from the Senate—had been strongly demonstrated at intervals ever since the beginning of Compton's administration. At that time, in 1946, the Committee of Forty adopted a plan for general college graduation requirements. Under this plan, students selected certain courses in the humanities, social sciences, and natural sciences as a means of acquiring the basic elements of a general education. This program remained unchanged in its objectives and general pattern of operation to the end of the 1970s, except for the addition of new courses. Indeed, a great deal of concern arose over the number of unsuitable offerings added to the list, which grew from 120 in 1946 to 175 in 1973.

Efforts to replace these amorphous general university requirements with a rational list arose in the middle of the 1970s. Special action was needed, as the list of courses had risen to 312 and included many that were little more than fragments of broad fields of learning, while others were blatantly technical or professional. In 1980, a special committee headed by Professor Joseph Hindman reduced the number of these courses to 154. The refined list became official in the fall of 1985.[68]

The panel of courses was augmented by a new category entitled inter-cultural studies, a group of classes that were non-European and non-North American in content and designed to introduce students

Associate Professor of Zoology Kenneth V. Kardong directs research at WSU on poisonous snakes. In recent years he has done research on varieties from rattlesnakes to the rare Chinese species, the Fea's Viper. Professor Kardong became editor of the journal Northwest Science *in 1986.* (Washington State University News Service)

Further attempts to improve the caliber of educational performance arose on October 30, 1975, when the University Senate debated a proposal to require a minimum of forty-five semester hours of upper division work for graduation, to replace the thirty semester hour standard followed since 1971.

to parts of the world long neglected in American higher education. All students were required to take at least one three-hour course from a group of diversified studies, which ranged from the "History of Japan" to the "Philosophies and Religions of India." Reaching beyond what some still regarded as a "cafeteria" offering of disparate courses, the committee also began planning required introductory core courses, broadly cross-cultural, and projects to improve written communication.[69]

Further attempts to improve the caliber of educational performance arose on October 30, 1975, when the University Senate debated a proposal to require a minimum of forty-five semester hours of upper division work for graduation, to replace the thirty semester hour standard followed since 1971. The Senate timidly sent the measure back to committee, despite the fact that graduates of the preceding year had averaged 53.4 semester hours and even the college with the lowest requirements had not fallen below an average of 48 semester hours per student. Then, on January 15, 1976, the Senate cautiously raised the minimum standard for graduation to thirty-five hours for all upper division studies. Finally, on April 26, 1979, the Senate raised the minimum number of upper-division credits required for graduation to forty, where it has remained ever since.[70]

The faculty also made an effort to raise entrance standards for freshmen, a measure designed in part to place pressure on the high schools to improve their instruction. On May 7, 1981, the University Senate recommended raising admission requirements from a 2.50 grade point average to 2.80 (C plus). But, the administration, perhaps fearful of enrollment declines, rejected the proposal, suggesting instead that priorities for admission be established by means of a complicated indexing system.[71]

The Academic Affairs Committee, in response to Terrell's suggestion, then spent two years formulating a comprehensive plan. It included a priority indexing system, which was to be based on high school grades, Washington Pre-College Test scores (or other tests where the prescribed test was not available), plus consideration of courses attempted. This plan, adopted for introduction in September 1988, laid down a rigorous course sequence for Washington high schools students who hoped to attend WSU. It included four years of English (specifically requiring a year of literature), three years of mathematics (through trigonometry), three years of social science (including one year of history), two years of a foreign language, and two years of science, including one year of laboratory work. Originally, the Academic Affairs Committee had set a higher standard for the natural sciences, calling for three years, two which must were to include laboratory work. The Senate reduced the requirement to two years when it recognized that the state had many small high schools which could not to meet the higher standard.[72]

Student interest in the quality of the university's faculty paralleled this concern for curriculum. Evidence of this interest can be found in the 1960s, when student body committees began evaluating teachers and courses. Finally in 1966, Student Body President Tom Glover appointed an editor for a course critique, plans were drawn, and the project completed in 1967. It proved to be a difficult undertaking but yielded information on 225 classes out of 500 originally planned for investigation. The dual propose of the Course and Instructor Critique, published by the Associated Students in 1968, was to reward good teaching with publicity—hoping it might lead to material rewards from other quarters—and to "help students in planning their curricula—particularly that outside their major field." This first effort actually yielded little publicity for outstanding or popular teaching and the numerical analysis of professor's traits and competence must have proven difficult to interpret.[73]

Guidance of this student evaluation process fell into the hands of the professors when, a decade later, in 1977, the Academic Affairs Committee recommended a broad program designed to improve instruction and aid in evaluating faculty for tenure and promotion. No publication of results was planned, since the purpose of the instrument would not be to measure popularity or to provide a "finding aid" for students. To be sure, evaluation by students remained useful and desirable, but judgments of *expertise* were to be made by experts. Tentative plans called for trying out established instruments in use at the University of Washington, Kansas State University, and Purdue University. Lack of funds soon dashed hopes of purchasing whose plans for trial, and no local scheme emerged to be used university-wide. Interest remained high in the utility of assessment, however, and eventually all or virtually all of the colleges and departments adopted one plan or another for evaluation.[74]

The demand for improved and extended education at Washington State University in the 1960s included an extraordinary request that it participate with Eastern Washington University and Whitworth College in establishing a full baccalaureate program in nursing education in Spokane. The demand came from the Spokane League for Nursing and the Inland Empire Nurse's Association, both of which recognized that Spokane hospitals could not train enough nurses to meet local needs nor provide them with a full collegiate education. Such a new program might strongly complement the largest B.S. program in the State, that of the University of Washington.[75]

The three institutions, plus Fort George Wright College of the Holy Names, agreed in September, 1968, to operate this cooperative program, the first of its kind in the United States. Students would receive general education and pre-nursing at their regular collegiate institutions and then undertake two years of clinical training at the Spokane center. Experienced diploma nurses, with the training gained in hospital programs, might also obtain a B.S. degree through this program. The Intercollegiate Center for Nursing Education, the formal title, found its first quarters in the antiquated Spokane center of Washington State University's extension program. Financing the nursing program, otherwise largely dependent on institutional support and student tuition fees, received a great impetus in 1971 from a $529,175.00 in federal funds; granted by the National Institute of Health.[76]

The building, named the Warren G. Magnuson Intercollegiate Nursing Building, was dedicated by Governor Dixy Lee Ray on August 27, 1980, in the presence of a large number of civic and academic leaders. Spokane and the consortium had good reason to be proud of their achievements as represented in this structure.

The Intercollegiate Center clearly met a great need, as evidenced by the fact that it had 183 students in 1971-1972 and 374 by fall, 1973. This rapid increase led the consortium to move to new quarters in the Washington School on Ash Street, no longer in use as a public school. The first graduating class in May 1971, included thirty-four members, of whom twenty-one came from Washington State University, eleven from Eastern Washington University, and one, each from Whitworth College and Fort Wright College.[77]

Accreditation of the Intercollegiate Center had not been a problem as national agencies had been impressed with the consortium from the beginning. Nevertheless, the continued successes of the program emphasized the need for a modern clinical facility. Thirteen acres were purchased next to the Spokane Falls Community College and on June 9, 1978, ground-breaking for a $5,900,000 structure took place. Senator Warren G. Magnuson was instrumental in obtaining a $3,500,000 grant from Congress to make the structure a reality.

The building, named the Warren G. Magnuson Intercollegiate Nursing Building, was dedicated by Governor Dixy Lee Ray on August 27, 1980, in the presence of a large number of civic and academic leaders. Spokane and the consortium had good reason to be proud of their achievements as represented in this structure. It contains four classrooms, nine seminar rooms, a nursing practice laboratory, and a clinical and behavioral observation laboratory. The Betty M. Anderson Library serves the campus in Spokane and off-campus continuing education centers in Yakima and other eastern Washington cities.

Availability of facilities and the need for high caliber professionalism led to the introduction of the master's degree in nursing, with the first four graduates completing their work in 1985. Development of the graduate program has been modest, but in March of 1987 it had thirty-one students. What is disconcerting is the fact that the Intercollegiate Center's undergraduate enrollment has followed a national trend by declining to approximately 250 students in 1988 from 376 four years earlier. By the close of the 1980s decade, three schools remained in the program, Fort George Wright having closed its doors in 1982. Currently, except for ten Whitworth students, the student body is divided about equally between Washington State and Eastern Washington universities.[78]

The State of Washington and the Pacific Northwest have also suffered from a tendency of medical doctors in the region to set up practice in larger cities, leaving people in smaller towns and rural communities without adequate medical service. To overcome these problems, and to train an increased number of medical doctors at lower cost, the Medical School at the University of Washington entered into a contract with the Federal Bureau of Health Manpower Education (later, Bureau of Health Resources Development). As a part of their plan the University of Washington cooperated with Washington State University, University of Idaho, University of Alaska, and Montana State University in a program entitled "WAMI" to train an augmented portion of its first year medical students in basic medical sciences. The WAMI Program, it was expected, would soon enable the University of Washington to raise its first year class from 135 to 175 by this means. It was hoped that many WAMI students would desire to remain in rural settings they had experienced while attending one of the cooperating schools.

Washington State University began its partnership with the University of Washington in 1972, as did the University of Idaho. These contracts called for ten medical students to receive first year training at Pullman and nine at Moscow. Professors at the two universities taught classes, which met on one campus or the other, according to local needs. The program has been successful, as judged by student scores on examinations given to all participants from each of the five institutions. The number of WAMI students at Pullman in 1980 was 20 and in 1988 it was 19, eleven of whom were men, eight women. These totals have remained at the same level for many years.[79]

Veterinary Medicine, having been put on firm ground at the turn of the century by Dr. Sophus B. Nelson, nevertheless reached a low ebb in the 1960s and early 1970s. An American Veterinary Medical Association accreditation team granted "Full Accreditation" to the Veterinary College in 1965, but then drew attention and approbation from the bulk of its report by insisting upon the need for "minimizing intellectual isolation." More specifically, the signer of the letter concluded: "I would like to emphasize the necessity of considering moving the college of Veterinary Medicine to an area more conducive to increased accessions [more animals available for clinical experience] and active cooperation with research personnel in human medicine." Shortly after, the state association considered the need to move, according to a story in the Spokane *Spokesman-Review* of September 28, 1965. There is no evidence that Terrell or the Regents were unduly concerned about these opinions, undoubtedly being aware Seattle had few large animal clinical specimens and that cooperation with the University of Washington Medical School did not require living cheek by jowl.[80]

Matters drifted until June 1973, when Dr. Leo K. Bustad took over as the dean of the college. He had graduated from Washington State University in 1949 with a DVM degree (also holding two other degrees from the University), and in 1960 took a Ph.D. from the University of Washington in Physiology and Biophysics. Bustad had been most recently Director of the Radiobiology Laboratory at the University of California at Davis. He quickly discovered that the condition of the College of Veterinary Medicine verged on the desperate. As he reported later, "We had the lowest budget and the lowest staffing rate of any state supported veterinary medical department in the United States." He felt that the college stood in danger of losing every shred of accreditation. Thus, he began the task of trying to overcome years of "benign neglect," a term which he attributed to President Terrell.[81]

Improvement began when the University drew up a "shared curriculum" with the University of Idaho, admitting students from the latter institution to study veterinary medicine in Pullman. This pro-

Associate Professor of Clothing, Interior Design, and Textiles Catherine M. Bicknell received the Burlington Northern Faculty Achievement Award in 1987. Her background and experience has brought a rich, international perspective to teaching and research at WSU. Professor Bicknell received her training at the Royal College of Art in London and at Essex University. Prior to joining the faculty in 1979 she worked for several design firms in the United States and Britain and as a book designer for WSU Press. (Washington State University News Service)

gram, which began in 1974, under the sponsorship of the Western Interstate Commission on Higher Education (WICHE), admitted a handful of students from Idaho in its first two years. Then, in 1976, Oregon State University agreed to send twelve students from that WSU on a trial basis. The State of Oregon also appropriated $10,000 per student, eighty percent of which was designated for their studies at Washington State University. This arrangement had made a promising beginning, but then became immeasurably strengthened in 1979 when the State of Oregon entered into a permanent agreement.[82]

Numerous changes and innovations followed signal successes in obtaining construction funds. the most important being for the completion of a $13,000,000 Veterinary Science Building, which was dedicated on October 20, 1978. At that time, it was recognized as greatly facilitating development of the Washington-Oregon-Idaho program mentioned above. Seven years later, on April 5, 1985, the University renamed it the Bustad Building and described it as "an all-purpose structure considered the most complex on the Pullman Campus." The building housed laboratory animals for research and teaching, provided a 120 seat amphitheater served by the most modern audio-visual teaching equipment, and contained laboratories used by its "principal occupants," the Department of Veterinary Microbiology and Pathology and the Washington Animal Disease Diagnostic Laboratory.[83]

By 1983, when Bustad retired, the Veterinary College had added more than fifty new faculty and a host of additional aides. These developments, together with the above-mentioned facilities, enabled the program to gain full accreditation at last.

By 1983, when Bustad retired, the Veterinary College had added more than fifty new faculty and a host of additional aides. These developments, together with the above-mentioned facilities, enabled the program to gain full accreditation at last. By that time, too, the college could boast of 106 candidates for the Doctor of Veterinary Medicine degree, where only sixty had stood in 1972. The number of graduate students had risen even more spectacularly to 108 in 1983, as opposed to thirty-two a decade earlier. Of course, the triumph was not a mere matter of additional floor space. The enlarged numbers of 1983 were far better equipped than their predecessors had been in 1972.

Bustad could justifiably conclude in 1983 that the college had "one of the very finest basic science teaching facilities in the United States. . . ." The research facilities were "outstanding" and the "teaching museum "was good, The major need was for "more and better clinical facilities." The outstanding faculty, recipients of $2,500,000 in grants in 1982, as opposed to only $700,000 in 1972, he might well have had reason to believe, would ultimately take care of any deficiencies.[84]

Unfortunately, the College of Pharmacy, Washington State University's fourth health education unit, found itself the target of attacks in the years when veterinary medicine flourished. Criticism came from the University of Washington, which sought from time to time to monopolize all pharmaceutical training in the state, and from the Council on Post-Secondary Education, the state's watch dog for higher education. The latter agency entertained the possibility of closing the program in Pullman, declaring that its students lacked clinical experience.[85]

Acting Dean Larry Simonsmeier rebutted the Council's criticism by pointing out that Washington State University had solved the problem of clinical experience by placing students as trainees in Spokane hospitals and drug concerns for extended periods. Indeed, he did not hesitate to argue that his students received a more extensive clinical experience than did students at the University of Washington. In addition, he put forth an impressive claim that his college supplied most of the pharmacists needed in eastern Washington.[86]

As a matter of fact, in 1979, if not earlier, authorities at Pullman anticipated a plausible argument from the University of Washington that pharmaceutical education would be inferior if not associated closely with a medical school. Evidently, University of Washington failed to recognize the legitimacy of a close bond between veterinary medicine and pharmacy. In Pullman, on the contrary, authorities began planning a pharmacy-veterinary health complex which stood ready to function in 1981 when the College of Pharmacy moved into remodelled veterinary buildings, Wegner and McCoy Halls. Physical proximity prepared the way for close cooperation and interdisciplinary teaching and research, which included specialists from numerous other scientific units on the campus.[87]

The Council on Post-Secondary Education voted in September 1981, to retain both undergraduate pharmacy programs—at Washington State University and the University of Washington. Dean Simonsmeier's arguments and the lobbying efforts of loyal Washington State University pharmacy graduates prevailed, but the ever-present problem of limited resources entered into a codicil attached to the decision. The Council recommended that Washington State University reduce the number of entering students each year to between forty-five and fifty from the previous sixty to sixty-five. It also requested that the University of Washington lower entering enrollment from eighty to sixty students. It is unlikely that either university suffered from these reductions. Total enrollment at Pullman (including graduate students) dropped from 231 in 1981 to 192 in 1983 but rose in the fall of 1988 to 197.[88]

Compromises extended to graduate study when, on November 20, 1981, the Council required that Washington State University drop the Master of Science and Doctor of Philosophy programs in the pharmaceutical sciences. The grounds for this action came from a powerful argument of the University of Washington's School of Pharmacy that Washington State University's faculty and other resources were insufficient for a full doctoral program. Graduate study, thus, in the broad field would be offered exclusively at Seattle. In return, Washington State University adopted the Council's recommendation that it offer M.S. and Ph.D. degrees in pharmacology and toxicology. These sciences, as published in the *WSU Bulletin for 1987-89*, "are important to the maintenance of human and animal health, food resources, and environmental quality." The introduction of the graduate program to support these degrees was a tribute to WSU for

The College of Education was another of the University's professional schools facing strong pressure from on campus and from outside agencies to improve the training of its graduates.

creating its own health sciences complex and to the interaction of faculty not only from pharmacy and veterinary medicine, but from a half dozen other science departments, as well as the Department of Veterinary Science at the University of Idaho.[89]

Not all of Pharmacy's problems were solved by these changes, however, a matter forcibly called to the University's attention when, in June 1977, the American Council on Pharmaceutical Education announced that the undergraduate program "continues to be in non-compliance with Council standards." The Council had placed the College in an anomalous position by imposing an "unpublished probation," which immediately became widely known, while permitting its name to remain on the published list of accredited schools. Probation had remained a threat until lifted in June 1988. The council at that time removed the stain, stating that it was satisfied with certain staff increases, improved funding, and a new permanent administration.[90]

The College of Education was another of the University's professional schools facing strong pressure from on campus and from outside agencies to improve the training of its graduates. The college took its first step in 1972-1973 with the introduction of a special education option for elementary school teachers to meet the needs of the educationally handicapped. In a more thoroughgoing advance the College, with the support of the Academic Affairs Committee, introduced sterner requirements for teacher certification in 1984. Thereafter, candidates seeking to enter teacher training had to present thirty semester hours of college work with a 2.5 grade point average or better, instead of the minimal 2.00 (C grade). In addition, each applicant would be required to demonstrate reasonable proficiency in the basic skills of reading, writing, speaking, and mathematics. Though evidence showed that nineteen percent of the previous spring's Education majors would not have qualified for admission under the new regulations, the College faculty expressed confidence that such declines would be short lived.[91]

A more dramatic change occurred in the physical education programs, which also were administered by the College of Education. In 1983, after several years of consideration, the Faculty Senate abandoned the practice of separating physical education programs on the basis of gender. Finally agreeing that such differences were *minor*, where previously they had been regarded as *major*, the Senate on December 8, 1983, established a single Department of Physical Education, Sport, and Leisure Studies. This coeducational department, of course, also represented a triumph of the powerful social movement toward equality of the sexes.[92]

Increased efficiency and rationalization in all aspects of the operation of the College of Education seem to have been the goal of a recent administrative reorganization. In the principal change, in June 1985, the administration split the Department of Education (within the College of Education) into three specialized departments: (1) Elementary and Secondary Education, (2) Counseling Psychology, and (3) Administration and Supervision. In addition, on March 21, 1986, in an economizing step, administrators eliminated the vocational-technical education program. The main reason given was that its courses were so under-enrolled as to make the program atypical of the College. Whether elimination saved money remains unclear. After the practical skills courses were dropped, those dealing with management and direction of vocational programs found a home in the Department of Adult and Youth Education.[93]

Enrollment in the business curriculum of the College of Business and Economics (a title change from College of Economics and Business) grew rapidly in the 1970s to meet the needs of the economy. The popularity of business courses seemed to represent a student reaction against the radical activism and militant idealism prevalent among students in the late 1960s and early 1970s. Encouraged by the popularity of its undergraduate program, the College proposed to offer a Ph.D. degree, which won approval of faculty and Regents in 1970. The Council on Post-Secondary Education, however, rejected the request by one vote, unimpressed, in all likelihood, by the argument that a large number of doctors of philosophy would be soon be needed as teachers and researchers, and by the perfunctory description of the faculty and other resources needed for a doctoral program.[94]

Undergraduates remained undeterred by the Council's rejection of a Ph.D. program, flocking in large numbers to business courses. In fact, the crush became so great as to threaten to overwhelm existing facilities and faculty. Student clamor to major in business drove minimum certification standards well above the usual 2.00 grade point average (C grade). In addition, the College of Business raised minimum hours required for entry into the major to forty (mid-sophomore standing), including six hours in Business and Economics core courses. Scarcity of space forced marginal students out of this major or caused delays in their work. Inadequate facilities has also caused numerous otherwise qualified students to attend summer school in large numbers, a new phenomenon.[95]

The College of Business and Economics launched several special programs after failing with its petition for a Ph.D. degree. In 1974, a satellite of the Hotel and Restaurant program, (popular for some time on the Pullman campus) opened a branch in Seattle. After lengthy consideration, the University had contracted with Seattle University to serve as a host and provide the base of operations. Students continued to take two years in Pullman before moving to the Seattle University campus, where one-half of the final two years would be presented by the host institution and one half by faculty representing WSU. A most attractive feature of the Seattle program was the opportunity for greatly varied experiences in hospitality situations. This satellite program has proven helpful to the Hotel and Restaurant Administration programs and has attracted many internships from throughout the Puget Sound area.[96]

In 1983, the College geared up for a serious attempt to establish the Ph.D. program denied to it in 1970 by the Council on Post-Secondary Education. Dean Rom Markin characterized his College for the Board

The popularity of business courses seemed to represent a student reaction against the radical activism and militant idealism prevalent among students in the late 1960s and early 1970s. Encouraged by the popularity of its undergraduate program, the College proposed to offer a Ph.D. degree, which won approval of faculty and Regents in 1970.

of Regents as a "growth industry." Indeed, he claimed that it was the largest undergraduate program of its kind in the West. Its popularity was easily demonstrated. In 1978, for example, some 16.7 percent of undecided students (officially, "undeclared," not yet majoring) chose his College for their major studies. By 1982, that figure had grown to 21.5 percent. The faculty of 1983, which had been greatly enlarged and diversified, undoubtedly was better prepared than in 1970 to undertake guidance of a Ph.D. program. Best of all, perhaps, was the claim that the new course of study could be started with few new financial resources.

And launched it was, in July of 1984. the program is academic and scholarly, rather than professional, a category occupied by the Master of Business Administration degree. The doctoral program encompasses accounting, finance, management, marketing, and quantitative methods and was designed to prepare researchers for governmental and business institutions, as well as professorships at universities. The College claimed that a ready market existed for its doctoral candidates. Above all, authorities insisted that the WSU faculty needed the program in order to continue to develop intellectually and professionally.[97]

Graduate education in the last two decades of the University's first century has been shaped by numerous intellectual and scientific developments, all of which have moved professors to seek maximum autonomy and flexibility in developing their own programs. The greatest change probably has been the abandonment of university-wide foreign language requirements for the Ph.D. degree. That issue, long debated, came to a head early in 1967 when the Graduate Studies committee recommended permitting each department or program to determine its own intellectual tools—statistics, computers, mathematics, and even foreign languages, if desired.

The debate reached the Resident Instructional Staff meeting on May 25, 1967, when the traditionalists took the initiative in seeking to protect the foreign language requirement. In the end, they were defeated 164 to 76. Thereafter, each department might require its doctoral students to use such tools as were deemed best. In many cases, departments continued language requirements but it is notable that the new Ph.D.s in Business, Biochemistry, and Biophysics do not require a foreign language. Botany, a much older doctoral program, has recently switched from a required foreign language to making the decision dependent on the student's research.[98]

In the Spring of 1969, two years after the Resident Instructional Staff abolished the university-wide foreign language requirement for the Ph.D. degree, it elevated computer science, one of the new research fields, from a program to departmental status. In doing so, the staff, in effect, ratified the bold assertion of advocates that "application of computers promises to revolutionize society." The short history of the program, which had been started in 1963, justified a certain confidence among its practitioners as to its utility on the campus. Fourteen faculty (some on split appointments) were training some forty-five graduate students and offering courses to 800 enrollees. The Ph.D, offering had begun in 1966 and the Bachelor of Science degree began in 1970. This major, which also had ten graduate students in Richland, promised many educational advances, if not an entire "revolution."[99]

Departures into the interrelated areas within the fields of chemistry, physics, and biology produced several interdisciplinary graduate programs. In the spring of 1968, the faculty and regents approved a Master of Science degree in Environmental Science (as well as a B.S. degree), designed to investigate ways to improve the physical quality of life. Emphasis was on study of "interactions among living organisms and their environment," utilizing mathematics and computers. Further venturing into scientific interaction produced a Ph.D. degree in chemical physics in March of 1969. A year later, scientists started a doctoral program in biochemistry. This field (and biophysics) involved "application of methods and theories of chemistry and physics to the study of biological phenomena," according to the *WSU Bulletin, 1987-89.* The prestige of an inner circle of biochemists, it was hoped, would enable its members to set high standards for research accomplishments and to attract an additional small number of high caliber Fellows to the University. The vehicle for this development was an exclusive Institute of Biological Chemistry. The cost would be great—a separate building was contemplated at an early date—but from the prestige and achievements of the Institute's members benefits would flow to the entire institution.[100]

When, in September 1982, the Regents merged the College of Home Economics with the College of Agriculture (thereafter titled the College of Agriculture and Home Economics), the new arrangement laid bare the necessity for yet another major consolidation, this one at the departmental level. Each of the colleges already possessed its own department devoted to foods—Food Science and Technology in Agriculture and Human Nutrition and Foods in Home Economics. Merging the two departments, thus, followed quite naturally, becoming a micro-mirror image of the consolidation of the Colleges. The merger, had a powerful sanction provided by the prospect of economics and efficiency in administration, as well as greater opportunities for improved teaching, research, and extension. A year later, in April 1984, the Regents approved M.S. and Ph.D. degrees in Plant Physiology, another interdisciplinary field important to agriculture and to a number of other sciences. In petitioning for the program, Graduate Dean C. J. Nyman stated that plant physiology was much needed nationally. It had become another instance in which interdisciplinary work was absolutely essential to scientific discovery. In this case, researchers from agronomy, soils, botany, horticulture, biophysics, landscape architecture, plant pathology, biochemistry, and biophysics constituted the faculty. In addition, the new program had the support of the Institute of Biological Chemistry.[101]

In graduate engineering studies, change has been easy to measure. They began with a single integrated program in 1966, but soon expanded and branched out into a variety of areas of specialization within the various sub-disciplines of the field. The original doctorate

Professor Pappachan E. Kolattukudy came to WSU in 1980 to serve as the first director of Washington State University's Institute of Biological Chemistry. (Washington State University News Service)

In 1978, the administration established the International Program Development Office (IPDO) to coordinate the university's burgeoning activities abroad and on campus. Projects, past and present, have involved contracts with more than two dozen nations in the Middle East, Africa, Indonesia, Central America, and Asia.

was a Ph.D. in Engineering Science, an eclectic program that served very well in the absence of a sufficiently diversified faculty and other resources to permit degrees to be offered by the various departments. Within a few years, however, departments offered, in effect, separate programs under the rubric of Engineering Science. Nineteen eighty-four brought recognition of growing strength throughout the College of Engineering as the University introduced separate doctoral programs in chemical engineering, mechanical engineering, civil and environmental engineering, and electrical and computer engineering. Singling out particular fields, it was hoped, would attract more good students as well as create a national reputation in engineering.[102]

Serious attention to environmental research began in the College of Engineering as early as 1950 when an Air Pollution Center opened on campus. In 1973, research in the program came under the jurisdiction of the Department of Chemical Engineering and remained there for a decade. After that, the Department of Civil and Environmental Engineering administered the interdisciplinary program, which involved meteorology, atmospheric chemistry, pollution abatement, and "global climate issues and effects of atmospheric pollutants." A petition for a name change from Air Pollution Center to Laboratory of Atmospheric Research met no opposition when posed to the Faculty Senate on May 17, 1984. As Richard W. Crain, Jr., Acting Dean, College of Engineering, stated as justification for the broader implications of the new title: "The faculty have developed an international reputation through their atmospheric research which has been conducted around the world and in cooperation with scientists from other nations." The faculty, staff, and students of this program have collected data in places ranging from Antarctica, China, and the Caribbean, the Pacific, and many places within the United States.[103]

Washington State University continued to serve international economic development in Third World nations in the tradition established earlier in Pakistan (discussed in chapter seven). In 1978, the administration established the International Program Development Office (IPDO) to coordinate the university's burgeoning activities abroad and on campus. Projects, past and present, have involved contracts with more than two dozen nations in the Middle East, Africa, Indonesia, Central America, and Asia. Work has ranged widely over many fields of agriculture, veterinary medicine, home economics, rural sociology, and library development. The benefits have not been restricted to the host nations. Crops have been introduced from them into the United States, as have pest control methods, soil conservation experiences, livestock management, etc. All projects, as well, have trained students from host nations, yielding experiences valuable to the general educational process. In summation of her study of "International Development at Washington State University, 1945-1987," Evelyn Rodewald wrote that "The International Program Development Office has become part of the university program with goals and a purpose which fit into the overall scope of Washington State University."[104]

Study abroad programs, which involve exchanges of students, or, simply, registering Washington State University students to attend foreign universities for a summer, semester, or year represent another international activity of considerable importance. In 1970, at the inception of the current program, a mere nine students studied at foreign institutions. Attendance, however, grew eleven fold over the next thirteen years to ninety-eight in 1983. Enrollment almost doubled in the 1984-1985 academic year and the total for 1989-1990 (including the summer of 1990) is forecast to be 206.

Director Vishnu N. Bhatia anticipated the continued sharp rise in program enrollment and strongly commended its utility to undergraduates interested in international trade, economics, diplomacy, and the like. The reasons for the mounting interest were two-fold. First, the summer international program in Copenhagen and other attractive cities met the traditional interest in European culture, not only with courses but with an opportunity to experience a lively cosmopolitan existence. Second, Washington State University recently has added new dimensions to its overseas exchange programs by reaching into countries long closed to American institutions of higher learning. The first step in this direction came in 1983 when WSU established a formal agreement with universities in Sichuan Province in southwestern China. The second came in 1988 when officials from WSU and Far Easter University of Vladivostok in the Soviet Union inaugurated a formal cultural and scientific exchange program that will involve many students and professors, East and West. Developments of this kind foreshadow the demise of the Cold War and are preparing Washington State University for a new era of global education.[105]

Chapter Nine

On the Brink of a New Century, 1977-1985

THE IMPORTANT ADVANCES THAT WASHINGTON STATE UNIVERSITY EX-
perienced in the post-World War II era were sufficient to suggest to
its supporters and critics that the future would be filled with achievements and honors. As the end of the first one hundred years
approached, the University's adherents would find it a commonplace
to celebrate "the land-grant tradition," whether defending time-
honored obligations and prerogatives or advocating educational
innovations and greater democracy and freedom in social relationships. Nevertheless, theirs was not a wholly free choice. They could
hardly expect that past accomplishments would eliminate tensions
and conflicts within society, or that financial bonanzas would be
available to provide a means to make wide the path to future
achievement.

In 1977, thirteen years before the University's centennial, a proposal to remove Washington's sales tax from food and medicine
posed a new dilemma for higher education. It was difficult to argue
that the institution should favor retention of such a regressive, un-
democratic measure as the tax on the necessities of life in order to
finance higher education. In November 1977, a commanding majority, fifty-four percent of Washington's electorate, voted to abolish the
tax on necessities. The action reduced net state revenue by
$127,000,000 and forced Governor Dixy Lee Ray to declare a "hiring
freeze" for all state agencies. In early January 1978, the Office of Fiscal
Management in Olympia ordered a spending reduction at Washington State University that amounted to "8.5 percent of anticipated state
funds."[1]

In his report to the Regents, President Terrell appeared bewildered
at the turn of events. In some departments "he had sensed a real spirit
of optimism" because they had enjoyed vastly increased research
funds from the federal government and other outside agencies. On
the other hand, he was reported as declaring that the University
"could not exist successfully" in view of a projected budgetary loss of

OPPOSITE: *The south entrance to the
Washington State University campus.
In the foreground from left to right are:
Stephenson Hall North, the Stephenson
Hall Dining Complex, Stephenson Hall
East, and Stephenson Hall South. In
the background, from left to right, are
Orton and Rogers halls.* (Washington
State University News Service)

$5,500,000 from the abolition of the food and medicine tax. An irony in this turn of events, one that probably was not lost on Terrell or those who listened to his words: outside agencies would keep research alive WSU, but people of the state appeared to care little about supporting higher education. The University Senate's Budget Committee, usually a resourceful critic of the administration, sought only to urge Terrell to place the highest funding priorities on instruction, organized research, and libraries. In a kind of bemused wonderment the committee observed that the governor's mandate "comes on the heels of a decline so severe that the current support of instruction in real terms [i.e., the number of full time faculty per 1,000 full time students] would have to be increased by twenty-eight percent to return to the level of a decade ago."[2]

President Terrell viewed Governor Ray's budget for 1981-1983 as being inadequate for the needs of higher education and urged the Council of Presidents (of Washington's public colleges and universities), to work hard to increase appropriations. In spite of his professed long-term optimism he could only admit to the Regents and the WSU Foundation that the funding of public higher education in Washington had declined from 15.2 percent of the state's operating budget in 1969-1971 to 10.4 percent as represented by the governor's budget request for 1981-1983. He acknowledged that the "campus capers" of students in the late 1960s and early 1970s had lowered the legislature's confidence in his institution.[3]

President Terrell and his administrators had other sources of anxiety, however, particularly in the realm of state politics. In 1979, the state government had taken control of the community colleges, which, Terrell anticipated, would increase the competition for education funds. Then, also in 1979, the voters adopted Initiative 62, a measure designed "to limit the rate of growth of state government" by placing restrictions on the rate of tax increases. Basic education (kindergarten through the twelfth grade) was singled out as an "essential service" to be protected, but higher education was not mentioned in the legislation.[4]

On September 24, 1981, at the opening of a new academic year, the faculty gathered in the CUB Auditorium to learn about the latest turn of events. It was another grave moment because the biennial budget had left an operations base that was 15.6 percent less than that of July 1980. Washington's newly elected Governor John Spellman had discovered in the meantime that the proposed budget was still too expensive and exacted further operating reductions of 10.1 percent from Washington State University and all other state agencies. Terrell underscored the severity of the order by indicating that the new reduction would remove $1,000 per student from the budget and would, in his opinion, sink the University, to fiftieth place among the states in funding higher education. At that point he reported his intention to ask the Board of Regents for the power to declare a state of financial exigency. The faculty was silent as it filed out of the auditorium.[5]

Professors had good reason to be anxious for the future. The Regents granted the financial exigency the next day, September 25, creating a situation in which tenure guarantees might cease to apply if fiscal shortfalls forced the administration to eliminate functions, positions, or even whole units. Albert Yates, Executive Vice-President and Provost, lightened the gloomy atmosphere for a moment, at least, on October 16, 1981, when he assured the Regents that, although the administration was holding up all applications for admission in the second semester, none of the classes for that term would be cancelled. In addition, he reported that salary increases planned for October 1, 1981, had gone into effect. Late in that month, the Senate, after deploring another possible round of devastating budget reductions, reaffirmed its established position that instruction occupied the first priority in funding, followed by organized research and libraries. After noting that $735,000 in state appropriated funds for 1981-1982 were earmarked for intercollegiate athletics, the University Senate turned much of its discussion to that subject. That body adopted its budget committee's assertion that it "doubts [that] it is in the best interest of WSU's primary missions [sic] to continue this level of state funding in a time of financial exigency."[6]

The meaning of financial exigency became clearer at the Regents' meeting of December 16, 1981, which generated a formidable volume of minutes. Yates warned the Regents that if Governor Spellman signed the legislature's recently passed budget, the University would be forced to reduce its operating expenditures by another 5.4 percent, a total of $10,400,000. On those grounds, he recommended continuance of the state of financial exigency. William Iulo, Chair of the University Senate, advocated rescinding the state of exigency, on the grounds that there was "virtually unanimous questioning on the campus of the need for continuing under the financial emergency." In opposition, James Short, representing the Steering Committee of the independent Association of Research Professors, sided with the administration. In the debate, too, the administration assured faculty members that it intended to follow tenure provisions as far as possible and also would honor the priorities whereby instruction would be funded first.[7]

There were, in fact, staff eliminations and program alterations. The number of such cases remained small and the final results did not confirm the faculty's worst fears about wholesale changes being made without its consent or advice. The Criminal Justice Department lost two and one-half faculty positions, some forty-seven percent of its staff. Thereafter, the Political Science Department absorbed the program as an aspect of public administration. The Department of Office Administration (in the past: Secretarial Studies) was dropped, eliminating two tenured faculty. Finally, the minorities programs—Black Studies, Asian/Pacific American Studies, Chicano Studies, and Native American Studies—were consolidated into the Department of Comparative American Cultures.[8]

Faculty members in general, however, continued to be troubled by what they perceived to be a threat to the whole tenure process and

•

The meaning of financial exigency became clearer at the Regents' meeting of December 16, 1981, which generated a formidable volume of minutes. Yates warned the Regents that if Governor Spellman signed the legislature's recently passed budget, the University would be forced to reduce its operating expenditures by another 5.4 percent, a total of $10,400,000.

•

to their prerogatives in determining curricula and programs. The Faculty Affairs Committee declared on January 14, 1982, that the Regents should remove the state of financial exigency at their next meeting. Their reasons were set forth plainly: The budget had not suffered as much as the administration had expected—being reduced only 4.7 percent instead of a predicted ten to twenty percent. Meanwhile, the committee claimed that faculty morale had been "devastated," by the threat to tenure rights. The administration was reminded of the difficulty of recruiting new faculty under such circumstances. Finally, the committee noted that the University of Washington had already removed its emergency status, returning the school to normal operating conditions.[9]

But further threats from the governor's office to slash the budget still more left the University administration determined to continue with the emergency. The University Senate opposed continuance to no avail. Then, with little warning, on June 4, 1982, President Terrell removed the exigency, stating simply that to do so was in the best interest of the institution. He cautioned, however, that resources remained meager and would be carefully and sternly allocated. Indeed, he warned that it might be necessary to install emergency controls again in the future.[10]

When Governor Spellman imposed a $4,400,000 cut that summer, major organizational changes seemed imminent. An exigency was not imposed, however, as President Terrell chose instead to offer a more conservative and seemingly less-than-adequate line of action. Indeed, he prefaced his policy statement to the Board with a kind of valedictory on his administration. He praised the institution for maintaining "high quality instruction" and for having fulfilled the traditional land-grant college missions in agriculture, engineering, home economics, and veterinary medicine. The other professional schools, he also assured the Regents, had to be maintained if the institution was to retain its integrity. None of these programs had been built at the expense of the liberal arts and sciences, in his view. The latter, indeed, had been "strong components of Washington State University" since Bryan's administration and "had been strengthened every decade."[11]

When Terrell directed the Regent's attention to the realities of cutting expenses drastically he added only a plan for the merger of the Colleges of Agriculture and Home Economics. The merger, though, seemed like a hasty move in the sense that little opportunity had existed to produce counter proposals before the Regents took up the matter at its meeting on September 16 and 17, 1982. Advocates of independence for the College of Home Economics feared that the loss of identity would hamper its work. On the other hand, faculty members on the reorganization committee blurted out certain hard facts of academic life, namely, that Home Economics faculty had always been underfunded and that it would enjoy better financing when under the Agriculture rubric. Then, too, Home Economics was far from losing its role in the university, since two flourishing departments of the College of Home Economics were transferred intact to

Public Services Librarian Alice Spitzer has been an active participant in the development of curricula within the library system, the English Department, and a variety of foreign study programs. She has served on the All-University Writing Committee and has participated in several overseas library programs sponsored by the International Development Office. In 1988 Librarian Spitzer was given the Library Superstar Award by the Center for Research Libraries. (Washington State University News Service)

Agriculture—the Departments of Child and Family Studies and Clothing, Interior Design, and Textiles. In addition, the Department of Human Nutrition and Foods was merged with Agriculture's Food Science and Technology Department, to the benefit of both. The Regents, greatly impressed by the academic value of the merger, as well as by the hope that it would save money, voted to conclude the action at the earliest possible moment.[12]

The specter of perennial financial insecurity experienced in the 1970s and early 1980s—not restricted to Washington State University, of course—was accompanied in 1977 by specific threats to dismantle forty-nine programs within the state's institutions of higher learning, ten such courses of study being at Pullman. The agency threatening this action was the Council on Post-Secondary Education, established by the state legislature in 1970. Originally titled the Council on Higher Education, it had been created as an advisory body that might propose alterations in the curricula and other matters concerning the administering of higher education. Since the law governing the Council also served notice that governing boards of the state's colleges and universities would continue in their traditional roles as administrators of their respective institutions, the Council might well have felt the ambiguity of its role. Investigating Washington State University's graduate programs and the curricula at other schools might strengthen the Council's position, as well as contribute to the educational process.[13]

On the other hand, the faculty and administration had no reason to be complacent about WSU's status, since the Council reported to various legislative committees and to the governor's office, all of which represented potential sources of adverse action. Furthermore, the council's staff recommendations struck at the heart of Washington State University's graduate program when, in the Spring of 1977, it recommended the elimination of Ph.D. degree programs in English, Geology, History, Pharmacy, and Political Science. President Terrell quickly challenged this proposal, declaring, according to the minutes of a Regents' meeting, that the doctoral programs in question were "central to the mission of WSU." Shortly thereafter the Council also proposed to investigate undergraduate programs. Terrell is reported to have "lashed out" at this "shocking idea of wholesale decimation." His response was supported by both the undergraduate and graduate student governing bodies.[14]

The outcries were directed at the council's staff, which had not yet finished its investigations. Subsequently, the staff abandoned efforts to eliminate graduate study in Political Science and Geology, concentrating instead on the advanced degrees in English, History, and Pharmacy. Upon making the staff's report to the Regents on June 3, 1977, Pat Callan, the executive director of the Council, defended his organization's mandate from the legislature to recommend a role and mission for each institution.[15]

The Council's staff, he reported, had scrutinized the costs of the doctoral programs in question and found them too high. Then, in a paradoxical vein, the staff criticized the programs for their low rate of

Professor of Botany and Zoology John Thompson. At the age of thirty-six in 1988, he was one of the youngest scholars ever elected to the American Association for the Advancement of Science. (Washington State University News Service)

degree conferrals and while at the same time arguing that the doctors trained were flooding professional fields already overcrowded. It was perhaps at the end of that report that Regent Robert Strausz suggested to his fellow members that the Board of Regents direct its president to write to the public, voting members of the Council to make its position clear. The letter-writing task should consist, first, of commending the public members for removing objections to Political Science and geology. Second the Regents should record their objections to plans to remove History, English, and Pharmacy from the graduate program. Finally, he asked the members to join him in stating that they "believed that the CPE staff have not taken full recognition of the historical role which the Board of Regents have played in the governance of this institution over the last 87 years."[16]

The contention reached a head in June 1977, when the council's public members rejected staff recommendations by a vote of 6-2, thereby insuring the retention of the Ph.D. programs in English, History, and Pharmacy, along with the M.A. in Philosophy. Retention of these programs, together with those in Political Science and Geology, represented a victory for Terrell and the entire University. The triumph, though, did not banish all qualms or uncertainties, for the departments involved were admonished to do some cost trimming. The doctorate in Pharmacy had not escaped financial and resource difficulties, which led to its ultimate demise in 1981, being replaced by two specialized Ph.D. degree programs, a matter discussed in chapter eight. The University also suspended the Philosophy master's degree in 1980. It has not been reinstated. Other degrees rounding out the ten criticized were dropped without the University's objection.[17]

The council's admonitions to trim program costs could hardly have met with the faculty's favor. Such reductions portended ill for faculty salaries. Indeed, between 1971 and 1983, there were but two appreciable general salary increases: the first a 10.5 percent raise granted in April 1973, and the second of twelve percent issued in the Spring of 1975. In spite of those increases, the faculty fell behind a seven-state average by five to eight percent. Unfortunately, the situation did not change materially during the next few years, but grew worse during the financial exigency of 1981-1982. The administration had to postpone issuing a salary increase scheduled for October 1982, until June 1983. These developments were followed by a "dry year" in 1983-1984, with no salary increases.[18]

Meanwhile, the faculty had not been idle. In 1971, certain of its representatives lobbied the Council of Presidents and legislative committees, but had no success in gaining higher salaries. Two years later, the faculty created the Faculty Council, a body independent of University authority, and directed it to not only obtain improved salaries but also to seek to promote the right of collective bargaining by law. The council soon had over 700 members and, for a time, was accepted as a body representing legitimate faculty interests. Influential faculty headed the organization and worked assiduously, but ultimately, without success, to gain collective bargaining. Many faculty, disliking anything resembling a labor union, joined with administrators to oppose collective bargaining. Terrell feared that collegiality would be lost forever if a collective bargaining element were introduced into campus politics.[19]

Perhaps it was the last straw for professors who had not received a raise in 1983 to learn that they might not gain additional increases before 1985. In any event, that dismal news produced a strong adverse reaction in the Faculty Senate. By an overwhelming vote, the senators demanded that the administration explain "what the relative importance faculty salary increases have among the University's priorities." Especially troubling to the Senators was their perception that the administration had reported "publically on several occasions that the State Legislature has treated the University particularly well in budgeting allocations or that faculty morale has improved markedly during the past year."[20]

Dr. Yates responded earnestly and at length in a January 5, 1984 memorandum, which the Senate took up on February 16, 1984. Faculty salaries had a high priority, he reported, for "by any reasonable standard . . . they are below what they should be and what they need to be, even after the economic condition of the state is taken into account." He assured the senators that no lobbying possibility had been overlooked but the only tangible plan he had— a sign of the poverty of the state—was to ask the legislature to move the effective date of an already voted salary increase of 6.7 percent from January 1, 1985 to a date six months earlier. In a highly collegial moment, Yates concluded with a strong affirmation of faith in the "core of the faculty . . . which [he said] is the heart of the institution and constitutes the chief architect of our character and culture." He then asked for cooperation from the senatorial leaders as the administration sought to properly reward the faculty.[21]

Faculty concerns for perquisites reached beyond salaries and promotions, of course, to retirement program and tenure provisions. Faculty and administration, alike, had reason to be proud of improvements in the retirement system during the 1970s and 1980s. First, the calculation for pension payments was changed from a formula based upon fifty percent of the average salary over the highest ten years of service to fifty percent of the top two years, which, of course, should be considerably higher. To be eligible, pensioners had to have served the University for at least twenty-five years and have reached sixty-five years of age. In 1978 employees gained the right to work until seventy years of age, erasing the requirement that they retire at sixty-five. The change was in response to federal legislation prohibiting forced retirement at an earlier age. The state legislature followed with its own measure to protect the right of state employees over the same cause and the Regents entered such a regulation into the practice of the institution. Thus, professors and other staff might continue to work until age seventy if physically able.[22]

Conversely, the University, following passage of a new state law in 1982, permitted employees to retire early under a special dispensation available only until January 1, 1983. The legislature had drawn

•

Dr. Yates responded earnestly and at length in a January 5, 1984 memorandum, which the Senate took up on February 16, 1984. Faculty salaries had a high priority, he reported, for "by any reasonable standard . . . they are below what they should be and what they need to be, even after the economic condition of the state is taken into account."

•

The liberation of women could not, however, take place without involving a new set of parental entanglements for the University. If a moral dilemma could be exorcised, a set of practical problems remained. The living units had to be made secure at a reasonable hour of the night to protect the individuals who were at home.

up a measure for the mutual benefit of both individuals and the institution. Lawmakers had anticipated that state agencies might be forced to reduce staffs in whole or part in the event of another fiscal emergency. The new law provided the means to compel early retirements in order to make staff reductions with a minimum of litigation. The inducement was a dispensation allowing employees to retire if they had served twenty-five years, or if they were fifty-five years old and had served the institution for ten years. These retirees would enjoy full actuarial benefits. In addition, such a scheme, it was thought, would enable the University to replace senior staff members, obtaining, in the process, a younger staff with new ideas. This plan was followed in 1983 with provision for fully funded retraining of forcibly retired professional staff for new positions within the University.[23]

The effect of the special dispensation upon academic programs was restricted largely to the loss of the courses taught by certain retiring professors. No programs were dropped and no tenured professors were fired, as financial exigency a second time was avoided. The number of faculty and staff who took advantage of early retirement was appreciable, if not precisely calculable. In 1982, some fifty seven faculty, fifty-one classified staff, and one member of the exempt staff accepted early retirement. In the previous year, with no retirement option, only twenty faculty but fifty-two classified staff had retired. Since few if any programs were drastically modified, probably few employees entered the fully funded training program. Nevertheless, these early retirements helped the University to balance its budget and to meet the guidelines laid down by the state, in spite of supplementary payments which the institution had to make to early retirees' pensions.[24]

The administration's concern for faculty well being went beyond improving retirement insurance to reviewing tenure requirements. In 1976, the Regents had approved tenure for part-time professors who had at least a fifty percent appointment. Further changes came in 1979 when the Faculty Affairs Committee sharpened and clarified procedures for evaluating professors seeking tenure. The *Faculty Manual* published in October 1980 stated that instructors and assistant professors of not less than half-time employment were to be considered for tenure during their sixth year instead of the customary fifth year. The authority for this decision is not clear since action taken by the Board of Regents on June 3, 1983 belies that statement. At that time the Board apparently made the fresh decision that tenure for assistant professors was to be considered during the sixth year, rather than the fifth. Also, as a means of stiffening requirements for tenure, the Board approved recommendations coming from the University Senate two weeks earlier to reduce instructorships to non-tenure track positions, to eliminate deferral of tenure, and to abolish it for appointments of less than three-quarter-time employment, except under extraordinary circumstances.[25]

Early in 1984, an intimation of possible changing attitudes toward judging faculty achievement came when the Faculty Affairs Committee pondered a revised annual review statement. At stake, of course, were tenure, promotion, and salary increases. As the chairman reported, the members had considered encouraging increased creative activity among the faculty. After some debate in committee and in the Faculty Senate (recently substituted for the University Senate), the Senators accepted a set of criteria for judging faculty eligibility for tenure which broadened appreciation of contributions to knowledge, arts, and humanities.

Whereas the 1980 edition of the *Faculty Manual* conservatively and rather narrowly noted that it was "the policy of the University to encourage *and within its means to facilitate* original creative research," the Committee offered a broader and more inclusive interpretation. As it found its way into the 1984 *Faculty Manual*, it became "the policy of the University to encourage and facilitate original creative activity *on the part of all faculty.*" For the first time, too, scholarly activity unequivocally included arts and humanities— performances, exhibits, awards, etc. and affirming that the arts and humanities were on a par with the sciences and technologies in the realm of achievement.[26]

While faculty were enjoined to seek achievement through their various talents, double standards under which women students lived and constraints on their actions were diminished. In 1967, in the period of student unrest already considered, a Women's Hours Evaluation Committee had denied the moral validity of special lockdown hours for women residing in University housing as long as it did not apply equally to men. Following that committee's recommendations, the University issued a new edict whereby, beginning in the Fall of 1967, that no women students except freshmen would be required to return to their residences at a fixed hour. As the Dean of Women reported the new plan to parents of women students, "The Head Residents or Housemothers will not be responsible for making decisions concerning your daughter's week-ends away from the campus."[27]

The liberation of women could not, however, take place without involving a new set of parental entanglements for the University. If a moral dilemma could be exorcised, a set of practical problems remained. The living units had to be made secure at a reasonable hour of the night to protect the individuals who were at home. "The crux of the problem seems to be this:" according to the Committee's philosophical statement, "the development of a system that will allow a woman to express her individuality, maturity, and responsibility, while at the same time providing for the security of the living group during late hours."[28]

The special protection of freshmen women by means of the lockdown continued until September, 1969, when Terrell rescinded closing hours for second semester freshman women. The president extended the privilege of no closing hours to all women the following year. In the next major development, which also came in 1969, junior women gained the right to live off-campus, an opportunity which fully one-fourth of the class took advantage of immediately. Sophomore women also gained that right in 1970.[29]

Joan Burbick joined the WSU Department of English and American Studies faculties in 1976. She is widely published, and among her accomplishments is the development of a summer curriculum at WSU based on the "American Sense of the Land." She is the author of Thoreau's Alternative History: Changing Perspectives on Nature, Culture and Language *and the recipient of the 1986 Norman Foerster Prize for her essay "Emily Dickinson: The Economics of Desire."* (Washington State University News Service)

The freshman live-in rule came under vigorous debate in 1976, with the Regents evenly divided but finally retaining it. Regents' President H. H. Hayner broke a tie by voting to retain the lockdown, on the grounds that important scholastic benefits came from group living. In 1979, however, the restriction was changed to read that all "single undergraduate freshmen under twenty years of age" are required to live "their first semester in organized living groups."[30]

In 1987, debate arose again as to the desirability of requiring freshmen to live for a full year in University housing. Public hearings and other inquiries indicated that students generally opposed the measure while perhaps sixty percent of recently admitted high school graduates and their parents favored it. The Regents approved the return to the one year requirement, in part at least for economic reasons—that is, to fill the dormitories. An additional argument which perhaps was persuasive, was that students living on campus had earned higher grade point averages than those living off-campus. But George Bettas, Director of Residence Living, denied that such arguments addressed the real issues contained in the proposal, stating, as reported in the *Evergreen*, that "It is a statement of the philosophy of this University . . . grade point average is a small part of it, [the rule] heightens the residential nature of WSU."[31]

Another major development in liberation of the sexes, and also in breaking down the geographical separation of men's and women's quarters, came in 1969 when the University granted a three months trial in Co-Ed visitation—that is, permitting persons of the opposite sex to be guests in a student's room. The short trial proved eminently satisfactory, as students enjoyed these visits on week-end afternoons and evenings. Subsequently, co-ed visitation became a regular feature of campus life. Accompanying that program, however, in testimony to continued surrogate parental concerns was a code of etiquette which in 1973 became incorporated into the State of Washington's *Administrative Code*. Finally, in that year, came the ultimate proposal—to permit twenty-four hour visitation. It drew heavy debate at a Regents' meeting and elsewhere and the issue might have been killed except for a timely compromise. By it, all sleeping floors were closed to visitors between two and six-thirty in the morning. In addition, those living units wishing more restricted hours might have them by resorting to secret ballot elections.[32]

Twenty-four hour visitation might suggest banishment of all biases inherited from the past. But, the golden age had not arrived. Homosexual and lesbian conduct, present but unpublicized, had not been freed either from guilt feelings or discrimination. The presence of gays came gradually to the attention of the campus when the Gay Awareness Committee lost support from student activities fees in a student election held in 1978. Thereafter, the group reorganized as the Gay People's Alliance, seeking to provide mutual assistance.[33]

When, in the spring of 1980, the Associated Students and the University Senate approved a resolution to prohibit discrimination for sexual preference, considerable emotional opposition welled up. At a public hearing on April 15, with eighty people present, some fifty

A 1985 management course taught by Professor Robert De Fillippi, is shown being taught in a WSU classroom in Pullman and supplied via microwave over the Washington Higher Educational Tele-Communication System (WHETS) to locations in the Tri-Cities, Spokane, and Vancouver, Washington. (Washington State University News Service)

spoke out in opposition to the measure, often citing religious reasons or venting opinions that homosexual behavior would tear at the fabric of American life. The Board of Regents, deluged with mail offering further opposition, refused to consider the anti-discrimination resolution. When the same issue surfaced again in February of 1985, the Associated Students' Senate killed the debate by refusing to restore financial support for the Gay Peoples' Alliance by a vote of 10-8. Since that time, actions to remove this discrimination have gained little support.[34]

Developments in intercollegiate athletics, in the last two decades of the University's first century, came to parallel closely the life of the institution in public relations, financing, and changing attitudes toward women. A fire on April 4, 1970, foreshadowed problems of this period. The fire destroyed half of the south stands of the antiquated, wooden Rogers Field bleachers, the football and track and field facility. Authorities lost little time in collecting private funds for reconstruction. Only thirty-two months later, the Regents dedicated the modernized structure as Martin Stadium (named after former Governor Clarence D. Martin). Haste characterized the decision to rebuild, for without a complete stadium the Cougars probably could not have remained in the Pacific-8 Conference (today's PAC-10).[35]

The Administration's dedication to participation in PAC-8 athletics, particularly football, had been made clear at various times, notably on October 13, 1967, when the Stanford University's football team defeated the Cougars by a score of 31-10. Following the disappointing outcome, WSU Coach Bert Clark complained that he had no first-rate players for offense and that his team had been "out-fought" and "out-couraged." His statements raised a storm of controversy when he blurted out "As it looks now, we shouldn't even be in this conference, but I must say there may come a tomorrow." Later Clark declared his words had been "misinterpreted," but his retraction, unconvincing at best, came too late. President Terrell announced without equivocation that "We regard our membership [in the PAC-8] as most appropriate and expect our association with this excellent conference to continue indefinitely." There was "no tomor-

Associate Professor of Comparative American Cultures and Marketing Talmadge Anderson founded the Western Journal of Black Studies *in 1977. Since that time, Anderson has served as editor of the journal, which has grown in stature to become one of the leading Black Studies publications in the United States.* (Washington State University News Service)

row" for Coach Clark, as he resigned before the next football season.[36]

In this period, financial problems proved to be endemic for intercollegiate athletics just as they had been traditionally for academic programming. In 1975, when President Terrell, once again, felt it necessary to reaffirm the University's commitment to the PAC-8 Conference, he coupled it with warnings about finances. It was, he said, "essential" to reduce costs of athletics in order to wipe out a sizable deficit within the next five years.[37]

Even as the administration talked of removing deficits, it began consideration of an enlarged and transformed stadium. Time was of the essence in this matter since the Conference had decreed that WSU must increase its football seating by more than 10,000 in order to be able to provide substantial minimum payments to visiting teams. The president and regents went beyond the bare minimum by deciding to construct an Academic Center as a part of the stadium complex. Only private funds and other material assistance were to be sought and used in the stadium portion of the project. The Academic Center, which became the facility of a computer science program, constructed with state funds, escaped controversy. The stadium, however came under scrutiny since $175,000 in student activity funds were used in construction despite pledges made to the contrary.[38]

Massive amounts of donated work in excavation and engineering added great value to the construction, marking hectic months of activity and a tight production schedule. In addition, the Cougar Club (the athletic booster organization) sponsored the relocation and building of a modern track and field facility (Mooberry Track) and a new baseball park (still named Bailey Field), near the golf course. A large football crowd witnessed the dedication of the new Martin Stadium on October 13, 1979. These installations completed a remarkable round of development of intramural as well as intercollegiate athletic and artistic exhibition facilities. The Beasley Performing Arts Coliseum, the crowning achievement, opened in 1973, providing a beautiful and utilitarian center for music, drama, and convocations, as well as basketball (played on Friel Court).[39]

Athletic funding—whether for facilities, games, or scholarships—had grown to a point where it disturbed faculty who believed it might threaten academic programs. Ninety-six professors of the College of Engineering, having suffered a decline in funding for many years, sought redress from the Regents in March, 1981, in a petition calling for "decisive steps" to "be taken immediately to reverse this trend with the goal of achieving parity with other instructional units on campus." Professor Richard Tinder, of Electrical Engineering, who presented the petition, faithfully recited the complaints, including the unhappy note that Engineering's funding had dropped from eighty-nine percent of formula in 1972-1973 to fifty-three percent in 1981. Further evidence that the situation had become intolerable came from the fact that their funding had declined to seventeen percent below the University's average. At the same time, the engineers anticipated a rapid rise in enrollments.[40]

Professor Tinder ventured beyond the petition's terms to declare that the engineers believed that instructional funds had been used for athletics. He also expressed the opinion that misuse of funds had been widespread. He and many others may not have been unprepared for what followed: President Terrell arose to acknowledge the truth of the first point, that academic funds had been transferred to athletes. But, on the other hand, he firmly rebutted any implication of wrong doing, declaring that no state laws had been broken. In fact, he asserted, the state funds in question had been appropriated to the University with the proviso that the president was to distribute them to various units as needed. In this light, the Board of Regents received the petition but laid it on the table to be forgotten and gather dust.[41]

As a matter of fact, the engineers hastened, at the next meeting of the University Senate, to refocus attention on the main issue of the dispute. They denied having sought to pit themselves against athletics. Instead, as the minutes thereafter revealed, the petition had been meant to seek equity for all faculty. This closing of ranks was strengthened when the Faculty Council, delivered the following message: "We believe that the time has come for our university administration to provide frank and honest answers to the many questions which are being asked publicly and privately regarding budgetary matters." The Budget Committee of the University Senate joined in this request.[42]

Vice President G. A. Hartford responded for the administration in April and May, 1981, providing voluminous data that unequivocally demonstrated the integral part that athletics played in the University's budget. His reports even showed an effort to finance women's athletics, when the administration refunded to the men's program some $150,000 which had been originally paid over to the women's program. But, the Senate Budget Committee claimed that the reports, though extensive and detailed, remained incomplete, leaving questions unanswered. It was, for example, impossible for the committee to discover which, if any, academic programs might have lost funds to athletics.[43]

The Budget Committee was satisfied that the use of state funds to support intercollegiate sports had an "adverse effect" on academic programming. The committee stated bluntly that "direct support of intercollegiate athletics should be sought openly from the legislature through the appropriations process." But, far from seeking *carte blanche* for sports funding, the Senate recommended that the administration reaffirm a policy attributed to Governor Dan Evans's administration whereby sports established on the basis of athletic scholarships should receive no state aid for direct costs. On the other hand, those activities not possessing athletic scholarships should be eligible for state monies to meet their direct costs. The plan, promoted by the Council on Post-Secondary Education, could not meet the needs of the University's athletic program. Even the Budget Committee took an ambivalent attitude toward the Evans' formula, as it recognized that athletics were making "an important contribution toward the public image of WSU."[44]

*Biochemist Clarence A. "Bud" Ryan
was elected to the National Academy of
Sciences in 1986. He was the first WSU
scientist to be accorded this
distinction. A member of the WSU
faculty since 1964, Professor Ryan is
widely known for his research into
plant defense mechanisms against
insect attack.* (Washington State
University News Service)

Nevertheless, Professor William Iulo, Chairman of the Budget Committee, in an open letter to the Regents, published April 28, 1981, revealed that the faculty on the committee "were startled by the size of both state and nonstate funds devoted to intercollegiate athletics and concerned about the procedures used to provide state funds for this purpose." Viewing the 1981-1983 budget proposed by Governor John Spellman certainly produced concern. It contained $8,700,000 in funds from all sources which were budgeted for the direct costs of athletics. That figure constituted approximately 3.5 percent of the University's total budget. Subsumed under that figure were $700,000 in student fees to be paid to athletics and $1,200,000 in state funds evidently appropriated for other, unnamed, purposes, but actually used for direct costs of athletics. Women's programs were aided to the amount of approximately $300,000, an amount not in any sense equitable.[45]

The issue of athletic funding had become such a sore point to many faculty by the Spring of 1981 that it drove them to an abortive movement to force President Terrell to resign. The action began when the Faculty Council, mindful of a wide-spread impression of misuse of institutional funds, asked the WSU Retirees Association to conduct a poll among the faculty, asking two questions. 1) Should the president resign? 2) Was his management of affairs satisfactory?

Of the 1,198 questionnaires mailed, 1,120 were completed, certainly a high rate of return. Forty-nine percent believed the president should resign, but forty percent did not. The remaining eleven percent ventured no opinion, which helped to make the vote inconclusive. Regarding the second question, sixty-seven percent stated that they were not satisfied with Terrell's performance, while twenty-seven percent defended it. Thus, many who voted dissatisfaction with his performance did not equate their criticism with a call for dismissal. The Regents did not find the faculty poll convincing in any sense. They needed but ten minutes in executive session on June 5, 1981, to give strong vote of support to President Terrell to continue in office until his retirement.[46]

Another issue connected with athletic funding did not disappear so easily from public attention as had the results of the poll. The administration soon found itself more firmly entangled than ever in the politics and funding of sports when it faced litigation. This development came when a group of women athletes and their coaches filed suit against the University in the so-called Blair Case. The appellants sought damages for discrimination and injunctions restraining further discrimination against women athletes. The principal point, of course, had to do with unequal funding for men's and women's programs. On January 3, 1983, Judge Philip H. Faris, of the Superior Court of Whitman County, ruled "substantially in favor of the plaintiffs," but excluded football from consideration in the funding formula, declaring that it occupied a unique role in WSU's sports program.[47]

The appellants carried their case to the State Supreme Court, which reversed Faris's exclusion of football from calculations of inequality.

The Court, on the other hand, upheld the University's "cross appeal" to permit "each sport to benefit from the revenue it generates," but cautioned that such benefit could not be had at the expense of equality between the sexes. The justices' decision repeated statistics showing that sex discrimination was widespread in WSU's sports program. Illustrative of the inequities, the majority decision noted the discrimination in the sums available for men's and women's athletic scholarships. In 1981, the men had $478,052 while the women had only $150,000. In summary, the justices invoked "injunctive relief" whereby the Supreme Court would keep the entire matter under its jurisdiction, being ready "to take whatever further action is consistent with [their] opinion." As a result, the University has made continued efforts to obtain financial relief from the legislature to balance expenditures between the athletic programs for men and women.[48]

The changes that took place in the campus life in the 1960s and 1970s called attention to the need to improve the physical environment. In 1969, President Terrell established a University Planning Council to follow-up on the Study Council reports, seeking to provide the physical implementation for academic goals. The Planning Council's report noted, for example, that the Study Councils of 1968 had emphasized a strong interest in the inter-relatedness of all knowledge and prophesied that interdisciplinary studies would become popular. The Planning Council accepted the challenge to suggest new facilities to make interdisciplinary work possible. In the process, it sought to define and establish a physical "continuum" whereby the circulation of people and communication over the campus would be relatively fluid.[49]

The planners proposed that the historic division of the campus into concentric circles, one at the top of College Hill and one around its base, would be the ideal pattern for future development. The hill top, the area enclosed within Spokane Street, Stadium Way, and Colorado Street, should remain an intensively developed area of "general academic interest facilities." In other words, the hill top in the future should bear more academic structures, high rise, devoted to general education. To attain fluid movement and to provide tranquility and a healthful environment, it should, above all, become a pedestrian mall, closed to private automobiles.[50]

The peripheral area at the base of the hill, the planners decided, (in recognition of past development), would be oriented laterally, devoted to residence halls, specialized programs such as agriculture and engineering, and athletic and recreational fields. Farm Way, stretching east from Stadium Way, would provide space for service buildings. The committee gave some thought, too, to a bus system to link all areas.[51]

Actually, even the mall idea reflected earlier action as much as it did innovation. The University had begun laying the groundwork for a mall on September 12, 1966, when sections of Wilson and Library Roads were chained off from seven o'clock in the morning to six in the evening, Mondays through Fridays. This procedure eliminated automobile traffic and street noises from the vicinity of Van Doren

●

The changes that took place in the campus life in the 1960s and 1970s called attention to the need to improve the physical environment. In 1969, President Terrell established a University Planning Council to follow-up on the Study Council reports, seeking to provide the physical implementation for academic goals.

●

Hall, Holland Library, Bryan Hall, Wilson Hall, College Hall, and Compton Union Building. It represented only the first step, for the mall was supposed to lend an air of culture and provide opportunities for inspired thought and the exchange of ideas. Construction of that phase began in the summer of 1968 when the chained off areas were paved with concrete and brick and the surroundings landscaped. In 1975, the Physical Facilities Sub-Committee of the Planning Council reaffirmed support for the removal of all auto traffic and noise from the top of College Hill. To demonstrate good faith, the committee proceeded to block off all traffic in front of the new Owen Science and Engineering Library (named for Regent Frances Owen).[52]

In addition to promoting its practical goals, the University Planning Council proposed to change the nature of the institution from one with virtually a majority of lower division students to one emphasizing the upper division and graduate studies. The prospect might have appeared dim at that time since enrollments were badly skewed in favor of freshmen and sophomores. Of the 1971 student body, only eleven percent were graduate students while forty-nine percent were in the lower division. Optimists noted that demographic authorities freely predicted a rapid rise in University enrollments in the next quarter century, which might make it possible to change the population mix of students, sending great numbers of freshmen and sophomores to community colleges, and finding the vast sums needed for greatly increased upper division and graduate education. The goal became that of increasing graduate students to twenty-five percent of the student body. With the projected expansion of graduate education, went unspoken expectations of prosperity for the state and generous appropriations needed for attaining increased prestige in a a number of research fields.

On August 3, 1979, in a confident mood after the legislature had granted a relatively generous budget, Terrell announced to the Board of Regents that he expected WSU to be invited to join the exclusive, research-conscious Association of American Universities within five years. In order to attain this goal, WSU would require a more generous state budget than any experienced in his administration and, in addition, perhaps ten times the previous research grants from outside sources. As he surveyed the scene that bright summer day, the president was keenly aware that his institution had risen from its national rankng of 110th for receipt of outside funding ten years earlier to fifty-sixth place in 1979.

But as time passed, Terrell's hopes for dramatic change slowly eroded. The expected major enrollment increases never materialized at WSU, or anywhere else in the state for that matter; thus, his efforts to transform the population mix on campus were defeated. The record enrollment at WSU, reached in September 1980 was 17,468. Thereafter the numbers fell off, totaling only 15,567 in 1988. That figure was only about a thousand students more than the number who attended the school in 1971. Another stumbling block to revamping the University was the fact that the lower-division population had dropped only six percent to approximately forty-three percent of the over-all student body. Under the circumstances, lower division instruction and general education had to remain high priorities. The added sums needed for research were as absent as were the projected hordes of additional graduate students.[53]

The anticipated enrollment explosion drew much of the administration's attention to student housing. In fact, in 1969, six hundred more students registered than the 12,500 projected, leaving a number—somewhere between 100 and 300 people—forced to reside at the University of Idaho for several weeks. Anticipation of another housing shortage in 1971 led the administration to the novel construction of 144 "turn-key" apartments. Under the plan, a general contractor developed all aspects of a garden apartment community from breaking ground to installing residences, streets, and lawns. The turn-key apartments also permitted the housing officials to accede to student demands for smaller and more diversified living units than the dormitory.[54]

The administration built more turn-key apartments in 1975 and 1976, at which time occupancy rose to approximately 1300 people, a small number consisting of families and the great majority being single students. On the strength of projections by a state agency that an additional 600 students would register for the fall of 1977, more apartments were planned. They were never built, however, after the Regents questioned the projections in the light of census data that indicated a decline in student population after 1980. The administration soon began to plan the razing of the World War II demountable housing which, because of low rents, had remained popular among student families for many years. Finally, in 1983 and 1984, the administration, with a sense of relief because of safety hazards and high cost of maintenance, had them demolished.[55]

In fact, the best indicator for gauging the utilization of student housing may be residence hall occupancy. The peak came in the fall of 1975 when twenty-six residence halls were in operation. They housed a total of 5,889 students, almost equally divided between men and women. Five of these halls were co-educational, as was the Graduate Center. Ferry Hall, which had for some time served graduate students, was razed in 1975, making way for an expansion of the biological sciences complex. Subsequently, declines in occupancy rates forced closure of several halls, or in some cases transforming them for other uses. In 1988-1989, only 4,786 students lived in residence halls, creating a serious financial dilemma for student housing planners. Forcing freshmen to live in dormatories, a matter discussed earlier, might be the last attempt made to restore the dominance of traditional dormitory arrangements. Other plans for revamping vacant space, included turning double-occupancy dorm rooms into single student rooms. That solution may sustain a tightly cohesive campus community.[56]

The campus took on a serene appearance in late spring and summer of 1971, a matter normally taken for granted. But it required the fresh observations of architects from a Houston, Texas, firm to express its charm. They reported that "Washington State [University]

Professor of Food Science and Human Nutrition Charles W. Nagel pioneered research in the growing of wine grapes in the Pacific Northwest. Because of research by Nagel and other WSU scientists, the State of Washington has become one of the leading wine-growing regions in the United States. (Washington State University News Service)

Glenn Terrell Friendship Mall at night.
(Historical Photograph Collections,
Washington State University Libraries)

has a generally pleasant campus. In the summer the preponderantly red brick buildings, varying in shades from soft rose red to a deep rich burgundy, form a dramatic contrast to the green of the lawns, the gold of the ripening wheat on distant hills, and the spectacular cloud-filled sky which seems to envelope the land."[57]

Had they returned on Sunday afternoon of May 18, 1980, they would have been startled to see "tons of dustlike, volcanic ash" falling on Pullman and the campus, as it did over large parts of eastern Washington. They would have found themselves experiencing the aftermath of an eruption by Mount St. Helens in the Cascades. Professor Don A. Dillman, a rural sociologist at WSU, has reported the event in an interesting chronicle. He wrote: "Last year's total eclipse of the sun made Pullman dark, but there was no comparison to the total void I then saw through our patio window. Street lights were on, appearing hazy in the fog-like darkness. The only light . . . in our backyard was reflected from the kitchen . . . A closer look at the entire backyard with help from the outdoor light showed only gray as the ash continued to fall, like small particles of gently driven snow."[58]

Thus began ten days of turmoil, almost ten years to the day since the student's strike over war and racial discrimination. Confusion reigned the next morning, Monday, when President Terrell first declared classes open but later announced that they would be closed, amid much anguish and wasted effort. Driving vehicles or other movement outside was so hampered by swirling dust that the speed limit, where driving on campus was permitted, was posted at ten miles per hour. For the most part, people were advised to stay at home. Terrell's confusion, in retrospect, was understandable, since probably no one on campus had experienced an ash fallout, but the mistakes might have been avoided had he tried the out-of-doors before advising others to do so.[59]

The University remained closed through Thursday on the advice of health specialists, with students penned up in their residences. The exception for most people came when they ventured outside to clean roofs, sidewalks, and streets of the heavy and hard-to-manage dust. A debate as to whether the University should close immediately, skipping final exams (slightly more than one week away), ended when President Terrell decreed that the term would be completed.[60]

In the meantime, students, staff and faculty alike suffered psychological as well as physical discomforts and ailments connected with their inactive, cooped-up conditions. Students flocked to the health service complaining of persistent coughs, headaches, and irritation in the chest. The authorities had quickly established an emergency medical leave for which approximately 3,500 students eventually applied. Taking examinations had, in effect, become optional.[61]

There probably were no lasting effects for the students, most of whom left the Palouse within two weeks. Perspective and research into the contents of the ash disabused notions that it threatened permanent damage. Faculty exhibited their own kind of maladjustment. When classes resumed on Friday, Chronicler Dillman found his office work "inefficient." So, he drifted over to the Faculty Lounge in the Compton Union Building for coffee. When he arrived he found, as he explained: "There is no place to sit, one of the few times I can recall there being so many people in it. Finally locating a chair with a group of other Department of Sociology faculty, I learn why. They, too, have found it difficult to get work restarted. Some are commiserating about the difficulty of giving a coherent early-morning lecture, when the one that preceded it was given so long ago, seeming like ancient history to both instructor and student."[62]

Subsequently, the administration laid elaborate plans for a possible reoccurrence of eruptions, which has not been the case. Otherwise, since youth rebound quickly from disaster, the ash fall might in itself be considered the only permanent effect. It represented, in a small way, a latter-day addition to the loess which had blown in from the western mountains eons ago, created the Palouse Hills, and the campus site.[63]

$\mathscr{E}$pilogue

Searching for Identity in the Second Century

President Glenn Terrell retired on July 1, 1985, having completed eighteen years of service to Washington State University. But when he left the president's office for the last time, past struggles did not disappear, leaving a clean slate for his successor. Indeed, a financial controversy had risen once again just six months before he retired.

The controversy concerned Terrell's income for the final six months of his tenure. On November 16, 1984, the Board of Regents secretly raised his salary 19.3 percent, from $88,885 to $106,000. Accidental disclosure of the sub rosa action raised a furor among students, faculty, and the public—both for the size of the increase and for an alleged violation of Washington's law requiring meetings of public bodies to be open. In early December, Terrell "backed off," asking the Regents to defer action on the salary matter until he retired, remarking also that they should center attention, rather, on the salary for his successor.[1]

Bowing to criticism and a possible citation for law violation, the Regents met in open session on January 18, 1985, to take up the salary topic once more. They refused to by-pass completely a raise for Terrell, but placed it at the more modest level of $94,840. That sum amounted to a 6.7 percent increase, a rate equivalent to average salary increases for the faculty at that time. In justification for its action the Board praised Terrell's performance extravagantly, but in actuality they were at least equally concerned about attracting superior candidates for the WSU presidency.

The Board's final tribute to the outgoing president came two days before his retirement when they declared the walkway system at the top of College Hill to be the Glenn Terrell Friendship Mall. In so doing, they acceded to his request that if he were to be commemorated, it should be through honoring his association with people, especially students. The idea of naming the mall after him was appropriate since Terrell had always found it a good location for meeting and greeting people.[2]

After a nation-wide search for Terrell's successor, the Board of Regents selected Samuel Howard Smith to serve as the eighth

OPPOSITE: *The clock on Bryan Tower.* (Historical Photograph Collections, Washington State University Libraries)

Samuel H. Smith, eighth president of Washington State University. (Washington State University News Service)

president of Washington State University. The new chief executive assumed the duties of office on July 1, 1985. Dr. Smith, dean of the College of Agriculture at Pennsylvania State University, as well as director of the Agricultural Experiment Station and the Cooperative Extension Service, was forty-five years of age. A native of California, he had engaged in undergraduate and graduate studies at the University of California at Berkeley, earning the Ph.D. in Plant Pathology in 1964. There followed a career in teaching, research, and administration, first at Berkeley (1964-1969) and then at Pennsylvania State University. He had become dean of agriculture at the latter institution in 1981.[3]

On assuming his new duties President Smith might well have pondered Glenn Terrell's "farewell address" to the Regents on June 28, 1985. On that occasion, the retiring president discussed in somber terms the financial difficulties of the preceding years. Terrell did not stop with a recounting of travail, however, earnestly arguing that WSU must gain equality with the University of Washington, especially in financial terms, if it was to carry out the ambitious programs contemplated. More than money was involved, though. Standing before the Board for the last time, Terrell reminded his hearers that to perform at their best, WSU's professors and administrators needed to have a great faith in themselves and their institution. "We need never apologize for any part of our institution nor should we ever accept being second best. We have a proud history and, more important, a bright future, provided we solve our financial problems. . . ."[4]

For those who would still apologize, Terrell offered his own deep commitment to the University. It was time to crush negativism, he said, a matter which he put into perspective by decrying a time-worn myth about WSU's location. He rebutted, he said, "this nonsense we have been hearing recently about the anachronistic nature of a research university located in a place like Pullman, Washington . . . our location is similar in position and geography to some of America's most distinguished Universities—for example, the University of Illinois, Indiana University, Cornell University, the University of Iowa, and Purdue University." He then urged the development of satellite campuses, invoking the conventional wisdom: "branching out is a land-grant tradition."[5]

Far from disagreeing with Terrell's final remarks, the Smith administration has maintained a continuity with its predecessor in its approach to on- and off-campus developments. President Smith's address at his formal inauguration on March 21, 1986, contained a list of four major objectives that had their beginnings earlier. The four, which have remained firmly fixed as the end of the twentieth century looms, called for, first, a restructuring of the undergraduate curriculum to emphasize core courses and integrated learning and a writing program which would be imbedded in the curriculum from the freshman through the senior year.[6]

A second objective was to establish branch campuses in three areas "underserved" by higher education—Spokane, the Tri-Cities, and Vancouver. Third, the new administration sought to raise research and graduate work to a level necessary to reach top ranking for the University, seemingly adopting Terrell's objective of gaining membership in the Association of American Universities. That is, the proposal was to single out certain departments or programs noted for research and then provide them with special funding. Fourth, to support the faculty, it was promised a step-salary system as a means of attaining equity in funding, and perhaps as a means of hastening the day when sufficient funds for salaries would be available.[7]

As a matter of fact, Smith expressed cautious optimism to the faculty about the institution's financial condition after a meeting of the legislature. Encouraging appropriations—though modest—for salaries and institutional development had been gained. The satellite campuses had inched nearer to full development, while sufficient funds for a state-wide telecommunications system were obtained. Through the latest developments in such a network the University would be able to link all parts of the state to it via "electronic classrooms." Thus the wildest dreams of preceding generations appeared to be nearing reality.[8]

When President Smith addressed an annual leadership conference of the University on September 8, 1988, his audience was made aware of significant developments concerning the branch campuses. Also added to the satellites were plans for a technical institute in Spokane to be conducted in cooperation with other Spokane-area institutions of higher learning. All of these units were weighted heavily toward technical training in fields as disparate as engineering, business administration, health physics, graduate training in teaching, and supervision of public schools. Undergraduate liberal arts programs are contemplated but plans are modest and projections are for a slower paced implementation.

Communities involved in these satellite campuses expect to find "a key" to economic well-being through a better-trained work force that would attract new industry. Place-bound students (unable to travel for schooling to existing campuses) hoped to obtain a general education or technical training (or both) at branch campuses. Meanwhile, the legislature seemed ready to fund the construction of necessary buildings and facilities on a substantial basis.[9]

The flagship campus in Pullman, too, has witnessed significant recent developments. Seventy-five million dollars in contemplated and on-going construction and remodelling have changed its skyline and brought larger and more sophisticated teaching and research facilities and equipment to the student body and faculty. In 1988-1989, two hundred and seven outstanding high school seniors were attracted to the campus by generous Glenn Terrell Scholarships, the product of a highly successful drive to accumulate scholarship funds by the WSU Foundation. Perhaps the most significant recent construction has been a great expansion of the chemistry building, a new section providing opportunity for the most sophisticated chemical research. Of greater popular use will be the Lewis Alumni Centre, a general meeting place created by remodelling a large beef cattle barn.[10]

Executive Vice President and Provost Albert C. Yates was hired by President Glenn Terrell in 1981. During the first years of the President Samuel H. Smith's tenure, Yates, a Ph.D. in Theoretical Chemical Physics from Indiana University, served as chair of the President's Commission on General Education, which developed the first major undergraduate general educational reform at WSU since 1946. (Washington State University News Service)

Professor of History LeRoy Ashby joined the Washington State University history faculty in 1972. The author of numerous scholarly books and articles, he is best known on campus as an outstanding teacher. Among his awards, he was the recipient of the 1983 Faculty Excellence Award in Instruction. In 1986 Professor Ashby gave the keynote address at President Samuel H. Smith's inauguration. (Washington State University News Service)

President Smith, in his address to the 1988 leadership conference also incorporated references to the growth of shared governance, the faculty being offered a larger role in the university's decision-making process. Shared governance remains a fragile relationship between faculty, students, and the administration, which may be injured or shattered at moments of conflict or stress. A recent lengthy study of faculty stress at WSU, for instance, revealed that a great deal of suffering had resulted from anxiety. The data reported centered upon the individual faculty member's stress resulting from strained interpersonal relations and feelings of personal inadequacy and frustration.[11]

Still, Chairman Walfred Peterson, of the Stress Study Committee, was not satisfied that the investigation had delved into all areas of stress. In an article published on April 8, 1988, he found a neglected source of stress in the threatened rapid transformation of the university. Such changes leave the individual in doubt as to the character of the University, perquisites available, and its demands upon the person. Peterson wrote on this matter: "A special quality in our stress results from WSU's uncertainty about its core nature. True, we are a land-grant university, a fact which settles major aspects of our identity. For other aspects, we are and have been seeking our identity for over two decades. The record shows the process."[12]

The records show that the faculty has been articulate in criticizing the new programs and plans. Meeting the demands inherent in new situations, whether in creating new campuses or revamped general education, would seem a drain upon already tight budgets which squeeze faculty as well as existing programs. The chances that a depressed government or a willing electorate will find all needed funds seems almost chimerical. As Peterson reported, "It'll come out of our hides," was a prevalent remark or belief of many faculty.[13]

President Smith, on the other hand, surveying the same scenario, addressed the question of stress in institutional terms. The University stood, he contended, on the threshold of great, new accomplishments which required sublimating stress into a "gutsy ambition to excel." The need was to educate all willing and able students, regardless of race, sex, or creed. They should be prepared well in the knowledge of life as well as in the skills their society needs. Success means steadfastly seeking to educate for the needs of society by utilizing the newest and most fruitful means available. In this fashion can the "people's university" be realized, thus fulfilling the mission of the land-grant movement.[14]

In the midst of his celebratory resumé of Washington State University's attainments and goals, President Smith paused to say "I see us insisting that our valued role as a university of opportunity continues in meaningful ways. *We are not on a course to become an elitist, homogeneous university.*" In this denial, Smith spanned the years from the founding of the college in 1890 to his own day. The school of George Lilley and Enoch Bryan indeed had been a small, homogeneous institution, elitist in the sense that few people mentally or physically could reach across Washington to its portals in the earliest

Lewis Alumni Centre, a one-hundredth birthday present to the people who make up the greater Washington State University community, was made possible by private gifts to the University through the WSU Foundation. The fully redesigned structure is named in honor of Seattle residents Jack and Ann Lewis, the parents of WSU graduates and million-dollar donors to the project. The chief architects for the remodeling of this former animal science facility were Robert Grossman, WSU class of 1959, and Steve McNutt, WSU class of 1971. (Washington State University News Service)

years. Nevertheless, Enoch Bryan had been the great spokesman for the modern university when he fought to enlarge the college's horizons, curriculum, and student body. The vision of the "people's university" began with him and gradually unfolded in the course of the century.[15]

In the future, this institution should progress further toward the goal of equality of opportunity, which is a hallmark of its land-grant mission. It should, also, following the time-honored goals of all true universities, redouble its efforts to discover knowledge and truth, ethics and aesthetics, and to protect fearlessly freedom of discourse and teaching, as well as research, in all these matters. The preservation of the people and their society, depends upon these efforts. In this role, Washington State University should include all disciplines of knowledge and learning as well as fundamental training for the professions, acknowledging that learning is holistic, taking place in the mind and psyche of the individual, and becoming in the process, a special and, indeed, unique gift to the person and to society. Endeavors of lesser magnitude would certainly be unworthy of the "People's University."[16]

Notes

Chapter One

1 The designation of the college was established in section 4 of the Enabling Act of March 28, 1890, entitled *An Act to Create a Commission of Technical Instruction, and to Establish a State Agricultural College and School of Science,* found in *Session Laws of the State of Washington, enacted by the First Legislature, Session of 1889-90,* pp. 260-266. Subsequent title changes were (1) to Washington Agricultural College, Experiment Station, and School of Science, as found in the *Third Annual Catalogue of the Washington Agricultural College, Experiment Station, and School of Science, 1893-94;* Pullman, Washington, 1893-1894 (2) to State College of Washington in 1905, and (3) to Washington State University in 1959.

2 President George Lilley and the editor of the local weekly newspaper, however, were "most agreeably surprised to find forty-seven present. . . ." See "Retrospective, Pullman Thirty-one Years Ago," Pullman *Herald,* January, 1923, clipping attached to *First Annual Catalogue. . . of the State Agricultural College and School of Science, 1891-1892,* Washington State University Libraries. The total enrollment of eighty-four is found in the compilation, "Total Enrollment Since 1892," Registrar's Office, WSU, but it offers no breakdown of enrollees as to class. Enoch Albert Bryan, *Historical Sketch of the State College of Washington, 1890-1925* (Pullman: Alumni and Associated Students, 1928), pp. 6-8.

3 *Regents Record,* Vol. 1, June 23, 1897, p. 325. *Sixth Annual Catalogue of the Washington Agricultural College, Experiment Station, and School of Science,* 1896-1897, p. 25.

4 Johansen, Dorothy O. *Empire on the Columbia: A History of the Pacific Northwest,* Second Edition. (New York: Harper and Row, 1967), pp. 339, 340, 607.

5 Roger C. W. Bjerk, "A History of Pullman, Washington, 1876-1910," (M. A. Thesis, Washington State University, 1965), pp. 37-42, tells the story of site selection interestingly but incorrectly lists May 30 as the date of site selection and places the victory celebration on Sunday when it actually took place the Monday following. Stores were closed rather than churches. The quotation from Letterman is inaccurate in Bjerk but may be found in the Pullman *Herald* for May 2, 1891. That from Bjerk is found in his thesis on pp. 40 and 41. Spokane Chronicle, April 27, 1891; Pullman Herald,May 2, 1891; Regent's Record Vol. 1, May 1, 1891, pp. 5-8; Session Laws of the State of Washington, Session of 1891, pp. 335,336. Documents pertaining to the actual date of site selection are found in "Official Report . . . Board of Commissioners. . . ." Folder 292, Bryan Papers.

6 Bjerk, Chapter 3, especially pp. 37, 38; Pullman *Herald,* May 2, 1891.

7 Parker's article was reprinted in the Pullman *Herald,* December 25, 1891.

8 E. V. Smalley, "In the Palouse Country," *The Northwest Magazine,* 10 (September 1892): 21-30 (quotations on pp. 24, 25).

9 *An Act Donating Public Lands to the Several States and Territories Which May Provide Colleges for the Benefit of Agriculture and the Mechanic Arts* (The Morrill Act), *Statutes at Large,* 12, ch. 130, pp. 503-505 (quotation is from p. 504).

10 For general discussion of the early history of the land-grant colleges and agricultural experiment stations, see among others, Edward Danforth Eddy, Jr., *Colleges for Our Land and Time: The Land-Grant Idea in American Education* (New York: Harper and Brothers, 1956), and Allan Nevins, *The State Universities and Democracy* (Urbana: University of Illinois Press, 1962). On the development of experiment stations, see Alfred Charles True, *A History of Agricultural Experimentation in the United States, 1607-1925* (Miscellaneous Publication No. 251, Department of Agriculture, 1937). The nature of scientific research in agriculture in Pullman is discussed in Robert W. Hadlow, "A History of the Development of Scientific Research at the Washington Agricultural Experiment Station in Pullman, 1890-1940" (M. A. thesis, Washington State University, 1987). For a general appraisal of agricultural science, see Margaret W. Rossiter, "The Organization of the Agricultural Sciences," in Alexandra Oleson and John Voss, *The Organization of Knowledge in Modern America, 1860-1920* (Baltimore: Johns Hopkins University Press, 1979), pp. 211-248, but especially p. 240.

11 Eddy, pp. 103, 104.

12 *Ibid,* pp. 100-102 (quotation from p. 102, italics are mine).

13 Johansen, chapter 21; Washington, *An Act to Create a Commission of Technical Instruction and to Establish a State Agricultural College and School of Science, Session Laws,* 1889-90, pp. 260-266 (quotation is from p. 262). Bryan, *Historical Sketch,* p. 16.

14 *Ibid.,* p. 263

15 Lacking in this statement was the idea of providing a broad cultural education for the masses which would rank with the best provided by private universities. For this law, see *Session Laws of the State of Washington, Session of 1891,* Chapter 145, pp. 334-341.

16   *Regents Record,* Vol. 1, April 22, 1891, p. 2; May 1, 1891, p. 5 (quotation "for one year"). Judge Thomas Neill, "Incidents in the Early History of Pullman and the State College of Washington" (Pullman *Herald,* 1922), typescript, p. 22.

17   [R. B. Botting,] "George Lilley, President May, 1891, to December, 1892." Subtitle "Biography," [1943] rough draft. Folder George Lilley, Office of the President (Research, Lewellen, Lilley, Miscellaneous) WSU 132; Pullman *Herald,* May 16, 1891; Bryan, *Historical Sketch,* pp. 9, 10, 83.

18   *Regents Record,* Vol. 1, May 22, 1891, pp. 8-11; Bryan, *Historical Sketch,* pp. 83-85.

19   *Regents Record,* Vol. 1, November 16, 1891 (quotation), p. 16; December 1, 1891, p. 43.

20   *Ibid.,* 45, 46; Bryan, *Historical Sketch,* pp. 9-12, 83.

21   *Regents Record,* Vol. 1, December 1, 1891, pp. 44, 45.

22   *Faculty Minutes,* Vol. 1, January 12, 1892, pp. 1, 2.

23   From the Pullman *Herald,* [January 15, 1892], in "Retrospective, Pullman Thirty-one Years Ago," in Pullman *Herald,* January 19, 1923.

24   *Faculty Minutes,* Vol. 1, February 4, 1892; Regents Record, Vol. 1 February 9, 10, 1892, entire set of minutes; February 18, 1892 pp. 88-94. A close study of the academic records of the students present in the first few years substantiates the generalization about the actual curriculum and the absence of sharp distinctions between preparatory and collegiate courses. (Registrar's Office). For pharmacy and domestic science, see the various college catalogs, 1891-98 through 1895-96.

25   *Regents Record,* Vol. 1, February 9-11, 1892, entire set of minutes; February 18, 1892, pp. 96, 97.

26   *College Record,* February, 1892.

27   *Faculty Minutes,* Vol. 1, February 22, March 2, March 4, April 8, all of 1892; *College Record,* February and April, 1892.

28   Bryan, *Historical Sketch,* pp. 204, 205. A complete file of the *College Record,* is found in Manuscripts, Archives, and Special Collections, Washington State University Libraries.

29   *Ibid.,* February, March, April, May and November, 1892. *Faculty Minutes,* Vol. 1, April 29, June 3, and June 10, 1892. For an authoritative record of athletic competition during the early years, see Richard B. Fry, *The Crimson and the Gray: 100 Years with the WSU Cougars* (Pullman: Washington State University Press, 1989), pp. 1, 37.

30   Term Examinations, reported on in the Faculty Meeting of March 18, 1892, substantiate the claim that a large number of examinations were for sub-collegiate courses. The situation could only have been the same in June.

31   *Regents Record,* Vol. 1, May 17, 1892, p. 125; June 16, 1892, p. 143; July 20, 1892, pp. 154-159.

32   *Ibid.,* Vol. 1, November 15 and 17, 1892, pp. 203, 204.

33   Edmond S. Meany to Board of Regents, Washington Agricultural College, November 11, 1892, and Meany to John W. Heston, March 24, 1893, Meany Letterpress Book (1891-1893). The Meany Papers are located in the University of Washington Records Center. *College Record,* December 1892.

34   Meany to John H. McGraw, November 11, 1892, Meany Letterpress Book (1891-93), (quotation) is representative of numerous letters found in the Meany Papers. See Bryan's judgment regarding Piper in his *Historical Sketch,* p. 94.

35   *Regents Record,* Vol. 1, December 28, 1892, pp. 239, 240; May 6, 1893, p. 250; Bryan, *Historical Sketch,* pp. 99, 100, 125; Pullman *Herald,* March 3, 1893.

36   *Regents Record,* Vol. 1 November 15, 1892, pp 201, 202; December 12, 1892, pp. 225; January 18, 1893; p. 244; May 8, 1893, p. 251'Pullman *Herald,* January 20, 1893 (quotation "Well Known in Pullman") and March 3, 1893; Bryan, *Historical Sketch,* p. 100 (quotation "an odd genius"), p. 124.

37   *Regents Record,* Vol. 1, October 26 and 29, 1892, pp. 187, 188; November 15 and 16, 1892, pp. 190-195.

38   *Annual Report of the Board of Regents of the Agricultural College, Experiment Station, and School of Science of the State of Washington,* November 1, 1892, pp. 3, 4, 6-9 (with quotations found on pp. 4, 6).

39   *College Record,* November 1892.

40   *Ibid,* April 1892 (quotation); *Annual Report of the Board of Regents,* November 1, 1892, pp. 17, 18.

41   *College Record,* April 1892 (both quotations).

42   *Regents Record,* Vol. 1, December 12, 1892, pp. 226, 227. Spokane *Review,* December 14, 1892 (quotation); George Lilley to A. H. Smith, November 11, 1892 and Lilley to S. B. Conover, November 19, 1892, both letters found in Vol. 1, General Correspondence, (Outgoing); Bryan Papers. Suggestions of a vendetta by Regent Smith against President Lilley are found in "The Removal of Mr. Lilley," editorial, Spokane *Review,* December 15, 1892

43   [B. R. Botting] "George Lilley, President, May, 1891, to December, 1892," rough draft of a biographical sketch, Folder "George Lilley," Office of the President, (Research, Lewellen, Lilley, and Miscellaneous), WSU 132.

44   Spokane *Chronicle,* December 14, 1892; *Regents Record,* Vol. 1, December 12 and 13, 1892, pp. 227-229 and 231-233; Bryan, *Historical Sketch,* pp. 97, 98.

45   Spokane *Review,* December 22 (quotations) and 24, 1892 and February 17, 1893; *Regents Record,* Vol. 1, December 28, 1892, p. 238. Bryan, *Historical Sketch,* pp. 97-98.

46   *Ibid.,* p. 98, states that "The disgraceful episode injured the college for many years thereafter and rendered difficult the task of reconstruction." *Regents Record,* Vol. 1, December 28, 1892, p. 238. The editorial in the Colfax *Commoner* was reprinted in the *College Record* for January, 1893, and its exaggerations commented on in the latter.

47   Spokane *Review,* December 15 and 24, 1892; *College Record,* January 1893.

48   Spokane *Review,* December 24, 1892 (quotation); [R. B. Botting] "John W. Heston, President, December 1892 to September 1893." Undated biographical sketch, Folder "John W. Heston," Office of the President (Research, Lewellen, Lilley, and Miscellaneous), WSU 132.

49   *College Record,* January, 1893; John W. Heston to J. R. Bellinger, February 3 [1893], Vol. 1, General Correspondence (Outgoing), Bryan Papers.

50   Pullman *Herald,* March 3, 1893; Bryan, *Historical Sketch,* pp. 101, 102. Text of the Report of the Agricultural College Joint Investigating Committee is found on pp. 543-547 (quotation).

51   John W. Heston to J. A. Arrasmith, April 4, [1893], Vol. 1, General Correspondence (Outgoing), Bryan Papers. Heston's letters to the true appointees were dated April 4 and 8, [1893]; Bryan, *Historical Sketch,* 555-556; [John Heston] "Minutes of Organization of the Board of Regents. . . ," May 4, 1893, Vol. 1, General Correspondence (Outgoing), Bryan Papers.

52   *Regents Record,* Vol. 1, May 10, 1893, pp. 288-289; *College Record,* March, 1893. (quotation) Heston to Charles R. Conner, May 12 [1893], and Heston to J. W. Stearns, June

2, [1893], both found in Vol. 1, General Correspondence, (Outgoing), Bryan Papers.

53   *Regents Record,* Vol. 1, May 24, 1893, pp. 292, 293; *ibid.,* June 14, 1893, pp. 296-298; *ibid.,* Vol. 2 April 1897, pp. 316, 317; Faculty *Minutes,* Vol. 1, May 26, 1893; A review of Steinle's academic records substantiate the weak character of his senior studies (Registrar's office).

54   *Ibid.,* Vol. 1, June 14, 1893, pp. 296-298; see also, Meeting of August 21, 1893, pp. 347, 348.; *Regents Record,* Vol. 1, August 21, 1893, p. 347.

55   *Regents Record,* Vol. 1, July 22, 1893, pp. 339-340; Bryan, *Historical Sketch,* pp. 114, 115; Bryan, "Reminiscences of Early History of the College and Pullman (Under the auspices of the Chamber of Commerce) Undated, but 1930s, Folder 267, Bryan Papers.

56   [E. A. Bryan,] Autobiography, a manuscript untitled and undated, Folder 279, Bryan Papers; Bryan, *Historical Sketch,* pp. 113-115.

57   The oration on "Character" appears originally to have been a student address because of Bryan's reference to the "recent death" of François Guizot, noted French historian and statesman, who died in 1874. In the midst of a longhand manuscript written on Vincennes University stationery from the 1880s there is inserted an obviously newer, typed section, quite substantial, with references to the Washington Agricultural College. Bryan to Professor Irion, Elberton, Washington, May 25, 1898 (Letterbook, 1895-1898, Correspondence to Students and about Internal Affairs) reveals that the lecture on "Character" had been given several times recently and that it would be given again on May 27, 1898. The speech on "Character" is found in Folder 267, Bryan Papers. Quotation is from p. 12 of the document. See also, Bryan, Baccalaureate Address to the Graduating class of Vincennes University on June 7, 1891, Item 168, Folder 256, Bryan Papers.

58   Bryan, "Reminiscences of Early Pullman and the College," Folder 267, Bryan Papers (Both quotations). The population of Pullman in 1890 was 868 (U. S., Bureau of the Census, *U. S. Census of the Population, 1960,* Vol. I: *Characteristics of the Population,* Part 49, p. 49-10.

59   *Regents Record,* Vol. 1, May 10, 1893, p. 274; *ibid.,* June 6, 1893, pp 310-312; Bryan, *Historical Sketch,* pp. 103, 104; Pullman *Herald,* June 16, 1893.

60   *Regents Record,* Vol. 1, June 16, 1893, pp. 310-312; *ibid.,* June 17, 1893, pp. 314-318; *ibid.,* September 30, 1893, p. 372; *ibid.,* Vol. 2, April 23, 1895, p. 144; *ibid.,* Vol. 2 June 27, 1895, p. 186; Session Laws of 1895, pp. 120, 121. The town leaders in question were A. G. Fariss, M. C. True, and H. J. Webb (*Regents Record,* Vol. 1, June 17, 1893, pp. 314-316.

61   Bryan, *Historical Sketch,* pp. 113, 121-123, 144, 157 (quotation regarding Spillman). [Bryan], "Founders of the College: W. J. Spillman," Folder 267, Bryan Papers; "Radio Talks, Founders of the State College: Elton Fulmer," *ibid.*

62   *Third Annual Catalogue . . . 1893-94,* pp. 5, 11-16, 31.

63   *Ibid.,* p. 32 (quotation on mathematics courses), 36 (quotation on chemistry courses), 41 (quotation on Piper's courses), and 45, 46.

64   *Ibid.,* pp. 49-52 (quotation on p. 51).

65   *Ibid.,* pp. 49, 50, 63 (quotation on "advanced technical courses"), 64, 65.

66   *Ibid.,* p. 76.

67   He also had to deal with debts piled up by his predecessors, a matter he handled with considerable aplomb: see Bryan to Carl Fischer, New York, October 11 and 26, 1894,

Vol. 2, General Correspondence (Outgoing), Bryan Papers. Other evidence of his myriad functions is found in Bryan Papers, Vols. 1 and 2.

68   *Third Annual Catalogue . . . 1893-94,* pp. 51, 52. See, myriad activities illustrated in numerous outgoing letters from Bryan to various constituents, publishers' of textbooks, etc., in Bryan Papers, Vol. 2, 1894-95. On his anxiety over the "Lilley Crowd," see Bryan to Blandford, May 3, 1894, Vol. 1, General Correspondence (Outgoing), Bryan Papers.

69   Bryan to Messers. E. and H. T. Anthony and Co., New York, November 9, [1893]; *Regents Record,* Vol. 2, August 21, 1894, p. 90.

70   [Bryan] to Hon. L. R. Grimes, State Auditor, November 14 [1893], Vol. 1, General Correspondence (Outgoing), Bryan Papers. Bryan to The Commissioner of Education, Washington, D. C., December 9, 1893, (quotation), Vol. 1, General Correspondence (Outgoing), Bryan Papers.

71   Bryan to A. C. True, November 24, 1893; Bryan to Charles R. Conner, December 21, 1893 (quotation); Bryan to L. C. Read, June 23, 1894; Bryan to the Commissioner of Education, August 25 [1894], all found in Bryan Papers, Vol. 1. Bryan in his *Historical Sketch,* p. 124, contradicted an earlier statement to True (above) that Read taught music after hours, by stating he had been hired to teach music rather than as an assistant in the experiment station.

72   *Regents Record,* Vol. 2, January 15, 1894, pp. 8-9; February 19, 1894, pp. 16-18; E. R. Lake to H. S. Blandford, February 26, 1894; Lake to Bryan, April 10, 1894, General Correspondence (Incoming), Bryan Papers. Bryan to H. S. Blandford, May 3, 1894, Vol. 1, p. 302; H. S. Blandford, Walla Walla, to E. R. Lake, March 2 [1894], (quotation "to wreck the college"), General Correspondence (Incoming), Bryan Papers. *Regents Record,* Vol. 2, April 2, 1894, pp. 28, 29. Bryan, *Historical Sketch,* p. 156 (quotation "retired").

73   H. S. Blandford, Walla Walla, to "Friend Bryan", April 28, 1894, (quotation), General Correspondence (Incoming), Bryan Papers; E. A. Bryan, "[Report] to the Board of Regents, June 18, 1894," Report to the Board of Regents, 1894-1916, WSU 136. Se also, Bryan, *Historical Sketch,* pp. 153-154.

74   [Bryan] "To the Board of Regents of the Washington Agricultural College and School of Science [1895], pp. 1-7" (quotation on "collegiate work," p. 1; "industrial classes," p. 3), Report to the Board of Regents, 1894-1916, WSU 136.

75   *Ibid.,* pp. 1-7 (quotation on "difficulty," p. 5; on "the nature of the work," p. 6, 7.).

76   Bryan, *Historical Sketch,* pp. 1-3, 86-92, 226, 309.

77   *Fourth Annual Catalogue of the Washington Agricultural College, Experiment Station, and School of Science, 1894-95,* pp. 20-22, 28 (quotation on p. 22); [Bryan] Report of the President . . . to the Secretary of Agriculture [1895], unpaged, on the mechanical arts building and program (Report to the Board of Regents, 1894-1916, WSU 136).

78   *Fourth Annual Catalogue . . . 1894-95,* p. 20. Bryan, *Historical Sketch,* p. 156.

79   *Ibid.,* pp. 166-169; *Evergreen,* June, 1895. [The student newspaper had its title partially altered from time to time but in this work it will merely be titled *Evergreen*]. Bryan, "Address Delivered on the Occasion of the Dedication of the Administration Building of the Agricultural College and School of Science, of the State of Washington, June 26, 1895," (quotations on p. 2), Folder 286, Bryan Papers.

80 *Fifth Annual Catalogue . . . 1895-96,* pp. 76-87; *Sixth Annual Catalogue . . . 1896-97,* pp. 23, 24, 103-106. The first announcement of pharmacy courses is found in the *First Annual Catalogue . . . 1891-92,* pp. 26, 41, but exhaustive studies by Allan I. White makes it clear that no classes were held before 1896 (see his "History of Washington State University College of Pharmacy, 1891-1988, Chapter 1, typescript).

81 *Sixth Annual Catalogue . . . 1896-97,* pp. 115, 116.

82 *Seventh Annual Catalogue . . . 1897-98,* p. 85.

83 *Fifth Annual Catalogue . . . 1895-96,* pp. 102, 103.

84 *Faculty Minutes,* Vol. 1, October 6, 1893; Pullman *Herald,* November 17, 1893, December 1, 1893; *Evergreen,* April, 1896, (quotation).

85 *Faculty Minutes,* Vol. 1, December 3, 1893; *ibid.,* April 17, 1896, p. 141; Pullman *Herald,* February 22, [1896], April 25, 1896.

86 *Ibid.,* November 23, 1894.

87 *Evergreen,* March, April, June, 1895; *Spokesman-Review,* June 9, 1895 (quotation).

88 *Evergreen,* June 1896; *Spokesman-Review,* November 10 and November 29, 1895.

89 F. B. Gault, Moscow, to E. A. Bryan, August 20, 1895, General Correspondence (Incoming), Bryan Papers.

90 *Evergreen,* June, 1896 (quotations); *Faculty Minutes,* Vol. 1, May 31, 1895.

91 Bryan to The Manager, Football Team, University of Idaho, December 2, 1896, Vol. 6, General Correspondence (Outgoing), Bryan Papers; Bryan to E. R. Chrisman, Moscow, April 27, May 10, *ibid.*; November 20, 1897, Vol. 7, General Correspondence (Outgoing); *ibid.*, F. B. Gault to Bryan, December 1, 1897, General Correspondence (Incoming), *ibid.*

92 Committee (W.A.C. Athletic Association) to Athletic Association, University of Idaho, March 31, 1898, Vol. 7, *ibid.*; *Faculty Minutes,* Vol. 1, June 24, 1898; June 25, 1898, (quotation on p. 211); June 2, 1899.

93 Bryan, *Historical Sketch,* pp. 203, 204, 282, 285. *Spokesman-Review,* November 26, 1898.

94 Bryan, "To the Board of Regents of the Washington Agricultural College and School of Science, June, 1897," pp. 3, 4, in a folder titled "Report to the Board of Regents, 1894-1916," WSU 136.

95 See below, notes 96, 97 for descriptions of the arduous duties of proctors and inspectors.

96 *Faculty Minutes,* Vol. 1, October 1, 1894, September 23, 1895, December 13, 1895.

97 *Ibid.,* Vol. 1, October 19, 1894.

98 *Ibid.,* Meetings of January 24, February 7, 17, and 18, 1896, reveal a heavy advising load; and May 11, 1896. On scholarships, see *Regents Record,* Vol. 2, April 23, 1896, p. 273 and *ibid.,* Vol. 1, May 1, 1896.

99 *Faculty Minutes,* Vol. 1, May 11, 1896.

100 Bryan to W. G. Preston, Waitsburg, October 11 [1895] (quotation), Correspondence to Students and About Internal Affairs, Bryan Papers; *Faculty Minutes,* Vol. 1, October 11, 1895 and October 15, 1895, June 25, 1896, February 8, 1897.

101 *Ibid.,* February 8 and 15, 1897.

102 *Ibid.,* April 2, 1897.

103 The records on this bomb explosion are voluminous but the basic facts and charges may be found in the following: *Regents Record,* Vol. 2, June 24, 1897, p. 330; *Faculty Minutes,* Vol. 1 June 7 and 8, 1897; Bryan to H. C. Miller, Port Angeles, June 9, 1897, Correspondence to Students

and About Internal Affairs, Letterpress Book, 1895-1898, pp. 308-310; *Spokesman-Review,* June 11 and 12, 1897.

104 Two letters herewith represent a great many more: P. H. Winston, Spokane, to E. A. Bryan, March 28, 1896 (quotation), General Correspondence (Incoming), Bryan Papers, and Bryan to Winston, April 30, 1895, Vol. 3 General Correspondence (Outgoing), *ibid.; Spokesman-Review,* June 11 and 12, 1897.

105 Judge Buck's letter has not been found but was commented on in detail in the Pullman *Herald,* April 4, 1896, while Smith's appeared in the April 6, 1896 edition of the *Spokesman-Review; Faculty Minutes,* Vol. 1, April 13, 1896, pp. 139, 140 (quotations); Pullman *Herald,* April 11, 1896; *Regents Record,* Vol. 2, April 21, 1896, pp. 259-261; *Evergreen,* January, 1897.

106 E. A. Bryan, Untitled reminiscences, undated, Folder 267, Bryan Papers; Bryan, *Historical Sketch,* pp. 181, 186, 187; Bryan to Governor J. R. Rogers, Olympia, September 10, 1897, Vol. 7, General Correspondence (Outgoing), Bryan Papers; *Regents Record,* Vol. 2, September 16, 1897, pp. 349-353; Bryan to Charles R. Conner, Spokane, September 18, 1897, Vol. 7, General Correspondence (Outgoing), Bryan Papers; John R. Rogers, Olympia to E. A. Bryan, October 22, 1897, General Correspondence (Incoming), *ibid.*

107 John R. Rogers, Olympia, to Bryan, November 18, 1897, General Correspondence (Incoming), Bryan Papers; Bryan to Rogers, December 11, 1897; and Bryan to George M. Witt, Harrington, January 29, 1898, Vol. 7, General Correspondence (Outgoing), *ibid.*

108 Bryan to Witt, February 19, 1898, *ibid.*

109 Bryan to Albert E. Egge, Iowa City, Iowa, June 27, 29, 1896, July 6, 1896, (quotation) Vol. 5, General Correspondence (Outgoing) *ibid.* Egge to Bryan, July 13, 1896, General Correspondence (Incoming), *ibid.*; Bryan to Egge, July 6, 1896, *ibid.*

110 Bryan, "Report of the President to the Board of Regents, June 30, 1898," p. 5, 6, *Report to the Board of Regents, 1894-1916,* WSU 136; *Regents Record,* Vol. 3, June 19, 1899, p. 45.

111 *Faculty Minutes,* Vol. 1, April 2, 1897 (quotation); April 30, 1897 (quotation); Bryan to Prof. F. Berchtold, Corvallis, Oregon, April 10, 1897, Vol. 6, General Correspondence (Outgoing), Bryan Papers.

112 Pullman *Herald,* June 5, 12, 1897; *Regents Record,* Vol. 2, June 22, 1897, pp. 325, 326, lists the class of seven: Jesse E. Hungate, Bachelor of Letters; Mary C. Johnson, Bachelor of Letters; Orin Stratton, Bachelor of Science, Civil Engineering; Carl Estby, Bachelor of Science, Civil Engineering; Emma J. Hardwick, Bachelor of Science, Botany; Edward Kimmel, Bachelor of Science, Economic Science and History; George Nixon, Bachelor of Science, Electrical Engineering.

113 Spokane *Chronicle,* June 25, 1897.

114 *Spokesman-Review,* June 25, 1897, carried the text of Bryan's speech.

115 Bryan to T. R. Tannatt, Farmington, June 28, 1897, Vol. 6, General Correspondence (Outgoing), Bryan Papers.

116 *Evergreen,* November, 1897, (Quoting the jokes); Pullman *Herald,* November 27, 1897; *Regents Record,* Vol. 2, November 26, 1897, p. 365 (quotation on "a cordial relation").

117 Bryan, "Some Recent Changes in the Theory of Higher Education," 1899 [*sic*], Folder 247, Bryan Papers, unpaged.

118 Bryan, "The Present Status of Scientific Education and How it Came to Pass," Speech, December 27, 1929, Folder 247, "Articles Concerning Higher Education," *ibid.*; Bryan to John W. Pratt, Seattle, March 21, 1899, (quotation "omitted many" and "to make a central thought"), Vol. 8, General Correspondence (Outgoing), Bryan Papers.

119 Bryan to R. C. McCroskey, Garfield, January 12, 1899; Bryan to H. W. Canfield, Colfax, February 24, 1899; Bryan to A. C. True, Washington, D. C., February 28, 1899, Vol. 8, General Correspondence (Outgoing), *ibid.*; Bryan, *Historical Sketch*, p. 198.

120 *Ibid.*, pp. 255-257; Attachment to Bryan to the *Post-Intelligencer*, May 10, 1899, Vol. 8, General Correspondence (Outgoing), Bryan Papers.

121 Harold Preston to Bryan, April 27, 1899, General Correspondence (Incoming), *ibid.*; Bryan to Preston, May 2, 1899, Vol. 8, General Correspondence (Outgoing), *ibid.*; Seattle *Post-Intelligencer,* May 5, 1899 (quotations "the people," "rebuke") May 15, 1899 (quotation "commented upon"). Bryan's reply to the newspaper's criticism of his position is found in a letter to the editor, May 10, 1899, Vol. 8, General Correspondence (Outgoing), Bryan Papers.

122 Colfax *Commoner,* May 12, 1899.

123 Bryan to Barton W. Everman, Washington, D. C., May 16, 1899, (quotations), Vol. 8, General Correspondence (Outgoing), Bryan Papers.

Chapter Two

1   Bryan, "The Report of the President to the Board of Regents of the Washington Agricultural College and School of Science, June 30, 1900,", Report to the Board of Regents, 1894-1916, WSU 136.

2   Bryan, *Historical Sketch*, p. 214; Bryan, "The Dedication of Science Hall, State College of Washington [*sic*], June 20, 1900, unpaged typescript, (Quotations), Folder 286, Bryan Papers.

3   Bryan, "Report of the President to the Board of Regents, June 30, 1898, pp. 2, 3 (Quotation), Report to the Board of Regents, 1894-1916, WSU 136.

4   Bryan, "Dedication of Science Hall, June 20, 1900," unpaged, Folder 286, Bryan Papers. On the structure of Science Hall, see J. Meredith Neil, "Administrators, Architects and Campus Development: Washington State University, 1890-1905," *Journal of the Society of Architectural Historians*, Vol. 29 (May, 1970): 152. Bryan, *Historical Sketch*, p.212 (quotation).

5   J. Meredith Neil, p. 153; Press Release on the dedication of Science Hall [and Ferry Hall], June 20, 1900, Folder 286, Bryan Papers.

6   Bryan, "Annual Report of the President of the College to the Board of Regents, June 30, 1901," Report to the Board of Regents, 1894-1916, WSU 136. Numerous examples of fear and criticism of the University of Washington may be found in the Bryan Papers over duplication of courses, contention as to which institution should possess the School of Mines, etc. See especially, *ibid.*, passim. *Regents Record*, Vol. 3, June 17, 1901, p. 160.

7   *Faculty Minutes*, Vol 1, May 29, 1900, and June 19, 1900; May 8, 1901.

8   *Faculty Minutes*, Vol. 1, October 2, 1901.

9   Bryan, "Annual Report to the President of the College to the Board of Regents, June 30, 1901," pp. 15-19; Report of the Board of Regents, 1894-1916, WSU 136; *Regents Record*, Vol. 3, August 15, 1898, p. 1.

10   Bryan, *Historical Sketch*, pp. 243-245 (Quotation on p. 245); Bryan, "Annual Report of the President of the College to the Board of Regents, June 30, 1901," pp. 15, 16, Report to the Board of Regents, 1984-1916, WSU 136.

11   Bryan, "Annual Report for 1902-1903," *ibid.*, pp. 1, 2.

12   *Regents Record*, Vol. 3, December 8, 1905, p. 367 and April 4, 1906, p. 376; Bryan, *Historical Sketch*, p. 250 (Quotation).

13   *Regents Record*, Vol 3, April 6, 1904, pp. 308, 309; Solon Shedd to the President [Bryan], May 20, 1904, Department of Geology Papers, WSU 84; Shedd to Bryan, May 21, 1915, *ibid.*

14   Bryan, *Historical Sketch*, pp. 253, 254 (Quotation); *Regents Record*, Vol. 3, October 11, 1904, pp. 324, 325; Robert Hadlow, "A History of the Development of Scientific Research at the Washington Agricultural Experiment Station in Pullman, 1890-1940" (M.A. Thesis, WSU, 1987), p. 42; *Regents Record*, Vol. 4, June 16, 1908, p. 46.

15   Bryan, *Historical Sketch*, pp. 241-245, 306-309; *Regents Record*, Vol. 3, April 5, 1905, pp. 338, 339.

16   For pharmacy, see *ibid.*, Vol. 3, April 5, 1906, p. 379 and *Sixteenth Annual Catalogue of the State College of Washington*, 1907, pp. 131, 132. For veterinary science, see *Regents Record*, Vol. 3, April 5, 1906, p. 379 and 383; *ibid.*, June 18, 1906, p. 385; L. M. Koger, College of Veterinary Medicine, Washington State University, unpaged.

17   *Regents Record*, Vol. 3, April 5, 1906, p. 379; *Fifteenth Annual Catalogue of the State College of Washington,* 1906, pp. 87-92, 111-113.

18   Bryan, Annual Report. . . June 30, 1904, to the Board of Regents, Reports to the Board of Regents, 1894-1916, pp. 9, 10; Bryan, *Historical Sketch*, p. 264; *Faculty Minutes*, Vol. 1, March 28, 1906. *Regents Record*, Vol. 3, September 16, 1902, p. 237; *ibid.*, June 21, 1905, p. 357. This outburst of creative energy also produced the first course in agricultural economics, offered by the Department of Economic Science and History (first appeared in *Fifteenth Annual Catalogue of the State College of Washington, 1906*, p. 76), On Sampson's distinguished services, see *Regents Record*, Vol. 4, June 16, 1908, p. 47.

19   *Ibid.*, Vol. 3, April, 1905, pp. 338, 339; Bryan, "Annual Report for June 30, 1905 to the Board of Regents," p, 2, Report to the Board of Regents, 1894-1916, WSU 136 (Quotations).

20   *Regents Record*, Vol. 3, September 3, 1900, p. 114; October 15, 1900, p. 124; October 1, 1901, p. 182. On art in the curriculum see *Tenth Annual Catalogue of the Washington Agricultural College, Experiment Station, and School of Science, 1900-1901*, pp. 133-134. *Faculty Minutes*, Vol. 1, February 12, 1902.

21   Bryan [To whom it may concern?], August 25, 1902, Vol. 16, General Correspondence (Outgoing), Bryan Papers; *Regents Record*, Vol. 3, September 6, 1902, p. 238; Bryan, *Historical Sketch*, pp. 262, 263 provides a succinct description of the construction of the conservatory. *Regents*

Record, Vol. 3, January 14, 1905, p. 327; June 21, 1905, pp. 353-355; April 5, 1906, pp. 376, 377.

22 *Regents Record*, Vol. 4, April 4, 1907, p. 3; Bryan to W. B. Strong, May 3, 1907, Vol. 31, General Correspondence (Outgoing), Bryan Papers; Bryan to Kimbrough, May 3, 1907, *ibid*; *Regents Record*, Vol. 4, June 19, 1907, p. 20; *ibid.*, September 26, 1911, pp. 307-309; Bryan, Special Report to the Board of Regents, September 26, 1911, Report to the Board of Regents 1894-1916, WSU 136; Bryan, Annual Report of the President for June 30, 1911, with the Budget for 1911-1912, p. 13, *ibid.*

23 Bryan to Prof. Weginer [*sic*], Tacoma, April 10, 1900, Vol. 9, General Correspondence (Outgoing), Bryan Papers; Bryan to Mrs. Annie M. Sonenson,[*sic*] Chehalis, April 13, 1900, *ibid. Ninth Annual Catalogue of the Washington Agricultural College, Experiment Station and School of Science, 1899-1900*, pp. 153, 154; Bryan, "The Report of the President, June 30, 1900," Report to the Board of Regents, 1894-1916, WSU 136, pp. 6, 7; Bryan "Annual Report of the President, June 30, 1901," p. 11a; *ibid.* Bryan to J. S. Keeney, Pullman, June 15, 1900, Vol. 9, General Correspondence (Outgoing), Bryan Papers.

24 To that correspondent, Bryan also stated there would also "be a thorough review in all of the branches" necessary for becoming licensed to teach school (Bryan to L. T. Miller, Oakesdale, May 19, 1900, *ibid.*).

25 "Annual Report . . June 30, 1904, to the Board of Regents, p. 12; Report to the Board of Regents 1894-1916, WSU 136; Bryan, "Annual Report of June 30, 1905, to the Board of Regents," p. 3, *ibid.; Fifteenth Annual Catalogue of the State College of Washington, 1906*, pp. 147-149.

26 Bryan to H. W. Canfield, Colfax, February 11, 1902, Vol. 14, General Correspondence (Outgoing), Bryan Papers; *Regents Record*, Vol. 3, February 8, 1902, pp. 200-203; *ibid.*, May 24, 1902, p. 218; Bryan to E. A. Brown, February 26, 1903, Vol. 17, General Correspondence (Outgoing), Bryan Papers; *Regents Record*, Vol. 3, May 24, 1902, pp. 212, 213; Bryan to Dr. G. B. Wilson, Olympia, February 28, 1903, Vol. 17, General Correspondence (Outgoing), Bryan Papers; Bryan, *Historical Sketch*, p. 226 relates that the legislature granted $33,000 to complete the building in 1903.

27 Bryan to [E. J.] Durham, January 19 (Quotation) and 26, 1903, Vol. 17, General Correspondence (Outgoing), Bryan Papers; Bryan to Herman D. Crowe, Olympia, January 20, [1903], *ibid.*; Bryan to Dr. G. B. Wilson, Olympia, January 30, 1903, *ibid.*

28 Bryan, "Annual Report, June 30, 1905, to the Board of Regents," Report to the Board of Regents, 1894-1916, WSU 136.

29 *Regents Record*, Vol. 3, October 1, 1901, p. 181; Bryan to Assistant Attorney General Ross, Olympia, April 15, 1902, Vol. 15, General Correspondence (Outgoing), Bryan Papers; Bryan to S. A. Calvert, Land Commissioner, Olympia, August 24, 1903, Vol. 19, *ibid*; *Regents Record*, Vol. 3, September 18, 1903, pp. 278-285; Bryan to Senator Pogue, January 19, 1905, Vol. 23, General Correspondence (Outgoing), Bryan Papers; *Regents Record*, Vol. 3, January 13, 1905 and April 5, 1905, p. 337. An ambitious plan to place the Board of Regents in control of State College lands was introduced by Senator J. L. Pogue on February 6, 1905 under the following title: Senate Bill Number 136, State of Washington, Ninth Regular Session, Washington State Legislature. The bill died in committee. On Bryan's continued vigilance see Bryan to Land Commissioner

Rose, Olympia, May 15, 1907, Vol. 31, General Correspondence (Outgoing), Bryan Papers; Bryan *Historical Sketch*, pp. 245-250.

30 Bryan, *Historical Sketch*, pp. 255-258; "Change its Name, Says Mr. Bryan," *Spokesman-Review*, January 8, 1905 (editorial); Bryan to W. D. Barkhuff, Everett, January 16, 1905, Vol. 23, General Correspondence (Outgoing), Bryan Papers; Bryan "to the Members of the State Legislature" [1905], broadside, Folder 267, *ibid.*

31 Session Laws of the State of Washington, Ninth Session, 1905, Chapter 53, p. 83.

32 Robert W. Hadlow, "A History of the Development of Scientific Research at the Washington Agricultural Experiment Station in Pullman, 1890-1940," (M. A. thesis, Washington State University, December, 1987), pp. 27-30.

33 *Ibid.*, pp. 30, 31 (Quotation), 38-48.

34 *Ibid.*, pp. 45, 46 (Quotations).

35 Bryan, "Annual Report of the President for June 30, 1911, with the Budget for 1911-12," pp. 5-7, Report to the Board of Regents, 1894-1916, WSU 136; Bryan to W. H. Paulhamous, Sumner, May 31, 1902, Vol. 15, General Correspondence (Outgoing), Bryan Papers.

36 Session Laws of the State of Washington, 1891, Chapter 145, pp. 336, 337; Bryan, *Historical Sketch*, pp. 518, 519.

37 *Ibid.*, p. 519; David A. Brodie to Bryan, March 17 and April 6, 1899, March 22 and May 28, 1901, General Correspondence (Incoming), Bryan Papers; Bryan, *Historical Sketch*, pp. 518-520; Bryan to Brodie, March 14, 1903, Vol. 18, General Correspondence (Incoming), Bryan Papers.

38 Hadlow, "A History of the Development of Scientific Research at the Washington Agricultural Experiment Station in Pullman," p. 39; Bryan, *Historical Sketch*, p. 519; W. H. Paulhamus to Bryan, July 22, 1907 (Quotation), General Correspondence (Incoming), Bryan Papers; Paulhamus to Bryan, March 18, 1911, *ibid*; Bryan, "Annual Report of the President, June 30, 1911, with the Budget for 1911-12," Report to the Board of Regents, 1894-1916, WSU 136.

39 Bryan, *Historical Sketch*, pp. 512-515; Donald W. Meinig, *The Great Columbia Plain, A Historical Geography, 1805 to 1910* (Seattle: University of Washington Press, 1968), Chapter 13; Bryan, "Annual Report of the President for June 30, 1911, with the Budget for 1912," Report to the Board of Regents, 1894-1916, WSU 136; *Regents Record*, Vol. 5, February 6, 1914, pp. 88-93; *ibid.*, April 7, 1914, PP. 137-143.

40 Bryan, *Historical Sketch*, pp. 512-517; Meinig, *The Great Columbia Plain*, p. 413 (Quotation); *Regents Record*, Vol. 5, August 6, 1915, pp. 177-179; October 20, 1915, pp. 194-197; Bryan, [Report] to the Board of Regents, February 22, 1915, Report to the Board of Regents, 1894-1916, WSU 136.

41 Hadlow, "A History of the Development of Scientific Research at the Washington Agricultural Experiment Station in Pullman," p. 13; Bryan, *Historical Sketch*, pp. 487-488..

42 Hadlow, "A History of the Development of Scientific Research at the Washington Agricultural Experiment Station in Pullman," pp. 39-41.

43 [O. L. Waller], "Report to the Board of Regents by the Acting President, December 20, 1911," Report to the Board of Regents, 1894-1916, WSU 132; Bryan, "Annual Report of the President of the College, June 30, 1912," *ibid.; Regents Record*, Vol. 5, April 9, 1915, p. 154.

44 Bryan, *Historical Sketch*, p. 536-538; Bryan, Report of the President of the College to the Board of Regents, April 14, 1913" (Quotation), 1916, WSU 136; Bryan, "Report to the Board of Regents, November 24, 1913, *ibid.; Regents*

Record, Vol. 5, June 12, 1913, pp. 72, 73.

45 Bryan, *Historical Sketch*, pp. 306, 307 (Quotation); Hadlow, "A History of the Development of Scientific Research at the Washington Agricultural Experiment Station in Pullman," p. 42.

46 Bryan, "Annual Report of the President to the Board of Regents, June 30, 1907," (Quotations), Report to the Board of Regents, 1894-1916, WSU 136; *Faculty Minutes*, Vol. 1, June 18 and 19, 1907.

47 *Regents Record*, Vol. 4, October 9, 1907, p. 25; Bryan, *Historical Sketch*, pp. 305, 306.

48 Bryan to Professor Fulmer, October 26, 1909, Vol. 41, General Correspondence (Incoming), Bryan Papers; Bryan, "Annual Report of the President, June 30, 1910, (Quotation), Report to the Board of Regents, 1894-1916, WSU 136; Bryan in his *Historical Sketch*, p. 327, called Fulmer "dean of the faculty."

49 Bryan to Dean Elton Fulmer, January 7, 1910, (Quotation), Vol. 42, General Correspondence (Outgoing), Bryan Papers; Bryan, Annual Report of the President for June 30, 1911, Report to the Board of Regents, 1894-1916, WSU 136.

50 Bryan, "Annual Commencement Report of the President to the Board of Regents, June 10, 1914, *ibid.*

51 Bryan, *Historical Sketch*, pp. 337-339, 352-357; Bryan, "Annual Report of the President of the College for the Academic Year ending June 30, 1912, (Quotation), Report to the Board of Regents, 1894-1916, WSU 136.

52 *Regents Record*, Vol. 5, June 11, 1912, pp. 4, 5; Bryan, "Annual Report of the President of the College, June 30, 1912," Report to the Board of Regents, 1894-1916, WSU 136; Bryan, *Historical Sketch*, pp. 363, 364.

53 Anonymous, A description of the Department of Domestic Science. Not dated but "From the 1910 Files," Bryan Papers (Quotations). Bryan, *Historical Sketch*, pp. 241-243. Compare *Catalogue of the State College of Washington, 1908*, pp. 115-117, with *Twenty-Fourth Catalogue, 1915*, pp. 221-227.

54 *Sixth Annual Catalogue of the Washington Agricultural College, Experiment Station, and School of Science, 1896-97*, pp. 129, 130; *Eighteenth Annual Catalogue of the State College of Washington, 1909*, pp. 53-54; *Faculty Minutes*, Vol. 2, March 9, 1911; Ibid., Vol.3 May 1, 1914; ibid., June 26, 1911; Bryan, "Annual Report of the President of the College to the Board of Regents, June 30, 1913," Report to the Board of Regents 1894-1916, WSU 136.

55 *Eighth Annual Catalogue of the Washington Agricultural College, Experiment Station, and School of Science, 1898-99*, p. 25 (Quotation "a prosperous town"); Bryan to Prof. Barton W. Everman, Washington, D. C., May 16, 1899, (Quotations on life in Pullman), Vol. 8, General Correspondence (outgoing), Bryan Papers.

56 James C. Mohr, "Academic Turmoil and Public Opinion: The Ross Case at Stanford," *Pacific Historical Review*, Vol. 39 (February, 1970): 39-61; Laurence R. Veysey, *The Emergence of the American University*, (Chicago: University of Chicago Press, 1965), pp. 383-407; Bryan to Prof. W. J. Ashley, Cambridge, Mass., May 22, 1901, Volume 12, General Correspondence (Outgoing), Bryan Papers; Bryan to Prof. F. W. Taussig, Cambridge, Mass., May 22, 1901, *ibid.*, (Quotations).

57 *Regents Record*, Vol. 3, December 15, 1900, pp. 131, 133 (Quotation); ibid., June 19, 1902, p. 229; *ibid.*, June 18, 1902, p. 226; Bryan to Dr. Albert E. Egge, Spokane, June 6, 1900, Vol. 9, General Correspondence (Outgoing), Bryan Papers; Egge to Bryan, April 3, 1901, General Correspon-

dence (Outgoing), *ibid.*; Landeen, *E. O. Holland and the State College of Washington*, pp. 195, 196, 329. For size of faculty and percentage of loss, cf. *Eleventh Annual Catalogue, 1902* with *Regents Record*, Vol. 3, June 18, 1902, p. 226.

58 *Regents Record*, Vol. 3, September 6, 1902, pp. 234, 235.

59 Bryan to Adjutant General, Washington, D. C., June 29, [1903], Vol. 18, General Correspondence (Outgoing), Bryan Papers; Bryan to Inspector General, Washington, D.C., July 24, 1903, *ibid.*; Bryan to Captain Edward Kimmel, Ft. McHenry, Maryland, July 24, 1903, *ibid.*; Bryan, *Historical Sketch*, pp. 239, 240.

60 Bryan, "Annual Report of the President to the Board of Regents, June 30, 1907," (Quotation), Report to the Board of Regents, 1894-1916, WSU 136; Bryan to Governor M. E. Hay, Olympia, December 8, 1909, Vol. 41, General Correspondence (Outgoing), Bryan Papers. *Regents Record*, Vol. 5, June 11, 1912, p. 7; J. J. Browne to Bryan, December 21, 1905, General Correspondence Incoming, Bryan Papers.

61 Bryan, "Annual Report of the President of the College to the Board of Regents, June 30, 1913," Report to the Board of Regents, 1894-1916, WSU 136.

62 Bryan, "Annual Report of the President of the College to the Board of Regents, June 30, 1913," (Quotation), *ibid.*; Bryan *Historical Sketch*, pp. 348 and 348n; "Frank Albert Golder," *Washington Historical Quarterly*, Vol. 20 (January 1929): 157-158.

63 *Regents Record*, Vol. 4, April 12, 1910, pp. 191, 192; Bryan to Governor M. E. Hay, Olympia, December 8, 1909, Vol. 41, General Correspondence (Outgoing), Bryan Papers.

64 *Ibid.* (Quotation); On Attorney-General Bell, see Hay to Bryan, December 29, 1909, General Correspondence (Incoming), *ibid.*; Hay to Bryan, December 15, 1909, *ibid.*

65 *Regents Record*, Vol. 3, June 18, 1902, p. 227; [Bryan], October Meeting, 1915, [of the Board of Regents], Report to the Board of Regents, 1894-1916, WSU 136.

66 Roger C. W. Bjerk, "A History of Pullman, Washington, 1876-1910," pp. 103-112; *Regents Record*, Vol. 4, April 1, 1908, pp. 33 (Quotations), 34.

67 Bjerk, pp. 103-112.

68 *Regents Record*, Vol. 4, August 6, 1908, pp. 63-67 (Quotation); *ibid.*, December 3, 1908, p. 86; Bryan, *Historical Sketch*, pp. 313, 314.

69 *Spokesman-Review*, March 8, 1901, quotation; *ibid.*, March 9, 1901.

70 *Faculty Minutes*, Vol. 1, March 14, 1901.

71 Bryan to Lyman L. Goodwin, Kalama, March 14, 1900, Vol. 9, General Correspondence (Outgoing), Bryan Papers; R. Winsor, Seattle, to Bryan, June 16, 1903, General Correspondence (Incoming) and Bryan to Winsor, June 23, 1903, Vol. 18, General Correspondence (Outgoing), *ibid.* Although Bryan (in *ibid.*) states that they treat students as young men and women rather than as children, the evidence of the parental spirit is overwhelming. *Faculty Minutes*, Vol. 1, April 4, 1902.

72 Bryan to Prof. Elton Fulmer, December 9, 1909, Vol. 41, General Correspondence (Outgoing), Bryan Papers; *Regents Record*, Vol. 4, April 6, pp. 241, 242, and April 7, pp. 252, 253, 1911. Bryan, "Annual Report of the President for June 30, 1911, with the Budget for the Year 1911-12," (Quotation), Report to the Board of Regents, 1894-1916, WSU 136.

73 Bryan to J. A. Crosby, April 9, 1910, Vol. 43, General Correspondence (Outgoing) Bryan Papers; Bryan to the Cook,

Stevens Hall, April 26, 1910, *ibid.*; Bryan to Professors Elton Fulmer, O. L. Waller, and R. W. Thatcher, April 27, 1910, *ibid.*

74 Bryan, *Historical Sketch*, p. 404, 406-407; *Regents Record*, Vol. 5, October 5, 1914, pp. 119, 120.

75 *Ibid.*, Vol. 4, December 3, 1908, pp. 86, 87; *Spokesman-Review*, December 13, 1908 (Quotation of headline). The whole story may be followed in both the Pullman *Herald* and the *Spokesman-Review* for the duration of the show; *Catalogue of the State College of Washington, 1908*, pp. 30, 31 (Quotation on college building).

76 Bryan, "Annual Report of the President for June 30, 1911, with the Budget for the Year 1911-12," Report to the Board of Regents, 1894-1916, WSU 136; *Faculty Minutes*, Vol. 2, June 15, 1911 and Vol. 3, November 3 and 17, 1911; Bryan, *Historical Sketch*, pp. 400-412.

77 Bryan, "Annual Report of the President of the College to the Board of Regents, June 30, 1913,"(Quotation "It will tend to give unity"), Report to the Board of Regents, 1894-1916, WSU 136; Bryan, *Historical Sketch*, pp. 350-352 (Quotations are Bryan's characterizations of McCroskey's views).

78 *Faculty Minutes*, Vol. 2, June 15, 1911, and Vol. 3, November 1 and 17, 1911; *Evergreen*, May 12, 1914 and May 28, 1915; Bryan, "Annual Commencement Report of the President to the Board of Regents, June 10, 1914," Report to the Board of Regents, 1894-1916, WSU 136.

79 *Evergreen*, May 12, 1914 and May 28, 1915 (Quotation).

80 *Faculty Minutes*, Vol. 2, June 15, 1911, and Vol. 3, November 11 and 17, 1911; *ibid.*, Vol. 3, June 3, 1915, and ibid., Vol. 4, November 4, 1915.

81 *Ibid.*, Vol. 3, June 3, 1915.

82 *Evergreen*, May 9, 1900; Bryan, *Historical Sketch*, pp. 286, 287.

83 *Faculty Minutes*, Vol. 1, June 21, 1900, April 8, 1901.

84 *Ibid.*, Vol. 1, May 12, 1903; Bryan to Byron Stimmel, Rossland, B. C., August 11, 1903, Vol. 19, General Correspondence (Outgoing), Bryan Papers.

85 *Faculty Minutes*, Vol. 1, June 10, 1902 (Quotation "all members"); *Evergreen*, June 18, 1902, October 9, 1902, and October 16, 1902.

86 Bryan, "Colleges for More Than Sport," *Spokesman-Review*, October 1, 1905, Part 1, p. 3; Record of an Interview given by President E. A. Bryan on "Summer Athletics," No date, c. 1903, Folder 307, Bryan Papers; Bryan to President Thomas F. Kane, Seattle, September 28, 1905, Vol. 26, General Correspondence (Outgoing), *ibid.*; Bryan to *The Evening Telegram*, Portland, November 26, 1909, Vol. 41, General Correspondence (Outgoing), *ibid.*

87 Lengthy correspondence between Presidents Bryan and Kane concerning athletics is scattered through the Bryan papers for 1905, the following being prominent: Bryan to Kane, October 17, 25, and November 6, 1905, Vol. 26, Bryan Papers (Outgoing); Kane to Bryan, September 23 and October 13, 1905, Folder 128, *ibid.*

88 Bryan, *Historical Sketch*, pp. 289-291.

89 *Ibid.*, pp. 318, 394, 395 (Quotation).

90 *Ibid.*, pp. 398, 399; Bryan divulged the information that the track was flawed, thus disallowing the world record for Nelson; in Bryan to President James M. Hamilton, Bozeman, Montana, April 25, 1910, Vol. 43, General Correspondence (Outgoing), Bryan Papers.

91 This story unfolds in a series of 1904-1905 letters from Bryan to elementary and high school principals: Vol. 23, *ibid.*; and the *Spokesman-Review*, May 14, 1905, part 1, pp. 1 and 4.

92 H. M. Cook, Colfax, to Bryan, January 17, 30, (Quotation), 1905, General Correspondence (Incoming) Bryan Papers; Bryan to Miss Myra H. Butler, Cheney, October 23, 1905, Vol. 26, (Outgoing), *ibid.*

93 Bryan to F. Lewis Clark, Spokane, January 18, 1905, Vol. 23, *ibid.*; *Regents Record*, Vol. 3, April 5, 1906, p. 377; Ibid., Vol. 4, April 9, 1909, p. 96 (Quotation "heartily approved"); *Ibid.*, June 28, 1909, p. 145; Bryan to W. J. Kerr, Corvallis, November 4, 1909, Vol. 41, General Correspondence (Outgoing), Bryan Papers.

94 Bryan to *The Evening Telegram*, Portland, November 26, 1909 (Quotation "intellectual," "clash of brute force"); Bryan to J. Newton Colver, Spokane, December 2, 1909 (Quotation "manliness, courage," etc.); Bryan to N. W. Durham, Spokane, December 4, 1909, all from Vol. 41, General Correspondence (Outgoing), Bryan Papers.

95 Bryan to W. S. Kienholz, February 28, 1910, Vol. 42, *ibid.*; Bryan, "Report of the President to the Board of Regents, April 6, 1910," Report to the Board of Regents, 1894-1916, WSU 136; *Regents Record*, Vol. 4, April 11, 1910, pp. 185-187 (Quotation "guilty as charged"); ibid., April 13, 1910, pp. 198, 199; Bryan to W. S. Kienholz, April 13, 1910, Vol. 43, General Correspondence (Outgoing), Bryan Papers.

96 Bryan, "Report of the President to the Board of Regents for the February Meeting, 1914," (Quotation "a splendid spirit"), Report to the Board of Regents, 1894-1916, WSU 136; *Regents Record*, Vol. 5, April 7, 1914, p. 135; Dietz claimed also to have played at Carlisle before becoming an assistant coach (See Pullman *Herald*, May 28, 1915); *Twenty-fifth Annual Catalogue of the State College of Washington*, 1916, p. 26; *Spokesman-Review*, January 1 and 2, 1916 (Quotation from Eckersall).

97 *Regents Record*, Vol. 4, May 13, 1908, pp. 43, 44; Bryan, "Annual Report of the President to the Board of Regents, June 30, 1908," Report to the Board of Regents, 1894-1916, WSU 136 (Quotation "monstrous").

98 Bryan, "Annual Report of the President of the College for the Year Ending June 30, 1910," (Quotation "intolerable"), *ibid.*; *Regents Record*, Vol. 4, February 28, 1912, p. 318; Bryan, "Presidents Report to the Board of Regents, Commencement Session, 1914-1915," Report to the Board of Regents, 1894-1916, WSU 136; Bryan [Report] to the Board of Regents, February 22, 1915, *ibid.* Earlier, in the summer of 1911 Clothier had cruised 14,000 acres of Cowlitz County, which may have been regarded as a trial run. On the matter see *ibid.*

99 Bryan, "Annual Report of the President for the Year Ending June 30, 1910," (Quotation "jealousy and rivalry," and "its efforts primarily"), *ibid.*

100 *Regents Record*, Vol. 5, December 14, 1914, p. 127; Stenographic Report of the Remarks of President Bryan before the Joint Committee of the Senate and House of Representatives on Education, January, 1915," Folder 243, Bryan Papers; Bryan, "Annual Report of the President of the College to the Board of Regents, June 30, 1913," Report to the Board of Regents, 1894-1916, WSU 136.

101 *Ibid.*; Gates, *The First Century at the University of Washington*, pp. 117, 125 (Quotation); Bryan, "Presidents Report to the Board of Regents at the Commencement Session," 1914-1915, Report to the Board of Regents, 1894-1916, WSU 136. Bryan, "Annual Report of the President of the College to the Board of Regents, June 30, 1913," Report to the Board of Regents, 1894-1916, WSU 136.

102 *Ibid.*

103 *Regents Record*, Vol. 5, June 8, 1915, pp. 171-175; *Twenty-Fourth Annual Catalogue of the State College of Washington, 1915*, pp. 8-28.

104 *Regents Record*, Vol. 5, October 20, 1915, pp. 187, 188; Bryan, *Historical Sketch*, pp. 415-417 (Quotation on p. 417); Landeen, *E. O. Holland and the State College of Washington*, pp. 1-18.

Chapter 3

1 E. O. Holland, "Washington State College: Its Place and Opportunity to Serve," Inaugural Address, January, 1916, typescript found in "Addresses by E. O. Holland" (The State College of Washington, 1936), Office of the President (Holland). (Quotations on pp. 1, 3, 4, and 9).

2 Landeen, *E. O. Holland and the State College of Washington*, pp. 34, 35 (Quotation, pp. 34, 35); Edwin T. Coman to President Henry Suzzallo, September 13, 1915, Folder 61, Office of the President (Holland). E. O. Holland to Ernest H. Lindley, Bloomington, Indiana, May 6, 1916, Folder 177, *ibid.*

3 Landeen, pp. 35, 36 (Quotation). On expenditure for higher education, see Bureau of Education, Department of the Interior, "A Survey of Educational Institutions of the State of Washington," (Bulletin, 1916, No. 26), pp. 40-42.

4 Landeen, pp. 36-40. (Quotations on 37, 38).

5 *Ibid.*, pp. 40-47.

6 *Spokesman Review*, January 17, 1917.

7 *Ibid.*

8 *Ibid.*, January 25, 1917.

9 Charles M. Gates, *The First Century at the University of Washington*, p. 149; Bryan, pp. 50-56; *Spokesman Review*, January 24, 1917. For the text of the law see: *Session Laws of 1917*, Chapter 10, "Regulating Courses of Instruction at State University, College, and Normal Schools," pp. 34-35.

10 Gates, p. 149; *Spokesman-Review*, January 24, 1917; *Session Laws of 1917*, Chapter 10.

11 Landeen, p. 55 (quotation), 56-58.

12 Seattle *Post-Intelligencer*, January 2, 1917, clipping in Folder 343, Office of the President (Holland); Holland to George W. Dodds, Spokane, March 16, 1917, Folder 386; Holland to W. H. Cowles, Spokane, March 31, 1917, and Cowles to Holland, April 3, 1917, both in Folder 367, *ibid.*

13 Edwin T. Coman, Spokane, to Holland, March 13, 1917, Folder 697, *ibid.*; Holland to Coman, March 15, 1917, Folder 364, (Quotations) *ibid.*; *Regents Record*, Vol. 5, April 6, 1917, pp. 298, 299; Landes to Holland, April 13, 1917, Folder 487, *ibid.*; *Biennial Report of the Board of Geological Survey of the State of Washington*, 1917-1919, p. 16.

14 Holland to Coman, December 5, 1917, Folder 364, Office of the President (Holland); Holland to Coman, July 10, 1918, Folder 697, (Quotation) *ibid.*; *Twenty-Fourth Biennial Report of the Superintendant of Public Instruction*, June 30, 1918, pp. 145, 146; *Thirty-Second Annual Catalogue of the State College of Washington*, 1923, p. 277; *Report of the Superintendant of Public Instruction*, June 30, 1928 to June 30, 1936, pp. 102-106; *Fifty-Fourth Announcement of the State College of Washington for 1946*, p. 120.

15 William C. Kruegel to Holland, March 17, 1916, Folder 21, Office of the President (Holland); *Regents Record*, Vol. 5, May 12, 1916, pp. 225-229; Landeen, p. 165; *Regents Record*, Vol. 5, August 31, 1916, pp. 258, 259; *ibid.*, November 4, 1916, pp. 271, 272 (Quotation).

16 O. L. Waller to Holland, May 9, 1916, Folder 88, Office of the President (Holland); Holland to W. D. Dodd, Goldendale, October 31, 1916, Folder 89; Holland to Olive E. Otis, Spokane, September 7, 1916, Folder 209 *ibid.* Joseph Ashlock, Holland's aide, wrote much public relations material, but it was done under Holland's supervision (see Ashlock to E. M. Duffy [Corvallis, Oregon], April 25, 1916, Folder 89, *ibid. Regents Record*, Vol. 5, June 15, 1916, pp. 254-256.

17 George Steyart, Tonasket, to Holland, November 1, 1916, Folder 255, Office of the President (Holland) (Quotation "smoldering" radicalism); and Holland to Steyart, November 6, 1916, *ibid.*

18 Landeen, pp. 59-65.

19 *Regents Record*, Vol. 5, April 13, 1917, p. 85; June 13, 1917, pp. 319, 320; and January 28, 1918, pp. 346, 350 (Quotation); L. F. J. [LeRoy] Jackson to Prof. W. G. Beach, Seattle, May 8, 1917, Folder 391, Office of the President (Holland).

20 Louis F. Hart, Olympia to Holland, April 27, 1917, Folder 438, *ibid.*; Holland to Hart, May 5, 1917, Folder 438, *ibid.*

21 Holland to Victor H. Engelhard, Louisville, Kentucky, July 19, 1917, Folder 399, *ibid*, quotation; *Regents Record*, Vol. 5, May 22, 1918, pp. 375, 376; Holland to Frank L. Blanchard, New York, June 27, 1917, Folder 339, Office of the President, (Holland).

22 *Regents Record*, Vol. 5, June 14, 1917, pp. 328, 329; *Faculty Minutes*, April 30, May 7, 8, 9, October 10, all of 1917; January 23, February 14, 1918. For the resolution on protecting young men from the evils of prostitution, see *Regents Record*, May 2, 1917 (Quotation).

23 *Regents Record*, Vol. 5, May 22, 1918, p. 373-376; Landeen, pp. 115, 116, 120-131.

24 *Regents Record*, pp. 122-130 (Quotation on p. 130).

25 *Faculty Minutes*, Vol. 4, August 2, 1918; September 20, 1918. A pre-nursing course was approved by the Faculty on September 28, 1918, probably as a war measure (*Faculty Minutes*, Vol. 4). For a discussion of war aims elsewhere, see Carol S. Gruber, *Mars and Minerva: World War I and the Uses of the Higher Learning in America* (Baton Rouge: Louisiana State University Press, 1975), pp. 240-244.

26 Landeen, p. 131; *Faculty Minutes*, Vol. 4, September 13, 1918; December 10, 1918; and February 7, 1919.

27 On the character and history of the pandemic, see Alfred W. Crosby, Jr., *Epidemic and Peace, 1918* (Westport, Connecticut: Greenwood Press, 1976), pp. 19-25, 311-325, and *passim*. The narrative of the development of the disease on the campus may be followed in great detail in the *Pullman Herald*, a weekly, from October 11-December 6, 1918; see also, the *Evergreen*, a weekly, especially October 4 and December 11, 1918. *Regents Record*, Vol. 5, November 19, 1918, pp. 397-407 and November 20, 1918, pp. 408, 409, 415. Landeen, p. 118.

28 *Thirteenth Biennial Report of the Board of Regents of the State College of Washington*, June 30-, 1918, pp. 9, 10.

29 J. N. Emerson to Holland, April 4, 1917, Folder 390, Office of the President (Holland).

30 *Regents Record,* Vol. 5, April 28, 1919, pp. 429-431; Vol. 6, January 22, 1920, pp. 10 (Quotation) 11, 15, 16; February 17, 1920, pp. 18-25; April 21, 1920, p. 40. The Association of Professors probably represented only a minority of the faculty. On February 16, 1920, Vice-President O. L. Waller represented 75 faculty and staff, non-members of the Association, in seeking salary increases for all employees, according to the *Regents Record,* Vol. 6, Feb. 16, 1920, pp, 16, 18.

31 *Faculty Minutes,* Vol. 4, February 14, 1918.

32 *Fifteenth Biennial Report of the Board of Regents of the State College of Washington,* June 30, 1922, pp. 3-5; *Faculty Minutes,* Vol. 4, January 28, 1921, and Vol. 5, May 20, 1924.

33 Examination of *Time Schedules* from 1922 to 1926/27 turned up no evidence of any offerings of honors courses, (Time Schedules located in the Registrar's Office); *A Ten Year Report of the Board of Regents* (Monthly Bulletin of the State College of Washington, Vol. 18, March, 1936), pp. 9, 10 (Quotation).

34 *Regents Record,* Vol. 6, June 14, 1921, p. 133; *Thirty-First Annual Catalogue for 1922,* p. 293; Ten Year Report of the Board of Regents, p. 56.

35 *Regents Record,* Vol. 6, April 8, 1922, p. 188; *Faculty Minutes,* Vol. 4, May 17, 1922. On Master's degree requirements, see also *Thirty-First Annual Catalogue for 1922,* pp. 50, 51.

36 *Regents Record,* Vol. 6, June 13, 1923, p. 266.

37 *Regents Record,* Vol. 6, June 13, 1923, p. 266 and Vol. 5, January 29, 1918, p. 353; *Fourteenth Biennial Report of the Board of Regents of the State College of Washington, June 30, 1920,* p. 11 (Quotation), 12.

38 F. F. Nalder, Berkeley, to Holland, June 3, 1919, Folder 1076, Office of the President (Holland); Holland to Nalder, June 10, 1919; and Holland to Nalder, July 16, 1919, *ibid.*

39 Nalder to Frank H. Arnold, Spokane, September 20, and Nalder to Holland, October 7, 1919, *ibid.; Fourteenth Biennial Report to the Board of Regents of the State College of Washington, June 30, 1920,* p. 12 (Quotation "fifty miles"); *Fifteenth Biennial Report of the Board of Regents of the State College of Washington, June 30, 1922,* p. 10 (Quotation "180,000 persons"); "To Make Good Music Popular," *Spokesman-Review,* November 24, 1919, clipping found in Folder 1079, Office of the President (Holland).

40 Nalder to Holland, February 7, 1924, Folder 2084, *ibid.* Evidence of the kinds of instruction which might have been offered, see newspaper clipping, Lewis and Clark [High School] *Journal,* May 21, 1923, Folder 1858, *ibid.;* C. P. Brewer, Spokane, to Frank H. Barnard, May 9, 1923 and Holland to Brewer, May 11, 1923, Folder 1858, *ibid.* Brewer was the instructor in both salesmanship courses, in Spokane and Walla Walla. For an adverse comment on the Walla Walla course, see Walla Walla Union, June 21, 1924, clipping, Folder 2084.

41 Nalder to Holland, April 21 [1923], Folder 1858, *ibid.;* Nalder to Holland, March 28, 1924, Folder 2084; (Quotation "a grim and silly mistake" and "The College is simply off the earth"); Nalder to Holland, April 24, 1924, *ibid.* Testimony that Holland also objected to the term "cow college" is given by Herman J. Deutsch in an interview with the author, April 22, 1971.

42 *Twelfth Biennial Report of the Board of Regents, June 30, 1916,* pp. 26-28; *Thirteenth Biennial Report of the Board of Regents, June 30, 1918,* p. 10; *Regents Record,* Vol. 5, October 9, 1917, p. 339, and Vol. 6, January 22, 1920, pp. 9, 10; *Fourteenth Biennial Report of the Board of Regents of the State College of Washington,* June 30, 1920, pp. 3-5; *Regents Record,* Vol. 6, November 3, 1923, pp. 287-289. Enrollment information needed for comparison with housing capacity is found in "Total Enrollment Since 1892, Registrar's Office.

43 *Regents Record,* Vol. 6, August 26, 1921, p. 141; August 27, 1921, pp. 152, 153; October 25, 1921, p. 155; and January 28, 1922, p. 165.

44 *Regents Record,* Vol. 6, April 2, 1923, pp. 238-243; *Twelfth Biennial Report of the Board of Regents, June 30, 1916,* p. 24 (Quotation).

45 Landeen, pp. 164.

46 Landeen, pp. 172-177. *Session Laws of the State of Washington,* Session of 1921, p. 528; and Extraordinary Session, 1925, pp. 95, 96.

47 Landeen, pp. 172, 173; *Regents Record,* Vol. 6, October 27, 1922, p. 228; and June 13, 1923, pp. 268-271; "Complaint and Brief of the University of Washington and Brief of the State College of Washington and Decision of the Joint Board of Higher Curricula," Office of the President (Holland), with quotation on pp. 17, 18.

48 "Complaint and Brief of the University of Washington and Brief of the State College of Washington and Decision of the Joint Board of Higher Curricula," *ibid.,* pp. 41-58, with quotation "an outlaw curriculum" found on p. 28.

49 The feud between Hartley and Suzzallo started during World War I when Hartley, lumber tycoon, fought bitterly against Suzzallo, federal arbitrator, who forced the eight hour working day on the lumber industry, Gates, pp. 165, 166, 168-170; Landeen, pp. 246, 251 (Quotation).

50 *Spokesman-Review,* April 1, 1926; *Regents Record,* Vol. 6, April 5, 1926, pp. 436-440; The work on Wilson Hall and the Mechanic Arts Building was completed in 1927 and the construction of the gymnasium-armory was finished in 1928, *A Ten Year Report of the Board of Regents,* 1926-1935 (Monthly Bulletin of the State College of Washington, Vol. 18, March, 1936), p. 21.

51 *Regents Record,* Vol. 6, April 5, 1926, pp. 436-439 (Quotation on p. 436). The census figures which Holland presented vary somewhat from those in the Registrar's "Total Enrollment Since 1892," but not enough to damage his conclusions. *Regents Record,* Vol. 6, April 5, 1926, p. 439. The other colleges included the comparable institutions in Oregon, Montana, Kansas, Indiana, and Iowa.

52 Landeen, pp. 152-155; *A Ten Year Report of the Board of Regents,* pp. 14-17.

53 *Regents Record,* Vol. 6, February 11, 1926, p. 432; *Twenty-Eighth Biennial Report of the Superintendant of Public Instruction,* June 30, 1926, p 184. *Seventeenth Biennial Report of the Board of Regents of the State College of Washington,* June 30, 1926, p. 15.

54 *Regents Record,* Vol. 6, February 20, 1928, pp. 139-141; and, June 8, 1928, p. 174; *A Ten Year Report of the Board of Regents of the State College of Washington,* 1926-1935, p. 16.

55 *Regents Record,* Vol. 7, June 8, 1928, p. 174.

56 *A Ten Year Report of the Board of Regents of the State College of Washington,* 1926-1935, p. 59, for Master's Degrees earned prior to 1926. It incorrectly lists 490

Master's degrees for 1926-1935. See, instead, the Registrar's "Washington State University—Historical Record of Master's Degrees Granted," which lists 380. *Faculty Minutes,* Vol. 5, May 26, 1927.

57 *Fourteenth Biennial Report of the Board of Regents of the State College of Washington, June 30, 1920,* p. 13; *Ten Year Report of the Board of Regents,* pp. 45-47; Koger, College of Veterinary Medicine; *Regents Record,* Vol. 6, September 27, 1920, pp. 86-90.

58 *Ten Year Report of the Board of Regents, 1926-1935,* pp. 11-14 (Quotation on p. 13).

59 Lawrence J. Golicz, "A History of Washington State University Libraries from 1946 to 1949" (Unpublished M. A. thesis, Washington State University, 1968); *Ten Year Report of the Board of Regents 1926-1935,* pp. 63-65 (Quotation on p. 63).

60 *Regents Report,* Vol. 7, July 7, 1927, p. 92.

61 [Joseph L. Ashlock] Secretary to the President to P. P. Claxton, Washington, D.C., March 14, 1916, Folder 55, Office of the President (Holland); *Regents Record,* Vol. 5, April 30, 1919, p. 432; Vol. 7, June 1, 1930, pp. 402, 403; April 1, 1931, p. 456; and Vol. 8, January 16, 1932, pp. 9-11.

62 *Regents Record,* Vol. 8, October 13, 1934, pp. 298, 299 (Quotation).

63 *Regents Record,* Vol. 7, June 8, 1928, p. 174; and September 8, 1928, p. 199.

64 *Regents Record,* Vol. 7, September 8, 1928, p. 203; June 1, 1930, p. 394; and Vol. 8, October 3, 1931, p. 1 (Quotation).

65 Indeed, there was no guarantee of leaves *without pay* to pursue advanced studies. Witness the case of Professor George Severance, Vice-Dean of the College of Agriculture. The Regents refused his request for the leave described above on grounds of creating a bad precedent. See *ibid.,* Vol. 5, April 30, 1919, p. 432.

66 *Ibid.,* Vol. 5, April 4, 1917, p. 287; and June 30, 1917, p. 322.Landeen, p. 99; *ibid.,* Vol. 7, February 20, 1928, p. 142; January 28, 1930, p. 347; and August 28, 1930, p. 420. *Spokesman-Review,* January 30, 1930; Dayton *Chronicle-Dispatch,* February 6, 1930.

67 Landeen, pp. 239, 240; *Regents Record,* Vol. 8, December, 1934, p. 320; and April 6, 1935, pp. 328, 329.

68 "Total Enrollment Since 1892," Registrar's Office; *Seventeenth Biennial Report of the Board of Regents of the State College of Washington, 1926,* p. 14 (Quotation).

69 Interview with Herman J. Deutsch by the author, April 22, 1971 (Second Tape), (Quotation); "Church Statistics" [1923-1924], single sheet, Folder 2245, Office of the President (Holland).

70 Ernest [Marchand] to Leslie [Marchand], September 24, [1916], Folder 185; Mrs. C. A. Marchand, Bridgeport, to the President of W.S.C., October 2, 1916, Folder 185; Holland to Mrs. Marchand, October 9, 1916, Folder 185; Mrs. Ethel Burgess to Holland, September 27, 1917, Folder 347; Mrs. F. R. Price to Holland, September 26, 1916, Folder 222; Dr.

E. A. Archer, Pullman, to Holland, October 19, 1916, Folder A; Office of the President (Holland).

71 Mrs. Nellie W. Denman, Spokane, to Holland, February 1, 1917, Folder 377; Holland to Mrs. Denman, February 8, 1917; *ibid. Faculty Minutes,* Vol. 4, March 17, 1916; October 3, 1919, October 15, 1921;

72 *Faculty Minutes,* Vol. 4, March 29, 1918, November 3, 1916, January 23, 1918, March 7, 1919, November 10, 1919, November 25, 1919.

73 *Faculty Minutes,* Vol. 5, May 27, 1924 (Quotation); June 10, 1924; February 1, 1926; December 9, 1926.

74 Landeen, E. O., pp. 372, 373; *Regents Record,* Vol. 7, July 7, 1927, pp. 101-103; November 10, 1927, pp. 125-129; April 9, 1928, pp. 169, 170; September 8, 1928, pp. 216-219.

75 *Regents Record,* Vol. 7, April 3, 1929, p. 263; August 28, 1930, p. 413; Landeen, p. 154.

76 Silas E. Stiles, Shelton, to Holland, December 11, 1925, Folder 2406, Office of the President (Holland); Holland to Stites, December 15, 1925 *ibid.* Holland reported regarding a game with the University of Montana, played in 1916, that he was pleased with the fighting spirit of the team and its rooters (Holland, Memo: "Montana Game," Folder 8434 *ibid.*).

77 *Post-Intelligencer,* December 2, 1916. *Regents Record,* Vol. 6, June 6, 1922, p. 203; Vol. 5, October 12, 1919, p. 475; Vol. 6, September 24, 1923, p. 275; Vol. 6, December 29, 1924, p. 357; Vol. 6, March 11, 1925, p. 359; Vol. 6, June 16, 1925, pp. 384-389.

78 Landeen, pp. 390-392; *Regents Record,* Vol. 7, September 27, 1926, p. 18.

79 Landeen, pp. 385-389, Landeen also summarizes the remarkable achievements of Boxing Coach Isaac "Ike" Deeter, whose athletes won numerous titles, including the National Collegiate in 1937. *Regents Record,* Vol. 7, September 27, 1926, p. 19; *Minute Book,* Athletic Council, WSC (1927-51) p. 10 (Quotation).

80 *Regents Record,* Vol. 7, September 27, 1926, p. 18; and May 30, 1931, p. 482.

81 A. S. Goss to Presidents Spencer and Holland, September 10, 1931, Folder 3826, Office of the President (Holland); Holland to Goss, September 19, 1931 and Goss to Holland, October 28, 1931, Folder 3826; *ibid.*

82 Holland to Goss, May 31, 1932, Folder 4075; *ibid.* Washington State Grange, "Master's Address by Albert S. Goss . . . Tacoma, Washington, June 7-10, 1932," Folder 4075; *ibid.* Quotation from the address. Ace Smith is reported as giving golf lessons in *Summer School Journal,* June 23, 1932 (Included in *Evergreen,* September 1931 through August 1934). Secretary to President Holland to Goss, June 24, 1932, Folder 4075, Office of the President (Holland).

83 Washington State Grange, "Master's Address by Albert S. Goss, . . . Tacoma, Washington, June 7-10, 1932, *ibid.; Seattle Times,* June 19, 1932, quotation.

Chapter Four

1   *Regents Record*, Vol. 8, April 5, 1932, pp. 27-37.
2   *Ibid.*, February 27, 1933, p. 93; June 3, 1933, pp. 144-155. Landeen, p. 223.
3   *Regents Record*, Vol. 8, March 26, 1933, p. 105; *ibid.*, April 8, 1933, pp. 119 (Quotation), 120; Landeen, p. 183, 184
4   *Regents Record*, Vol. 8, March 26, 1933, pp. 104, 105.
5   *Ibid.*, Vol. 7, April 3, 1929, p. 247; *ibid.*, March 26, 1933, pp. 105-106; *ibid.*, Vol. 8, April 8, 1933, p. 113; Hadlow, "A History of the Development of Scientific Research at the Washington Agricultural Experiment Station in Pullman, 1890-1940," pp. 80-83; Landeen, pp. 183-185.
6   *Regents Record*, Vol. 8, July 21, 1933, pp. 167-171; *ibid.*, May 15, 1934, p. 242.
7   *Ibid.*, June 3, 1933, pp. 156-158; *ibid.*, February 27, 1933, p. 92; *ibid.*, March 26, 1933, p. 110; *ibid.*, April 25, 1934, p. 228; *ibid.*, April 8, 1933, p. 121.
8   *Ibid.*, Vol. 8, April 25, 1934, pp. 224-231; p. 228 (Quotations).
9   *Ibid.*, April 25, 1934, p. 229 (Quotation "superior members"); *ibid.*, June 9, 1934, pp. 263, 264 (Quotation "heaviest administrative and teaching loads" on p. 263).
10 *Ibid.*, Vol. 9, October 2, 1936, pp. 86-89.
11 *Ibid.*, Vol. 9, September 12, 1936, pp. 77, 83; *ibid.*, Vol. 9, April 7, 1937, pp. 127-136.
12 *Ibid.*, Vol. 8, February 8, 1936, pp. 484, 485; *ibid.*, Vol. 9, April 1, 1936, pp.14-16, p. 14 (Quotation); Vol. 8, February 8, 1936, pp. 484, 485; *ibid.*; Vol. 9, April 7, 1937, pp. 136-140. For enrollment statistics see "Total Enrollment Since 1892" (Registrar's Office).
13 *Regents Record*, Vol. 8, April 22, 1935, pp. 348-350; *ibid.*, May 29, 1935, pp. 354, 355; *ibid.*, Vol. 9, April 1, 1936, p. 11.
14 *Ibid.*, pp. 16, 17; *ibid.*, May 15, 1936, pp. 37, 38; *Biennial Report of the Board of Regents of the State College of Washington, April 1, 1937*, p. 28.
15 Regents Report, Vol. 8, November 14, 1935, pp. 445, 446.
16 Hadlow, pp. 81, 82, 88-95; *Regents Record*, Vol. 8, June 3, 1933, pp. 156-158; *ibid.*, July 21, 1933, pp. 167-171.
17 Hadlow, pp. 95-99; Margaret Rossiter, "The Organization of Agricultural Sciences," in *The Organization of Knowledge in Modern America, 1860-1920,* eds. Alexandra Oleson and John Voss (Baltimore: The Johns Hopkins University Press, 1979), p. 228 (Quotation, "Seemingly unaware"); *Fifty-first Annual Report of the Washington Agricultural Experiment Station (1941)*, pp. 5, 6 and *Fifty-third Annual Report. . . , ibid.*, (1943)., pp. 5, 6. Obituary: "Norman Golding, WSU Cheese's Creator," Pullman *Daily News*, November 10, 1984.
18 *Regents Record*, Vol. 8, October 19, 1935, pp. 435, 436; *ibid.*, Vol. 9, April 25, 1936, pp. 21, 22; *ibid.*, Vol. 8, November 14, 1935, p. 444.
19 *Ibid.*, Vol. 8, February 8, 1936, p. 483; Donald E. Heller to E. O. Holland, May 8, 1936, Folder 5204, Box 177, Office of the President (Holland); Don G. Abel to C. C. Todd, February 9, 1938, Folder 5690, Box 198, *ibid.*, Herman J. Deutsch to E. O. Holland, June 22, 1938, Folder 5540, Box 192, *ibid.* In an interview, October 11, 1989 (by the author) Dr. Lawrence R. Stark, Assistant Archivist, WSU, recounted examples of materials collected and their importance to future historical writing.

20 *Regents Record*, Vol. 8, February 8, 1936, pp. 483-485 (Quotation on p. 483); Holland to W. D. Griffin, February 11, 1936, Folder 5040, Box 170, Office of the President (Holland); Holland to Griffin, October 27, 1937, Folder 5273, Box 180, *ibid*; W. D. Griffin, "The Story of the Portraits Painted by Worth D. Griffin. . . . [1947], W. D. Griffin Papers.
21 W. D. Griffin, Untitled Report, 1935, Folder 4788, Box 158, *ibid.*; Griffin to Holland, May 17, 1938 (Quotation), Folder 5509, Box 190, *ibid*; Griffin, "The Story of the Portraits Painted by Worth D. Griffin. . . ." [1974], W. D. Griffin Papers; *A Ten Year Report of the Regents of the State College of Washington, 1926-1935*, pp. 55, 56; *Regents Record*, Vol. 8, November 5, 1932, p. 87; *ibid.*, June 3, 1933, p. 154,; *ibid.*, December 11, 1935, p. 456. Details for inauguration of advanced degrees are found in *Bulletin of the Graduate School for August 1928* (Monthly Bulletin of the State College, 11), pp. 66-69 and *Regents Record*, Vol. 10, April 24, 1940, p. 45; Board of Regents, *Six Year Report . . . April 1, 1945*, p. 66.
22 *Regents Record*, Vol. 8, May 29, 1935, p. 355.
23 *Ibid.*, Vol 11, July 19, 1943, pp. 161, 175. Clark and Dakin are listed as Associate Professors of English in *The State College of Washington, Catalog Issue, 1952-53 and 1953-54*, p. 14.
24 *Regents Record*, Vol. 6, June 10, 1924, p. 314, 327; Anderson, Ida Lou, Faculty Personnel Records, (Faculty Personnel Office); *Thirty-Fourth Annual Catalogue of the Sate College of Washington, June, 1925*, pp. 272, 293; May K. Anderson, "Sixteen Years of Devotion," *Ida Lou Anderson, A Memorial* (1941), pp. 8, 9.
25 Edward R. Murrow, ". . . And Reverenced All," *ibid.*, pp. 18, 19; Robert A. Sandberg, "A Man and His Teacher," speech to WSU Symposium "Commemoration of the 75th Birthday of Edward R. Murrow," April 22, 1983 (Quotation "Her goal") Cage 4596, WSU Archives; E. O. Holland, "Great Teachers Make Great Universities," in *Ida Lou Anderson, A Memorial*, pp. 20 (Quotation "hundreds" and "to see themselves objectively"), p. 21.
26 *Regents Record*, Vol. 10, February 27, 1942, pp. 322-324; *ibid.*, May 29, 1942, pp. 416, 417; *ibid.*, August 8, 1942, pp. 468, 474.
27 *Session Laws of the State of Washington, 1937*, Chapter 223, "Annuities for Teachers and Employees of State Educational Institutions," p. 1132; R. B. Heflebower to President R. E. McConnell, Ellensburg, June 11, 1937, Folder 5137, Box 174, Office of the President (Holland); Heflebower to Holland, April 4, 1939, Folder 5876, Box 207; *ibid.*, *Regents Record*, Vol. 9, June 3, 1939, p. 430.
28 Partial employment for elderly professors may be followed in *ibid.*, Vol. 10, April 24, 1940, pp. 51, 52; June 1, 1940, p. 81; and October 5, 1940, pp. 95, 96.
29 *Faculty Minutes*, Vol. 6, March 10, 1941; *ibid.*, June 5, 1941; *Regents Record*, Vol. 10, October 10, 1941, p. 291; *ibid.*, November 24, 1941, pp. 307-313; Session Laws of the State of Washington, 1943, Chapter 262, pp. 800, 801; *ibid.*, 1947, Chapter 223, pp. 944, 945. For a comprehensive statement of the program, see the *Faculty Manual of the State College of Washington, January, 1949*, pp. 70-77.

30 "Total Enrollment Since 1892" (Registrar's Office).

31 *A Ten Year Report of the Board of Regents, 1926-1935*, pp. 8, 9; *ibid.* (Quotation on p. 9); Interview of Robert Sandberg by William Stimson, June, 1987 (WSU Oral History Project); *Evergreen*, June 28, 1933, August 8, 1933.

32 Peter E. Kragt, "How I Make Both Ends Meet," [February, 1932], Folder 4182, Box 135, Office of the President (Holland), quotations. Another example of "baching" is found in Interview with Robert Sandberg by William Stimson, June 1987 (WSU Oral History Project); *Evergreen* February 21, 1936.

33 *Evergreen*, January 20, 1933 (editorial) and August 8, 1933. *Regents Record*, Vol. 8, November 14, 1935, p. 451; *ibid.*, April 1, 1936, p. 10; *Evergreen*, February 21, 1936. The evidence that "baching" continued into 1936 is found in the *Evergreen*, February 21, 1936.

34 *Ibid.*, Vol. 8, April 1, 1936, p. 10; Pullman *Herald*, December 25, 1936 and January 1, 1937.

35 *The History and Activities of the State College of Washington, 1937-1939, (Twenty-fourth Biennial Report of the Board of Regents)*, pp. 33-41 (Quotation on p. 40).

36 *Ibid.*, p. 35.

37 *Ibid.*, pp. 152-156 (Quotation, "have acted," p. 155, and "many fraternities," p. 152).

38 Mary Jane Levi, "The Evolution of Student Government at Washington State College (Seminar Paper, Department of History, WSU, April, 1987), pp. 1, 4-7; *Evergreen*, May 1 and 15, 1935, November 1, 1935, April 29, 1936, May 13, 1936; Interview with Lawrence Giles by Marjorie B. Grunwald, May 8, 1986 (WSU Oral History Project).

39 Landeen, pp. 367-369. *Evergreen*, February 24, 1936. On student solidarity see, *Evergreen*, May 6 and 8, 1936, and November 1, 1935.

40 *Ibid.*, May 4 and 6 (Quotations) 1936; Spokane *Spokesman-Review*, May 6, 1936 (Quotations).

41 Landeen, p. 369; *Evergreen*, May 6 and 7, 1936.

42 Landeen, pp. 370, 371; *Regents Record*, Vol. 9, June 6, 1936, pp. 49, 58; V. H. DeBoldt, Seattle, to Holland, June 23, 1936 and Holland to DeBoldt, July 3, 1936, Folder 5014, Box 169, Office of the President (Holland).

43 The faculty voted a $1.00 fine per class missed. See *Minutes of the Faculty Organization*, May 7, 11, 1936, Folder 1934-45, Box 1, Faculty Executive Committee Records (WSU Archives).

44 *Faculty Minutes*, Vol 6, December 1, 1938. On smoking, see *Regents Record*, Vol. 10, February 27, 1940, pp. 16, 17, *ibid.*, April 24, 1940, pp. 53, 54; June 1, 1940, pp. 59, 60; October 4, 1940, p. 87; October 18, 1940, pp. 122, 123, all in *ibid.*

45 *State College of Washington. Board of Regents Six Year Report, April 1, 1945*, p. 64; F. L. Pickett to Holland, February 2, 1938, Folder 5530, Box 191, Office of the President (Holland); "Total Enrollment Since 1892 (Registrar's Office)."

46 Board of Regents Six Year *Report . . . April 1, 1945, pp. 63, 64;* Shirley L. Thomas, "Paul H. Landis: Businessman, Professor and Writer" (Unpublished Essay, American Studies Seminar, January 29, 1970) Cage 4203 (WSU Archives), Quotation "irksome and exhausting"; *Regents Record*, Vol. 11, December 11, 1942, pp. 15, 32.

47 Thomas, "Paul H. Landis"; Landis to Holland, January 17, 1940, Folder 6096, Box 217, Office of the President (Holland); Holland to Landis, January 22, 1940, *ibid.*; Landis to Holland, February 5, 1941, Folder 6484, Box 233, *ibid.*;

48 Board of Regents, *Six Year Report for the Period Ending April 1, 1945* (State College of Washington Bulletin, November 15, 1945), p. 66. Those departments granting doctoral degrees in this period included agronomy, botany, chemistry, entomology, horticulture and plant pathology, *ibid.*

49 *Regents Record*, Vol. 9, September 22, 1939, pp. 457, 458; *ibid.*, Vol. 10, February 28, 1942, p. 347 (Quotation); Carl F. Ruess, Paul H. Landis, and Richard Wakefield, *Migratory Farm Labor and the Hop Industry on the Pacific Coast, with Special Applications to Problems of the Yakima Valley, Washington* (State College of Washington, Agricultural Experiment Station, Pullman, Washington, Bulletin No. 363, August, 1938).

50 B. A. Perham to George Gannon, Pullman, September 2, 1938, Folder 5523, Box 191, Office of the President (Holland); *Regents Record*, Vol. 9, September 14, 1938, pp. 345, 346.

51 *Ibid.*, Vol. 10, June 1, 1940, p. 80.

52 *Ibid.*, April 18, 1941, p. 161.

53 Holland, "Forward," *Research Studies of the State College of Washington*, Vol. 1 (June 28, 1929), p. 3; *Regents Record*, Vol. 8, May 29, 1935, p. 360; *Research Studies*, Vol. 3 (September, 1935), (quotation is taken from the masthead).

54 [Holland], "Notes for the Meeting of the New Members of the Faculty - October 7, 1936," Folder 5033, Box 170, Office of the President (Holland), unpaged, quotations. For evidence on Holland's close attention when a professor petitioned to have a telephone in his office, see Holland to H. J. Deutsch, September 11, 1935, Folder "Pres. E. O. Holland Correspondence," Box 7, H. J. Deutsch Papers; Deutsch to Holland, September 21, 1935, *ibid.*, and Holland to Deutsch, September 24, 1935, *ibid.*

55 [Holland], "Notes for the Meeting of the New Members of the Faculty - October 7, 1936," Folder 5033, Box 170, Office of the President (Holland).

56 *Faculty Executive Committee Minutes*, January 22, 1934, Folder 1934-45, Box 1, Faculty Executive Committee; *ibid.*, February 10, 1934; *ibid.*, June 1, 1934; *ibid.*, September 19, 1934; Annual Report of the Executive Committee . . . September 13, 1935, *ibid.*, (WSU Archives).

57 *Faculty Executive Committee Minutes*, November 19, 1935 and January 9 1936, *ibid.*

58 *Ibid.*, September 19, 1934. The voters approved Initiative 94 at the November 6, 1934 general election, as found in *Session Laws for 1935*, Chapter 2.

59 *Evergreen*, January 6, March 8, March 19, March 22, April 19, all of 1937. Holland to Dr. W. T. Foster, Newton, Mass., September 24, 1937, Folder 5278, Box 180, Office of the President (Holland), quotation; Holland to Foster, December 7, 1937, *ibid.*

60 B. R. McElderry and four others to Holland, September 18, 1936, Folder 1934-45, Box 1, *Faculty Executive Committee Records* (Quotations); *Faculty Executive Committee Minutes*, September 24, 1937 and October 8, 1937, *ibid.*; *Minutes of the Faculty Advisory Committee*, November 9, 1937, *ibid.*; R. B. Heflebower to Holland, July 21, 1938, *ibid.* (Faculty Executive and Advisory Committee records are located in the WSU Archives.)

61   *Regents Record*, Vol. 9, October 2, 1937, p. 208; *ibid.*, Meeting of April 12, 1938, p. 255; *ibid.*, Meeting of April 10, 1939, p. 395.

62   Landeen, pp. 185, 186.

63   *Ibid.*, p. 186 (Quotation); *Regents Record*, Vol. 9, April 9, 1939, pp. 368, 369.

64   *Ibid.*, Vol. 9, April 10, 1939, pp. 385-389.

65   Holland to Governor Clarence D. Martin, Olympia, March 7, 1940, Folder 6146, Box 220, Office of the President (Holland); *ibid.*, March 20, 1940; Martin to Board of Regents, March 21, 1940, *ibid.*; *Regents Record*, Vol. 10, February 27, 1940, pp. 15, 16.

66   Holland, "The Educated Citizen and His Responsibilities," Commencement Address, June 10, 1935, (Quotation "enlightened"), Folder 8426, Box 298, Office of the President (Holland); Holland, "Straight-Thinking in a Disordered World," Commencement Address, June 6, 1938, (Quotation "straight-thinking"), *ibid.*; Holland, "Commencement Address, State College of Washington," June 3, 1940 (Quotation "this small army"), *ibid.*

67   Holland, "Victory Gardens," transcription of a Radio Address, March 21, 1943, Folder 8440, Box 300, *ibid.*

68   *Regents Record*, Vol. 11, January 3, 1944, pp. 247, 248; Press releases [January, 1944], Folder 7618, Box 273, Office of the President (Holland); Spokane *Spokesman-Review*, February 5, 1944 (Editorial); Arlington (Washington) *Times*, February 3, 1944, Folder 7632, Box 274, *ibid.*; Holland to H. J. Deutsch, February 10, 1944, Folder 7618, Box 273, *ibid.* Box 274 of the papers of the Office of the President (Holland) contains a great deal of information on the activities of the institute.

69   C. F. Barnes, Richland, to Glenn Jones, July 19, 1944, Folder "W.S.U. General College Extension", Box 7, H. J. Deutsch Papers; Interview with H. J. Deutsch by George A. Frykman, January 24, 1971.

70   Holland, "The College and Public Relations," July 24, 1944, Folder 8426, Box 298, Office of the President (Holland).

71   *Regents Record*, Vol. 9, April 9, 1939, p. 384; *ibid.*, September 22, 1939, p. 472; *ibid.*, Vol. 11, March 21, 1944, p. 295; *Board of Regents, Six Year Report for the Period Ending April 1, 1945*, pp. 12, 13 (Quotation).

72   "Total Enrollment Since 1892" (Registrar's Office).

73   Board of Regents, *Six Year Report for the Period Ending April 1, 1945*, p. 88.

74   Interview with H. J. Deutsch by George A. Frykman, June 24, 1971; "Wartime Training Programs at the State College of Washington," March 1, 1942, bound in *State College of Washington Bulletin*, Vol. III, March 1, 1942; "Report of the Faculty Advisory Committee," May 25, 1942, Folder "WSU-War Curriculum," Box 8, Cage 111, H. J. Deutsch Papers (Quotation "Today *Trained* Men and Women," p. 12); *Faculty Minutes*, Vol. 6, lists temporary "War Year Courses," pp. 471-477.

75   On the "signal failure," see Interview with H. J. Deutsch by George A. Frykman, June 24, 1971; on another colleague's conclusions, see Interview with H. J. Wood by George A. Frykman, January 26, 1972. Todd's statement is found in his report in the Board of Regents, *Six Year Report for the Period ending April 1, 1945*, p. 38.

76   H. J. Deutsch to E. O. Holland, October 21, 1942, Folder 6898, Box 248, Office of the President (Holland).

77   Landeen, pp. 67-69; Board of Regents, *Six Year Report for the Period ending April 1, 1945*, pp. 44-46.

78   *Ibid.*, pp. 60-63; Landeen, p. 69.

79   *Regents Record*, Vol. 11, December 11, 1942, pp. 16, 17, 32; "College of Sciences and Arts," Board of Regents, *Six Year Report for the Period ending April 1, 1945*, pp. 37-39.

80   E. C. Johnson, "College of Agriculture," *ibid.*, 1945, pp. 11, 16, 20; Johnson, "Agricultural Experiment Stations," *ibid.*, 23-25 (Quotation on pp. 24-25).

81   *Regents Record*, Vol. 11, December 11, 1942, pp. 13, 32; *ibid.*, July 19, 1943, pp. 152, 153; *ibid.*, May 23, 1943, p. 138; *ibid.*, September 6, 1943, pp. 187, 192, 193; *ibid.*, March 21, 1944, pp. 275, 276; Board of Regents, *Six Year Report for the Period ending, April 1, 1945*, pp. 15, 16; Homer J. Dana, "Engineering Experiment Station," *ibid.*, pp. 36, 37.

82   C. C. Todd, "College of Sciences and Arts," Board of Regents, *Six Year Report for the Period ending April 1, 1945*, pp. 38, 39, 40.

83   *Ibid.*, pp. 38, 39 (Quotation), 40.

84   *Regents Record*, Vol. 10, June 29, 1942, p. 541.

85   "Dedication of H. V. Carpenter Hall," October 22, 1949 (pamphlet), Folder "Homer Jackson Dana," Box 66, VF 2438; Landeen, pp. 340-347.

86   *Regents Record*, Vol. 11, April 19, 1943, p. 112.

87   *Ibid.*, July 19, 1943, p. 143 (Quotation).

88   *Ibid.*, Vol. 10, October 10, 1941, p. 289; Lawrence Golicz, "A History of Washington State University Libraries from 1946 to 1949," (Unpublished M. A. Thesis, 1968, WSU), pp. 7-14.

89   *Evergreen*, November 5, 1937 (editorial).

90   W. W. Foote to Holland, October 11, 1937, Folder 5321, Box 182, Office of the President (Holland); Golicz, "A History of Washington State University Libraries from 1946 to 1949," pp. 1, 2, 11, 12; *Evergreen*, November 15, 1937; Holland to C. O. Johnson, December 18, 1943, Folder 7294, Box 261, Office of the President (Holland); *Regents Record*, Vol. 10, October 10, 1941, pp. 289, 290.

91   Golicz, "A History of the Washington State University Libraries from 1946 to 1949," pp. 13-15; Gates, *The First Century at the University of Washington*, p. 164 (Quotation); *Regents Record*, Vol. 11, November 1, 1943, pp. 215, 216, 225.

92   *Evergreen*, November 14, 1932 (Quotations "revitalizing" and "epic struggle") and November 16, 1932 (Quotation "daring coup" and "good piece of work").

93   *Ibid.*, November 27, 1933; *Regents Record*, Vol. 8, November 24, 1933, pp. 198, 199.

94   *Faculty Minutes*, Vol. 6, March 20, 1941 and December 6, 1942; *ibid.*, February 16, 1942; *Regents Record*, Vol. 10, August 8, 1942. *Evergreen*, December 12 and 15, 1942.

95   *Ibid.*, March 16, 1942 (Quotation "whereby students"); Claudius O. Johnson and H. J. Deutsch to Holland, March 18, 1942, Folder 6898, Box 248, Office of the President (Holland); Johnson to Holland, March 23, 1942, *ibid.*; *Evergreen*, March 20, 1942 and March 6, 1942 (Quotation "terrific").

96   *Ibid.*, April 22, 1942.

97   *Ibid.*, April 10 and 12, 1942; *ibid.*, May 1 and 2 (Quotation "their country's war effort"), 1942.

98   Frank T. Barnard, Registrar, to Holland, December 8, 1942, Folder 7014, Box 252, Office of the President (Holland); Barnard to Holland, December 11, 1942, *ibid.*; *Evergreen*, December 12 and 15, 1942; *ibid.*, January 12, 1943.

99   *Ibid.*, December 15, 1942.

Chapter Five

1   *Regents Record,* Vol. 11, March 20, 1944, pp. 277, 278; *ibid.,* March 21, 1944, pp. 277 (Quotation), 278, 279.

2   *Ibid.,* pp. 277-283; *ibid.,* July 5, 1944, pp. 363, 364.

3   Members of the College Advisory Committee present were Professors Leslie L. Chisholm, Education, and Emmett B. Moore, Civil Engineering, Frank T. Barnard, Registrar, according to *ibid.,* August 12, 1944, p. 393; *ibid.,* August 21, 1944, p. 394.

4   *Current Biography, Who's Who and Why,* 1952, pp. 114-116; *Time,* February 12, 1945, pp. 74 and 77; *Who's Who in America,* Vol. 27, pp. 495, 496; James R. Blackwood, *The House on College Avenue; The Comptons at Wooster, 1891-1913,* (Cambridge, Mass.: MIT. Press, 1968).

5   Copy of a telegram, Wilson Compton to the Board of Regents (invitation to the Presidency of the State College of Washington), August 21, 1944, Box 9, Compton Papers.

6   Seattle *Times,* October 22, 1944, in Scrapbook of Newspaper Clippings, 1944-1951, Box 2, *ibid.*

7   New York *Post* description is reported in: *Current Biography, Who's Who and Why,* 1952, p. 116. He also was described in the Post as a Republican, an "active Presbyterian layman." The number of professional societies and social clubs he belonged to suggested a very gregarious personality of the upper middle class, *ibid.* Interview with H. J. Deutsch by George A. Frykman, April 22, 1971.*

8   *Regents Record,* Vol. 11, October 17, 1944, pp. 430-434; Compton to Senator Wallgren, November 14, 1944, Box 9, (Quotations), Box 9, Compton Papers; Compton to H. E. Goldsworthy, December 1, 1944, *ibid.*

9   Compton to H. E. Goldsworthy, November 13, 1944, *ibid.;* Spokane *Spokesman-Review,* October 8, 1944, Scrapbook of Newspaper Clippings, 1944-1951, Box 2, *ibid.* Numerous other favorable newspaper clippings are found in this scrapbook.

10 "Dr. Compton Sees State's Problem," Wenatchee *Daily World,* c. December 1944 or January, 1945, (Quotation "a school as fine as MIT."), Scrapbook of Newspaper Clippings, 1944-1951, Box 2, *ibid.*; Wenatchee *Daily World,* April 23, 1945, *ibid.*

11 "Predicts Great Era for Region," Spokane *Spokesman-Review,* March 14, 1945, (Quotation "electrified" and "trans-Pacific relations"), *ibid.*; Compton, "What the State May Expect from the State College of Washington," Speech, March 30, 1945, Box 8, *ibid.*

12 Interviews with Herbert J. Wood, January 26, 1972; Herman J. Deutsch, April 22, 1971 (First and second tape); Allen I. White, April 14, 1982, all by George A. Frykman; Interview with Robert Sandberg, June 1987 by William Stimson (WSU Centennial Oral History Project); Compton to Members of the Faculty, January 27, 1945, Box 8, Compton Papers; Bob Sandberg to Bill Stimson, April 6, 1987, describes Holland's administration as bequeathing a formidable autocratic opposition that Compton had to disperse (Letter in possession of William Stimson).

13 Interview with Allen I. White, April 14, 1982, by George A. Frykman; Compton to Members of the Faculty, January 27, 1945 (Quotation "wits and wisdom"), Box 8, Compton Papers; *Regents Record,* Vol 11, April 4, 1945, p. 476.

14 "Action of the Board of Regents, State College of Washington, June 19, 1945, Box 8, Compton Papers (Quotation "in principle"); *Regents Record,* Vol. 12, June 19, 1945, pp. 64, 73, 74; Compton to Deans and Directors [copies to faculty], February 19, 1946, Box 12, *ibid.*

15 Compton, "Frontiers Unlimited," [Inaugural] Address, December 11, 1945, Box 8, *ibid.,* (Quotation "we are the guardians," p. 2; "No man," p. 2; "effective individualism," p. 10).

16 *Ibid.,* pp. 13-15; [Compton] Untitled Speech on Institutes, Early 1945, Box 8, *ibid.*; *Regents Record,* Vol 12, November 5 and 6, 1945, pp. 157-163; *ibid.,* December 10 and 12, 1945, pp. 192, 196, 197; Board of Regents, Biennial Report, 1945-1947, pp. 1, 3-6; *ibid.,* Biennial Report, 1947-1949, pp. 90-93.

17 "Total Enrollment Since 1892" (Registrar's Office); Compton to A. L. Brown, November 24, 1945, Box 10, Compton Papers.

18 "Total Enrollment Since 1892" (Registrar's Office); *Board of Regents, Biennial Report, 1947-1949,* Table 7, IV; *ibid.,* 1951-1953, p. 37; "Non-Extension Students Registered, Fall Term" (a chart), Registrar's Office. For the faculty-student ratios, see the *Board of Regents, Biennial Report, 1945-1947,* p. 9. For the quotation "Inconveniences were many," see *ibid.,* p. 8.

19 Compton to Board of Regents, September 20, 1945, (Quotation), Box 9, Compton Papers; *Board of Regents, Biennial Report, 1945-1947,* pp. 11, 12.

20 *Regents Record,* Vol. 12, February 7, 1946, p. 230; Faculty Executive Committee Minutes, January 29, 1946, Box 1, Folder 1945-46, Faculty Executive Committee Records; Memo to President Wilson Compton and the FEC from S.E.H. [Stewart E. Hazlet], March 6, 1946, Box 1, *ibid*; *Regents Record,* Vol. 12, April 3, 11, 12, 1946, p. 262 (Quotation). Faculty Executive Committee records are located in the WSU Archives.

21 Pullman *Herald,* July 5, and 26, 1946; *Regents Record,* Vol. 12, July 22 and 23, 1946, pp. 405-407; W. C. (Wilson Compton), "Statement for Files," October 7, 1946, Box 12, Compton Papers.

22 Press Release: "Statement of October 4, 1946 on Proposed Extension Branch of Washington State College at Fort George Wright, Box 12, *ibid.;* Interview of Robert Sandberg by William Stimson, April 4, 1987. Compton to Institute of Agricultural Sciences and others, November 5, 1947, Box 15, Compton Papers (Quotations). See Folder 132, "Fort George Wright, 1946," Box 12, *ibid.,* for evidence. Robert Sandberg, Compton's Executive Assistant, argued in his interview with William Stimson (June, 1987) that Compton had wanted to move everything except agriculture and perhaps engineering to Spokane but the Spokane Chamber of Commerce blocked it (see pp. 33, 34 of transcript). Sandberg, indeed, signed some of the letters and notes indicating that the State College plan was only to accommodate the overflow of veterans.

23 *Board of Regents, Biennial Report, 1945-1947,* pp. 11 (Quotation), 12; Compton to Board of Regents, September 16, 1946, Box 13, Compton Papers, "Total Enrollment since 1892," (Registrar's Office); Press Release, November 30, 1946, Box 11, Compton Papers.

24   Observations and experiences of the author.

25   G. Beryl Roberts to E. H. Hopkins, October 8, 1947, Box 15, Compton Papers; Compton to James E. McCluskey, Spokane, August 6, 1947, with attachment "Regarding a Petition Concerning Housing for Married Students at Washington State College, July 28, 1947," Box 15, *ibid.*

26   R. F. Rathjen, "Military Hill Housing Project Report," February 25, 1948, Box 1, Office of the President (Compton); Compton to Residents of College Owned Houses on Military Hill, June 2, 1949, Box 4, *ibid.*; E. H. Hopkins to Carl Pettibone, September 12, 1949, *ibid.*; Hopkins to Pettibone, October 20, 1949, *ibid.*

27   *Regents Record,* Vol. 12, April 3, 11, 12, 1946, pp. 263, 314; Registrar, "Announcement of Revised Requirements," State College of Washington . . . April 15, 1946, Box 11 Compton Papers; Memorandum: Compton to Registrar H. M. Chambers and Director of Admissions Claude Simpson, June 24, 1946, Box 11, *ibid.*

28   Claude Simpson to Compton, October 1 [1946], Box 11, *ibid.*

29   *Regents Record,* Vol. 13, April 2, 1947, pp. 93, 144, 145; *Board of Regents, Biennial Report, 1947-1949,* pp. iv, v.

30   Compton to Associated Students of the State College of Washington, November 15, 1946, (Quotations "camping out," and "In my home"), Box 11, Compton Papers. Compton to Members of the Board of Regents, September 16, 1946, Box 13, *ibid.*

31   Board of Regents, Biennial Report, 1945-1947, pp. 15, 16 (Quotation "There were long lines"); Compton to the Associated Students of the State College of Washington, November 15, 1946, Box 11, Compton Papers (Quotation "good humored patience").

32   *Board of Regents, Biennial Report, 1945-1947,* pp. 8, 9, 11; Departments of History and Political Science, Sociology and Anthropology, and others, to Compton, June 21, 1946, (Quotation); Box 11, Compton Papers.

33   "Space Use by the College of Engineering," unsigned, attached to G. E. Thornton, "Report-1946," Box 13, *ibid.*

34   Harold E. Culver to Stanley A. Smith, November 4, 1946, Box 12; *ibid.*, Culver to E. H. Hopkins, November 6, 1946, Box 12, *ibid.* (Quotation); "(7) College of Engineering and School of Mineral Industries," Unattached 3 pp., of unidentified report, not dated or signed, Box 13, *ibid.*

35   *Board of Regents, Biennial Report, 1945-1947,* pp. 12, 13, 22-25; Pullman *Herald,* September 27, 1946.

36   W. C. [Wilson Compton] to Deans and Directors, January 15, 1946, Box 12, Compton Papers, in which he stated, regarding the State College, "that next to its students the most important concern is its teachers. . . . I believe these two interests are fundamentally inseparable and I hope and believe you will help me keep them so."

37   *Regents Record,* Vol. 12, December 10-12, 1945, pp. 196, 197; *ibid.*, January 14, 1946, pp. 201, 202, 211-214; Press Release, December 12, 1945, Box 10; Compton Papers, Faculty Executive Committee to President Compton [April or May, 1946], Box 11, *ibid.*, Compton to J. C. Knott, February 12, 1946, Box 11, *ibid.*; Compton to E. H. Hopkins, July 26, 1946, Box 11, *ibid.*; Edwin C. Johnson and C. L. Simpson to Compton, July 19, 1946, Box 11, *ibid.*

38   W. C. [Wilson Compton] to Deans and Directors January 15, 1946, Box 12, (Quotations); *Board of Regents, Biennial Report, 1947-1949,* pp. 81-83; *The State College of Washington Faculty Manual (January, 1949).* On his apposition to "administration by crony," see *Regents Record,* Vol. 13, April 18 and 19, 1947, pp 178-179.

39   The report was a "Communication from the Faculty Executive Committee to President Compton, February 8, 1947, Box 1, Folder 1946-47, Faculty Executive Committee Records (Quotations on pp. 1, 3). The author of the report was S. T. S. [S. Town Stevenson].

40   S.T.S., "On the Problems of an Institution of Higher Education [Shortened title]," February 8, 1947, Box 15, Compton Papers; [James Quann], Office of the Registrar, "A Brief and Sometimes Annotated History of the WSU General Studies Program," (September 12, 1985), pp. 1-5. The 30 semester hour requirement represented the minimum standard for those majoring at the end of the freshman year and applied to designated departments only. Additional requirements prevailed for those adopting a major after the first two years (See *ibid.*, and *The State College Catalogue for 1947,* pp. 88, 89).

41   Professor P. J. Rempel provided the philosophical statement which the Educational Policies Committee endorsed. It is quoted in [James Quann], "A Brief . . . History of the WSU General Education Program," p. 4. The integrated courses appeared for the first time in the Fifty-fourth Announcement of the State College of Washington for 1946, pp. 163, 164; *Board of Regents, Biennial Report, 1947-1949,* pp. 8, 12, 13, 17, 18.

42   *Regents Record,* Vol. 13, April 18, and 19, 1947, p. 179.

43   S.T.S. to Compton, May 28, 1947, Box 15, Compton Papers; Press Release: Washington State College, May, 1947, Box 15, *ibid.*; *Regents Record,* Vol. 14 November 26 and 27, 1948, p. 257; Interview with Allen A. White by George A. Frykman, April 14, 1982; "The State College of Washington, its Expansion, its Plans (Report)" Box 15, Compton Papers.

44   *Ibid.*; Interview with Herbert J. Wood by George A. Frykman, January 28, 1972; A. O. Shaw and 11 others to Wilson Compton, April 19, 1949, (Quotations "arbitrarily minimized" and "awkward"), Box 3, President's papers (Compton); Memo: Compton to E. H. Hopkins, undated, (Quotation "there is genuine resistance"), Box 3, President's Papers (Compton).

45   Memo: E. H. H. [Hopkins] to Compton, April 26, 1949, Box 3, President's Papers (Compton); J. L. Ellis to Compton, July 7, 1949, and September 10, 1949, *ibid.*; *Regents Record,* Vol. 15, September 15 and 16, 1949, pp. 8-10; Eleanor Newell to E. H. Hopkins, September 23, 1949, Box 3, President's Papers (Compton); Emmett L. Avery to E. H. Hopkins, April 8, 1947, Box 15, Compton Papers.

46   *Regents Record,* Vol. 13, April 18 and 19, 1947, pp. 147, 174. *Board of Regents, Biennial Report, 1945-1947,* p. 82, but note that the School of Music and Fine Arts acted independently in reporting activities in Board of Regents, Biennial Report, 1947-1949, pp. 81-84. On eliminating the Graduate School of Social Work, see *Regents Record,* Vol 12, October 1 and 2, 1945, pp 120, 121; *ibid.*, Vol. 14, April 20, 1949, pp. 402-409.

47   *Board of Regents, Biennial Report, 1947-1949,* p. 4; *Regents Record,* Vol. 14, December 28 and 29, 1948, p. 270; *ibid.*, Vol. 15, March 30 and 31, 1950, p. 152.

48   *Ibid.*, Vol. 13, April 18 and 19, 1947, pp. 147, 176-179 (Quotations on p. 179).

49   Washington State University President's Committee, "Recommendations . . . Approved . . . by the President's Committee and Submitted to President Compton (1945), Sections R-1 and R-2; *Board of Regents Biennial Report, 1945-1947,* pp. 17, 18; *ibid.*, pp. 84-87; *State College of Washington, Annual Catalogue 1949,* pp. 97-100.

50   *State College of Washington Annual Catalogue, 1948*, p. 198.

51   Betty Milne, "Cosmopolitan Club History, 1910-1940," Box 1, International Students (Quotation); List of Members of the Cosmopolitan Club, 1926, "Minutes of the Cosmopolitan Club, 1925-1926," Box 1, *ibid.*; Untitled roster, Envelope of the Cosmopolitan Club, Box 1, *ibid.* International students' papers are found in the WSU Archives.

52   Betty O. Milne, Seattle, to Office of Student Affairs, WSU, May 27, 1970, Folder "WSU Cosmopolitan Club Papers, 1938-1940," Box 1, *ibid.*

53   Hsu Pin Ling and others [to Dr. E. F. Gaines, 1935] "Addressed to the Chinese Students in the State College of Washington," Folder "Chinese Students Club, Box 1, *ibid.*; "The Filipino Club of the State College of Washington: Pictures and Programs, Old and New," Folder Filipino Club, Box 1, *ibid.* On Japanese students, see untitled list [1942] of WSC students of Japanese extraction, Box 249, Office of the President (Holland).

54   *Laws of Washington, Session Laws, 29th Session, January 8-March 8, 1945*, Chapter 236, p. 704; Washington (State) University, President's Committee, "Recommendations . . . Approved . . . By the President's Committee and Submitted to President Compton" (1945), Section N-9.

55   Claudius O. Johnson and Six others to Wilson Compton, April 16, 1946, Folder "Committee 1946," Box 11, Compton Papers; *Laws of Washington, 1949 Session Laws of the State of Washington, 1949*, pp. 133-134.

56   "Enrollment Data Book II," Registrar's Office.

57   Ivan Putman to Wilson Compton, September 29, 1948, Box 1, President's Papers (Compton); Putman to Compton, October 30, 1948 *ibid.*; Putman to Compton, Hopkins, and Craig, March 22, 1951, Box 8, *ibid.*

58   Putman to Compton, *ibid.*; Putman to Compton, October 30, 1948, Box 1, *ibid.* Conversation with Clair McNeal, Assistant Director of Admissions, W.S.U., October 9, 1987, on quota restrictions of foreign students as advisable in order to retain the free communication among different groups on the campus. Putman to Compton, Hopkins and Craig, March 22, 1951, Box 8, Office of the President (Compton).

59   Washington (State) University, President's Committee, "Recommendations . . . Approved . . . By the President's Committee and Submitted to President Compton," (1945), (Quotations), Section T-12; [Wilson Compton], "Tentative Suggestion of Changes," February 5, 1947, Box 15, Compton Papers.

60   Washington (State) University, President's Committee, "Recommendations . . . Approved by the President's Committee and Submitted to President Compton," (1945), Section T-12. The role of the Faculty Executive Committee is described by H. J. Wood in his interview of June 26, 1972, reported by George A. Frykman. Board of Regents, *Biennial Report, 1947-1949*, pp. 81-83.

61   *Faculty Manual of the State College of Washington* (January, 1949), pp. 50-55 (date of approval is on p. 54). For information on the Organization of the Resident Instructional Staff and other staffs, see *ibid.*, pp. 24-32.

62   *Ibid.*, pp. 59-61 (Quotation on p. 61).

63   *Ibid.*, pp. 48, 49, 61. *Regents Record*, Vol. 14, October 15 and 16, 1948, p. 168 (Quotation).

64   [Wilson Compton], "Tentative Suggestions of Changes," February 5, 1947, Box 15, Compton Papers; *Regents Rec-*

ord, Vol. 13, April 2, 1947, p. 91; Memo: "History of Faculty Evaluation Program," from Faculty Executive Committee to the Resident Instructional Staff [December, 1948], Box 1, Faculty Executive Committee Records; *Board of Regents, Biennial Report, 1947-1949*, pp. 81, 82.

65   *Faculty Manual of the State College of Washington, (January, 1949)*, pp. 56-61 (Quotations are from p. 59, italics in the original).

66   *Board of Regents, Biennial Report, 1947-1949*, pp. 82; *Faculty Manual for the State College of Washington, (January, 1949)*, pp. 63, 64; Faculty Executive Committee Minutes, October 17, 1950, and January 9, 1951, Box 2, Faculty Executive Committee Records; *Regents Record*, Vol. 14, October 15 and 16, 1948, pp. 168-16.

67   Lawrence J. Golicz concluded that Compton placed a new library near but not at the top of this list of priorities, behind a general classroom building and structures for the new institutes. See his "History of Washington State University Libraries from 1946 to 1949," pp. 60-66. But see also Robert Sandberg to S. A. Smith and C. L. Hix, July 13, 1946, Box 11, Compton Papers; Compton to Board of Regents, July 18, 1945, Box 9, *ibid.*

68   Herman J. Deutsch, "Report of the Special Committee on the Library, Appointed September 1, 1945, to Compton, Box 9, *ibid.*; Observations of the present author.

69   Golicz, "History of Washington State University Libraries from 1946 to 1949," p. 56-58.

70   *Board of Regents, Biennial Report, 1947-1949*, pp. 75-77.

71   Compton to Holland, January 4, 1945, found in Exhibit E in *Regents Record*, Vol. 11, February 5 and 6, 1945, pp. 466, 467 (Quotations on p. 467); Golicz, "History of the Washington State University Libraries from 1946 to 1949," p. 51.

72   Herman J. Deutsch, "Report of Special Committee on the Library, appointed September 1, 1945, to Compton, (Quotation on p. 6), Box 9, Compton Papers.

73   *Regents Record*, Vol. 12, July 22 and 23, 1946, p. 417; Golicz, "History of Washington State University Libraries from 1946 to 1949," pp. 19-23. The present author, who was Assistant Librarian and Chief, Social Sciences Division, of Holland Library, 1951-1953, here adds his recollections. See, also, A. I. White to Compton, February 22, 1947, a memo: "Proposal for a Reorganization of the College Library," Box 15, Compton Papers.

74   Recollections of present author. "Program for a New Library at Washington State College, June 10, 1947," attached to G. D. Smith to Compton, *c* June 10, 1947, Box 15, Compton Papers.

75   *Ibid.*, p. 1 (Quotation: italics in the original); Golicz, "History of the Washington State University Libraries from 1946 to 1949," pp. 51-61.

76   *Ibid.*, p. 47; Dudley Pratt, a prominent Seattle sculptor, created "Nature Boy," according to *ibid.*, pp. 60, 61.

77   *Ibid.*, pp. 61-67.

78   *Regents Record*, Vol. 13, November 21 and 22, 1947, p. 393.

79   "Report on the Policies and Program of the State College of Washington Library, March, 1949," Box 4, President's Papers (Compton); "Modular Library under Construction, The State College of Washington, Pullman, Washington," *The Architectural Record*, Vol. 104 (July, 1948):102-109 (Quotation on p. 102); Golicz, "History of the Washington State University Libraries from 1946 to 1949," pp. 80-89. Recollections on delay in moving into the library are those of the present author.

80   Paul H. Landis, "The Graduate School," Board of Regents, *Biennial Report, 1945-1947*, p. 96; Landis to Compton,

November 9, 1945, Box 9, Compton Papers; Stewart E. Hazlet, "The Graduate School," Board of Regents, *Biennial Report, 1947-1949*, p. 68.

81   Note from Wilson Compton to H. K. (Herbert Kimbrough), undated but attached to Landis to C. L. Hix, April 11, 1945, Box 9, Compton Papers; Compton to Dean H. Kimbrough, April 17, 1945, Box 9, *ibid.*; *Regents Record*, Vol. 12, April 23, 1945, pp. 20, 21. Graduate assistantships are sometimes referred to as fellowships. In either case, the positions required one-half time duty.

82   Landis, "The Graduate School," *Board of Regents Six Year Report for the Period Ending April 1, 1945*, pp. 63-65; Landis to Compton, February 6, 14, and 24, 1945, Box 9, Compton Papers; *Regents Record*, Vol. 12, April 23, 1945, pp. 20, 21.

83   Stewart E. Hazlet to Compton, April 1, 1946, Box 11, Compton Papers; Faculty Executive Committee to President Compton [not dated but April or May, 1946], *ibid.*

84   *Ibid.*

85   Departments of History and Political Science, Sociology and Anthropology, and Economics to Compton, June 21, 1946, (Quotation), Box 11, (Signed by Herman J. Deutsch, Fred Yoder, and Daniel Barth); *ibid.*, Compton to Members of the Advisory Board, Institute of Agricultural Sciences, January 7, 1947, Box 14, *ibid.*

86   *Board of Regents, Biennial Report, 1947-1949*, p. 5.

87   Glenn Jones to Compton, March 28, 1947, Box 14, Compton Papers (italics are in the original text). Memorandum: Norman Braden to Glenn Terrell and Wallis Beasley, April 1, 1968, attached to Memorandum: Allan H. Smith to John M. Cronlund, November 7, 1972, Folder "General Extension Service," Box 8, Office of the President (Terrell); [Glenn Jones], "Biennial Report of Community College Service . . . July 1, 1947 to May 30, 1949," pp. 1-7, Box 3, Office of the President (Compton).

88   [Glenn Jones], "Biennial Report of Community College Service . . . , July 1, 1947 to May 30, 1949," Box 3, Office of the President (Compton). In 1947, the State College joined in a cooperative program with the General Electric Company to operate "The Graduate School of Nuclear Engineering," for company employees (Wilson Compton to F. E. Johnson, August 12, 1947, Box 14, Compton Papers and Johnson to Compton, August 30, 1947, *ibid.*).

89   [Glenn Jones] "Biennial Report of Community College Service . . . , July 1, 1947 to May 30, 1949," pp. 7, 16 (Quotation), Box 3, Office of the President (Compton).

90   *Ibid.*, pp. 7, 14, 15; Richard Bray to Glenn Jones, April 12, 1949, Box 3, Office of the President (Compton); Compton to E. H. Hopkins, May 4, 1949, *ibid.*; W. C. [Wilson Compton] to Glenn Jones, December 21, 1949, *ibid.*; Bray to Jones, December 28, 1949, *ibid.*

91   Richard Bray to Glenn Jones, April 12, 1949, Box 3, *ibid.*

92   Class enrollments are found in Enrollment Data Book, I (Registrar's Office); Board of Regents, *Biennial Report, 1945-1947*, pp. 100-106.

93   *Regents Record*, Vol. 11, December 11, 1942, pp. 16, 17; *Fifty-Third Announcement of the State College of Washington for 1945*, pp. 233-236; *Regents Record*, Vol. 11, April 5, 1945, p. 477; *ibid.*, Vol. 12, July 20, 1945, p. 80; "Memorandum of Basic Understanding Between the State College and St. Luke's Hospital . . . ," Box 13, Compton Papers.

94   C. Clement French to Nursing Education Committee, May 28, 1954, Box 16, Office of the President (French); "Student Enrollments as of 12/31/54," [in collegiate schools of nursing in Washington], Box 17, Office of the President (French); C. Clement French to Dean S. T. Stephenson, March 19, 1956, Box 36, *ibid.*; French to Charles Gonser, Spokane, June 6, 1956 and Gonser to French, September 13, 1956, Box 36, *ibid.*; Compare *State College of Washington Catalogue, 1958-59 and 1959-60*, pp. 158, 159 with *ibid.*, 1956-57 and 1957-58, pp 262, 263, for termination of program.

95   Compton to Dean E. C. Johnson, August 17, 1945, Box 9, Compton Papers; Compton to The Board of Regents, August 20, 1945, Box 10, *ibid.*; Compton to Dean E. C. Johnson, August 20, 1945, Box 9, *ibid.*

96   "Horticulture Advisory Report, February 7 and 8, 1946," Box 11, Compton Papers.

97   Frank A. Riches, "Report of the Animal Husbandry Advisory Committee," February 8, 1946," Box 11, Compton Papers; Compton to Deans and Directors, February 19, 1946, (Quotations. Italics in the original), Box 12, *ibid.*

98   *Board of Regents, Biennial Report, 1945-1947*, pp. 26-30, 39-46.

99   *Ibid.*, pp. 39-42; *Board of Regents, Biennial Report, 1947-1949*, pp. 45-51.

100 *Biennial Report of the State College of Washington, April 1, 1949 to March 31, 1951*, pp. 10-12 (Quotation on p. 11).

101 *The State College of Washington Catalog, 1950*, pp. 123-125. Some of the sixteen percent farming were farm managers, suggesting that they, in some cases, probably were businessmen. On this and other statistics and developments, see *Biennial Report of the State College of Washington, April 1, 1949 to March 31, 1951*, pp. 8, 9.

102 Press Release, December 12, 1945, Box 10, Compton Papers; "A Report on the Work of the Division of Industrial Research . . . April 1, 1945 to December 31, 1945, to Compton, January 25, 1946, Box 9, Compton Papers; Board of Regents, *Biennial Report, 1945-1947*, pp. 43-46, 53-60; *ibid.*, 1947-1949, pp. 30-35; *Biennial Report of the State College of Washington, 1949-1951*, p. 15.

103 Board of Regents, *Biennial Report, 1945-1947*, p. 60; *ibid.*, 1947-1949, pp. 33, 34; *ibid.*, 1949-1951, p. 16.

Chapter Six

1   Pullman *Herald*, December 14, 1945; Interview with Herman J. Deutsch by George A. Frykman, April 22, 1971.

2   [Doris Pierson], "Greetings: For the Students, The State College of Washington," *The Inauguration of Wilson M. Compton as President of the College*, Vol. 1, Compton Papers; *Evergreen*, December 14, 1945 (Quotations "charming" and "unscheduled"); Interview with Herbert J. Wood, by George A. Frykman, January 26, 1972 (Quotation "she got more applause.")

3   [Doris Pierson,] "Greetings" (Quotation "deep satisfaction"), The Inaugural of Wilson M. Compton, Vol. 1, Compton Papers; interview with Herman J. Deutsch by George A. Frykman, May 13, 1971; Interview with Herbert J. Wood by George A. Frykman, January 26, 1972. E. H. Hopkins, "The Essentials of a Student Personnel Program," *College and University*, July, 1948 (reprint), Quotations, Box 13, Vertical File 763 (Speech to the American College Personnel Association, May 29, 1948).

4   E. H. Hopkins to the Resident Instructional Staff, February 15, 1949, Box 4/7, Office of the President (Compton). Hopkins to Resident Instructional Staff, December 12, 1949, *ibid.*

5   *Evergreen*, October 22 and 29, 1948; Selma Streit to E. H. Hopkins, September 12, 20, 1949, Box 4/1, Office of the President (Compton); Streit to Dean J. C. Clevenger. September 24, 1952, Box 11/2, Office of the President (French); *Regents Record*, Vol. 14, December 28, 29, 1948, pp. 271-273.

6   Claude Simpson to E. H. Hopkins, June 2, 1949, Box 3/5, Office of the President (Compton); Special Committee of Fraternity and Sorority Rush to the Board of Regents, December 15, 1949, Box 3/5, *ibid.*; E. H. Hopkins to Wilson Compton, December 15, 1949, *ibid.*; *Regents Record*, Vol. 15, September 16, 17, 1949, P. 110. There is a plethora of comments and reports on women's enrollments in Box 1/9 of Office of the President (Compton). Most notable is an untitled report from the Educational Policies Committee, November 1, 1948, attached to E. H. Hopkins to R. A. Sandberg, November 1, 1948, *ibid.* See, also, W. W. Bleasner to R. A. Sandberg, October 30, 1948, *ibid.*

7   E. H. Hopkins to R. A. Sandberg, November 1, 1948, and attached untitled report from the Educational Policies Committee, November 1, 1948, *ibid.*

8   *Regents Record*, Vol. 12, July 19-21, 1945, p. 112.

9   Joe R. Matsen, " Request by the Students at the State College of Washington for College Union Building Construction," [1949] Box 3/1, Office of the President (Compton); Matsen to Members of the Board of Regents, April 8, 1949, *ibid.*

10 *Ibid.*, (Quotation "desperate"); Matsen, "Request by the Students . . . for College Union Building Construction," *ibid.*, (quotation "our students"); *Evergreen*, April 13, 1949. The dedication is discussed below.

11 E. H. H. [Hopkins] to the Chairmen of Student-Faculty Committees, September 12, 1949, Box 3/4, Office of the President (Compton); Interview with Herbert J. Wood by George A. Frykman, January 26, 1972.

12 *Regents Record*, Vol. 14, October 15, 16, 1948, pp. 168, 210-213 provides a full summary of regulations and laws

dating back to 1931, governing outside speakers and forbidding communist speakers; *ibid.*, November 26, 27, 1948, Box 2/4, Office of the President (Compton); *Evergreen*, October 22, 1948 (Quotation).

13 *Regents Record*, Vol. 14, October 15, 16, 1948, pp. 168, 210-213; *ibid.*, November 26, 27, 1948, pp. 236, 237; Dorothy W. McPherson to Wilson Compton, November 3, 1948, Box 2/4, Office of the President (Compton); *Evergreen*, October 22, 1948 (Quotation).

14 Dorothy W. McPherson to Wilson Compton, November 3, 1948, Box 2/4, Office of the President (Compton); *Regents Record*, Vol. 15, September 16, 17, 1949; (Quotations) *Evergreen*, October 22, 1948 and March 7, 1949; Pullman *Herald*, March 11, 1949.

15 *Ibid.*; January 9, 1948.

16 *Ibid.*

17 *Evergreen*, February 23 and 27, 1948; Spokane *Spokesman-Review*, February 26, 1948; *Endicott Index*, February 27, 1948.

18 "Washington State College Budget, 1949-1951," February 28, 1949 (Quotations "mistakenly," a modification of "mistake," "until this additional amount is restored"), Box 4/1, Office of the President (Compton).

19 Wilson Compton to Administrative Officers and Departmental Chairmen, January 17, 1949, Box 3/4, *ibid.*

20 "Press Release," April 12, 1949, Box 3/2, *ibid.*; *Session Laws of the State of Washington, 1949*, p. 946.

21 E. H. Hopkins to Wilson Compton, April 4, 1949, (quotations on p. 1, Box 3 Office of the President (Compton); Stewart E. Hazlett to Compton, March 21, 1949, *ibid.*

22 E. H. Hopkins to Wilson Compton, May 20, 1949, *ibid.*, For quotes on the Student Activities Program, see Hopkins to Compton, April 4, 1949, *ibid.*

23 *Regents Record*, Vol. 15, April 12 and 13, 1951, pp. 440-442, 447, 448.

24 *Ibid.*, April 27, 1951, pp. 475, 476, 479, and 480. "A Statement by Wilson Compton . . . May 4, 1951, attached to Compton to WSC Advisory Boards, May 15, 1951, Box 24, W. E. Carty Papers, WSU Archives.

25 *Ibid.*, p. 480.

26 *Ibid.*, pp. 514-518; Seattle *Post-Intelligencer*, April 29, 1951; *Evergreen*, May 1, 1951.

27 *Ibid.*, May 1, 1951.

28 *Faculty Minutes*, Vol. 8, May 3, 1951.

29 *Evergreen*, May 8, 1951, (Quotation carries Compton's inaccurate appraisal of the roster of the Board of Regents. A comparison of the Board rosters in Catalogs for 1949-51 reveals the fact that there were four new Regents on the board of seven.

30 Sandberg (Interview with William Stimson, June 1987) comments on disorderly meetings and on Mrs. Compton's helpful as well as meddling activities on campus and in town (WSU Centennial Oral History Project, WSU Archives).

31 *Who's Who in America*, Vol. 27, 1952-53, p. 1602. For seniority in service on Board of Regents, see *Annual Catalogs, State College of Washington*. McAllister's book was published by Revell in 1948. George Gannon, former Regent, accused McAllister of dominating the Board to the detriment of the administration (*Spokesman-Review*, May

30, 1951) and Compton on June 2, 1951 named McAllister and Camp as disruptive in the months before his resignation, "A Statement by Wilson Compton, . . . June 2, 1951," Box 8/2, Office of the President (Compton). Allen I. White (Interview with George A. Frykman, April 14, 1982) indicated that McAllister and Camp came to the campus to make investigations, probably without the knowledge of other Regents.

32 Interview with Allen I. White by George A. Frykman, April 14, 1982; Interview with Robert Sandberg by William Stimson, June, 1987, (Quotation). On Brumblay's resignation see Spokane *Spokesman-Review,* May 1, 1951.

33 *Faculty Minutes,* Vol. 8, May 28, 1951.

34 *Ibid.*

35 *Ibid.,* Vol. 8, June 6, 1951.

36 Dr. William A. Pearl, Professor of Mechanical Engineering, served as interim Acting President, *Regents Record* Vol. 16, October 1, 1951, p. 103; *ibid.,* October 26, 1951, pp. 139 (Quotations).

37 *Faculty Minutes,* Vol. 8, November 9, 1951; *Regents Record,* Vol. 16, November 23, 1951, pp. 196 and 211. The *Faculty Minutes* for November 9, 1951, indicate that the Master of Education degree was approved at that time, but a comparison of the *Graduate School Bulletins* for 1949-1950 and 1953 indicates it had existed before. Also, the *Graduate School Bulletins* reveal the nature of the change that degree underwent.

38 *Regents Record,* Vol. 16, February 24 and 25, 1952, pp. 247, 248; Alan Rogers, Ellensburg, to C. Clement French, College Station, Texas, December 26, 1951, Box 4, C. Clement French Papers, Cage 310; Charles E. McAllister, Spokane, to French, College Station, Texas, January 28, 1952, *ibid.*; *Who's Who in America,* Vol. 27, 1952-53, p. 855.

39 Interview with C. Clement French by Harold Helton, May 18, 1983, WSU Centennial Oral History Project, WSU Archives; *Regents Record,* Vol. 16, February 24 and 25, 1952, pp. 247, 248, 332; *ibid.,* April 22, 1952, p. 332.

40 Interview with C. Clement French by Harold Helton, May 18, 1983; Spokane *Spokesman-Review,* April 11, 1952 (Quotation).

41 Interview with C. Clement French by Harold Helton, May 18, 1983 (Quotation); Spokane *Chronicle,* April 17, 1952, clipping in Folder "W.S.C. Inaugural, 1 June, 1952," Box 4, C. Clement French papers, Cage 310; For the relationship between the two Episcopalian leaders, see French to Robert A. Magill, Lynchburg, Virginia, December 7, 1951, *ibid.*: French to McAllister, March 5, 1952 and McAllister to French, November 10, 1951, *ibid.*

42 Interview with C. Clement French by Harold Helton, May 18, 1983, quotations; Petition #63, To the Board of Regents of the State College of Washington [1952], Box 12/4, Office of the President (French).

43 Interview with C. Clement French by Harold Helton, May 18, 1983.

44 *Ibid.*; *Faculty Minutes,* Vol. 8, April 17, 1952.

45 Interview with Allen I. White by George A. Frykman, May 26, 1982, discusses French's low-key administration. On Commencement, see *Evergreen,* June 3, 1952, and Pullman *Herald,* June 5, 1952. On dedication, see *Evergreen,* October 23 and 27, 1952, and Pullman *Herald,* October 30, 1952. French's deliberate, cautious style is revealed in an exchange with Gordon H. Coe, Editor of the Spokane *Chronicle.* See telegram, Coe to French, March 7, 1952, and letter, French to Coe, March 10, 1952, both found in Box 4, C. Clement French Papers, Cage 310.

46 Faculty Executive Committee Meeting, December 4, 1951, folder 1952, Box 2, Faculty Executive Committee Records; January 15, 1952, Folder 1951-54, *ibid.*; *Regents Record* Vol. 6, January 19, 1952, p. 221.

47 Faculty Executive Committee Meeting, June 6, 1952, Folder 1951-52, Part 2, Box 2, Faculty Executive Committee Records.

48 *Ibid.,* December 15, 1953, Folder 1953-54, Box 2, *ibid.*; February 18, 1954, *ibid,* (Quotation).

49 *Regents Records,* Vol. 16, May 30, 1952, p. 371 (Quotation); Fred A. Dudley and Carl Stevens to C. Clement French, S. T. Stephenson, and C. L. Barker, "Faculty Salaries in the Next Biennium," June 12, 1952; Faculty Executive Committee Minutes, 1951-1952, Faculty Executive Committee Records. This report also contains a comparison of State College salaries with six other state universities.

50 *Regents Record,* Vol. 16, May 30, 1952, p. 371 (Quotation), *ibid.,* Vol. 17, November 28, 1957, p. 2; S. T. Stephenson to Carl Pettibone, November 12, 1952, Box 10, Office of the President (French).

51 *Ibid.,* Office of the President (French). The general funds had been reduced from $10,763,089 to $9,485,328 in March, 1951.

52 Stephenson to Maynard Hicks, June 23, 1953, (Quotation), Box 13/2, Office of the President (French); Stephenson to Norman Braden and eleven others, December 15, 1953, Box 15/1a, *ibid.,* "Total Enrollment Since 1892" (Registrar's Office).

53 *Regents Record,* Vol. 17, February 11, 1954, p. 313; *ibid.,* Vol. 18, March 25, 1955, p. 89.

54 Stephenson to French, November 12, 1953, Box 13/3, Office of the President (French).

55 Faculty Executive Committee Meeting, April 12, 1955, Folder 1954-55, Box 2, Faculty Executive Committee Records.

56 *Faculty Minutes,* Vol. 10, September 15, 1964.

57 *Ibid.,* Vol. 9, May 9, 1957; *ibid.,* March 26, 1957 (Quotation); *Session Laws of the State of Washington, 1957,* Chapter 299, pp. 1198-1201; Referendum Bill No. 10, *ibid.*; *Evergreen.* November 25, 1958; *Session Laws of the State of Washington, 1959,* p. 1781.

58 Dean S. T. Stephenson served as the president's mentor in this matter, pointing out the history of Compton's plan, its strengths and weaknesses. See Stephenson to French, April 17, 1952 Box 12/1, Office of the President (French); French to the Deans and Others, January 26, 1953, box 14/2, *ibid.*; *Faculty Minutes,* Vol. 8, January 26, 1953.

59 French to Dean Henry Schmitz, Minneapolis, March 27, 1952, Folder: "WSU [sic] Inauguration, 1 June 1952," Box 4, French Papers, Cage 310; French to Schmitz, March 23, 1954, Box 16/2 Office of the President (French); Schmitz to French, January 28, 1954, and French to Board of Regents, February 16, 1954, Box 17/1 and 17/4, respectively; *ibid.*

60 *Ibid;* French to Schmitz, November 2, 1953, Box 14/3, *ibid.*

61 *Ibid.,* H. P. Everest to French, April 13, 1954, Box 16/2, *ibid.*; *State College of Washington Catalog, 1956-57 and 1957-58,* pp. 168, 169; French to Stephenson, April 21, 1954, Box 16/2, Office of the President (French).

62 John P. Nagle to E. H. Steffen, January 5, 1954, Box 15/4, *ibid.*; *Regents Record,* March 19, 1960, p. 157; *ibid.,* May 6, 1960, p. 294; *Session Laws of the State of Washington,* 1961, Vol. 2, Chapter 71, p. 1488.

63 Pullman *Herald,* January 25, 1952; Faculty Executive Committee Minutes, January 29, 1952, Folder 1952, Box 2,

Faculty Executive Committee Records (Quotation "to clarify").

64 Memorandum to French from the Faculty Executive Committee, February 10, 1953, Folder 1953, *ibid.;* Fred Dudley to French, February 10, 1953, Box 13/1, Office of the President (French); French to Dudley, February 19, 1953, Box 10, *ibid.*

65 *Session Laws of the State of Washington, 1950 and 1951,* Chapter 254, pp. 793-803.

66 *Ibid, 1955,* Chapter 377, pp. 1545, 1546; *Regents Record,* Vol. 18, June 14, 1955, p. 196. No evidence can be found of prosecutions of faculty or staff on the matter of oaths, but Annette K. Meinhart, who was Director of the Office of Faculty Personnel at the time, has stated that no one, to her knowledge, was removed from the University's rolls. See Meinhart to Robert Hadlow, July 21, 1988 (in possession of George A. Frykman). For an account of the history of the 1931 and 1955 laws, see Jane Sanders *Cold War on the Campus: Academic Freedom at the University of Washington, 1946-1964,* (Seattle: University of Washington Press, 1979), passim, but especially pp. 168-171.

67 Spokane *Spokesman-Review,* September 13, 1951. For comprehensive documentation on the institutes of international affairs, see files entitled "The Current Incident," "Related Incidents," and "Recommendations" in Box 10/5 (1952), Office of the President (French); *Regents Record,* Vol. 16, June 30, 1952, p. 407; Fred A. Dudley to Members of the Faculty Executive Committee, July 31, 1952, Box 2, Faculty Executive Committee Records.

68 *Regents Record,* Vol. 19, April 20, 1959, pp. 142-144.

69 *Ibid.,* Vol. 20, March 17, 1962, pp. 34, 35; *Evergreen,* February 23, March 20, May 2, 1962; *Regents Record,* Vol. 20, May 1, 1962, pp. 48, 54; *ibid.,* Vol. 20, March 6, 14, 1964, p. 219.

70 "A Review of the Decline in the Purchasing Power of the Faculty Salaries at Washington State College," [1952], Box 10/7, Office of the President (French).

71 R. D. Tousley to S. T. Stephenson [not dated but June 1952], Box 10/4, *ibid.; Regents Record,* Vol. 18, August 6, 1956, p. 331 (Quotation "imperative") The number of resignations was not listed.

72 *Ibid.,* April 27, 1957, p. 392; October 1, 1955, p. 241.

73 French to All Members of the Faculty, September 16, 1953, Box 13/3, Office of the President (French); French to Faculty and Staff Residents of College Housing, September 24, Box 15/7, *ibid.*

74 "Percentage of Students Housed in College-Operated Residence Halls, Selected Midwestern and Pacific Coast Institutions, Fall, 1954," Box 15/7, *ibid.*

75 *Evergreen,* October 21 and 24, 1952; French to J. C. Clevenger, October 30, 1952, quotation "a drinking school," Folder 12/1, Office of the President (French); J. C. Clevenger to WSC Faculty [1953], "Student Conduct and Disciplinary Action," Box 13/2, *ibid.* For an exchange of letters concerning the Crosby sons, see Bing Crosby to French, August 12, 1952, Box 10/5, *ibid.;* and French to Crosby, September 2, 1952, *ibid.*

76 John D. Lillywhite to French, June 8, 1954, Box 15/1a, *ibid.*

77 French to Lillywhite, June 16, 1954, *ibid.*

78 J. C. Clevenger to All Members of the College Staff, September 20, 1954, Box 15/1a, *ibid*; Victor Dauer and J. C. Clevenger to the Faculty, September 13, 1955, Box 17/a, *ibid.*

79 *Regents Record,* Vol. 19, January 19, 1959, pp. 121, 122; *Evergreen,* January 20, 1959.

80 *Ibid.,* January 23, 1959, quotation; *Regents Record,* Vol. 19, January 19, 1959, p. 122.

81 *Evergreen,* January 23, 1959.

82 *Regents Record,* Vol. 19, April 5, 1961, pp. 394-396.

83 *Evergreen,* March 11 and April 22, 1964.

84 Golden Romney to French [undated but 1952], Box 10/3 (1952), Office of the President (French).

85 *Ibid.,* French to Victor O. Schmidt, November 17, 1952, *ibid.;* Schmidt to French, June 30, 1954, Box 16/5, *ibid.*

86 Romney, "Report of the Athletic Department, January 18, 1954," quotation, Box 16/1, *ibid.;* French to Members of the Board of Regents, February 16, 1954, Box 17/1, *ibid.*

87 Helen G. Smith to French, December 28, 1953, Box 16/5, *ibid.* French to Smith, January 5, 1954, *ibid.*

88 French to Members of the Board of Regents, February 16, 1954, Box 17/1, *ibid.,* French to Emmett Moore and Golden Romney, May 24, 1954, quotation, Box 16/5, *ibid.*

89 *Regents Record,* Vol. 177, May 19 and 20, 1954, p. 395.

90 *Evergreen,* October 5, 1954.

91 French, to Victor O. Schmidt, Los Angeles, December 17, 1956, Box 33/5, Office of the President (French); clipping of editorial San Francisco Examiner, December 6, 1956, attached to *ibid.* See editorial from the Pasadena *Star-News,* December 7, 1956, attached to *ibid.* San Francisco *Chronicle,* December 6, 1956; Victor O. Schmidt and Bernard Hammerbeck, "Action on Major Rules Violations, Pacific Coast Intercollegiate Conference, August 6-8, 1956," Box 33/7, Office of the President (French); San Francisco *Chronicle,* January 4 and 5, 1957; Seattle *Post-Intelligencer,* June 14, 1962.

92 *Regents Record,* Vol. 19, May 1, 1958, P. 28; *ibid.,* Vol. 19, September 19, 1958, p. 99; *ibid.,* Vol. 20, July 20, 1962, pp. 78, 79. For a defense of the WSU's legitimate role in the new conference by a third party, see L. H. Gregory, "Greg's Gossip," in the Portland *Oregonian,* June 17, 1962, attached to French to Gregory, June 29, 1962, Folder "Athletic Association of Western Universities, 1962," Box 5, Office of the President (French).

93 Harry M. Cross to Rixford K. Snyder, May 7, 1964, Folder "AAWU, 1964," Box 13, *ibid.* For a thoughtful statement of the program at Washington State College, see Bill Tomaras to Stan Bates, May 31, 1956, Box 33/5, *ibid.*

94 Wallis Beasley, Robly Williams, and Arthur R. Kooker, Report of Financial Aid Committee to the Council of the AAWU on the Subject of "Rhodes-type Scholarships," August 27, 1964, folder "AAWU, 1964," Box 13, *ibid.*

95 *United States Statutes at Large,* Vol. 12, Chapter 80, The Morrill Act, Section 4, p. 504. Eddy, *Colleges for Our Land and Time;* pp. 64, 65, 93, 94, 163-165, 223-226.

96 On Bryan's ideas and attitudes, see his *Historical Sketch,* pp. 24-27, 158, 159, and elsewhere in passing. In 1969 the Educational Policies Committee discovered the error in the 1925 catalog while considering whether academic credit should be granted for military training. (Report of the Project Committee of E.P.C. . . , December 15, 1969, Folder "Correspondence and Memoranda, 1969-72," Military Education Committee, University Archives 163. See, also, *Annual Catalog, 1925,* p. 315 and *ibid., 1933,* p. 274.

97 "Report of the Project Committee of EPC on Academic Credit for R.O.T.C. at Washington State University, December 15, 1969," Folder "Correspondence and Memoranda, 1969-72," Military Education Committee, University Archives, 163.

98   *Regents Record*, Vol. 18, July 22, 1957, p. 463; "Resolution for addressing the 1961 state legislature on removing mandatory military training of WSU students, Folder "Military Science and Tactics, 1960," Box 4, Office of the President (French), 1961. *Regents Record*, Vol. 20, November 19, 1965, P. 407. *Revised Code of Washington*, Vol. 4, Titles 28-34 (1951-1965), Chapter 28.80.130; *ibid.*, Chapter 28.80.135 (1961). The Regents threw out Rule 140 requiring basic ROTC on May 29, 1961. See *Regents Record*, Vol. 19, May 29, 1961, p. 411.

99   *Ibid.*, Vol. 20, November 19, 1965, p. 407; "Report of the Project committee of EPC. . . ," December 15, 1969,

Folder "Correspondence and Memoranda, 1969-72," Military Education Committee, University Archives 163.

100 *Evergreen*, March 20, 1970.

101 "Resident Instructional Staff Minutes, Thursday, March 19, 1970," a single set of minutes, mimeographed, Folder "Correspondence and Memoranda, 1969-72," Military Education committee, University Archives 163.

102 "Report of the Project Committee of EPC. . . , December 15, 1969," Folder "Correspondence and Memoranda, 1969-72," *ibid.*

Chapter Seven

1   *Regents Record*, Vol 17, April 7, 8, 1954, p. 364, (Quotation "at this time"); *ibid.*, Vol. 19, January 16, 1958, p. 8 (Quotation "interest"); E. L. Avery to Honorable Henry L. Schumacher, February 9, 1959, Folder 1958-59, Box 3, Faculty Executive Committee Records; Avery to various members of the Legislature, February, 1959, *ibid.*, *Regents Record*, Vol. 19, March 9, 1959, p. 129.

2   S. Town Stephenson to R. L. Albrook, P.A. Anderson, and ten other professors, September 24, 1953, Box 31/6, Office of the President (French); *Regents Record*, Vol. 17, November 20, 21, 1953, pp. 260, 261; *ibid.*, Vol. 18, March 29, 1957, p. 387.

3   *Regents Record*, Vol. 19, April 5, 1961, p. 391; *Evergreen*, September 23, 1983, (Quotation); Spokane *Chronicle*, March 7 and 9, 1961; *Regents Record*, Vol. 20, September 6, 1963, p. 180 Spokane *Spokesman-Review*, December 31, 1957.

4   Pullman *Daily News*, April 13, 14, 1985; *Evergreen*, February 11, 1986; Spokane *Spokesman-Review*, October 7, 1987.

5   *Faculty Minutes*, Vol 19, May 19, 1960; cf. *WSU Graduate Bulletin, 1959-1960*, pp. 26, 27, with *ibid.*, 1960-1961, p. 27.

6   *Faculty Minutes*, Vol 9, December 15, 1960; cf. *WSU Graduate School Bulletin, 1959-1960*, p. 19, with *ibid.*, *1960-1961*, pp. 19, 20.

7   *Faculty Minutes*, Vol. 9, May 25, 1961, which contains a memo, French to S. T. Stephenson, June 5, 1961 reporting the boards' approval. Discussion of the American Studies program is, in part, based on recollections by the present author. "Program Statement for the Ph.D. Program in American Studies"(Revised May 1, 1975), prepared by Charles E. Blackburn (WSU, January, 1976). In the possession of the present author.

8   Committee for the Program in American Studies, Minutes, Meeting of January 29, 1969 (In possession of the present author), "A List of American Studies Ph.D. Dissertations Reported to the *American Quarterly*, May 1, 1969 issue (corrected reissue, May 28, 1969, in possession of the present author); "Enrollment of Majors by Class and Department, Fall Semester, 1988" (Registrars' Office). "Program in American Studies, Washington State University, 1970-71" (in the possession of the present author), quotation.

9   Observations by the present author who participated in developing cooperation while serving as Assistant to Dean Donald Farner of the Graduate School.

10 *Ibid.*, *Faculty Minutes*, Vol. 9, December 20, 1961; *Regents Record*, Vol. 20, January 8, 1962, pp. 21, 22; *ibid.*, vol. 20, September 6, 1963, p. 180 (Quotation).

11 "Report of the Engineering Study Council, June 1968", (Study Council Reports are available in the WSU Archives), pp. 9, 10, 20-22; *Regents Record*, Vol. 20, June 21, 1964, p. 206.

12 "Report of the Engineering Study Council, June, 1968," pp. 20-24, 27, 28.

13 *Regents Record*, Vol. 20, January 9, 1965, p. 311; "The Science Development Program at W.S.U.: A Progress Report Submitted to the N.S.F. in Support of a Science Development Grant," (January 1965-February, 1966) p. I-1, VF1087, WSU Archives.

14 *Ibid.*, pp. I-2 through 7.

15 *Ibid.*, pp. II-22 through 25, pp. IV-1, 5, 11-13, pp. V-2, 3.

16 *Ibid.*, pp. V-8, 9 (Table 6).

17 *Ibid.*, pp. V-8, 9 (Table 6).

18 *Ibid.*, p. V-2.

19 Harold W. Dodgen, Grant proposals, [c.1967] in Folder "Faculty Vitae," Department of Chemistry, WSU; "Departmental Science Development Proposal, November 2, 1967," in Folder "Chemical Physics Proposed Document," personal papers of Dr. Harold W. Dodgen, Fulmer Hall, WSU; Robert H. Linnell, National Science Foundation to Harold W. Dodgen, June 5, 1968, *ibid.*, *Regents Record*, Vol. 21, June 10, 1968, p. 132; Interview with Harold W. Dodgen, by Robert W. Hadlow, September 2, 1988.

20 *Regents Record*, Vol. 21, October 20, 1967, p. 86; *ibid.*, January 5, 1968, p. 96.

21 Report of the Biological Sciences Study Council at Washington State University, 28 May 1968, pp. ii, 1.

22 Allan M. Cartter, *An Assessment of Quality in Graduate Education* (Washington, D. C., American Council on Education, 1966), pp. 42-63. "Report of the Biological Science Study Council at Washington State University, 28 may 1968," p. 4.

23 *Ibid.*, p. 4.

24 Biological Sciences Study Council, "Dissent" (October, 1968), pp. 1, 2.

25 "Report of the Physical Sciences Study Council (May, 1968), pp. 15-17 (Quotation on p. 15).

26 Report of the Ten Year Plans of the Academic Units in the Division of Science, "Chemistry: Departmental Analysis and Plans," [c.1966], Box 3, WSU 154, WSU Archives; *ibid.*, "Physics: Departmental Analysis and Plans," [.1966],

(Quotation on p. 24).; *ibid*, "Geology: Departmental Analysis and Plans," [c.1966].

27 *Ibid.*, "Chemistry.".

28 "Report of the Social Sciences Study Council (1968)", p. 43 (Quotation), 45, 46; Press Release, September 13, 1966, Folder "Johnson Tower," WSU News Bureau.

29 [Mary J. Kientzle,] "Psychology at Washington State University: A Brief History," [1976] Cage 4514, WSU Archives. Recollections of the present author concerning the dispensary building and its uses. Academic Vita: Dr. Clare Thompson, Office of Faculty Personnel, French Administration Building.

30 "Report of the Social Sciences Study Council (1968)", pp. 22, 45, 46 (Quotation).

31 *Ibid.*, pp. 8-13, 50 (Quotation).

32 *Ibid.*, p. 50 (Quotation "the social sciences are in a unique . . . position"); Appendix 30, "Report of the Social Science Study Council (1968), unpaged, quotation "an intellectual focus," attached to W. Beasley to Planning Council, May 23, 1969."

33 "Report of the Social Sciences Study Council (1968), pp. 14, 53, 54, 56, 57, (Quotations on pp. 53, 54).

34 *Ibid.*, pp. 3, 25-30 (Quotation on p. 3).

35 T. H. Kennedy to Glenn Terrell, August 30, 1968, Folder "College of Sciences and Arts, 1968," Box 3, Office of the President (Terrell); *WSU Catalog 1972-73*, pp. 165-170; to be compared with *ibid., 1970-71 and 1971-72*, pp. 156-1959.

36 "Report of the Humanities Study Council, June 1, 1968," pp. 21, (Quotations), 22. On teaching Latin and Greek, compare *WSU Catalog, 1966-67 and 1967-68*, pp. 121, 122, with *Ibid., 1970-71 and 1971-72*, pp. 156, 157.

37 "Report of the Humanities Study Council, June 1, 1968," pp. 1-6 (Quotations).

38 *Ibid.* pp. 6, 11-13 (Quotations "the myth" is on p. 12, "horizons of this university" is on pp. 11, 12), 17-21, Italics are those of the present author.

39 Petition (For an American Studies Ph.D. degree program) from Departments of English and History to the Committee on Graduate Studies, 1961 Folder "Historical Files on American Studies at WSU, American Studies Records (Office of the Director); Nelson Ault and Raymond Muse to George A. Frykman, Graduate School, May 4, 1961, *ibid.* A. W. Thompson to C. Simpson, February 1, 1961, *ibid.* Other information from recollection of George A. Frykman.

40 Robert O. Johnson to All Interested Persons, June 5, 1981, WICHE office Files, American Studies, Office of the Director. Johnson to Stanton Smith, Graduate School, August 5, 1980, *ibid.*, "Regional Graduate School Participation Data, 1982-83", *ibid.*, WSU Graduate School Bulletin, 1986, p. 17. The English doctorate became available in 1965, Literary Studies in 1968. See *Regents Record*, Vol 21, July 26, 1968, p. 134, and *Ibid.*, Vol. 20, July 16, 1965, p. 374. *WSU Catalog, 1987-89*, p. 92.

41 "Report of the mathematical Sciences Study Council, June 14, 1968," Frontispiece, pp. 3-11, 23.

42 *Ibid.*, p. 8. (Italics are those of the present author.)

43 *Ibid.*, pp. 39, 42, 47 (Quotation "step backward"), 48, 49.

44 *Ibid.*, pp. 33-35; E. Alden Dunham to C. J. Nyman, May 22, 1970 (in possession of the present author). General discussion of the proposed degree is based on the present author's experience with a proposed Doctor of Arts program for the Department of History in the Summer of 1970. That proposal was not accepted. On the D. A. in Mathematics, see *University Senate Minutes*, Vol. 1, November 9,

1972, p. 2 and *Regents Record*, Vol. 22, March 30, 1973, p. 181.

45 "Economics Sub-Committee of the Economics and Business Study Council Final Report, June 1968," pp. 1, 2, 9-15.

46 "Business Administration Sub-Committee's Final Report" in "Report in Economics and Business Administration Study Council, June, 1968", pp. 3-7, 15-26 (Quotation "they were not meeting the needs" on p. 7), (Quotation "must contribute" on p. 6.).

47 "Report of the Agricultural Study Council, Washington State University, June 1, 1968," pp. 25-29.

48 *Ibid.*, p. 30. Italics are found in the original text).

49 *Ibid.*, pp. 30, 31.

50 *Ibid.*, pp. 30-35, 38 (Quotation), 39.

51 "Home Economics Study Council Report, June, 1968," pp. 1 (Quotation), 2, 14-17; Earl McGrath and Jack T. Johnson, *The Changing Mission of Home Economics, A Report on Home Economics in Land-Grant Colleges* (New York: Teachers College, 1968), pp. ix, x, 1-5.

52 "Home Economics Study Council Report, June, 1968," pp. 4, 5, 6-9.

53 *Ibid.*, pp. 3, 4, 11, 18-27.

54 [L. M. Koger] College of Veterinary Medicine, Diamond Jubilee, 1899-1974 (1974).

55 "Report of the Veterinary Medicine Sub-Committee," in "Report of the Professional Education Study Council, (1968), Section I, pp. 156, 157 (Quotation, "Intellectual isolation"); *ibid.*, Section II, pp. 163-172.

56 *Ibid.*, Section II, p. 202 (figure 5); *ibid.*, Section I, pp. 147-150.

57 *Ibid.*, Section I, pp. 132-134; *ibid.*, Section II, pp. 175-177 (Quotation on p. 177)

58 "Report of the Pharmacy Sub-Committee," in "Report of the Professional Education Study Council (1968), Section I, pp. 42-44 (Quotation is on p. 44)

59 "Report of the Pharmacy Sub-Committee," in "Report of the Professional Education Study Council (1068), Section I, pp. 72-75, (Quotation "incapacitation" on p. 73), *ibid.*, pp. 64-69 (Quotation "modest" . . . "appears to be sound.")

60 Evelyn Rodewald, "International Programs at Washington State University, 194-1987" [a copy is in the possession of the present author], pp. 6-13.

61 *Regents Record*, Vol. 16, April 22, 1952, p. 338; J. Russell Andrus to C. C. French, December 9,, 1953, Box 13/7, Office of the President (French); *Regents Record*, Vol. 16, April 22, 1952; Rodewald, pp. 13, 14.

62 *Ibid.*, *Regents Record*, Vol. 19, June 1, 1959, p. 150 (Quotation).

63 Rodewald, pp. 14, 15.

64 *Regents Record*, Vol. 19, September 11, 1961, p. 484; Rodewald, pp. 14, 15 (Quotation).

65 *Ibid.*, pp. 28, 31 (Quotation), 32.

66 *Regents Record*, Vol. 22, March 28, 1975, p. 408; Rodewald, pp. 17-19.

67 *Ibid.*, p. 19.

68 *Ibid.*, pp. 20-24. Four projects in this group have been supported by the Consortium for International development (CID): Egypt, Sudan, Yemen, and Jordan Highlands. See Rodewald, p. 26-28.

69 Theodore Doty, "Washington State University in West Pakistan, 1954-1969: An Evaluation of Technical Assistance to Higher Education for Agriculture and Economic Development" (Ph.D. dissertation WSU, 1971) P. 207, as found in Rodewald, p. 14 (Quoting Doty), 15.

70 *Ibid.*, p. 32.

71 *Faculty Minutes,* Vol. 9, October 15, 1959; *Regents Record,* Vol. 19, October 23, 1959, p. 229; *Faculty Minutes,* Vol. 9, May 17, 1960 (Quotation).

72 *Ibid.,* May 17 and 26, 1960; *Regents Record,* Vol 19, May 30, 1960, p. 308.

73 *Ibid.,* Vol. 20, October 20, 1961, p. 4; *ibid.,* January 21, 1964, p. 211; *ibid.,* October 28, 1966, p. 488. Gene I. Maeroff, "Honors Programs Spreading," New York *Times,* January 30, 1979, Clipping in file, "Honors Programs," WSU News Bureau. [V.N. Bhatia], " The First Decade of a University Honors Program, A Report of the First Ten Years (1960-70) of the University Honors Program at Washington State University," p. 27 (Office of the Honors Program) Table 1: Honors Program Enrollment Statistics, Fall, 1988, (Office of the Honors Program).

74 *Ibid.,* p. 17 [V. N. Bhatia] "The First Decade of a University Honors Program," p. 17..

75 *Ibid.,* p. 29.

76 *Ibid.,* p. 31 (Quotation "They do not accept"); *ibid.,* p. 32 (Quotation "I think every class I teach"). Other evidences of closer attention to honors than to other students comes from the early admonitions that the former would get continuous advising (*Regents Record,* Vol. 19, May 17, 1960, p. 827) and the development of an Honors Center for use by its enrollees ("The First Decade of a University Honors Program   .   .   . at WSU," p. 9).

77 Recollections of the present author who, as Assistant to the Dean of the Graduate School Donald S. Farner, participated in establishing this program.

78 *Ibid., Regents Record,* Vol. 20, January 8, 1962, pp. 23, 25; *Graduate Study, WSU Bulletin,* 1966-67 and 1967-68, p. 8.

79 "Annual Report of the Dean of the Graduate School and Vice-Provost for Research, 1985-86 (Office of the Graduate School) p. 17. *University Senate Minutes,* Vol. 1, December 14, 1972, pp. 14, 15.

80 *Regents Record,* Vol. 18, April 5, 1961, p. 392.

81 *Ibid.,* Vol. 20, March 6 and 14, 1964, pp. 214, 219.

82 *Ibid.,* March 22, 1965, p. 333.

83 Debate on rising enrollments was not recorded, but the registrar's statistics in "Total Enrollment Since 1892" (Registrar's Office) attest to the increasing numbers. Educational Policies Committee, Vol. 15-16, November 26, 1962 (Quotation "the entering freshmen).

84 *Ibid.,* December 6, 1962, *Faculty Minutes,* Vol. 9, December 18, 1962; Regents Record, Vol. 20, March 2, 1963, p. 120.

85 *Ibid.,* Vol. 20, October 20, 1961, p. 7; *ibid.,* November 24, 1961, p. 14, *ibid.,* October 19, 1962, p. 101.

86 *Ibid.,* October 20, 1961, p. 7.

87 *Ibid.,* p. 101; *Faculty Minutes,* Vol. 10, September 15, 1964.

88 *Ibid.*

89 *Regents Record,* Vol. 20, August 28, 1964, p. 282.

90 The Board of Regents had expressed dissatisfaction at a meeting on April 7-8, 1954 (*Ibid.,* Vol. 17, p. 350) *Ibid.,* March 22, 1965, p. 336, (Quote "Continuing"), April 16, 1965, p. 346; *Faculty Minutes,* Vol. 10, Memorandum, C. C. French to J. W. Spielman, June 21, 1965 and memorandum, French to L. L. Madsen, July 1, 1965.

91 French to Milton Durham, May 6, 1965 (Quotation) Folder "Presidents' Office, 1965," Box 21, Office of the President (French), VA 84-29; *Regents Record,* Vol. 20, May 31, 1965, pp. 355, 371-373.

92 *Ibid.,* p. 355; *ibid.,* May 30, 1966, p. 445; *ibid.,* August 29, 1966, p. 471.

93 *Ibid.,* March 18-19, 1966, p. 433; April 16, 1966, p. 436, June 11, 1966, p. 465. November 30, 1966, p. 495. Terrell's appointment so recorded in *ibid.,* February 24, 1967, pp. 8, 9; *ibid.,* Vol. 21, March 31, 1967, p. 19; *ibid.,* May 5, 1967, p. 32.

94 Dorthy R. Powers, "A Student's President: WSU's Dr. Terrell Says Today's Students are Brighter, Better Informed, and More Sophisticated, *Spokesman-Review,* October 1, 1967, Box 1a, Glenn Terrell.

95 *Who's Who in America,* 39th Edition (1976-1977), Vol. 2, p. 3113. *Spokesman-Review,* February 25, 1967.

96 *Evergreen,* March 15, 1968. The editorial is unsigned but Mark Reese probably wrote it.

97 Glenn Terrell, "Inaugural Address," in *The Inauguration of Glenn Terrell as Seventh President of Washington State University,* March 17, 1968, (Pullman, Washington), pp. 6-8.

98 *Ibid.,* pp. 10, 11; Howard R. Bowen, "The Changing role of the University in Contemporary Society: The University in America: 2,000 A.D." in *ibid.,* pp. 17, 18, 20, 21.

99 Terrell "Inaugural Address," in *ibid.,* pp. 11,12/

100 *Regents Record,* Vol. 21, September 20, 1968, p. 166.

101 *Ibid.,* P. 167; *ibid.,* October 25, 1968 pp. 178, 179   .   .   . Information on Bishop's career is found in Microfiche Records, Office of Faculty Personnel.

102 *Evergreen,* April 30, 1968, "Marmes Man" was named after Roland J. Marmes, owner of the ranch on which the archaeological site is located, in southeastern Washington. See Roald Fryxell and Richard D. Daugherty, "A Human Skeleton from Sediments of Mid-Pinedale Age in Southeastern Washington," *American Antiquity,* Vol. 33, No. 4, 1968, p. 512.

103 David G. Rice, "Preliminary Report of the Marmes Rock Shelter Archaeological Site (Pullman, WSU Laboratory of Anthropology, 1969), p. 6. The fight to save the site is detailed in Marmes News Service (WSU), found in WSU News Bureau files. *Spokesman Review,* February 2, 1969. Quotation from Fryxell is found in Marmes News Service, February 24, 1969.

Chapter 8

1   "Preliminary Report of the Student Life Study Council, June 7, 1968" pp. iii-viii (Quotation is on p. viii).

2   *Evergreen*, September 22 and 26, 1967.

3   "Preliminary Report of the Student Life Study Council, June 7, 1968," p. 5 (Quotations). Professor Bruce Anawalt served as chair of this council. Other faculty and staff members were: Matthew G. Carey, Richard W. Dingle, Robert H. Ewalt, Robert A. Johnson, Willis E. Sibley, John A. Smetana, and Ruth Warnke. Student members were: Peggy Bachhuber, Annette Buchwalder, Katherine A. Harda, Thomas F. Kingen, Arthur G. Kidman, Cheryl E. Knighton, Marc R. Mutz, Neville Spadafore, and Alan Waugh.

4   *Ibid.*, pp. 22, 28, 29, 36-40, 43.

5   *Ibid.*, pp. 26, 27, 47-52, 61-69, and 85 (Quotation).

6   *Ibid.*, pp. 52 (Quotation "demanded"), 53 (Quotations "favorably impressed" and "may not."); Faculty Minutes, May 16, 1968.

7   Willis E. Sibley to Leon Luck, February 26, 1968, attached to Memo on E.P.C. Meeting, March 7, 1968, *Educational Policies Committee*, Vol. 22, not paged. Italics are those of the present author. The Editor and Managing Editor of the *Evergreen* supported the anticipated plan in an April 23, 1968, editorial.

8   "Proposal for a Pass-Fail Grading System Experiment, and other Matters" (to Leon Luck from Project Committee, February 26, 1968, Educational Policies Committee, Vol. 22, unpaged; meetings of April 4 and 18, 1968, unpaged, *ibid.*; *Faculty Minutes*, Vol. 10, Meeting of May 16, 1968; *ibid*, May 22, 1969.

9   *Ibid.*, Vol. 11, Meeting of May 4, 1971; *University Senate Minutes*, Vol. 3, May 13, 1976, pp. 12-15; *ibid.*, May 12, 1977, pp. 22-24; "Registrar's Report   .   . Spring 1984" (March 27, 1984), bound in *Academic Affairs Committee*, Vol. 38, March 27, 1984.

10 "Preliminary Report of the Student Life Study Council, June 7, 1968, p. 5 (Quotation); Lewis M. McNew to Terrell, May 24, 1968, Folder 109, General Correspondence of Committee on Social Responsibility, 1968, UA 85-26, President's Files; *Regents Record*, Vol. 21, June 10, 1968, p. 132; *ibid.*, September 20, 1968, p. 169.

11 Board of Control Minutes, February 19, 1969, and attachments (Quotation), Folder 112, Box 7, Archives 164. Quotation is found in attached memorandum to President Terrell and others, "WSU's Experimental Education Program," from Board of Control [February 19, 1969]. Louis McNew to Terrell, July 23, 1968, Folder 109, General Correspondence, Committee on Social Responsibility, 1968, UA 85-26, President's Files.

12 June Bierbower, "HEP," *Washington State Review*, Vol. 11 (Winter, 1967), 9; *Evergreen*, April 22 and 23, 1969; "High School Equivalency Program," *News Bulletin* of August 23, 1971, File " High School Equivalency Program," WSU New Bureau. "High School Equivalency Program," clipping from *Spokesman-Review*, Sept. 7, 1979, News Bureau files. *HEP: High School Equivalency Program*, p. 2 (Bulletin: Department of Education, no date).

13 *Board of Control Minutes*, October 18, 1967, folder 79, box 5, ASWSU President's Records, Archives 164; *ibid.*, October 25, 1967; Memo: to Steve Kikuchi from Leon Luck, March 1, 1968, Folder 91, Box 6, *ibid*; Committee on Student Bill of Rights and Responsibilities to Board of Control, February 19, 1968, Folder 79, box 5, ASWSU President's Records; *Board of Control Minutes*, November 8, 1967, *ibid.*; Memo to Terrell from Board of Control, May 15, 1968, Folder 101, Box 6, *ibid.* (Quotation, "the student" is from ""Policy Statement," attached to Board of Control Minutes, October 25, 1967, Folder 79, Box 5, *ibid.*) Reese's statement is from the *Evergreen,* March 6, 1968.

14 *Course and Instructor Critique*, (1968), p. iii (Quotation)iv, v; *Board of Control Minutes*, January 17, 1968, Folder 79, Box 5, ASWSU President's Records, Archives 164.

15 "Viet Nam Opinion Poll," with totals, File 78, Box 6, *ibid*; *Evergreen*, March 13, 1968.

16 Student-Faculty Committee to End the War to WSU Faculty, April 22, 1968, Folder "Unrest", box 3, UA 85-26, Terrell Papers. *Evergreen*, April 26, 1968; *Regents Record*; Vol. 21, April 26, 1968, pp. 124, 125; *New York Times*, May 3, 1968; Johnetta Cole and 8 other faculty, to Terrell, April 24, 1968, Folder "Black People," Box 2, Terrell Papers, UA 85-26; Black Student Union to Terrell, April 24, 1968, *ibid.*

17 *Evergreen*, May 14, 1968 (Quotation); Spokane *Daily Chronicle*, May 10 and 13, 1968.

18 *Evergreen*, January 17, 21, 22, 24, 1969; February 5, 1969; March 4, 1969.

19 *Ibid.*, February 5, March 4, 7, April 18, 23, 1969; Interview with Edward M. Bennett by Robert Hadlow, October 30, 1985, WSU Centennial Oral History Project. Quotation is found in the *Evergreen*, April 23, 1969.

20 "A Letter from Glenn Terrell," January 22, 1969. broadside, Folder "A Letter from Glenn Terrell," quotation, Terrell Papers, WSU Archives 162; *Evergreen*, October 7, 8, 9, 23, 30, 1969. The Blue-Ribbon Committee of Faculty and Administrators supported Terrell in a report in the *Evergreen*, October 30, 1969.

21 *Ibid*, October 15, 16, 1969 (quotation "several thousand"); Daniel J. Evans to Richard M. Nixon, October 27, 1969 (quotations "they all shared one thing" and "Their Voices"), Folder "State Governor, 1969," Box 4, Terrell Papers, UA 85-26.

22 *Faculty Minutes*, Vol. 11, May 5, 1969; *Evergreen*, May 2, 7, 9, 1969. Several members of the faculties of existing departments expressed interest in teaching Black Studies temporarily, a situation which encouraged the Resident Instructional Staff to begin the program without delay in 1969, according to the *Faculty Minutes*, Vol. 11, May 5, 1969.

23 *Ibid.*

24 *Evergreen*, May 5, and 9, 1969; October 31, 1969; "Fall Semester's Ethnic Enrollment Data" (Registrar's Office). According to *ibid.*, 132 Blacks were enrolled in 1970. No figures are available for the year 1969.

25 *Evergreen*, May 5, 1970.

26 *Ibid.*, May 6, 1970

27 *Ibid.*

28 *Ibid.*, May 7, 1970

29 *Ibid.*, May 7, 8, 13, 1970.

30 *Ibid.*, May 19, 1970; *ibid.*, May 27, 1970.

31 *Ibid.*, May 19, 1970

32 *Ibid.*, May 26, 27, 28, 1970.

33   Concerning the last day of the strike, see *ibid.*, May 29, 1970. On the RIS meeting of May 28, 1970: The general description of the tense, somewhat chaotic scene at the plenary session is from my observations as a seated member of the RIS. The *Evergreen* on May 29, 1970, failed to describe fully the scene, stating that only 100 students were present, greatly underestimating the pressure of their numbers and possible intimidation and participation in procedures.

34   *Ibid.*, May 27-29, 1970; For the official proceedings and decisions, see RIS Meeting, May 28, 1970, as found in the *Faculty Minutes*, Vol. 11; *Summer Evergreen*, June 29, 1970.

35   Wallis Beasley to Claude H. Pair, November 19, 1970, Folder "Minority Studies 1969 [sic]," Box 5, UA 85-26, Terrell Papers; "Fall Semester's Ethnic Enrollment Data Since 1968" (Registrar's Office); Rudy Cruz to Stan Berry, October 23, 1970, Folder "Minority Studies, 1969," Box 5, UA 85-276, Terrell Papers; Willis E. Sibley to Harold A. Romberg, June 6, 1970, Folder "Faculty Support," Box 6, *ibid.*; Sibley to "Dear Colleagues," June, 1970, Folder "Unrest," *ibid.* Numerous letters from the public are found in Boxes 4 and 7, UA 85-26, Terrell Papers. A notable critical comment, ostensibly supported by conversations with many faculty and staff members is J. L. Kimzey, past president of the Alumni Association, to Harold A. Romberg, President of the Board of Regents, July 27, 1970, Folder "Unrest, 1970," Box 7, *ibid.* Carlton A. Gladder to President Terrell, April 18, 1970, Folder "Senators and Representatives, 1970," Box 5, *ibid.* Terrell to Gladder, April 18, 1970 [sic], quotation, *ibid.*

36   *Evergreen*, October 7, 8, (Quotation, "broad approval") 9, 1970, and my observations of this session. For the non-participation of the Native Americans, see the Native American Indian Student Association, "Third World Claims and the Strike: The Indian View," Folder "American Minority Studies, 1970," Box 5, UA 85-26, Terrell Papers (1970).

37   *Daily Evergreen*, November 4, 1970, March 10, 13, 1971. For the polls see *ibid.*, October 30, 1970 and March 23, 1971 (Quotation "generally favorable"). That the minority groups still experienced divisiveness may be gathered from the statements of Rutledge M. Dennis, a graduate student in Sociology, as found in the *Daily Evergreen*, March 11 and 13, 1971. The fault was that of "Whitey," in his estimation. The editor of the *Evergreen*, however, pointed out that the Blacks and Chicanos would not even sit together at the workshops, *ibid.*, March 11, 1971.

38   The B.A. degree program in Chicano Studies had been authorized to start in September, 1970, by the RIS Meeting of May 28, 1970 (see Faculty Minutes, Volume 11, for 1969-1971). "An Undergraduate Program in Chicano Studies," not dated, but 1970, Folder "Chicano Studies, 1970," Box 4, UA 85-26, Terrell Papers. *Evergreen*, February 9, 1971. Broadside: "Why Should People Have to Strike for Conditions That We Take for Granted?" (February 24, 1971), Folder "Unrest, 1971" Box 7, UA 85-26, Terrell Papers. *Evergreen*, March 11, 1971. President Terrell to Wayne J. Kerr, March 31, 1971 and Terrell to D.B. Leonard, April 12, 1971, both in Folder "Unrest, 1971," Box 7, UA 85-26, Terrell Papers. Also, Scott Hendrickson to Terrell, April 12, 1971, *ibid.* The census report is found in Santiago C. Estrada, "Semester News Letter," [March, 1973], Folder "Chicanos 1973," Box 1, UA 85-49, President's Papers.

39   Native American Indian Student Association, "Third World Claims and the Strike: The Indian View [1970], Folder "American Minority Studies, 1970," Box 5, UA 85-26, Terrell Papers. "Conference Draft Proposal: Center for the Development of Native American Programs," attached to Roberta Minnis to Dean S.R. Mitchell, April 30, 1971, Folder "Native American Indians, 1971," Box 6, *ibid.*; Mitchell to Allan H. Smith, May 25, 1972, Box 9, *ibid.*, and Smith to President Terrell, June 21, 1972, *ibid. University Senate Minutes*, Volume 2, February 27, 1975. pp. 5-8; *Annual Time Schedule, WSU, Fall and Spring Semesters*, 1975-76.

40   Asian-American Students Association to President Terrell, March 20, 1973, Folder "Asian Americans, 1973," Box 1, UA 85-49, President's Papers. Thomas L. Kennedy to Wallis Beasley, March 27, 1973, *ibid.*, supported the idea, to which Professors Francis Ho and Toshio Akamine added support the same day, *ibid.* The suit may be followed in "Compromise and Settlement Agreement . . . between the Spokane Japanese American Citizens League . . . and Washington State University," July 29, 1981, pp.5-8 (Office of the Assistant Attorney General, WSU). University Senate Minutes, Volume 4, April 26, 1979. For a statement of the ethnic objectives and philosophy of the supporters of an Asian-American program, see U.S. District Court for the Eastern District of Washington: *Spokane Japanese American Citizens League v. Regents of Washington State University* (September 18, 1978) (Office of the Assistant Attorney General WSU). For approval of the program, see the *Regents Record*, Vol. 23, June 8, 1979, p. 402.

41   Louis NcNew to All CAP Advisors, January 24, 1980, Folder "Chicano and Chicano Studies, 1980", Box 6, UA 88-04, President's Papers.

42   Census and Class Distribution, Fall [19]80, Registrar's Office; Fernando V. Padilla to Louis McNew, October 2, 1980, (quotation), Box 6, UA 88-04, President's Papers.

43   Census and Class Distribution, Fall [19]80 and Census Report and Class Distribution Report Fall [19]88 (Registrar's Office).

44   "A Letter from Glenn Terrell, May 7, 1971," Folder 1, Box 1, Papers of Nancy Porter, 1971-1976, WSU Archives.

45   WSU Commission on the Status of Women, "Report on the Status of Faculty Women, February, 1972," especially Tables 1 and 3, *ibid.*, Minutes of the Commission on the Status of Women, November 15, 1972; *ibid.*, "Promotion and Reclassification of Female and Male Classified Staff at WSU," (November 15, 1972, *ibid.*

46   "Improving the Climate for Women at Washington State University, A Report by the Ad Hoc Committee on Restructuring Programs for Women, February 3, 1988, pp. 1, 6, 7. According to this report, "minority women faculty at WSU constitute 5.3 percent of academic women faculty and 13.2 percent of administrative women faculty."

47   The WSU Commission on the Status of Women, "Report on the Status of Faculty Women," February, 1972, p. 12, Folder 1, Nancy N. Porter Papers, Cage 181. Annette M. Lopez to George Frykman, April 20, 1989, provided salary comparisons, 1972 and September 30, 1988, and Table 11, Salary Comparison, 1972.

48   U. S. President, Executive Order, "Equal Employment Opportunity, Executive Order 11375, Amending Executive Order 11246," *Federal Register*, (17 October 1976), Vol. 32, no. 201, pp. 14303-14304, microfilm, Title IX, Prohibition of Sex Discrimination, Education Amendments of 1972, *United States Statutes at Large*, Vol. 86, 1973.

49   "Title IX, Self-Examination," is a folder in Box 3 of UA 87-29, Affirmative Action Office, WSU Archives, which provides evidence on these points.

50   *Regents Record*, Vol. 23, February 16, 1979, p. 365; James Carroll to Wallis Beasley, February 2, 1979, Folder "HEW-Assurance of Complaints under Title IX, July 1976 [*sic*], Box 3, UA 85-29, Affirmative Action Office.

51   Terrell to Aldora Lee, March 5, 1980, Folder "Committees: Status of Women, 1980," Box 7, UA 88-04, President's Papers; Interview with Carol Gordon by Joanne Washburn, June 14, 1983, Folder "Carol Gordon," Box 7, Archives 202; Interview with Mary Lou Enberg by Joanne Washburn, June 27, 1983, Folder "Mary Lou Enberg, Box 5, *ibid.*

52   *Karen Blair, et al, Appelants, v. Washington State University, et al, Respondents, Washington Reports: Cases Determined by the Supreme Court of Washington*, 2nd Series, 108 (1987): 558-559; Pullman *Daily News*, May 18, 1988; editorial by Pete Dunlop, "Potential Victims Had Nice Smiles," *Evergreen*, July 26, 1988.

53   "Task Force on Continuing Education: Report to the WSU Commission on the Status of Women, February, 1975," Folder 2, Box 1, "Commission on the Status of Women," Archives 32; Sue Durrant to Wallis Beasley, August 22, 1975, Folder 4, Box 1, *ibid.*, and Beasley to Durrant, January 29, 1976.

54   Commission on the Status of Women, Minutes, March 11, 1975, Folder 12, Box 1, *ibid.*; Annjennette S. McFarlin to Marylee H. King, May 5, 1975, CWS Folder, Box 2, UA 82-27, Affirmative Action and Special Program General File; Indian Women to the Women's Commission, June 5, 1975 (Quotation "For Indian Women"), Folder 4, Box 1, Commission on the Status of Women, Archives 32.

55   Sue Durrant to Wallis Beasley, August 22, 1975, and Beasley to Durrant, January 29, 1976, both found in *ibid. WSU Bulletin, 1978-1980*, p. 287 (Quotations).

56   Census and Class Distribution, Fall [19]80 (Registrar's Office), p. 41 and Census Report and Class Distribution Report, Fall [19]88, (Registrar's Office), p. 179.

57   K. Fielding, Sub-Committee of Affirmative Action, of the Committee on the Status of Women, April 1, 1977, Folder 25, Box 2, Commission on the Status of Women, Archives 32; *Evergreen*, April 22, 1977.

58   *Ibid.*, April 22, 27, 28, 29, May 3, 10, 12, September 19, 30, 1977; "[Minutes of] Student Affairs Restructuring Task Force meeting, May 19, 1977," Folder 25, Box 2, Commission on the Status of Women, Archives 32.

59   WSU Commission on the Status of Women to the Board of Regents, June 1, 1977, *ibid; Evergreen*, September 30, November 1, 1977 (Quotation), *Regents Record*, October 28, 1977, p. 214.

60   *Ibid.*, Vol. 23, October 28, 1977, p. 214. See also *ibid.*, pp. 23, 24. For total enrollment in September, 1977, see "Total Enrollment Since 1892" (Registrar's Office).

61   *Regents Record*, September 27, 1977 carries a a review of Terrell's planned reductions which amounted to almost four million dollars and included saving $50,000 by cutting out the office of Vice president for Student Affairs; *Evergreen*, November 1, 1977, April 22, 1977 (Quotation, "a white man's club").

62   *Regents Record*, vol. 21, September 3, 1970, pp. 354-367 (Quotation on p. 354); *ibid.*, October 16, 1970, pp. 384-390.

63   *Educational Policies Committee*, Vol. 20, March 31, 1966; *Faculty Minutes*, vol. 10, May 26 1966; *ibid.* February 28, 1967; *ibid*, vol. 11, February 23, 1971.

64   *Regents Record*, Vol. 21, April 12, 1971, p. 419, 420; *ibid.*, Vol. 22, October 31, 1975, p. 490; Memo to RIS from T. J. Musik, Chairman of FSC, April 18, 1975, attached to RIS, May 6, 1975, subject; "Review Report of the WSU Senate: The First Three Years, 1971-1974, April, 1975," as found in *Faculty Minutes*, Vol. 12, May 6, 1975; *ibid.*, May 6, 1975 and November 29, 1978.

65   *University Senate Minutes*, Vol. 4, October 19, 1978, pp. 1-3; *ibid.*, Vol. 6, October 16, 1980, pp. 1-3 (Quotations on pp. 2, 3).

66   *Ibid.*, Vol. 8, October 7, 1982, p. 3, and March 31, 1983, pp. 19; *Regents Record*, Vol. 24, November 19, 1982, pp. 362, 363 and June 3, 1983, pp. 427, 428.

67   *University Senate Minutes*, Vol. 8, May 19, 1983, p. 4.

68   WSU President's Committee, *Recommendations . . . Approved by the President's Committee and Submitted to President Compton*, [1945], Section N-10, p. 1; [C. J. Quann], "A Brief and Sometimes Annotated History of the WSU General Education Program," September 12, 1985 (Office of the Registrar).

69   *Ibid.; Regents Record*, Vol. 25, November 18, 1983, p. 12.

70   *University Senate Minutes*, Vol. 3, October 30, 1975, pp. 4-6; *ibid.*, January 15, 1976, p. 8; *ibid.*, Vol. 4, April 26, 1979, pp. 10-12l *WSU Catalog 1987-89*, p. 25.

71   *University Senate Minutes*, Vol. 7, October 22, 1981, p. 1.

72   *Faculty Senate*, Vol. 9, May 19, 1984, pp. 39-44; *ibid.*, Vol. 10, October 4, 1984, pp. 22-26; *WSU Bulletin, 1987-89*, P. 13.

73   *Course and Instructor Critique* (Associated Students of Washington State University, 1968), pp. iii-v and *passim*, quotation on p. iii.

74   *University Senate Minutes*, Vol. 3, May 12, 1977, pp. 29-34; *ibid.*, Vol. 4, April 6, 1978, pp. 4, 5; *ibid.*, April 20, 1978, p. 2; *ibid.*, Vol. 6, October 16, 1980. p. 9.

75   "The Need for a Baccalaureate Degree in Nursing at Washington State University," May 25, 1965. Courtesy of Hilda Roberts.

76   "Baccalaureate Nursing Program," October 8, 1968 (brochure from the Intercollegiate Center for Nursing Education); Spokane *Chronicle*, September 19, 1968; Application for Permission to Establish a School of Professional Nursing, Folder 11, Box 1, Archives 54; "Intercollegiate Center for Nursing Education," no date, Folder 23, Box 1, Archives 54; *Faculty Minutes*, Vol. 11, March 25, 1969, pp. 5, 6; Memo to William G. Matlan from Regional Engineer ROFEC-X, Seattle (David Brown), April 5, 1971, Folder 103, Box 2, Archives 54; WSU News Service, June 14, 1971, for press release on the NIH grant.

77   WSU News Service release of May 10, 1971, report on the first graduating class; *ibid.*, for September 28, 1973, which provides numbers of students and information on leasing Washington School.

78   WSU News Service releases, December 13, 1974, August 9, 1977, June 9, 1978, July 25, 1980, August 18, 1980, August 22, 1980; *Spokesman Review*, June 10, 1978. Charlene E. Clark, "Setting for the Project: Leadership Spokane," May 13, 1988 (Draft Report), courtesy of Betty M. Anderson; *Regents Record*, Vol. 25, March 27, 1987, pp. 472, 473; *ibid.*, Vol. 24, January 30, 1981, p. 109. Charlene E. Clark, "Setting for the Project: Leadership Spokane," May 13, 1988.

79   *Regents Record*, Vol. 22, January 12, 1973, p. 170; *ibid.*, October 25, 1974, p. 366; *University Senate Minutes*, Vol. 3, October 16, 1975, pp. 10-12; "Enrollment of Majors by Class and Department," issued annually by the Registrar.

80   L. M. Koger, *College of Veterinary Medicine, Washington State University* (September, 1974, unpaged source of the quotations and the citation of the *Spokesman-Review*, September 28, 1965. *Regents Record*, Vol. 21, September 29, 1967, p. 72.

81   Koger; Vita of Leo K. Bustad, found in Bustad File, WSU News Bureau; *Evergreen*, February 6, 1985 (quotations); *Regents Record*, Vol. 22, June 2, 1973, P. 206.

82   *Ibid.*, Vol. 22, May 31, 1974, p. 313; *ibid.*, Vol. 23, June 4, 1976, pp. 39, 40. *Ibid.*, January 12, 1979, pp. 343, 344.

83   News releases from the WSU News Service September 28, 1978, and February 22, 1985 (Quotations); *Regents Record*, Vol. 29, March 29, 1985, p. 190.

84   Accreditation by the American Veterinary Medical Association might be granted, with numerous conditions, at several levels above non-accreditation. In 1982, WSU attained the zenith of uncontested accreditation. *Ibid.*, Vol. 24, June 3, 1983, pp. 424, 425 (Quotation on p. 425.).

85   *Ibid., July 25, 1980, p. 47;* Vol. 24, July 31, 1981, p. 170; *ibid.*, July 25, 1980, p. 47.

86   *Ibid.;* Lewiston (Idaho) *Tribune,* July 31, 1980, clipping in File "College of Pharmacy," WSU News Bureau.

87   *Pullman Herald*, November 21, 1979, clipping in File "College of Pharmacy," WSU News Bureau; *Regents Record*, Vol. 24, July 31, 1981, p. 170.

88   *Ibid.*, Vol. 24, September 25, 1981, p. 201; Press Release, *WSU News Bureau*, September 25, 1981 (File, "College of Pharmacy," WSU news Bureau); *Seattle Times*, September 24, 1981, clipping, File "College of Pharmacy, WSU news Bureau; Enrollment of Majors by Class and Department" for relevant years (Office of the Registrar).

89   *Regents Record*, Vol. 24, November 20, 1981, pp. 223, 224; *ibid.*, June 4, 1982, pp. 285, 286. On the University of Washington's argument, see Milo Gibaldi to George M. Beckmann, November 7, 1986; Beckmann to Albert Yates, November 24, 1986; and A. Robert Thoeny to Albert Yates, November 21, 1986, all attached to Yates to Frederick Gilbert, December 15, 1986, File "College of Pharmacy," WSU News Bureau. *WSU Bulletin, 1983-85*, pp. 264, 265; *ibid., 1987-89*, pp. 150, 151, quotation on p. 150.

90   Press Releases, WSU News Bureau, June 16, 1987 (Quotations); Pullman *Daily News,* June 21, 1988, File "College of Pharmacy," WSU News Bureau.

91   "Programs of Preparation Leading to Teacher Certification, August, 1973", in WSU [College of Education] Annual Progress Report Submitted to the Superintendent of Public Instruction, State of Washington, filed in VF 2848, "WSU Department of Education," WSU Archives. *Faculty Senate Minutes*, Vol. 9, April 19, 1984, pp. 25-30.

92   *Ibid.*, Vol. 9, December 8, 1983, pp. 4-14; *ibid.*, April 19, 1984, pp. 10-12; underlining is that of the present author.

93   Press Release, June 24, 1985, Folder "College of Education," WSU News Bureau. See *WSU Bulletin, 1987-89*, passim., for description of these departments. *Evergreen*, March 24, 1986; *WSU Bulletin, 1987-89*, pp. 37-40, to be compared with *ibid., 1983-85*, pp. 52, 312-318, for evidence that courses in vo-tech education were transferred to the Department of Adult and Youth Education.

94   *Faculty Minutes*, Vol. 11, March 19, 1970; *Regents Record*, Vol. 21, August 3, 1970, p. 318. Interview with Theodore

Saldin by Robert W. Hadlow, January 26, 1989 in which Saldin noted that the Council on Postsecondary Education refused by one vote to approve the Ph.D. program; Memo to Eugene Clark from Omer Carey, March 9, 1972, attached to Terrell to James M. Furman, Olympia, Washington, March 9, 1972, in Folder 336, Box 6, Office of the President (Terrell), UA 162. For name change, cf. *WSU Bulletin*, 1983-85, p. 49 with *ibid., 1985-87*, p. 64.

95   See "Certification of Major" and "Special Note", *WSU Bulletin, 1987-89*, pp. 22 and 29; *WSU Summer Session Catalog, 1987*, pp. 23-25.

96   *University Senate Minutes*, vol. 2, October 14, 1974, pp. 1-9; *Regents Record*, Vol. 22, October 25, 1974, p. 366; *ibid.*

97   *Faculty Senate Minutes*, Vol. 9, February 16, 1984; *Regents Record*, Vol. 24, July 18, 1983, pp. 437, 438 (Quotation on p. 438); *ibid.*, Vol. 25, July 23, 1984, p. 75; *WSU Graduate Bulletin, 1986-1987*, p. 50.

98   *Faculty Minutes*, Vol. 10, May 25, 1967; *WSU Graduate Bulletin, 1985*, pp. 40, 45,

99   *Faculty Minutes*, Vol. 11, March 25, 1969 (Quotation); *ibid.*, May 14, 1970; *Regents Record*, Vol. 22, October 24, 1974, p. 366. Notice of the B.S. in Computer Science first appeared in the *WSU Bulletin for 1972-73*, p. 122.

100   *Faculty Minutes*, Vol. 10, May 30, 1968; *Regents Record*, Vol. 21, July 26, 1968, p. 134; *WSU Graduate Studies Bulletin, 1970-71 and 1971-72*, p. 81 (Quotation "interactions"); *Regents Record*, Vol. 21, June 9, 1969, p. 219; *Faculty Minutes*, Vol. 11, March 19, 1970; *WSU Bulletin, 1987-89*, p. 56 (Quotation "the application"); *University Senate Minutes*, Vol. 5, March 13, 1980, pp. 4-7; *Regents Record*, Vol. 24, April 28, 1980, p. 21.

101   *University Senate Minutes*, Vol. 8, April 21, 1983, pp. 6-10; *Regents Record*, Vol. 25, April 27, 1984, p. 56; *WSU Graduate Bulletin, 1986-87*, pp. 193, 194. On the merger of the Colleges of Agriculture and Home Economics, see *Regents Record*, Vol. 24, September 16 and 17, 1982, pp. 327-331, 335-339; *ibid.*, June 3, 1983, p. 418.

102   *Regents Record*, Vol. 25, March 9, 1984, p. 29; *Faculty Senate Minutes*, Vol. 9, April 19, 1984, pp. 12, 13; *Regents Record*, Vol. 25, July 23, 1984, p. 75. The doctoral program available in Materials Science and Engineering continued to be that of the Ph.D. in Engineering Science, according to *ibid.*

103   *Faculty Senate Minutes*, Vol. 9, May 17, 1984, pp. 32, 33 (Quotation "The Faculty" on p. 33.); *WSU Bulletin, 1987-89*, p. 11 (Quotation "global climate").

104   "International Development: Washington State University," flyer (c. 1985, probably International Development Office), unpaged); Rodewald, "International Development at Washington State University, 1945-1987," p. 33 (Quotation "The International Program Development Office.").

105   *Regents Record*, Vol. 24, June 3, 1983, pp. 425, 426; V. N. Bhatia to George Frykman, October 17, 1988; Enrollment for 1988-89 is from Kathleen M. Bodley to George A. Frykman, March 24, 1989. *WSU Bulletin, 1987-89*, p. 10; Press Release on exchanges with Sichuan University, February 25, 1985, Folder "International Programs," WSU News Bureau. The first agreement with Sichuan University was signed in 1983, according to *ibid.* Announcement of the agreement with Far Eastern University appeared in the Pullman *Daily News* on November 24, 1988.

Chapter Nine

1   *Regents Record*, Vol. 23, September 28, 1977, p. 200; *Spokesman-Review*, November 10 and 11, 1977; *Faculty Minutes*, Vol. 12, November 9, 1977; *University Senate Minutes*, Vol. 4, January 12, 1978, p. 1 (quotation).

2   *Regents Record*, Vol. 23, November 18, 1977, p. 223 (Quotation "A real spirit of optimism" and "could not exist"); *University Senate Minutes*, Vol. 4, January 12, 1978, pp. 1-3 (Quotation "comes on the heels," p. 2).

3   *Regents Record*, Vol. 24, September 26, 1980, pp. 79, 80; *ibid.*, October 24, 1980, p. 90 (Quotation "Campus Capers").

4   *Ibid.*, An Act Relating to Community Colleges, *Laws of Washington* (1979), Vol. 2, pp. 1922-27; *ibid.*, pp. 2556, 2557.

5   *University Senate Minutes*, Vol. 7, September 24, 1981, pp. 1, 2, 9; *Regents Record*, Vol. 24, September 25, 1981, pp. 201, 202.

6   *Ibid.*, Vol. 24, September 25, 1981, pp. 201, 202, 210, 211; *ibid.*, October 16, 1981, p. 215; *University Senate Minutes*, Vol. 7, October 22, 1981, pp. 4-8 (Quotation "doubts" on p. 8). For an explanation of a state of financial exigency, see *Faculty Manual* (October, 1980), p. 30.

7   *Regents Record*, Vol. 24, December 16, 1981, pp. 227-229, 232-237. Quotation is on p. 228.

8   *Ibid.*, pp. 229-231; *ibid.*, July 26, 1981, p. 298; *ibid.*, June 4, 1982, p. 284.

9   *University Senate Minutes*, Vol. 7, January 14, 1982, pp. 8, 9.

10 *Regents Record*, Vol. 24, February 12, 1982, p. 243; *University Senate Minutes*, Vol. 7, April 22, 1982, pp. 13, 14; *Regents Record*, Vol. 24, June 4, 1982, pp. 283, 284.

11 *Ibid.*, September 16 and 17, 1982, pp. 327-331 (Quotations on p. 327); *University Senate Minutes*, Vol. 8, October 7, 1982, pp. 9-12, 16.

12 *Regents Record*, Vol. 24, September 16 and 17, 1982, pp. 335-339.

13 *Evergreen*, April 21, 1977; *Faculty Minutes*, Vol. 12, April 21, 1977; *Session Laws of the State of Washington, 1969* Chapter 277, pp. 2593 and 2598; *Revised Code of Washington*, 28B.80.

14 *Evergreen*, April 21, 1977; *Faculty Minutes*, Vol. 12, April 21, 1977, (Quotation "central"); *Evergreen*, May 25, 1977 (Quotations "lashed out," and "shocking idea,"), May 26, 1977.

15 *Regents Record*, Vol. 23, June 3, 1977, pp. 154, 155.

16 "Summary of Review of Six Graduate Programs: CPE Review, June, 1977," Folder "State: CPE, July to September, 1977," Box 2, UA 88-04, President's Papers; *Regents Record*, Vol. 23, June 3, 1977, pp. 154, 155 (Quotation).

17 *Evergreen*, June 20, 1977; *Regents Record*, Vol. 24, June 6, 1980, pp. 32, 33. An added degree, the doctor of Arts in Chemistry, not so widely heralded, was eliminated (*Evergreen*, June 20, 1977)

18 *Faculty Minutes*, Vol. 12, April 17, 1973, December 11, 1973, and October 21, 1975; *Faculty Senate Minutes*, Vol. 9, February 16, 1984, pp. 16, 17.

19 *Regents Record*, Vol. 22, November 19, 1971, pp. 33, 34; *Faculty Minutes*, Vol. 12, February 17, 1972; *ibid.*, December 20, 1972; *ibid.*, January 25, 1973; *ibid.*, April 17, 1973; *ibid.*, Vol. 12, April 30, 1974; *Regents Record*, Vol. 23,

January 25, 1980, pp. 494, 495; *ibid.*, Vol. 24, March 4, 1983, pp. 386, 387.

20 *Faculty Senate Minutes*, Vol. 9, November 10, 1983, p. 34 (Quotations).

21 *Ibid.*, February 16, 1984, pp. 16, 17 (Quotation "by any reasonable standard," on both pages); *ibid.*, p. 18 (Quotation "the core of the faculty").

22 *Regents Record*, Vol. 22, January 21, 1974, p. 274; *Faculty Minutes*, April 30, 1974; Public Law 95-256, *U.S. Statutes at Large*, Vol. 92, Pt. 1; *Washington Laws, 1979, 1st Extra Session* Chapter 159; *Regents Record*, Vol. 23, July 20, 1979, p. 418.

23 *Ibid.*, Vol. 24, April 26, 1982, pp. 271, 272; *University Senate Minutes*, Vol. 7, April 22, 1982, p. 12. Interview with Thomas L. Kennedy, Associate Dean, the Graduate School, by Robert W. Hadlow, January 19, 1989; *University Senate Minutes*, Vol. 8, May 5, 1983, pp. 29, 30; *Regents Record*, Vol. 24, June 3, 1983, pp. 419, 420.

24 *Bulletin/Calendar*, December 10, 1982 (WSU Archives).

25 *Regents Record*, Vol. 23, March 19, 1976, p. 15; *Faculty Manual, 1976*, p. 30; *University Senate Minutes*, Vol. 4, April 26, 1979, pp. 13-15; *Faculty Manual, 1980*, pp. 32, 33, cf. with *Faculty Manual, 1976*, p. 33; *Regents Record*, Vol. 24, June 3, 1983, p. 418.

26 Howard D. Copp, Chairman, FAC, February 23, 1984, memo found in Faculty Affairs Committee Files, 1984 (Registrar's Office); *Faculty Manual, 1980*, p. 28 (Quotation "the policy of the University," italics are those of the present author); *ibid., 1984*, p. 28 Quotations; italics are those of the author); *Faculty Senate Minutes*, Vol. 9, May 3, 1984, pp. 18, 19 (Quotation "the policy to encourage and facilitate") *Faculty Manual, 1980*, p. 28.

27 *Regents Record*, Vol. 21, February 24, 1967, p. 8; *ibid.*, March 31, 1967, p. 25; "A Summary of the Philosophy and the Proposal" [on Women's Hours and Locking of Residences], WSU, Associated Women Students, Hours Evaluation Committee, January 9, 1967, attached to Catherine M. Northrop to Parent, April 5, 1967, found in Folder 104, Box 6, ASWSU President's Records, Archives 164; Catherine M. Northrop to Parent, April 5, 1967 (Quotation), *ibid.*

28 "A Summary of the Philosophy and the Proposal: [on Women's Hours and Locking of Residences], WSU, Associated Women Students, Hours Evaluation Committee, January 9, 1967, (Quotations), attached to Catherine M. Northrop to Parent, April 5, 1967, found in *ibid.*

29 *Regents Record*, Vol. 21, May 23, 1969, p. 218; *ibid.*, May 1, 1970, p. 312.

30 *Ibid.*, Vol. 22, January 9, 1976, pp. 499, 500; *University Senate Minutes*, Vol. 4, March 22, 1979, p. 5 (Quotation).

31 *Evergreen*, May 6, 1987 (Quotation); *Regents Record*, Vol. 25, May 8, 1987, pp. 487-489 and 495, 496; *WSU Bulletin, 1987-89*, p. 17.

32 *Regents Record*, Vol. 21, February 17, 1969, p. 194; *ibid.*, Vol. 22, July 20, 1973, pp. 211, 212.

33 *Evergreen*, September 20, 1979.

34 *Ibid.*, April 15 and June 16, 1980; *Regents Record*, Vol. 24, June 6, 1980, p. 33; *Evergreen*, February 11 and 14, 1985, April 3, 1989.

35 *Evergreen*. April 4, 15, and 16, 1970; Interview with William B. Pence by Randy Bennett, not dated, but WSU Cen-

tennial Oral History Project, Box 15, Archives 202. On re-building the stadium, see *Regents Record*, Vol. 21, May 1, 1970, p. 311; Vol. 22, January 21, 1972, pp. 39, 40; *ibid.*, June 3, 1972, p. 94; *ibid.*, September 8, 1972, p. 134.

36   *Spokesman-Review*, October 15, 1967 (Quotations "out-fought and "out couraged" and "as it looks now"), October 17, 1967, (Quotations "misinterpreted" and "We regard our membership"); *Regents Record*, Vol. 21, October 20, 1967, p. 87.

37   *Ibid.*, Vol. 22, February 21, 1975, p. 400 (Quotation); *ibid.*, March 28, 1975, p. 409.

38   *Ibid.*, March 8, 1974, p. 279; *ibid.*, Vol. 23, January 12, 1979, pp. 345-350; *ibid.*, January 17, 1979, p. 353; *ibid.*, July 7, 1979, 411; *ibid.*, July 11, 1979, pp. 409-412; *ibid.*, October 19, 1979, p. 449. On the Academic Center, see *ibid.*, July 15, 1977, pp. 163, 164 and the *Spokane Chronicle*, October 31, 1979.

39   *Regents Record*, Vol. 23, January 12, 1979, pp. 345-350; *ibid.*, June 8, 1979, pp. 405-406; *ibid.*, October 19, 1979, p. 456; *ibid.*, November 10, 1979, p. 471. *Ibid.*, Vol. 24, November 21, 1980, p. 100; *ibid.*, June 5, 1981, p. 156. On the Coliseum, see: "Multi-Purpose Coliseum" (no date) and "Performing Arts Coliseum Fact Sheet (March 26, 1981), both found in Folder "Coliseum," WSU News Service.

40   "A Petition for Equitable Funding for the College of Engineering at Washington State University [January 28 1981, first date of circulation], (Quotation), Folder "College of Engineering, 1981," President's Office, French Administration Building; *Regents Record*, Vol. 24, March 6, 1981, p. 119.

41   *Ibid.*, p. 119; *University Senate Minutes*, Vol. 6, March 19, 1981, p. 1; *ibid.*, March 19, 1981, p. 1.

42   *Ibid.*, April 2, 1981, p. 1; Robert O. Johnson to G.A. Hartford, March 12, 1981 found in *University Senate Minutes*, Vol. 6, March 19, 1981, pp. 13-14 (Quotation on p. 13); *ibid.*, April 23, 1981, pp. 17-19.

43   *Ibid.*, April 2, 1981, pp. 12-16; *ibid.*, May 7, 1981, pp. 21-24; *ibid.*, April 23, 1981, pp. 17-19.

44   *Ibid.*, May 7, 1981, p. 20 (Quotations "adverse effect" and "important contribution") p. 21 (Quotation "direct support"), pp. 19-26.

45   William Iulo, "Open Letter to the Board of Regents of Washington State University," April 28 [1981], Quotation, Records of the Budget Committee, Senate Files in Registrar's Office. *University Senate Minutes*, Vol. 6, May 7, 1981, pp. 19-20. The budget: State of Washington, Budget, 1983-85 Biennium, submitted by Governor John Spellman, p. 636. I am indebted to Robert W. Hadlow, Research Assistant, for these figures and computations. From the figures available, it was impossible to be certain what percentage or amount of funds discussed were state-appropriated. That is, it was impossible to distinguish them from gifts, accruals, etc.

46   *Pullman Herald*, June 6, 1981; *Regents Record*, Vol. 24, June 5, 1981, p. 150.

47   *Blair v. Washington State University, Washington Reports: Cases Determined by the Supreme Court of Washington*, 2nd Ser., 108(1987): 558-579. Quotation is on p. 559.

48   *Ibid.*, pp. 559-562, 564- 569, 577. Quotations are on pp. 560, 561, 577.

49   "Washington State University Comprehensive Plan" [1971], pp. 1, 6, Planning File, WSU 186.

50   *Ibid.*, p. 6.

51   *Ibid.*

52   Press release "Terrell Mall," June 28, 1985, WSU News Bureau; *Evergreen*, September 23, 1966; *University Senate Minutes*, Vol. 2, March 13, 1975, pp. 2-4.

53   "Washington State University Comprehensive Plan," [1971], pp. 10, 13, 14, Planning File, WSU 186; Enrollment of Majors by Class and Department, Fall Semester, 1971-72," December 1, 1971 (Registrar's Office), "Enrollment by Majors by Class and Department, Fall Semester, 1988," *ibid.* Terrell described his goal regarding the American Association of Universities in *Bulletin/Calendar* August 3, 1979, pp. 1, 2 (WSU Archives). On the quest for entry into the American Association of Universities, see Comment by Walfred Peterson, "Committee to Release WSU Stress Study Report," *Bulletin/Calendar*, April 8, 1988, pp. 2, 3.

54   *Regents Record*, Vol. 21, September 12, 1969, p. 259; "Total Enrollments Since 1892," (Registrar's Office) *Regents Record*, Vol. 21, October 24, 1969, p. 269; *ibid.*, September 18, 1970, pp. 371 and 372; *ibid.*, Vol. 22, October 25, 1974, pp. 366, 367.

55   *Ibid.*, November 21, 1975, p. 496; *ibid.*, January 9, 1976, p. 4; *ibid.*, Vol. 23, July 16, 1976, p. 49; *ibid.*, October 22, 1976, p. 104; *ibid.*, November 19, 1976, p. 110; *ibid.*, Vol. 24, March 4, 1983, p. 382; *ibid.*, Vol. 25, March 9, 1984, pp. 32, 33.

56   "Family Housing at Washington State University," [1975] Folder "Housing." Box 3, Affirmative Action Office, UA 85-29; "Total Enrollment Since 1892," (Registrar's Office). Press Release: "Ferry Hall," March 3, 1975, WSU News Bureau; Information on Residence Halls and their occupants received from Housing and Food Service, May 3, 1989, courtesy of Mary Braun.

57   "Washington State University, Comprehensive Plan," [1971], Planning File, WSU 186, p. 31.

58   *Evergreen*, May 20, 1980 (Quotation "tons"); Don A. Dillman, "Mount St. Helens: Seven Gray Days in May," May 1980 (typescript), quotation "Last year's total eclipse", on p. 4.

59   *Evergreen*, May 20, 1980; Dillman, pp. 5-9.

60   *Ibid.*, pp. 15-19; *Evergreen*, May 21 and 23, 1980.

61   Dillman, pp. 29, 30; *Evergreen*, May 27, 29, and June 4, 1980.

62   *Regents Record*, Vol. 24, July 25, 1980, p. 47. Dillman, p. 28 (Quotations).

63   *Faculty Minutes*, Vol. 12, May 27, 1980; A.E. McCartan to President Terrell and Mayor Pete Butkus, June 4, 1980 (Office of Director of Safety, WSU); News Release on Mount St. Helens, File "Mount St. Helens," WSU News Bureau.

Epilogue

1   *Evergreen,* December 5, 7, 11-14, 1984 (Quotation on Dec. 14); *Faculty Senate Minutes,* December 13, 1984.

2   *Regents Record,* Vol. 25, January 18, 1985, pp. 144-148; *ibid.,* June 28, 1985, pp. 210, 211; Press Release. "Regents Name Mall for Terrell," June 28, 1985, Folder "Glenn Terrell Mall," WSU News Bureau.

3   *Regents Record,* Vol. 25, March 8, 1985, pp. 180, 181; *Who's Who in America,* 45th edition, 1988-1989, Volume 2, p. 2901; Press Release: "Samuel Smith is 8th President of WSU," Folder "Samuel H. Smith, WSU News Bureau.

4   Glenn Terrell, "Statement for the Board of Regents," June 28, 1985, Folder "Glenn Terrell," WSU News Bureau, pp. 1-4 (Quotation "We need never apologize" is found on p. 4).

5   *Ibid.,* pp. 3, 4 (Quotations "this nonsense" is on pp. 3,4); "branching out" is on p. 4.

6   Samuel H. Smith, "Inaugural Address," *The Inauguration of Samuel Howard Smith as the Eighth President of Washington State University,* March 21, 1986 (WSU News Bureau), pp. 27, 28.

7   *Ibid.;* "Institutional Planning" *The Path to Excellence, Washington State University* (1984), p. 18.

8   Samuel H. Smith, "About Our University," *Bulletin/Calendar,* September 4, 1987.

9   "Opening Address by President Samuel H. Smith at the 1988 Leadership Conference, on September 8, 1988," Tri-Cities, Washington, pp. 6,7 (WSU News Bureau). Samuel H. Smith, "Annual Spring Address to WSU Faculty Senate, Thursday, 13 April 1989" (WSU News Bureau); Much information on the history and plans for the branch campuses may be found in Washington State University, *Development Plan for Campuses in Spokane, Tri-Cities, and Vancouver,* Presented to WSU Board of Regents on May 6, 1988, passim.

10   "Opening Address by President Samuel H. Smith at the 1988 Leadership Conference on September 8, 1988," pp. 2, 3.

11   *Ibid.; Bulletin/Calendar,* April 15, 1988.

12   Walfred Peterson, "Committee to Release WSU Stress Study Report," *ibid.,* April 8, 1988, pp. 2, 3 (Quotation on p. 2).

13   *Ibid.* pp. 2, 3 (Quotation on p. 3).

14   "Opening Address by President Samuel H. Smith at the 1988 Leadership Conference on September 8, 1988," p. 8 (Quotation).

15   *Ibid.,* p. 7. Italics are those of the present author.

16   Among the many works available on the future of higher education, the following have played a role in these conclusions: Derek Bok in *Higher Learning* (Cambridge: Harvard University Press, 1986) points out the value of open competition among American universities for attainment of the "people's" higher education. Peter Drucker in *The New Realities: in Government and Politics/In Economics and Business/in Society and World View* (New York: Harper and Row, Publishers, 1989) stresses the urgency of developing computer sciences and techniques in the incipient "information age." Michael B. Katz, in *Reconstructing American Education* (Cambridge: Harvard University Press, 1987) alerts the reader to a crisis of integrity in higher education caused by the influence of governmental funding (and control) of research and by the influence of business in dictating the curriculum and objectives.

Bibliographical Essay

Secondary Works A brief selection relevant to this work

Before publication of *Creating the People's University: Washington, 1890-1990* and the other volumes that make up the *Washington State University Centennial Histories,* only partial accounts of the institution's past were available. The first was Enoch Albert Bryan, *Historical Sketch of the State College of Washington, 1890-1925* (Published by the Alumni and the Associated Students, 1928), a semi-autobiographical account especially useful for understanding the third president's land-grant philosophy and goals. The second was written by Professor of History William M. Landeen, under the title of *E. O. Holland and the State College of Washington, 1916-1944* (State College of Washington, 1950). Within this rather narrow administrative history Landeen managed to convey a sense of the school's traditional rivalry with the University of Washington. To the above should be added Charles M. Gates, *The First Century at the University of Washington, 1861-1961* (University of Washington Press, 1961) which provides a useful corrective against parochialism and another viewpoint on the rivalries of the two major universities of the State of Washington.

The best work available on the general history of the land-grant movement is Edward Danforth Eddy, *Colleges for Our Land and Time, the Land-Grant Idea in American Education* (New York: Harper and Brothers, Publishers, 1956) but it should be supplemented with Allan Nevins, *The State Universities and Democracy* (University of Illinois Press, 1962), a work that celebrates the growth of democracy through all the state universities, not merely the land-grant institutions.

The standard study of the birth and early development of the American university, as opposed to the nineteenth century college, is Laurence R. Veysey, *The Emergence of the American University* (University of Chicago Press, 1965). Important works dealing with more recent developments in European and American universities include the following: J. W. Chapman (editor), *The Western University on Trial* (University of California Press, 1983), which offers essays by international authorities on universities of the Western World, and Leslie W. Keopplin and David W. Wilson (Editors), *The Future of State Universities: Issues in Teaching, Research, and Public Service* (Rutgers University Press, 1985), which provides technical and detailed studies of the ways and means for reaching new goals and objectives in higher education.

Finally, there are two current works that address questions of future developments in higher education in very pointed ways, at times in terms polemical or strident, which are nonetheless authoritative and thought-provoking. These are Peter Drucker, *The New Realities: In Government and Politics/In Economics and Business/In Society and world View* (New York: Harper and Row, Publishers, 1989) and Michael B. Katz, *Reconstructing American Education* (Cambridge: Harvard University Press, 1987). A third work written in a more even temper is Derek Bok's, *Higher Learning* (Cambridge: Harvard University Press, 1986). For further information on these three books see note sixteen of the Epilogue.

Documentary and other Source Materials

Washington State University does not have a central collecting point for all of its official publications, records, and manuscripts pertaining to the institution. The *Regents Records* (minutes and addenda) are housed in the President's Office while the *Faculty Minutes*, including those of the Resident Instructional Staff (which are not distinguished from faculty in the citations in the notes), are located in the Registrar's Office. Also found in the Registrar's domain are the *University Senate Minutes,* the *Faculty Senate Minutes,* and the records of some faculty committees. The Registrar's Office also contains a complete file of college catalogs, a nearly complete set of time schedules, and enrollment statistics, current and historical.

The official Washington State University Archives, located in the Division of Manuscripts, Archives, and Special Collections of the Washington State University Libraries, possess the complete Office of the President's files of correspondence, memoranda, and reports, except for current materials. Under separate files are found some additional papers of the presidents, other administrators, and faculty. The WSU Archives also hold numerous minor collections of faculty committees, student government, women's and ethnic organizations, and files on particular movements or events, such as that on the student movements of the late 1960s and early 1970s. Tapes and transcripts of interviews conducted by the WSU Oral History Project and used in this study are found in the WSU Archives. Other interviews are in the possession of the present author.

Newspapers cited are found in the microfilm section of Washington State University's E. O. Holland Library. In addition, files of press releases and newspaper clippings located in the WSU News Bureau have been used. Several master's theses used in this work are found in Holland Library.

Index

Numbers in italic make reference to photographs.